SURVIVING YOUR DIVORCE

SURVIVING
Your
DIVORCE

A Guide to Canadian Family Law

MICHAEL G. COCHRANE, LL.B.

Canada's Bestselling Book on Separation and Divorce
6TH EDITION: EXPANDED AND UPDATED

Cataloguing in Publication data available from Library and Archives Canada

LegalIntel
151 Yonge Street, Suite 1800
Toronto, Ontario, M5C 2W7
www.legalintel.ca

ISBN 978-0-9948545-0-6 (paperback)
ISBN 978-0-9948545-1-3 (ebook)

Cover design by Peter Cocking
Text design by Nayeli Jimenez
Printed and bound in Canada

15 16 17 18 19   5 4 3 2 1

CONTENTS

Acknowledgements   x
Author's Note   xi

Introduction – Reality Check: Become an Informed Consumer   1
    Why I Can Provide Advice about These Matters   2
    What to Expect From This Book   3
    Smarter, Safer and Saner (and Savings, Too)   5
    What's Wrong with the Family Law System   9
    Being Your Own Lawyer?   11

Chapter 1 – Taking a Look at Ourselves: The Emotional Stages of Marriage Breakdown   13
    Some Observations on Marriage   15
    Emotional Stages   17
    Marriage Counselling: Getting Help to Cope   22
    Why Did This Happen? The Causes of Divorce   23
    Transition People: Cause or Casualty   24

Chapter 2 – Taking a Look at Lawyers: Take Charge of the Relationship   27
    Finding a Family Law Lawyer   28
    Conflicts of Interest   30
    Confidentiality   31
    The First Interview with Your Lawyer   32
    The Retainer (or What Everyone Else Calls a Contract)   34

Family Law and Legal Aid   37
If You Are Dissatisfied with Your Lawyer   37
Firing Your Lawyer   41

Chapter 3 – Taking a Look at the Process: Understanding Family Law and the Legal System   46
The Legal System: Civil Versus Criminal   49
Family Law and the Courts   50
The Rules of Court   54

Chapter 4 – Getting a Divorce: Dissolving the Marriage Vows   67
Grounds for Divorce   68
The Procedure for a Divorce   74

Chapter 5 – Dividing the Family's Property: Get Your Fair Share from the Marriage Partnership   83
What Is "Property"?   85
What Is Debt?   86
Financial Statements   87
Value of Assets and Liabilities   89
What Is Not Divided? Exempt Property   92
Date of Valuation   94
Unequal Division of Property Values   94
The Matrimonial Home   95
Pensions   97
Paying an Amount to Resolve Property   101
Some Tax Considerations   101

Chapter 6 – Obligations to the Children of a Divorce: Every Parent's Top Priority   106
Custody and Access: Understanding Terminology   107
Who Is a Child?   111
How Is Custody Determined?   113
Help from Professionals When Determining Custody   118
Hot Spots   120
Strategic Considerations   132

What Will We Tell the Children?   *139*
A Warning   *147*

Chapter 7 – Support: Financial Assistance after Separation   *151*
Child Support   *153*
Who Is a Parent?   *158*
Who Is a Child?   *159*
Hot Spots   *161*
Spousal Support   *170*
Parental Support   *180*

Chapter 8 – Common-Law Spouses Have Rights Too (Just Not the Same as Married Couples)   *183*
The Meaning of "Common Law"   *183*
Children in Common-Law Relationships   *185*
Spousal Support   *186*
Property Division for Common-Law Couples   *187*
Cohabitation Agreements   *193*

Chapter 9 – Settling Your Differences: Avoiding the Courtroom   *196*
Offers to Settle   *198*
Minutes of Settlement   *201*
Orders on Consent   *201*
Separation Agreements   *202*
Memorandum of Understanding   *210*

Chapter 10 – Not Settling Your Differences: Going to Court   *212*
The Courtroom   *214*
The Paper Chase   *216*
The Trial   *217*
Appeals   *225*

Chapter 11 – Alternatives to Court: Mediation, Arbitration and Collaborative Family Law   *229*
Mediation   *230*
Arbitration   *238*

Mediation/Arbitration *239*
Religious Arbitration *240*
Collaborative Family Law *240*
Strategic Considerations *241*

Chapter 12 – Enforcing Family Law Orders: Making an Order Stick *245*
Custody Enforcement *246*
Abduction *250*
Canada Customs and Travelling outside Canada *251*
Access Enforcement *253*
Support Enforcement *255*
Property Enforcement *260*
Personal Restraining Orders *262*
Contempt *263*

Chapter 13 – Grandparents and "Other Interested Persons" *266*
Grandparents: A Special Status *267*
"Other Interested Persons" *273*
Strategic Considerations *274*

Chapter 14 – Marriage Contracts and Cohabitation Agreements: Managing Your Relationship Contractually *278*
Marriage Contracts *279*
Cohabitation Agreements *283*
Setting Aside Domestic Contracts *285*

Chapter 15 – Family Law and Your Will *290*
Making a Will *290*
Divorce and Your Will *293*

Chapter 16 – Domestic Violence: A Common Feature of Marriage Breakdown in Canada *297*
Violence: The Myths *299*
Why Are Women Assaulted? *300*
Why Do Men Do It? *301*

What Can Be Done?   *302*
Strategic Considerations   *306*

Chapter 17 – How to Represent Yourself   *310*
A 10-Step Legal Framework for Your Case   *311*
50 Tips for Your Day in Court   *325*
Dealing with Lawyers   *328*
Dealing with Court Staff   *329*
Dealing with the Judge   *329*
Getting Help from Lawyers: The Limited Retainer   *330*
Legal Research   *331*
Internet Resources   *333*
How to Complain   *336*

Appendix A: Some Important Paperwork   *338*
A Retainer Form   *338*
A Separation Agreement   *341*
The Family Law Client History Form   *361*

Appendix B (To Be Attached to a Full Separation Agreement):
The Parenting Plan   *364*

Appendix C: Table of Common-Law Rights and Responsibilities   *375*

A Glossary of Family Law Terms   *377*
Index   *387*

ACKNOWLEDGEMENTS

I FIND IT hard to believe that this book has now been on bookshelves in Canada for over 25 years. The number of changes to family law and the ways in which these changes are affecting Canadian families continue to grow with each passing year.

In this sixth edition, I would like to again acknowledge the very positive responses I have had from readers. They continue to share the details of their own difficult separations and divorces with me. Their stories, along with my own experiences in the family law system with my clients, continue to deepen my understanding of family law in Canada and its impact on families.

I would like to acknowledge the wonderful support and expertise of the team put together by Page Two (www.pagetwostrategies.com), including Jesse Finkelstein, Trena White, Megan Jones, Robyn Read and Peter Cocking. I have worked with many editors, designers, proofreaders and publishers, big and small, over the years, but the work of Page Two in helping me and LegalIntel to bring this sixth edition to Canadians has been the best. Thanks to a first-class team.

I would also like to thank and acknowledge again the Law Foundation of Ontario, which provided a grant to assist me in the preparation of the first edition of this book.

Thank you to all of my clients and readers for your feedback.

AUTHOR'S NOTE

THE GOAL OF this book is to make you a more informed consumer of legal services in the family law area. It is designed as an overview and guide to Canadian family law. I want you to be smarter, safer, saner and to save your money.

Each family law case is different and the law varies from province to province, so the book's applicability to individual cases is limited. I cannot guarantee that the laws described will apply in your particular case. If you have a family law problem, please consult an experienced family law lawyer to determine how your circumstances may be affected by the law of your province.

My goal is not to help you avoid lawyers, but rather to help you deal with them confidently. I am personally alarmed at the number of Canadians who have been forced to represent themselves in our justice system. Perhaps they are representing themselves because they have lost confidence in their own lawyer, they can no longer afford to pay for legal services and do not qualify for legal aid, or they simply feel that they are in the best position to speak for themselves or their family. Regardless of their reason, self-represented people are presenting some major challenges to the family law system in Canada. Not understanding how the system works has added to the delays; mistakes are made and frustrations build. Judges, lawyers, court staff and those seeking justice in our family law system are all struggling. The family law system in Canada is not only in serious trouble, but it has become increasingly hostile to self-represented individuals.

Lawyers themselves often struggle to understand this crazy system of family law that has developed in Canada. I honestly do not know how self-represented people can cope with the pressures. I do understand that many self-represented people simply cannot afford to pay lawyers' fees. I urge these people in particular to take the time to develop a big-picture view of how the family law system works, or at least of how it is supposed to work. The system is in big trouble and it is not serving Canadians particularly well right now. No one is in the system by choice. When I have met individuals who are representing themselves, one comment that they have made about this book is that they had to read sections of it a couple of times in order to appreciate what was happening to them.

While self-representation is not something that I promote in this book, in response to the virtual flood of Canadians who are forced to represent themselves in our family courts, I have added Chapter 17, which is entirely dedicated to the subject. In this chapter I provide advice about how to build a framework for your case based on facts, evidence, law and common sense. I have included 50 tips on how to handle yourself on your day in court.

THROUGHOUT THIS BOOK I have used factual situations to illustrate some of the problems people encounter. While all of the circumstances described are real, names, places and some facts have been changed to protect people's privacy and the confidentiality clients enjoy with their lawyers.

I invite you to check out my website for regular updates on things of interest to people struggling with separation, divorce and other legal problems.

MICHAEL G. COCHRANE, B.A., LL.B.
Partner, Brauti Thorning Zibarras LLP, Toronto, Ontario
www.michaelcochrane.ca
www.btzlaw.ca

INTRODUCTION

Reality Check:
Become an Informed Consumer

THE INCREASING NUMBER of marriage breakdowns, common-law relationships and single-parent families; the recognition of domestic violence; the mobility of families; medical breakthroughs in conception, such as in vitro fertilization; and the rights of same-sex couples have all contributed to a growing complexity in family relations. Newspapers, magazines, television and the Internet provide us with the most intimate details of family disputes—"Grandparent seeks custody of grandchild," "Mother loses custody of children," "Father refuses to pay support," "Wealthy couple fights over family business"—and let's not forget the many cases of violence.

A great deal of legal information is now available online for Canadian families and individuals undergoing family crises; however, a lot of it is inaccurate and unreliable, either because it's not provided by lawyers or it's not information about Canadian law from Canadian jurisdictions. In addition, Canadian laws are different from province to province, while U.S. laws are very different from Canadian laws, so we need to be cautious when gathering information from online resources. Offline, self-help books are plentiful. And many people still get what little information they can second-hand from the experiences of friends and acquaintances who have gone through the divorce mill. But this is not enough to thoroughly inform and prepare a consumer, and as a result people experiencing family crises, separation and divorce often head into the marketplace of legal services without a clear sense of the family law system.

However, the cost of hiring lawyers for divorce and separation proceedings in court has moved well beyond the average person's means. In fact, lawyers often admit that they themselves could not afford to hire a lawyer if they needed one. And yet the issues of family law are complex, significant and emotionally charged for the people involved—the exact circumstances that call for reliable, educated and prudent advice.

This is what I call sage advice. As someone who has talked directly to thousands of consumers, I believe that ordinary Canadians with family law questions want more than gossip and anecdotes. Canadians need sage advice about their family law problems before they start to make informed decisions about their personal lives and the lives of their children, perhaps now more than ever before.

WHY I CAN PROVIDE ADVICE ABOUT THESE MATTERS

OVER THE LAST 35 years of practising law, I have had the unique opportunity to see Canadian family law from a number of perspectives, not the least of which is as a family law lawyer, down there in the trenches, in hand-to-hand combat, battling literally thousands of cases. Along the way I have also

- worked as a Senior Policy Advisor to the Attorney General of Ontario on Family Law Reform;
- chaired the Ontario Attorney General Advisory Committee on Enforcement in Family Law and the Ontario Attorney General Advisory Committee on Mediation in Family Law;
- authored several books on family law, including, in addition to *Surviving Your Divorce*, *Surviving Your Parents' Divorce*, *Do We Need a Marriage Contract?*, *Do We Need a Cohabitation Agreement?*, *Family Law in Ontario* and *Strictly Legal*;
- taught at the University of Ottawa Law School, Osgoode Hall Law School, Carleton University and Ryerson University; taught the

Ontario Bar Admission Course; and lectured as a part of the MBA Program at Schulich School of Business;

- trained as a mediator, a collaborative family law lawyer and at Harvard Law School in Negotiation and Advanced Negotiation;
- taken Intensive Trial Advocacy for the Courtroom;
- sat on the Executive of the Ontario Bar Association Alternative Dispute Resolution Section and the Editorial Board for the Ontario Bar Association magazine *JUST*;
- served as Ontario's representative on the Federal-Provincial-Territorial Committee on Family Law Policy and at the annual Uniform Law Conference of Canada;
- hosted a television show, *Strictly Legal*, and been a guest expert on numerous radio and television programs dealing with family law issues;
- lastly, I have been divorced myself, and remarried into a beautiful blended family.

The ways in which Canadians marry, cohabit, separate and divorce leaves a lot to be desired. I do not see any dramatic change in the law, or process, on the horizon; there is not a more humane, holistic, child-focused, less acrimonious and adversarial system on the way. So we need to deal with the realities of the system you face as you go through a separation and divorce.

When I meet with clients, I often tell them that moving through a separation and divorce is not unlike walking across hot coals. The best way to get across is to simply set your mind to it and, with purpose, walk across the hot coals. You get to the other side and remarkably your feet are warm, but they are not burned. It is the clients who walk out onto the coals and hesitate or turn back who ultimately end up with charred feet. When you are ready to separate and divorce, develop an appropriate plan, set your mind to it and then walk across the hot coals.

WHAT TO EXPECT FROM THIS BOOK

TWENTY-FIVE YEARS AGO when I described this project to a family law lawyer friend of mine, he said, "You're giving away all the secrets." He was right. That was my intent. This book tells you what experienced family law lawyers know about separation and divorce and the system. It is designed as a handbook for anyone who wants to know more about Canadian family law. Who will benefit from reading it?

- people who are separated and already involved in legal proceedings
- people who are thinking about separating
- people who are living common law—or thinking about it
- people who are thinking about getting married
- people who want marriage contracts—or who are being asked to sign one
- people who are involved in violent relationships
- people who have already been through the legal mill, but are still wondering what happened
- students studying law (who will find that this book provides a healthy reality check against what they may hear in academic settings)

A quick glance at the table of contents will give you an idea of some of the areas that I try to demystify for you, including:

- the emotional stages of marriage breakdown
- hiring and firing lawyers
- the family law court system
- the division of family property
- custody and access
- support
- the rights of common-law spouses
- domestic violence
- marriage contracts

Surviving Your Divorce is not about managing your relationship. It's over if you are reading this book. If you need relationship advice, consider my other books, *Do We Need a Marriage Contract? Understanding How a Legal Agreement Can Strengthen Your Life Together* and *Do We Need a Cohabitation Agreement? Understanding How a Legal Contract Can Strengthen Your Life Together.* (For further information about these titles, please visit www.michaelcochrane.ca and www.legalintel.ca.) This book is about surviving the gauntlet you must run in order to unravel your married lives and start afresh.

I have focused on a number of the hot spots that occur in family law cases. For example, in custody there is often conflict around the need for a parent to move, vacation planning, remarriage and even religion. In response to this, I have included in the appendix a full-draft Parenting Plan to help parents develop detailed solutions for custody of their children.

Other hot spots include new developments around the calculation of child support for joint custodial parents, or parents who have split custody. I've included new information about Spousal Support Advisory Guidelines and provided new and up-to-date information for common-law couples who continue to face challenges when dividing their property at the time of separation.

In the area of property, I have gathered new information on such problem areas as family loans, the developing problem of identity theft resulting from the details that people have included in financial forms, challenges in valuing assets and changes in pension law. I've also updated the chapter dealing with wills and estates, and some of the planning that's required as you move on to a new life after your divorce.

Take a quick look at Appendix A for some examples of the paperwork that you may face in a family law dispute, and refer to the glossary of legal terms to guide you through the legal mumbo-jumbo.

The information is provided in a way that makes it useful in all provinces (except Quebec) and the territories. While the specific names of documents, courts and procedures can vary from province to province, the broad principles and guidelines are very similar. I have tried to organize these guidelines by subject area and in a way that makes the most sense.

SMARTER, SAFER AND SANER (AND SAVINGS, TOO)

MY GOALS IN writing this book are fairly straightforward: I want you to become an informed consumer of family law legal services and to be able to protect yourself. If you do,

- you will save thousands of dollars in legal fees,
- you will have a great deal more control over your life,
- you will make better decisions for you and your family, and
- you will be smarter, safer and saner after the whole experience.

Will reading this book save you $1,000 in legal fees? If you read this book and apply some of the information before going to a lawyer about a family law matter, you will save at least $1,000. In some cases, you will save much more. The reason is simple: after reading this book, you will be a more informed consumer. You will know how to pick the right lawyer for your needs and how to tell the lawyer what you want for yourself and your children. You will have a good understanding of what our laws actually say about family problems and how "the system" works. In addition, you will learn when *not* to see your lawyer, which can be a significant saving in itself.

The best way to illustrate the potential savings in being an informed consumer is through some examples. The following situations are all drawn from cases I knew about while in private practice or while participating in the reform of our family laws.

The Battered Client

AN OLDER WOMAN arrived in a lawyer's office early one Monday morning still bearing the marks of a beating she had received more than a week earlier. She was accompanied by three lovely children who had at last persuaded her to leave their father, her abusive husband of 30 years. She had finally had enough and had left him the previous week. Where had she been for the past week? The first lawyer she had consulted was the real estate lawyer who had helped with the purchase of their home and occasional refinancing. He didn't "do" family law, but agreed to see her. After two interviews and the collection of some of her important documents; after telephone calls to the husband, who was holed up in the family home on an alcoholic binge; and after taking care of some other clients' important real estate deals, the lawyer gave his advice: he suggested she try to "work things out," especially since legal proceedings would be slow and expensive. A court order, he said, couldn't be obtained for months. With this advice she received a bill for $1,000.

She nearly took the advice until her eldest daughter encouraged her to get a second opinion from an experienced family law lawyer. Twenty-four hours after she arrived in that lawyer's office, she had an interim order for exclusive possession of the home, a restraining order against the husband, interim custody of the youngest child and a temporary support order. *Getting the right lawyer from the start makes a big difference.*

The Client in the Dark

A COUPLE WHO had been married for 11 years separated and began an informal schedule of moving their son between their two new households. The husband had some difficulty at work and stopped paying some of the family's bills. This created tension and they began to argue over the schedule of time for their son. The wife consulted a lawyer who immediately issued an application in the court which demanded financial disclosure from the husband to learn about his actual financial circumstances. The husband, partially in denial, set the lawyer's letters and documents aside assuming that he and his wife would "work things out the way they always had." More notices came, court dates were booked, and he refused to deal with the matter other than to assume that everything would be okay. The wife attended at court with her lawyer; the husband told her to tell the judge that they would work everything out. The judge was not impressed and made a court order that included $3,000 for legal fees incurred because the court appearance was a waste of time.

Knowing how the system works, and what the consequences of a court application are, before you go into the system makes a big difference—emotionally and financially. *Knowing how the system works before you go into it makes a big difference.*

The Bitter Client

GARY AND SHERRY Leskun were married in 1978. Sherry was about 10 years older than Gary and had two children from her previous marriage. They had their own child and blended everyone into a happy family life, that is until Gary worked hard to improve his credentials and ended up being transferred to a different company in a different city. Sherry injured her back, and got some further bad news that her position at a bank was being eliminated. The expectation was that she would move to join Gary in Chicago. Instead she learned that Gary wanted a divorce, as he had been having an affair. You can imagine Sherry's reaction. Their case went all the way to the Supreme Court of Canada in what was described by one judge as "the scorched earth policy" of an embittered Sherry. She was so hurt by his misconduct and deceit in the marriage that she was unable to make a new life for herself. One judge described it as "her life became the litigation." It consumed her every waking hour. It was a legal and emotional nightmare for both of them, because it was not motivated by finding a way to move on to two new, separate lives. It was motivated by anger. *Don't let anger be the only motivator in your divorce proceedings—it can cost you in the end, emotionally and financially.*

The Blindsided Client

A YOUNG COUPLE went to their respective lawyers to get a Separation Agreement. They were on relatively friendly terms and knew what they wanted, except for a couple of small concerns about their two children. Both suddenly found themselves being told not to discuss the matter with each other to avoid confusion during the settlement discussions.

His lawyer suggested that legal proceedings be commenced, as a precaution, and held in the file. If negotiations didn't go well, they could serve the proceedings and gain "strategic advantage." Discussions continued, but suddenly the proceedings were served on her at work in front of her friends. The papers said that her husband wanted custody, so she instructed her lawyer to file for custody, too. They were in court before they knew what hit them. The matter was adjourned to allow everybody to cool off. Cost? $3,500—each. What happened?

She heard from a friend that mediation (where an objective third person facilitates settlement discussions between the couple directly) should be tried. With a little help, they found a mediator, the original problem was solved and an agreement was reached for joint custody of the children.

The mediator's fees were $1,500. The clients wanted to know why the lawyers had not told them about mediation. His lawyer's answer? You didn't ask about it. Her lawyer's answer? She didn't believe in mediation.

The $7,000 in lawyer's fees was a waste, particularly in a year when finances were tight due to the separation and the new expense of maintaining two households. *Knowing all of your options for solving problems can make a big difference.*

I COULD FILL a book with similar examples of uninformed clients watching money slip away in the lawyer's office or in the legal system. This would be less likely to occur if people had a good idea of what awaited them and played a more active role in deciding what was going to happen to them, their children or their hard-earned property.

Clients in these cases could have saved a lot more than the $1,000 I mentioned earlier if they had gone to a family law specialist, if they had asked for written retainers and opinions before proceeding, if they had understood that the toughest lawyer may not be the best lawyer for them and if they understood that there is more to the settlement of family law cases than fighting it out in the courtroom.

Read this book. Save $1,000—maybe more. But, more importantly, gain some control over what will be a difficult time for you emotionally and financially.

WHAT'S WRONG WITH THE FAMILY LAW SYSTEM

IN TRYING TO explain what I think is wrong, I divide our system of family law into three general parts:
The Users: that's you, your spouse, your kids and your extended family—the people most affected by the experience of separation and divorce
The Process: the laws that are supposed to provide some predictability and guidelines for resolving issues, including the rules of evidence and court process and its alternatives, such as mediation and arbitration
The Guides: the lawyers and other professionals who should act as advocates and guide you through the process

1. The Users

LET'S CONSIDER FOR a moment the people who must use the family law process: people undergoing separation and divorce. This group is largely uninformed—or worse, misinformed—about what is about to happen and the decisions that will be expected of them. To make matters worse, at the time they are expected to make these decisions, they are angry, broken-hearted, depressed, in many cases mentally unwell, victims of violence or despairing and frequently unaware of their future needs. We are seeing more and more people in the family law system who have problems with alcohol, drugs, mental health and other disorders. Users of the system are very vulnerable.

2. The Process

WE THEN TAKE these poor, vulnerable souls and make them resolve their problems in a process that is adversarial, slow, often illogical, expensive, inflexible and controlled by people who are often very cynical and may not have any interest in family law matters. I have seen an increasing attitude from people in the system amounting to, "if you're here, you get what you deserve." At the same time, there is no emotional support in the system for the people who are looking for help.

You will notice a theme in this book that I will be repeating from time to time: the Canadian family law system is in crisis. As I did my research for this book, an experienced family law lawyer related to me an incident that he had seen in court where a terribly insensitive judge brought a self-represented individual to tears. The individual was simply pursuing his rights in the system and did not deserve the harsh treatment. Was the judge's attitude caused in part by his frustrations with the system? Perhaps.

You would be hard pressed to find someone in Canada who is familiar with our family law justice system and would be prepared to stand up and defend it as doing anything approaching an adequate job for Canadian families. It is not good for women, it is not good for men and it is certainly not good for children. Those who administer justice—whether they be judges, court staff or lawyers—are equally dissatisfied with the system. In my view, it is a billion-dollar drag on the Canadian economy and families' resources are devastated unnecessarily because of the way in which our family law system currently operates.

Here is the really bad news: no one is doing anything about it and it will in all likelihood get worse. What does this mean for you? It means that you have even more reason to understand what you are in for as you go forward with a separation and divorce. Read on.

3. The Guides

WHO IS BEST placed to help people through this maze? Lawyers, of course. But even this important decision—the selection of a personal guide to take people through the system—is often left to chance. I am always shocked to find that some people have actually selected their lawyers simply by using Google. I think if you do anything as a result of reading this book, it should be to select a competent lawyer who is sensitive to your needs. That decision alone can be half the battle. My goal is to make you an informed consumer of legal services, someone who is able to exercise control over yourself as a user of the system, control over the process and control over the lawyers; smarter, safer, saner, it starts with your lawyer.

BEING YOUR OWN LAWYER?

AS PREVIOUSLY EXPRESSED, it is not a goal of this book to convince you to go it alone, without a lawyer. (Although I know many of you have to go it alone and have no choice.) There is so much at stake when you tinker with your own case: support, property division and, most importantly, the best interests of your children are all at risk. You have no doubt often heard the expression "a person who represents himself has a fool for a client."

But the fact of the matter is that tens of thousands of Canadians are forced to represent themselves in family disputes. They are acting as their own guides in a hostile system not because they are fools, but simply because they have no choice. While Chapter 17: How to Represent Yourself surveys how this is making for some additional problems in the system, this text will arm you with knowledge that can help you, should you have no other choice than to meet the challenges yourself in self-representation.

CLOSING REMARKS

YOU SHOULD REALIZE that by reading this book, you are doing your part because you will have the information necessary to help your lawyer do a better job for you. Remember, lawyers should not just listen to your opinion, they should respect it. Your knowledge and confidence will undoubtedly speed up the process, save time and expenses as well as narrow the issues in dispute and facilitate a solution.

MY ADVICE

1. Don't be an accident waiting to happen—inform yourself about your rights.
2. Accept and deal with the system as it is—inform yourself about your options.
3. Get an experienced, affordable family law lawyer who respects and appreciates you as an informed consumer.
4. The legal system can be complicated; the process will chew up dollars and emotions.
5. If you must be your own guide, be prepared to work hard to deal with the system. This book will help. The only consolation may be that you are not alone.

TAKING A LOOK AT OURSELVES

The Emotional Stages of Marriage Breakdown

LAWYERS LOVE TO go to court. That's where all the real drama is played out—witnesses cross-examined, exhibits shown, legal arguments made and, almost anti-climactically, a judgment or some order is arrived at by the court. Plus—plain and simple—lawyers make more money going to court. But dramatic as that setting may be, lawyers also love to settle cases outside of court. They can often be found around courthouses leaning on walls, talking with pride about "the one they just settled," as if they had just wall-mounted some trophy. Good lawyers take pride in a good settlement.

I had a chance to eavesdrop before a meeting one day as a couple of family law lawyers—one senior, one very junior—traded banter about their recent settlements. The junior lawyer was bemoaning the fact that his client had just accepted a settlement that was, in his opinion, satisfactory. That's right—satisfactory—and the lawyer was surprised.

"I don't understand her instructions," he said. "I could have gotten her that settlement six months ago. Suddenly one morning my client waltzes into my office, instructs me to accept the offer of settlement that had been made months earlier. I couldn't believe my ears. After six months of vicious motions and really testy discoveries, six months of bloodletting, she wants to settle. She was like a different person... the same settlement was available six months ago..." The lawyer's voice trailed off in disbelief. He was totally baffled by the about-face of his client.

The senior lawyer nodded knowingly but added an observation. "Maybe she was a different person."

"No, it was her all right," the junior lawyer added with a laugh.

"I'm serious, maybe she was a different person; maybe she had changed." The senior lawyer bore down a little on the junior lawyer. "Maybe she had moved into that stage of acceptance where she felt comfortable restructuring her life."

"Stage? What stage?" The junior lawyer looked uncomfortable.

I thought to myself, *Uh oh—this lawyer is trying to help people involved in family problems and does not understand the emotional stages that most people move through during marriage breakdown.*

Not only must lawyers themselves understand these stages, but they also have an obligation to explain them to their clients at the very outset. Lawyers have an obligation to provide their clients with some perspective on where the clients are, emotionally, and where they may be headed emotionally, not just legally.

This poor young lawyer was destined to serve a never-ending string of family law clients who would constantly surprise him with seemingly unpredictable mood changes and apparently conflicting opinions and instructions. The lawyer's only explanation? "Wow, clients in family disputes sure are crazy!" His clients probably went away feeling that he was right about them, not knowing how or why their feelings could change so dramatically over a relatively short period of time.

Well, they are not crazy at all. They are simply being asked to make some of the most important decisions of their lives under the most painful and stressful of circumstances. It is difficult to be reasonable and sensible under such pressure. However, with a little help and perspective on the emotional changes, these difficult times can run considerably smoother.

Empathy for people undergoing family breakdown is possible if one understands the general stages through which they may pass. I say that they *may* pass through them because there are no guarantees that they will do so. I have vivid memories of clients who never quite got on with their lives. Some stayed stalled for five, even ten, years after the separation, not really wanting or needing to reconcile with their spouse, sometimes seething with a vague anger, but at the same time not knowing what to do next.

Others, of course, move quickly and smoothly through all the emotional stages and emerge after just a few months, ready for career changes, new loves and new families. I can't help but wonder whether having an "emotional perspective" on the family breakdown contributed in some way to them having a better sense of direction and control.

If you don't have a lawyer to explain these emotional stages to you, then you must inform yourself. Be objective. Look at these stages and then be honest with yourself—where are you emotionally?

SOME OBSERVATIONS ON MARRIAGE

I COULD EASILY devote an entire book to the subject of marriage in Canada. Most Canadians heading into marriage spend more time thinking about where they will hold the ceremony, who will take the pictures, what kind of flowers will be at the wedding and what will be served for dinner than they do thinking about the actual marriage itself. In other words, they spend more time thinking about the *wedding* than they do about the realities of marriage. In my view, we should not give people marriage licences unless they have taken some kind of course to prepare them for marriage. These courses would teach them about the meaning of having a mature love and about the realities of the challenges facing every marriage, and it would equip them with dispute-resolution skills so that when reality leaps up and bites them, they would have the skills to tackle the problem and develop a solution. Many Canadian marriages break an axle the first time they hit a pothole because they are not equipped to deal with a crisis.

Since lawyers see marriages at the point of separation and divorce, we hear the courts saying things such as "marriage is an economic partnership." It is treated as if a business is splitting up. Yet we see couples spend very little time doing due diligence on their future "business partner" in advance of the marriage. Marriages would be much more successful if couples performed more due diligence. As clinical as this may sound, it's reality. What is your future partner's track record with money? If he or she has gone bankrupt two or three times, brace yourself. If he or she has criminal convictions for domestic violence, fraud or other serious crimes, brace yourself. If your future partner has a history of health problems, mental or physical, then you had better brace yourself. All of these realities should be known in advance.

If you still choose to marry someone who has a terrible financial record, a history of criminal convictions or a propensity to mental health issues, then you are at least going in with your eyes wide open. (All of these comments apply equally to common-law relationships. For more information about strengthening marriages at the outset, see my books *Do We Need a Marriage Contract? Understanding How a Legal Agreement Can Strengthen Your Life Together* and *Do We Need a Cohabitation Agreement? Understanding How a Legal Contract Can Strengthen Your Life Together.* For further information about these titles, please visit www.michaelcochrane.ca and www.legalintel.ca.)

In 1969, Elisabeth Kübler-Ross, then medical director of the Family Service and Mental Health Center of South Cook County in Illinois, published a book entitled *On Death and Dying. Life* magazine described it as a "profound lesson for the living." Her observations on death and dying were formed on the basis of her experiences with terminally ill patients. She identified a number of distinct phases through which the terminally ill will pass.

Many experienced family law practitioners and mental health professionals have been struck by the parallels between the experiences of those who are dying and those undergoing a marriage or family breakdown. While these stages will not apply to every case, they provide a useful framework to understand where a person may be emotionally. This understanding is invaluable because it may provide clues to a person's motivation when instructing his or her lawyer.

Kübler-Ross identified the following stages:
1. Denial and Isolation
2. Anger
3. Bargaining
4. Depression
5. Acceptance

What follows is an attempt to adapt her analysis of terminally ill patients to those experiencing the loss of a relationship or family. Based on my 30+ years of doing this work, I think it is a very reliable way of looking at our emotional selves.

EMOTIONAL STAGES

Stage 1: Denial and Isolation ("It's not happening to me... something else is wrong.")

KÜBLER-ROSS IDENTIFIED A tendency to deny the fact of the illness when learning that one is terminally ill. This, she speculated, was meant to "act as a buffer after the unexpected shocking news," allowing the patient to collect himself or herself and to mobilize defences.

Our expectations of our marriages are not unlike our expectations about life—we expect to be immortal in both. These expectations are somewhat understandable given the rather spectacular pledges made at weddings. This is not to suggest that we should be more cynical about wedding vows, but rather that we should recognize the extremely high expectations with which we begin our marriages and live-in relationships. It is these huge expectations that come crashing down at separation. This appears to be true regardless of the number of marriages we enter into. I have encountered people who have married three and four times, each time with renewed confidence that this one is "the right one."

It is not surprising, therefore, that the first reaction to marital strain, marriage breakdown or many other problems in a family is denial. Something (his job's too much lately) or someone else (her family) must be to blame. A typical response is, "If I ignore this problem, it will blow over." More likely than not, this denial occurs or begins to occur well in advance of the actual separation. Some spouses report knowing something was wrong months or even years in advance of separation. They admit denying there was a problem—"Please let it be something else," "He'll change," "She promised it would never happen again," "She's just depressed." Sometimes it works and the problem appears to blow over. Of course, sometimes it is "something else." Relationships can and must go over many bumps. But many times it is just plain old denial of a fundamental challenge to the relationship or family.

If the marriage has indeed ended for one partner but not the other (as is usually the case, since one person is almost always way ahead of the other in separating), denial can be a powerful obstacle to a lawyer attempting to assist in the orderly severing of the knot. "Denying" clients may move from lawyer to lawyer in search of someone who will share their view, someone who will keep them in the marriage, someone who will keep the family together. It is not unlike the terminally ill patient who seeks a second, a third, even a fourth medical opinion. They search for someone who will keep their original expectation of immortality alive. I myself have met clients who have listened patiently as we worked through their issues, thanked me, paid their bill ... and gone right back to the troubled marriage or relationship and were only able to separate many years later.

So we should understand that for those experiencing marital difficulties or other family problems, a likely first response is to deny, deny, deny. This can be both tragic and painful for the people involved as well as family and friends who surround them. Imagine the difficulty in resolving any issue between spouses in such a predicament. One person is not ready to discuss a settlement because they don't even agree that there is a major problem. I remember one client who asked me to try to delay the divorce so that his wife would have time to "snap out of it." She was remarried by the time he clued in. Denial can be a huge obstacle to moving forward. Are you in denial? Is your spouse in denial?

Stage 2: Anger ("It is happening to me ... and I hate it.")

THE DENIAL STAGE is often followed by a partial acceptance of what has occurred. The issue or problem facing the couple can no longer be avoided, perhaps because one partner has taken unmistakable steps to confront the issue, like moving out and consulting a lawyer or actually starting divorce proceedings. The "patient" finally accepts the diagnosis, perhaps after multiple consultations with other "doctors." However, while the diagnosis is finally being accepted, denial may be replaced with anger because the client doesn't like what he or she hears and feels. The anger may be directed against the other spouse, family members, oneself (the harshest, perhaps) or the lawyers who may now be involved.

Sometimes, these angry clients talk of being made to look "foolish," of being "blind" or "stupid." Suddenly the other spouse has been taking advantage of him or her, apparently laughing all the while. The anger becomes white-hot.

Once the awful truth is accepted, a spouse may be left with little else but that anger at a frustrating, possibly humiliating, predicament (with a lot of "I told you so's" not really helping the situation). It is at this stage that people search for their lawyers. The other spouse may have forced the issue into the open by consulting a lawyer and having "the letter" sent (see Chapter 4: Getting a Divorce), and the truth is finally accepted by the denying spouse.

It is also at this stage that lawyers frequently receive their instructions to start legal proceedings, to go to court, to be tough and, in short, to vent the angry client's venom. The lawyer and client can ill afford these proceedings because they are not designed to advance the client's interests, nor will they make the client happy. If anything, such proceedings may produce only regrets and lawyers' bills. The client who offers instructions to a lawyer while in such a state of mind will never be happy and will later blame his or her lawyer for wasting time and money. With the client in this angry stage, we may be left with a person who no longer denies there is a problem but now confronts the issue with what is never a scarce resource—unproductive anger.

Beware—this stage has been known to last a long time. In my experience, this stage can also make people sick. Family law lawyers see clients with all manner of physical complaints caused by the stress of their anger. Are you reacting in anger? What is motivating you? What is motivating your spouse?

Stage 3: Bargaining ("If I do this, maybe you will do that.")

KÜBLER-ROSS DESCRIBES THIS next phase as an attempt to postpone the inevitable. The anger has not produced anything and subsides partially. But now promises, often unrealistic ones, are made in the hope of buying more time. The patient has accepted what is happening but now negotiates to postpone it. The same can be true of people in family breakdown.

The bargaining may manifest itself in overly generous settlement proposals—"She can have everything," or "I'm the one who left; he can keep the house." Sometimes the offer is no more than a weak attempt to ease guilt or to prove to the other spouse that "I'm not so bad after all." For some reason, men do this more often than women. Unfortunately, but not surprisingly, such promises are rarely wise or kept. The client's interests have not been advanced; in fact, they may have been harmed by this bargaining.

At this stage, we have a client whose anger may be subsiding but whose instructions are nonetheless tainted by unreal feelings. Lawyers and clients alike must be alert to these motivations and recognize that instructions during this phase of false bargaining are unlikely to produce lasting settlements. They will, however, produce a legal bill ... and you will wonder later what you are paying for. A settlement achieved during this phase can be a waste of money. I have met many clients who were filled with resentment for having entered into an unwise settlement for all the wrong reasons. Likewise, the person who has been told "you can keep the house" will be extremely disappointed when the false bargaining has to be abandoned as unrealistic. Are you motivated by feelings of guilt? Are you trying to improve your image in the eyes of your ex? Are you trying to move on too quickly to a new relationship? All elements of false bargaining.

Stage 4: Depression ("I'm losing my past and I have no future.")

THIS NEXT PHASE is identified by Kübler-Ross as one in which the terminally ill patient's sense of anger subsides, the false bargaining has ended unsuccessfully (as it had to) and a sense of great loss sets in. She identifies this depression as being two-edged—a reactive depression and a preparatory depression. Reactive depression is a reaction to the past loss. What the patient once had is now gone or is slipping away. Preparatory depression anticipates impending losses.

For the couple undergoing marriage breakdown, this "double depression" is understandable. Their reactive depression may be in response to the loss of things such as their best friend, their life partner, a sense of family, time with their children, the family home, the cottage, valued possessions and so on. At the same time, they must face the losses yet to come—the companionship of the spouse, the old network of friends and the plans that were made but will never materialize. Discovering that there will be no more anniversaries can hurt. In many cases both spouses must lower their expectations financially. A standard of living once taken for granted is gone.

Few clients in this state of mind are equipped to provide balanced instructions to their lawyer. Not only does the past generate feelings of sadness, but prospects for the future seem bleak as well. Sadness and loss of hope suddenly overwhelm everything. Negotiating on behalf of these clients is pointless for a lawyer. These clients do not care what happens. Where are you? In a dark place, not caring anymore? Can you reach out, can you wait to make these important decisions? Is there someone there to help?

Stage 5: Acceptance ("I've got things I want to do.")

FROM THE FOREGOING, it may appear that people are virtually never able to provide instructions to their lawyers. If they are not denying the problems, or angry or depressed, they are engaged in false bargaining. However, there *is* a time when clients are best equipped to make decisions, although lawyers may not always have the luxury of awaiting that moment. This stage is described by Kübler-Ross as a time when the patient is "neither depressed nor angry about his fate." It is a time of contemplation and almost void of feelings. The dying patient at this time has found some peace and acceptance.

In the case of marriage breakdown, the spouse at this stage will have accepted the end of the relationship and marriage and will not see the dispute or court process as offering a meaningful or desirable link with the other spouse. It is as if everything has become clearer. Settlement proposals suddenly seem worthy of consideration. If the marriage is truly over, then the final loose ends should be tied up. The chapter of life that was the marriage must be closed. Planning seems worthwhile, new events have meaning and the past is just that—past. What is also important at this stage is the client's willingness to reconstruct or start again. What is ahead is what is important. As corny as it sounds—what is past truly is prologue. When will you be ready to move on, to accept the future?

It is at this stage of acceptance that clients are best equipped emotionally to settle. (Please understand that by "settle" I do not mean "give up.") For the first time, perhaps in months or years, emotions are not obstructing their powers of reason. They are able to describe what is best for their children, what they need and what they want.

This is the stage to which, in my anecdote, the junior lawyer's client suddenly arrived. She had denied, she had been angry, she had been depressed. She had even tried a little false bargaining, too. But she ultimately accepted what had occurred and was ready to move on.

No one should be embarrassed about this experience because it is a natural evolution of feelings. I would be worried if it didn't occur. Of course, you should be angry and depressed—you are going through something that is awful. The best you can do sometimes is to just understand it, roll with it and recognize that it will all pass and you will move on.

MARRIAGE COUNSELLING: GETTING HELP TO COPE

IT CAN BE tough going through all of these emotional stages. Many of the male clients that I have met over the years deal with the breakdown of their relationship in stereotypical isolation. Their colleagues at work are often stunned when the separation is announced. Meanwhile, women have shared their problems with friends, family and co-workers. Two extremes: he tells no one; she tells everyone.

Men have said to me, "My God, I can't believe it. The whole neighbourhood knows!" And their wives shake their heads. "He refuses to talk to anyone. Even his family doesn't know!"

I suggest a little understanding of these ways of coping. Women typically have a wider circle of friends than men. Men don't share much with the few friends they have. For male readers: find someone to share your situation with. I don't mean somebody who will just say, "Yeah, I know what you mean, let's have another beer." Find someone who can offer some support and honest, objective suggestions. For the women: be sensitive to the limits that need to be respected when sharing details of the relationship. Reach out, but do it with discretion.

Why not get some professional help? Have you tried marriage counselling? If one more person tells me that they want to try marriage counselling but their spouse won't go ... Let me speak to the reluctant spouse directly: what exactly do you think will happen if you go? No one has died from marriage counselling. No one is stigmatized or shunned. It is confidential. Marriage counselling is always a help unless, of course, you can't speak the truth or hear the truth.

If you are afraid of the unknown, let me try to help. Imagine having a wise friend that both you and your partner like and trust. Neither of you is any closer to this friend than the other. You join your friend in a comfortable room and discuss the situation that you face or that you think you face. You take turns explaining it. The friend asks questions. Probes. Makes you think. Challenges you. Makes you think some more. Helps you identify some mistakes. Some strengths. Helps you say you're sorry. The friend keeps all of this in confidence and sends you off to work on some things. You can check in as often as you need.

I have never heard of a marriage counsellor making a couple stay together, though I have heard of marriage counsellors saving marriages that were unnecessarily headed for a split. But marriage counselling can also become separation counselling, and can make matters easier for the couple: marriage counsellors can help a couple come to a realization that their marriage is over, and then help them deal with that reality.

Go to marriage counselling. Go now. Keep going. Don't let a relationship die because you wouldn't work at it. Go down swinging. You won't regret it—no matter how it turns out. If you are worried about the expense, don't be. It is much less expensive than a lawyer. Rates range from $50 to $300 per hour. A great investment no matter how it turns out. (See, for example, www.theravive.com for family therapists in Canada.)

WHY DID THIS HAPPEN? THE CAUSES OF DIVORCE

THIS IS A question that is often posed during first interviews with clients. Why did this happen to me—I don't understand why we are separating. Certainly, in the marriage counselling that I have just recommended, you will have an opportunity as a couple to explore what happened in the marriage. In all my years of seeing marriages unravel, there have been many reasons why the relationship has ended, from the more expected causes—adultery, financial problems, falling out of love—to those that are less clear and definitive. All kinds of things happen to all kinds of relationships. What I have noticed, however, is that Canadians are unprepared for some of the challenges that are thrown at their marriages.

As I mentioned earlier, we make some rather spectacular promises when we marry, and ignore the very strong likelihood that at some point in time the marriage is going to face a challenge. By way of example, let's consider marriages faced with financial problems—a wife overspends on credit cards, a husband doesn't pay his taxes, someone makes poor investments. To address the problem, I've seen couples rush to the financial institution and simply increase their line of credit or their mortgage to pay the debt, without any regard for understanding how they got into the predicament to begin with or how they can make sure that it doesn't happen again. What Canadian families need are skills to deal with the challenges that arise in marriages. When I say skills, I mean dispute-resolution skills, including the ability 1) to identify what the real problem is; 2) to consider options for dealing with that problem; 3) to objectively evaluate the relative advantages and disadvantages of different ways of solving the problem; and 4) to then work together to deal with the problem in a way that does not simply cover it up, but prevents it from coming forward again.

Marriages can fail because Canadian couples don't work at solving problems very well, or they don't take the long view. If Canadian couples had the resources, skills, or even just a clear plan—based on the steps I'm suggesting in this book—they could take the long view instead of breaking down at the first challenge, not knowing how to recover.

TRANSITION PEOPLE: CAUSE OR CASUALTY

WHAT IS A transition person? Sometimes when a marriage is in trouble or over, you will meet someone. This person may be a great listener, fun and attractive. They are able to make you forget about all the problems in the marriage or the separation. Maybe they have already been through it themselves and can really empathize. The new relationship may have become one where the people in it are more than just friends.

Do these people cause the marriage to break down? Not really, though they can make a marriage breakdown happen faster. The marriage may already be in trouble, but the transition person helps you to make the move out of the marriage—at least emotionally or psychologically.

But suddenly you are out of the relationship and this supportive person may start to look different. They have served their purpose. However, the transition person may have expectations about where the both of you will go now together, in a new relationship, but you may have a different plan that doesn't necessarily include them.

I mention this for three reasons:

1. If you have a transition person in your life, be careful about feeling obligated to him or her. He or she may have been a great friend during a tough time, but that doesn't mean you have to be together for the rest of your lives.

2. If your spouse has used a transition relationship to exit the marriage, be aware of the role it played for him or her. In other words, don't blame the transition person for something that may have been happening anyway. Your issue is with your spouse.

3. If you are a transition person, go into these situations with your eyes open. It can be tough for you, too, if things don't evolve the way you expected.

CLOSING REMARKS

YOUR EMOTIONS WILL be very powerful as you move through separation and divorce, but they can't be allowed to rule your decision-making. Get a read on where you are with the emotional rollercoaster of feelings. Denial can be dangerous and delay action; anger and depression can sap you of the strength that you will need to deal with this intense period; false bargaining can be a dangerous, easy way out that you will regret later. Make sure you're ready to accept solutions because they're good for you, your children and your future.

MY ADVICE

1. Get an accurate read on where you are and where your spouse is emotionally.
2. Do not fall into the traps of denial, anger, depression and false bargaining.
3. Put your anger aside and focus on practical results.
4. Go to a marriage counsellor: if the effort doesn't save the marriage, it will certainly ease the separation.

TAKING A LOOK AT LAWYERS

Take Charge of the Relationship

O N THE SUBJECT of lawyers, it is difficult to know where to begin. No trade or profession has been so vilified in recent times as this group. Do we deserve it? A little bit. But it does not change the fact that at some point in time you are going to need one of us. This chapter provides a few insights into the legal profession, with a view to helping you make intelligent decisions about which lawyer to use and how to deal with him or her.

The harsh criticism of lawyers ignores two important things. First and foremost, there are many excellent lawyers. I know dozens of lawyers who genuinely care about their clients, their clients' families and their futures. Second, you must understand that clients can be responsible for much of their own misfortune in dealing with lawyers. I am not blaming these clients. They are hurt and angry and want to do something about it. They can lash out at everyone including their lawyer. However, if people are very poorly informed and very undemanding consumers of legal services, they set themselves up for problems. So, rather than debate whether all lawyers are sharks or not, let's focus on how to find a good lawyer—specifically, a good family law lawyer—and what to demand as an informed consumer once in his or her office.

FINDING A FAMILY LAW LAWYER

THE LAWYER YOU ultimately choose to represent you could be the single most important decision you make about your own case, so take some time to make it properly. It is not uncommon to hear non-family law lawyers remarking to family law lawyers, "How can you do that stuff?" or "If I wanted to be a social worker or psychiatrist, I wouldn't have gone to law school" or "Family law? It's not challenging enough—every case is decided on the facts, not the law," and so on. While lawyers recognize that a family law case is a legal matter and can be quite lucrative, they do not flock to this area of practice. Lawyer burnout is common because family law is emotionally charged. Files are injected with added intensity, stress, emotion and, too frequently, violence. Finding an experienced, humane and reasonably priced lawyer can be very difficult, so take your time.

A number of provinces have established a method of accrediting lawyers as specialists in fields such as family law, criminal law and so on. This represents a quantum leap for consumers who before had to rely on word-of-mouth, the Yellow Pages and hit-and-miss. The same lawyer who handled Granddad's will, Aunt Mary's car accident and Mom and Dad's real estate deal often inherits the family's first divorce. When the economy is in bad shape, or work is slow, lawyers who practise other areas of law such as real estate law or commercial work, and who have little or no experience in family law, often take on family law cases. This is more often than not a big mistake for them—and for you. Contact your provincial law society and ask if they have an accreditation system for family law lawyers and a list of those in your community. Get someone who knows family law.

In addition, some provincial law societies have established Lawyer Referral Services. These free services list lawyers in the province by city and preferred area of practice. It lets you pinpoint family law lawyers in your community. These referral services can also give you information about the availability of legal aid, which we will discuss in more detail later in this chapter. A lawyer who receives a client through this service will give the first half hour for free—not a bad deal if you are shopping around.

With systems such as accreditation and lawyer referral services, clients have a fighting chance to at the very least find an experienced family law lawyer. Assuming that you have found your way to a lawyer, let's consider in more detail what makes a lawyer the right choice for you.

In my opinion, the ideal family law lawyer is experienced, honest, a good listener, humane, has a sense of humour and is respected by his or her peers. This person does not lose sight of people, especially children, in the heat of practice. He or she is punctual, considerate and professional.

The ideal family law lawyer lets you participate in a discussion about your situation and is not afraid to tell you, at the outset, things you may not want to hear. Usually, after spending 30 minutes with this lawyer, you should be able to answer three questions:

1. Do I feel comfortable with this person?
2. Do I respect his or her opinion?
3. Does he or she respect mine?

Do not be influenced by designations such as Q.C. (Queen's Counsel). Ignore lawyers who bluster about past wins or big cases and have a hired-gun attitude. If somebody comes across as a stuffed shirt, they probably are.

You do not need the most expensive lawyer in town. I can assure you that he or she is not necessarily the best. You do not need the biggest law firm in the city, either. Do not pass over lawyers who may appear too young. They may have special skills. It is experience, not age, that counts.

Some clients have preferences for a lawyer of a particular sex. More women than men seem to practise as family law lawyers these days. I have met male clients who think a female lawyer is preferable because
• they can "control" her;
• they want their ex-spouse to see how "enlightened" they really are; or
• the judge will like them more if they have a woman lawyer. (Oh, brother! Now we know why the marriage had trouble.)

On the other side of the coin, we have the female client who thinks that she must have the toughest male lawyer to intimidate her husband and earn his respect. So the male lawyer becomes her personal gladiator.

These kinds of clients end up having fascinating conversations like, "My lawyer says your lawyer is ..." or "My lawyer has never heard of your lawyer and ..." They are ignoring the fact that they should be picking their own lawyer, not letting their spouse pick for them.

Family law has also become a bit of a battleground for the "rights" movements—fathers' rights, mothers' rights, grandparents' rights, women's rights and men's rights. There are lawyers out there who are fighting causes while they practise law, lawyers who describe themselves as a fathers' rights lawyer or lawyers who practise with a feminist perspective. This is not to say that these lawyers do not fulfill a role or make some important contributions to the law through, for example, test cases. If you want to be a test case and are prepared to pay for it, then that is your choice. I personally believe that these lawyers have an admitted bias and should be avoided. Their cause may become your cause—at your expense. You have enough to worry about without getting tangled up in someone else's agenda. Keep your eye on the ball: your needs, your children's needs, your money and your future.

In a similar vein, you do not want a lawyer who says things like:
- "I never send anybody to mediation ..."
- "I don't approve of joint custody ..."
- "I never agree to ..."

Their straitjacket probably doesn't fit you. You want more choice, not less.

You do want a lawyer who is going to actually *be* the lawyer. You do not want someone who meets you at the initial interview, sniffs the file and then passes it to a junior lawyer without consulting you, and the junior lawyer then proceeds to do all the work, including meeting with you, going to court and negotiating the issues. Know who you are actually hiring. It is one thing to have lawyers work as a team. It is another thing to have the work done by lawyers that you did not actually hire.

CONFLICTS OF INTEREST

YOU SHOULD ALSO be aware of any potential conflict of interest when hiring a lawyer. Do not use a lawyer who has previously done work for your spouse or your spouse's family. The lawyer may have information from these sources that will put him or her in a difficult position at a later date.

Another question that comes up frequently is, "Can we use the same lawyer?" This often appears to be a good idea, especially if the couple thinks separation and divorce is straightforward and that all issues are agreed upon. But one lawyer who is representing both sides cannot fairly represent each party's interest. If the lawyer discovers an issue that needs to be resolved in favour of one spouse or the other, he or she is immediately in a conflict of interest. In raising the issue, the lawyer may undermine the agreement that the couple thinks they have achieved. In the field of law, it is generally considered to be negligent for one lawyer to try to represent two parties to a separation.

In some cases, one client will go to see a lawyer and that lawyer will prepare all of the legal documents. The other client will never meet with the lawyer, but instead will receive a package of documents that he or she can then take to a lawyer for independent legal advice. There is no law in Canada that requires a person to obtain independent legal advice prior to signing, for example, a separation agreement or a marriage contract. Certainly it is recommended that both parties obtain independent legal advice, but not everyone can afford it and people cannot be forced to go see a lawyer. In such circumstances, it is not uncommon to see a clause put in the agreement expressly acknowledging that the individual had an opportunity to go see a lawyer, but expressly declined that opportunity and is signing the agreement voluntarily.

CONFIDENTIALITY

ONE OF THE most important features of the lawyer's relationship with the client is the promise of confidentiality. It is the basis of the client's trust and confidence in a lawyer.

To solve a client's problem, the lawyer must know everything about the client. In order to feel comfortable telling everything, the client must trust the lawyer to keep every word in confidence. Not only is indiscreet chatter about the personal details of clients' problems totally unprofessional and a breach of their trust, it is dangerous. It risks the law firm and lawyer's reputations and may be considered professional misconduct. The Canadian Bar Association's Code of Professional Conduct provides as follows:

> The lawyer has a duty to hold in strict confidence all information acquired in the course of the professional relationship concerning the business and affairs of his/her client, and he/she should not divulge any such information unless he/she is expressly or implicitly authorized by his/her client or required by law to do so.

This rule extends to the entire law firm and staff. Every lawyer is bound by this rule of confidentiality. The confidentiality is known as solicitor-client privilege. The lawyer cannot be forced to disclose confidential information even if the court orders it. The lawyer can only reveal the information if it is necessary to advance your case or if you expressly authorize it. In limited situations, such as to prevent a crime or to report child abuse, lawyers are able to breach this privilege.

THE FIRST INTERVIEW WITH YOUR LAWYER

AFTER YOU HAVE the names of several experienced family law lawyers, take the time to meet at least three of them. For the first interview, make a list of questions about the important issues. (See my first-interview outline later in this chapter.) In preparation for the interview, you may want to write out your own history of the relationship. Collect as many important documents as you can (marriage certificate, financial records, mortgage papers, previous orders or agreements and so on). During the interview, you'll want to be as complete and as frank as possible. The lawyer needs to know everything to be able to provide an objective analysis. Resist the temptation to colour the facts in your favour. I often ask a client, "If your spouse was sitting here listening, what would they say about your description of the marriage? What are they telling their lawyer?"

Before you meet with your lawyer for the all-important first interview, I would recommend that you examine the Family Law Client History Form in Appendix A. If you show up at the lawyer's office with this form completed, you will easily save yourself hundreds, if not thousands, of dollars in legal fees. All of the information that forms the basis for the lawyer's understanding of your situation will be there. Simply knowing the length of the marriage, the number of children or the basic asset picture for your family can accelerate his or her consideration of your situation. So step one is go to the form and fill it in.

Step two is sit back and imagine a meeting with me in the boardroom of my law firm in front of a large whiteboard upon which I have written the following seven headings:

1. Divorce
2. Custody
3. Access
4. Child support
5. Property
6. Spousal support
7. The other thing

During this first interview, my approach is to work through each topic, discussing some of the options that are available. So, for example, under *divorce,* we will look at the various grounds for divorce, such as adultery, cruelty or one-year separation. Under the heading of *custody,* we will look at some of the alternative approaches, such as sole custody, joint custody and shared parenting. In the area of *access* we consider various schedules and with *child support,* we will consider the respective best interests of the child (or children), the gross annual incomes of the parents and the Child Support Guidelines, which accurately predict the monthly amount of child support. Under *property,* we will review what is included in family assets and liabilities. Under the heading of *spousal support,* we will look at each spouse's needs, their respective abilities to pay and, in some cases, the impact of the marriage on career opportunities of a spouse.

But before we begin a consideration of any of those substantive issues, I want to talk about *the other thing.* I usually can't even begin to discuss the substantive issues before a client asks me "What do you mean by 'the other thing?'"

Each marriage has something that makes it unique. There is always something that affects the way in which the substantive issues are negotiated. Other things include mental health problems suffered by a spouse; the presence of violence or other abuse; alcoholism; drug addiction; gambling problems; extramarital affairs; criminal activities; financial catastrophes, such as bankruptcy; or the signing of a marriage contract that affects the division of property and spousal support. It can even include something as common as the parents of the separating couple being heavily involved in the care of their children, in their finances or even in the ownership of their home. This list is not intended to be an exhaustive list, but it illustrates the kinds of things that are going on in Canadian marriages that will affect the way in which the separation and divorce progress.

So, for example, if one spouse has had an extramarital affair and the way in which it was discovered was particularly humiliating or embarrassing for the other spouse, the emotions caused by that extramarital affair will affect the way in which the parties negotiate the separation and divorce. If the spouse has a mental health issue, or abuses alcohol and drugs, that too will affect the way in which the negotiations proceed. Some of these things may affect the substantive outcome of the divorce, but all of them will affect the way in which the issues are negotiated. In my experience, every separation and divorce has another "thing."

As you read the upcoming chapters, keep track of these seven categories and it will help you develop a reliable game plan for proceeding with your own separation and divorce.

THE RETAINER (OR WHAT EVERYONE ELSE CALLS A CONTRACT)

THE WORD "RETAINER" can mean a number of different things. It can mean the amount of money you give a lawyer up front. He or she may request the money to cover disbursements that will be incurred, such as couriers, court filing charges or similar, relatively small expenses. The amount of such a retainer can range from a few hundred dollars up to $10,000 or more. "Retainer" can also mean the actual contract the client signs to hire the lawyer to do the work. It is this type of retainer we will examine.

It never ceases to amaze me that a person will go into a lawyer's office, discuss the most intimate details of his or her life (details they have often never shared with anyone else) and then turn their whole life over to this virtual stranger without so much as discussing how much the lawyer charges per hour, the estimated time for completion of the work, the expected disbursements, billing policy or quality of work.

This same individual will leave the lawyer's office, go home and decide to get the house painted by a couple of university students. What do they do? First they ask all their neighbours about painters they have used and whether they would recommend them. Once they have found their painters, they spend an hour walking around the house, telling them exactly what they want and how they want it done. They demand written contracts, guarantees, a fixed date for completion and references. They want to control the kind of paint that is used and whether these budding painters have liability insurance. Once they have the estimate in hand and the students have jumped through every conceivable hoop, the client wants to "think it over."

The hapless students may make a couple hundred dollars if they get the job, while the lawyer on the other side of town is casually opening a file with what amounts to a blank cheque, having given few, if any, commitments.

How can this contradiction be remedied?

The answer is not to stop asking the painters for a written contract! Start asking your lawyer for one. The lawyer is not going to throw up his or her arms, stamp around the office or sulk as if you have offended them. Lawyers know what retainers are; we use them all the time. Do you think that business people who hire lawyers don't pin them down on the cost? Of course they do, and they insist on answers to a lot of questions. Why should decisions about your life be any different or any less important?

This need not be a painful experience—you are simply asking someone, supposedly a highly skilled professional, to give you a copy of his or her retainer form. Remember, it does not matter what lawyers call it, it is still a contract. It will describe the parties to the contract (you and the lawyer), the work that is to be done, the fee that will be charged for the work (hourly rate) and other important terms. A basic retainer, which I developed from my time in private practice, is included in Appendix A. You have my permission to photocopy the form (but, please, not other parts of the book) and present it to the lawyer (if they do not have their own retainer form).

If they hesitate at the use of a retainer, you don't want them to handle your case. There is absolutely nothing in the retainer provided that is unusual or offensive to an experienced lawyer. Do not hire a lawyer without a written retainer.

Consider asking that a term be incorporated into the retainer that places a ceiling on the fee that can be charged without further consultation and a further written retainer. Matrimonial proceedings that begin quickly (perhaps in anger) have a way of consuming bundles of money in a very short time. A clause that states simply, "Fees not to exceed $2,000 without prior further written authorization" can be a valuable inhibition for those lawyers tempted to litigate first and negotiate later. Ask to look at a sample retainer.

When describing the legal service to be provided, a simple "obtain divorce" is the equivalent of a blank cheque. (Would you ask the painter to simply "paint house"?) Insist on a specific description of the work and sign a retainer authorizing perhaps only the first few steps (see Chapter 4: Getting a Divorce). This again inhibits premature litigation and gives you control of the progress of work. If you are not satisfied with the work that has been done, don't authorize any more until you are.

As I mentioned earlier, lawyers must spend money from time to time. It costs almost $200 in court fees to start a divorce. It can cost as much as $300 to have a copy officially delivered to the other spouse (called "service"). There are dozens of small out-of-pocket items. When lawyers disburse or spend money on these items, they would prefer to use the client's money. Consequently, most lawyers ask for an amount up front as a deposit (sometimes also called a retainer). The amount varies depending on the type of case and the degree of complexity, but out-of-pocket expenses rarely exceed $500. In other words, be prepared to provide the lawyer with some money to be applied toward disbursements.

You will note that a paragraph in the retainer refers to client inquiries about fees and disbursements. At no time and under no circumstances should you ever feel inhibited about inquiring about the state of your account, the lawyer's disbursements or fee policy, or any other matter related to your file. Being in doubt or unclear in any way is an invitation for disagreement at a later date. If you are not sure, ask! If it's still not clear, ask again! Don't pay for something you do not understand.

I offer you one final caution concerning your relationship with the lawyer during the course of his or her work for you. Lawyers employ junior lawyers, articling students, support staff and secretaries to assist with the work. Without their assistance, little could be done. Do not think that your lawyer is shirking his or her responsibilities by delegating to support staff. On the other hand, you have hired a particular lawyer and you are entitled to meet with that lawyer on a regular basis to discuss your case.

I suggest that you discuss this matter during the initial interview. If you want personal attention, then tell the lawyer at the first interview, not on the eve of the trial or while trying to negotiate a final settlement.

FAMILY LAW AND LEGAL AID

EVERY PROVINCE HAS a form of legal aid for people who cannot afford legal services. This usually involves applying, passing a "means test" (they judge your neediness) and receiving a Certificate of Legal Aid. The lawyer to whom you present this certificate then renders his or her accounts to the provincial legal aid plan. The amount that can be charged for particular steps is defined by a fee structure called a tariff. Lawyers receive less money for legal aid work on an hourly basis than if they were hired "off the street." If you own property, in many cases legal aid will take a lien on your home. You then either pay legal aid when that home is sold or you have a repayment scheme. These plans are not funded well and it is a small number of people who qualify for legal aid. On the other hand, payment of the account is guaranteed.

IF YOU ARE DISSATISFIED WITH YOUR LAWYER

LET'S EXAMINE THIS in two parts—first, what is likely to make you unhappy, and second, what to do about your dissatisfaction.

Poor Communication

ONE OF THE chief complaints law societies receive from clients about lawyers is that they don't return telephone calls or e-mails promptly or, in some cases, at all. Why don't lawyers return telephone calls? The telephone is often the only means by which they can stay in contact with their clients, so why wouldn't the lawyers use it?

There are, I think, a variety of reasons. First, most lawyers are too busy to return every telephone call they receive in a working day. Second, in some cases it is just physically impossible. Lawyers are often out of the office, in court, on discoveries, travelling and so on. Third, many lawyers are procrastinators. If they have no good news, only bad news or no news at all, then they are less likely to pick up the telephone.

Experienced family law lawyers will use personalized answering services or e-mail, or will have their secretaries return calls, if they are busy. I have heard of lawyers who do not return telephone messages for weeks. This is inexcusable. I recommend a polite but firm warning after the first time it is a problem: "Return my calls promptly or I'll get someone who will."

Another complaint from clients is the lawyer's failure to keep them abreast of developments. An experienced family law lawyer will meet with the client regularly and provide, through periodic letters, reports on the status of the matter (called reporting letters). A good lawyer will not only report on the status of the matter but also summarize what happened, what options were open, which course was recommended, what the client's instructions were and any other considerations.

I place a great deal of emphasis on regularly written reporting letters, and for good reason. The goal of this book is to make you an informed consumer of legal services before you enter a lawyer's office. It will have taken some effort on your part to have achieved that status. It will only be maintained if your lawyer takes over the job of informing you about your own case. Reporting letters are no more than a form of continuing education about your own case, your options and how the legal system is working on your case. They provide a record of past decisions and enable you to make intelligent choices about the future. Insist on regular reporting letters.

Lawyers' Accounts

ANOTHER FREQUENT AREA of disagreement is the bills that are rendered by the lawyer during or at the end of a matter. I have already set
out the essential items that need to be discussed at the time the retainer
is signed. Another thing that you may wish to discuss is the method
of billing. If an accurate estimate can be given, some clients prefer to
be billed in regular monthly instalments rather than letting a huge bill
accumulate. Others cannot afford to pay until the case is finished and
successful. In either case, make a point of discussing with the lawyer the
method by which you would like to be billed.

Generally, lawyers will insist on billing the disbursements to you as
they are incurred. For example, if a $200 bill is incurred to serve the
documents on your spouse, then often that amount will be invoiced to
you immediately. If you have an amount on deposit with the lawyer for
the purpose of paying such disbursements, known as a "Disbursements
Only" account, you should receive a statement from the lawyer stating
that the disbursement was incurred and was paid out of the amount held
on deposit. Any account, whether for disbursements only or for legal
services rendered, should also include a specific description of what was
done to justify the fee.

Lawyers charge hourly rates, but for obvious reasons lawyers cannot work in blocks of one hour at a time on each file. Sometimes it is a
6-minute telephone call with the opposing lawyer, a 45-minute period
of preparation for court or 18 minutes of research on a particular issue.
To accommodate work of less than an hour, the lawyer divides his work
hours into tenths, or units of six minutes. Ten units of six minutes make
up each hour. The lawyer will, regardless of how much time was actually spent, never record less than 0.1 of an hour being spent on a matter,
because that is the smallest unit of their time. Some lawyers use a system by which they never record less than 0.2 regardless of how much
time was spent on the task. Ask the lawyer how he or she records time.

As the lawyer works through the day, he or she will keep track, either
by written docket or computer, of each tenth of each hour. For example,
the telephone rings and it's the client making an appointment and the
call lasts three minutes. The lawyer will fill out a time docket for 0.1 or

six minutes. (Yes, you get billed for phone calls. Time is money.) If the call lasted 12 minutes, the lawyer would fill out a docket for 0.2, two units of six minutes. As each docket is filled out, the lawyer writes down what service was rendered. A typical time docket could look as follows:

Mike C.—Jan. 5, 2015
10:00–10:06
Client—Brown #161
Telephone call re: husband's breach of restraining order 0.1

The lawyer accumulates these dockets, usually in the office computer system; when it is time to render an account, a full chronological list of all services is available for download. The account will also total the time and multiply it by the lawyer's hourly rate. Once any disbursements and HST or other taxes are added, you have a full account.

Insist on full, itemized statements of account, whether it be an interim or final account. Under no circumstances should you accept the old chestnut—one sheet of paper with "To Services Rendered— $15,000." You deserve a full statement of services.

What to Do When You Are Unhappy with Your Lawyer's Bill

THIS CAN BE a painful experience. You receive the lawyer's bill for the work done on your behalf. You may even be happy with the outcome, but the cost! It seems like a lot more than you originally estimated or were told it would cost. Can the subject be dealt with in any way other than simply paying and stewing or refusing to pay? Yes.

An important beginning would be to discuss the matter with the lawyer directly. Make an appointment to discuss the bill and be prepared to go through it line by line. You should have received an itemized statement of account. Remember, mistakes can be made, misunderstandings occur and they can readily be remedied. Lawyers often reduce bills to get them paid. They will write off a small amount to settle the matter.

Assessing the Account

HOWEVER, IF YOU are still dissatisfied, it is possible to arrange an appointment with a court official for you and the lawyer to have an independent third person assess or "tax" the lawyer's account. To arrange such an appointment, contact the local courthouse and speak to the Taxing Officer. You will be given an appointment and a notice that must be delivered to the lawyer.

Once at the meeting, you should be prepared with notes, your account and your retainer to discuss the agreement you thought you had with the lawyer. The court official will look at the retainer, the number of hours worked, the amount charged, the normal standard for such work, out-of-pocket expenses and so on. He or she has the power to reduce the account—and often does. It is never increased.

It is not an embarrassing hearing for either person. Lawyers' accounts are taxed or assessed all the time. It could save you several hundred dollars, maybe even more. There are some notable cases where lawyers' accounts were reduced to zero—that's right, zero. The officer thought the work was worthless and a court subsequently agreed when the decision was appealed by the lawyer.

Let's take a look now at what to do if, once you've assessed what's made you unhappy with your lawyer, you think it is better to part company with the lawyer.

FIRING YOUR LAWYER

A CLIENT MAY end the retainer or contract with the lawyer at any time. It may surprise you to learn that the lawyer cannot do likewise. The circumstances under which a lawyer can refuse to continue to act for a client are very, very limited. If a client asks a lawyer to mislead the court or do some other unethical act, the lawyer can refuse to continue representing the client. Similarly, if the client does not pay the lawyer, he or she can refuse to take any further steps. However, if the client provides instructions and pays the lawyer's account, the lawyer cannot refuse to act.

I think most clients are intimidated by the prospect of telling a professional that they are unhappy with the services rendered and intend to seek help from someone else. You will recall my analogy to the hiring of the college students to paint a house. Few people would have trouble putting an end to that work if they thought it was unsatisfactory.

If you hired a contractor to renovate your kitchen at a cost of $15,000 and the work was shoddy, the contractor uncommunicative and your instructions not followed, you would not hesitate to air your grievances. Why do we hesitate to do the same with a lawyer? The answer lies in part with our expectations and the vulnerability we feel at this point in our lives. In some cases clients don't want to waste the investment they have already made in this particular lawyer.

When we hire the kitchen renovator, we probably have a good idea of what we want, when we want it, what it should look like (designs, photographs from magazines and so on), when it will be finished and how much it will cost. This is not the case when we hire a lawyer. Instead, we have a very vague idea about what we want or need, no idea how quickly work can begin, no idea what it should look like when it's underway (never mind when it's finished) and no idea when it will be completed. We only fear how much the case will ultimately cost (perhaps more than the kitchen).

Unlike the kitchen, we have no way of knowing whether the legal work is being done, let alone done well. That makes it very difficult for us to complain.

If you followed the suggestions in the first half of this chapter, you will be in a much better position to evaluate your lawyer's performance. If you have a specific retainer, you will know whether or not your instructions are being carried out within the cost limits established.

Before dismissing your lawyer, take a few minutes to ask yourself what the real reasons are for your unhappiness. It might even be prudent to re-examine where you are emotionally. Reread the advice at the end of Chapter 1: Taking a Look at Ourselves, and reconsider the questions concerning motivation. You should also take a few minutes to consider the investment you have already made in this lawyer's handling of the problem. Be aware that when a new lawyer takes over the matter, many of the hours of preparation in familiarizing himself or herself with your case will be a duplication of time and expense. It is expensive to change lawyers, so make sure it is for the right reason.

All lawyers who practise family law are wary of the client who dismisses lawyer after lawyer and is always unhappy with the service. Experienced lawyers can see these clients for what they frequently are— spouses stuck in one of the stages described earlier. Like a terminal patient who denies the illness and shops for a second, third or fourth opinion, clients have been known to fire lawyers until they find one who will simply do as they are told. The client may be happy with that lawyer until they move on to the later emotional stages and suddenly look back on a lot of wasteful, angry litigation. The lawyer, perhaps out of inexperience or other motivation, will have always done as the client asked, but the client may not have been well served.

Assuming you are comfortable with your decision to fire your lawyer, what do you do next? Do not expect to pull this off without speaking to the lawyer face to face.

Most, if not all, law firms will only end a retainer after a personal interview has taken place to discuss why the problem arose. If you are intent on ending the retainer, schedule an interview with the lawyer, tell him or her what you wish to discuss and attend to the matter with the same resolve you would use to scold the painter or fire the kitchen contractor.

I have never argued with the client on such occasions. If they were unhappy, then I considered it their right to have a lawyer with whom they felt comfortable. Tell the lawyer what is on your mind and ask them to turn over the file with a written summary of its status (if you have not received one recently).

You should understand that you will likely receive an account for work done but not yet billed to you at the time the retainer comes to an end. If there are monies being held in trust by the lawyer, they will be applied toward the account and the balance (if any) returned to you.

Once paid, the lawyer has two obligations: first, to return your file to you promptly and, second, to render whatever assistance he or she can to your new lawyer. If a new lawyer has been found in advance of ending the retainer, your lawyer may be prepared to simply courier the entire file to the new lawyer.

The file that arrives at your new lawyer's office (or is turned over to you directly) may not be identical to the file you saw sitting in front of your former lawyer at the time the retainer ended. The lawyer does not simply slide the entire file into an envelope (or box in some cases). He or she is entitled to remove certain materials. However, the following items should be in the file:

- original legal documents (pleadings);
- letters written by you to the lawyer (originals);

- letters to the lawyer from the opposing lawyer or others (originals);
- copies of all other letters;
- originals of all evidence;
- legal research and memos of law (after all, you have paid for this research); and
- any other material needed to advance the case and not available elsewhere.

The lawyer may remove from the file such items as notes and memos to file, and a copy of legal research done to formulate his or her opinions.

Often a lawyer will turn over everything in the file but keep copies for his or her own records. The lawyer may do this if there is any concern that arguments may arise at a later date about the quality of work done.

Solicitor's Lien on the File

IF THE LAWYER is owed money for work done, he or she is entitled to be paid before releasing the file. Until paid in full, the lawyer has what is called a "solicitor's lien" on the file and its contents. Many people are familiar with a construction lien or mechanic's lien, whereby a worker or contractor can register notice on title to a piece of property that he is owed money for work done. The property cannot be mortgaged, sold or dealt with until the lien is paid. The same is true of a client's file with a lawyer.

CLOSING REMARKS

HIRING A LAWYER is a critical point in your handling of your own marriage or common-law relationship breakdown. It should be done from a position of power, which means from a position of being an informed consumer. The checklist set out at the end of this chapter can be consulted during the initial interview to ensure that the lawyer has a clear understanding of your needs as a client. If you have read the entire book and understand your own position emotionally and your legal needs in a reasonably specific way, your lawyer will know from the outset that the necessary standard of work and communication will be a high one.

In addition, if the lawyer is an experienced family law lawyer, he or she should welcome clients who are in touch with their own emotional and legal needs. You will be recognized and respected as a client who provides instructions from a position of informed self-interest and nothing less.

Should you determine that it is necessary to terminate your relationship with your lawyer, you can at least do so with confidence by following the guidelines above. Every client cannot be happy with every lawyer. The individual needs and idiosyncrasies of both are too diverse and personal to have perfect harmony. If you have followed the guidelines, you will have significantly reduced the likelihood of a mismatch. However, if your choice proved unfortunate or circumstances changed (e.g., a new lawyer in the firm took over the file), do not settle for less than you need and deserve. Examine your reasons for wishing to terminate the retainer. If you are confident in your decision, arrange the interview and find someone who can move your case to a conclusion quickly, inexpensively and, with luck, happily.

MY ADVICE

1. The lawyer works for you, not the other way around.
2. Hire only an experienced family law lawyer.
3. Check with your provincial or territorial law society and lawyer referral services to find lawyers who are experienced in family law.
4. Meet with a few lawyers for the sake of comparison of styles until you are comfortable. Focus on you, your children, your money and your future.
5. Go to the first interview with the Family Law Client History Form prepared (see Appendix A).
6. Get a written retainer (see Appendix A).
7. Monitor the work being done by your lawyer and get regular reporting letters.
8. If you're unhappy with your lawyer's work, speak up.

TAKING A LOOK AT
THE PROCESS

Understanding Family Law
and the Legal System

S OME GENERAL BACKGROUND knowledge about family law
is valuable if you are to become an informed consumer. I do not
intend to frighten, intimidate or bore you with the constitutional
intricacies of which jurisdiction, federal or provincial, has responsibility for laws that affect the family. You may be surprised to know that the
easy answer is that they both have responsibility and that they tried to
enact laws that complement each other.

Most people understand that the federal government has responsibility for such things as national defence or criminal law. These are
areas that affect the entire country and one law is therefore required for
everyone, regardless of the province in which they reside. We have a
Criminal Code that applies to everyone in Canada. The same is true of
the law of divorce.

Our Constitution provides that the federal government has responsibility for passing laws that permit people to divorce. The people of
Prince Edward Island use the same Divorce Act that is used by people
in British Columbia and Ontario. The procedural rules governing the
way in which the divorce is moved through the courts may vary from

province to province, but the substantive divorce provisions are the same in every province.

The applicability of the Divorce Act is triggered by one thing and one thing only: a request for a divorce, which is a court order dissolving a marriage. The Divorce Act only applies if a divorce is sought.

The Act provides guidelines for making orders concerning custody, access, support (for a spouse or a child) and, of course, the divorce itself. The Divorce Act does not say anything about dividing property, the matrimonial home or, for example, Marriage Contracts. Those issues also can be an important part of family law, so where are they dealt with? The answer lies in provincial law.

By virtue of our Constitution, the provinces have responsibility for laws concerning "property," including the way in which property is to be divided when a marriage breaks down. This means that if someone seeks a divorce and wants the court to divide the family's property, then provincial property division laws and federal divorce laws must work together.

If a couple separates, but they only want their family property divided (but they do not want a divorce), then the Divorce Act will not apply. Provincial law will provide the law for division of their property. But what if they also need to sort out custody of, access to and support of their children? Again, the answer lies in provincial law.

Each province supplies a complete package of alternative law in the event a couple does not seek a divorce, but needs legal assistance with property division, spousal support, child support, custody, access and dozens of other matters.

For example, consider Ontario provincial law. The Family Law Act sets out the law for property division on marriage breakdown. In combination with other provincial laws, it also sets out the means by which spousal and child support are calculated, special rules concerning the matrimonial home and the requirements for domestic contracts (Marriage Contracts, Cohabitation Agreements and Separation Agreements).

The Ontario Children's Law Reform Act sets out the law for determinations of custody and access and applies when a divorce is not sought. Each province has an equivalent law dealing with custody and access. We will look at all of these areas in more detail in upcoming chapters, but at this point we only need to see the interconnection between federal divorce law and provincial family law. They are designed to work together so that every combination is covered. Remember that when a divorce is sought, the Divorce Act does everything except divide your property. Provincial law always divides the family property.

There are other federal and provincial laws that are relevant to family law. Many of the provinces now have provincial enforcement agencies to collect support owed because of a court order or agreement. For example, Ontario passed the Family Responsibility Act, which sets out the structure and power of an agency that will collect support payments ordered under either federal or provincial law. In other words, the agency will enforce a support order, whether or not it was made as part of a divorce. Manitoba was the first province to establish a support enforcement program. Since then, every province has established some form of support enforcement assistance program. The degree of assistance may vary from province to province.

Federally, there is the Federal Orders and Agreements Enforcement Assistance Act, which provides information to those trying to track down support defaulters. It facilitates the work of the provincial enforcement agencies. The support enforcement area is a good example of recent attempts to enact complementary federal and provincial family laws in Canada.

In most cases, when a couple decides to separate and they cannot agree on how to settle their differences, an Application for Divorce is started in the court. It will also contain a request for division of property under the relevant provincial property law. In Ontario, between the Family Law Act and the Divorce Act, all the necessary court orders can usually be made, whether for custody, access, property division or the divorce itself. These different laws make up a patchwork designed to help the court sort out the problems experienced when a family splits up. Understand that there is no quick solution in the federal or provincial laws. If you and your spouse cannot agree, the law serves only as a guide and the judge decides for you.

THE LEGAL SYSTEM: CIVIL VERSUS CRIMINAL

THERE ARE SOME other basic elements of the legal system that should be understood in order to place your particular dispute in some context. Proceeding in the absence of some of this general knowledge would be ill-advised without knowing the rules.

In every province there are two distinct parts of the legal system— civil justice and criminal justice. Most people are familiar with the criminal law because so many news stories concern the justice system's handling of crime. Less well understood, but equally important, is the civil part of the justice system, which encompasses virtually anything not related to criminal justice.

Family law is but one of many areas being handled by our civil justice system. Legal disputes over wills, property, motor vehicle accidents, commercial contracts, defective products and family law are all handled within the system. Each province is the same in this respect. With minor variations, disputes concerning family law enter our civil justice system in much the same way as disputes over motor vehicle accidents or breaches of contract.

The differences between the civil justice system and the criminal justice system cause confusion for many people. In many cases the two systems operate in the same building, use the same judges, lawyers and court staff and, for all intents and purposes, look the same. But they are not.

Onus of Proof

THE TWO SYSTEMS, civil and criminal, do not reach conclusions in exactly the same way. The differences concern the amount of proof required to get the court to make a decision. This is generally called the "burden of proof." In a criminal case the Crown attorney (not district attorney or DA—that's in the United States) must prove "beyond a reasonable doubt" that someone is guilty of a crime. In other words, the judge or jury must be left with no doubts about this person's guilt. There must be no other reasonable explanation for what happened. In the civil justice system (including family law) the burden is different. A person must prove that his or her version is correct "on the balance of probability." This is a lower standard than the criminal system. Here each person tries to tip the scales in their favour with the proof. It doesn't have to be "beyond a doubt"; it just needs to be "probable."

Understanding this subtle but fundamental difference between a family law case and, say, a murder trial may change your approach to solving the problems in your own case. Family law judges are not trying to find out who is "guilty beyond a reasonable doubt." Rather, they are trying to choose between two possible solutions to the problem and pick the one that is on balance best for the family.

FAMILY LAW AND THE COURTS

IT IS A constant source of amazement to me as a lawyer and to those people who must use the courts for resolving family disputes that there is not simply one court capable of handling all family law problems. The provinces vary in this respect, but many of the provinces have more than one level of court for family law disputes. Ontario, for example, has three different courts: the Superior Court, the Unified Court and the Provincial Court. In Ontario, depending on the specific nature of the dispute, your geographical location, the wishes of the lawyers and the availability of court time, a person's request for help from the court could end up in one of three courts.

The Personnel of the Courts

WITHIN THESE FAMILY courts you may encounter a variety of people performing the functions that make the justice system operate. These people include:
- judges
- trial coordinators
- registrars, clerks and other court staff
- court reporters
- lawyers.

We will take a brief look at each person's role to understand the process of family law.

JUDGES

This job continues to hold great mystique for the Canadian public. It is admittedly a powerful position that gives this handful of men and women control over our property, our children and, in some cases, our liberty.

Judges are appointed to their position by either the federal or the provincial government. It is a job for life and can pay quite well compared with other jobs ($200,000+), and includes a pension and other benefits. They are free from political interference and cannot be fired or removed from the bench except in the most limited circumstances.

Most judges have been lawyers for at least 10 years and therefore have a certain degree of experience. They are not all people appointed for political favours, receiving payoffs for service to the political party that appointed them. In fact, by and large, we have good judges in Canada. The quality of Canadian judges continues to grow rather than decline.

Once appointed to the bench, judges are treated differently by their former colleagues and many complain that it can be an isolating experience. It can be difficult to relax publicly when so much decorum and respect is necessary for a judge's work.

The judge's function in the courtroom goes beyond simply rendering a decision at the end of the case. He or she must listen to the theory of each lawyer's argument, listen to the witnesses, watch their demeanour, take notes, rule on questions of evidence and control the entire courtroom process. The workload is often heavy and they must also manage court time closely as resources are scarce. It means following each and every question, protecting witnesses in some cases and prodding them in others.

It is a very difficult job and many a judge has sat in frustration as a lawyer did a poor job, knowing full well they could present the client's case better if they themselves jumped down and did it for the lawyer, but they can't. They sit patiently, taking notes of everything said, with observations or questions, and develop their own opinion about how the problem should be solved.

Most judges are called "Your Honour." When in doubt, use "Your Honour" and resist "Your Majesty" (which some poor witness called a judge in a traffic case; the judge was slow to point out the error). Judges expect lawyers to be clear and concise and witnesses to be direct, honest and easy to hear.

Sometimes a judge will give his or her reasons for judgment or decision at the end of a case; sometimes they do not and "reserve" or promise to give the decision later after they have thought about it.

TRIAL COORDINATORS

In some large cities, traffic is managed in one computerized control centre. The flow and volume of traffic is monitored, and when bottlenecks occur, traffic is diverted to an alternative route. This is essentially what a trial coordinator does for a living, except he or she manages the litigation flowing through the courts.

A large courthouse may have 10 or more courtrooms hearing motions, trials and even appeals. The trial coordinator ensures that the right judge gets the right case, at the right time, in the right courtroom. This means getting lawyers, clients (and their witnesses), court clerks and a court reporter to the same place as well. Last, and certainly not least, they must ensure that the judge has the court file and appropriate materials in advance of the hearing. Of course, once everything is ready to go, the clients may decide to settle, which means another group of ready, willing and able lawyers and clients must be found. And so it goes. Sometimes a matter scheduled for 30 minutes in Courtroom Number 1 suddenly stretches into a whole day, causing a bottleneck. Cases waiting for that judge and courtroom are then diverted elsewhere—or simply sent home to wait.

Some courts use a "fixed-date" method, which means that once the lawyers alert the court that they are ready for trial, the trial coordinator assigns them a fixed date for the hearing. This is easier on the lawyers and clients, but can result in downtime for the courts unless some creative overbooking is done to accommodate the inevitable out-of-court settlements that always seem to occur at the last minute.

REGISTRARS, CLERKS AND OTHER COURT STAFF

There is a barely visible world that processes the justice system's paperwork. Tens of thousands of lawsuits are started each year and your case is just one of the many files at the courthouse.

The registrar is the chief administrative officer of a particular judicial district. He or she is responsible for the staff of the courthouse and for ensuring that lawsuits are processed in accordance with the rules of the court. The registrar takes responsibility for opening files, checking documents for rule compliance, taking fees for filing and so on.

Important steps in lawsuits are not only recorded in the file kept at the courthouse but also logged in computerized record books. In this way, orders, judgments and other important matters can be tracked down relatively easily. The registrar's staff does many of these things, but he or she has ultimate responsibility for the local administration of justice.

The court staff also assists the judges and trial coordinator with making sure the right file and materials are available for hearings.

One of the less pleasant aspects of family litigation—any litigation for that matter—is the need to line up to file material at the courthouse. In larger cities the courts are very overburdened and court staff cannot keep up. It is not unusual to see law students or paralegals, or even secretaries, lined up at the courthouse waiting to file some important material. It is a stressful environment and a mystery to first-time observers.

COURT REPORTERS

Court reporters are used at trials, appeals and discoveries. In matters such as an important motion, they may also be used. Their sole purpose is to record everything that is said during the proceeding. This includes the opening introduction of the judge by the clerk right through oath swearing, to every question and answer.

Different methods are used by different court reporters. Some reporters use a steno mask, which is a large plastic device that fits over their mouth and nose. They simply repeat every word said by anyone who speaks, whether it is the judge, lawyer, witness or clerk. Other reporters take the proceedings down in shorthand with a pen (this is on the decline) and others use what is known as a silent typewriter. The typewriter is set up at the front of the courtroom and the reporter silently types the proceedings. In other cases, it is all on tape.

Technology is making real-time transcription a possibility. The reporters can produce (overnight if necessary) a transcript of the proceedings. This transcript is used to prove what was said by whom and can be used, for example, on an appeal. Often it is used to impeach a witness. This means to challenge his or her present statement by showing the person the transcript of what they said on a previous occasion under oath. This type of impeachment often ends with the brilliant question, "Were you lying then, or are you lying now?"

Most witnesses seem to forget about the court reporters as they go about their invisible work.

LAWYERS

Lawyers often refer to the opposing lawyer in the courtroom as their "friend." For example, the lawyer may say, "Your Honour, my friend's point is well taken; however, he neglected to mention that such ..." Clients are seen shaking their heads as if to say, "Hey, wait a minute, if he is such a good friend, how can he do a good job for me?" However, they may soon realize that the last thing that these two lawyers are is friends. They may have never met before or may dislike each other intensely. I have yet to hear one lawyer call another "my learned friend" without at least a hint of sarcasm or a smile—or both.

The reference is simply a courtesy developed to maintain some decorum or civility. Lawyers are reminded that they are merely advocates for clients who come and go, while they are there as adversaries day after day in the courts throughout their careers.

Many courts still require lawyers to wear their robes to court. These include the black cape, black waistcoat, wingtip-collar shirts and tabs. No one wears a wig to court and no one ever has in Canada—except perhaps a witness or two.

As a final note, if you see a jury in the courtroom, slowly stand up and, as quietly as possible, leave—you're in the wrong courtroom. Family law disputes are never heard by juries.

THE RULES OF COURT

YOU MAY RECALL the first time you played Monopoly and everyone sat patiently (well, nearly everyone) and listened while someone read out the rules. Markers were selected, a little money counted out, the dice were cast and away you went. Well, our court system, in its handling of family law matters, is not unlike that, except you are the marker and the money is real.

If you will bear with me for a minute I will "read the rules," so to speak. Remember, too, that this is a general overview. The court system, lawyers, court personnel and your own case respond to or initiate action by using sets of rules. These rules, which are very specific, actually have the force of law because they are regulations made pursuant to provincial law. Without these detailed rules, no one would know what to do next on a particular case. Everyone would be going off in different directions without any guidance or control or, worse yet, everyone would simply sit and do nothing.

Each province has its own set of rules governing procedure in its courts. These rules are known as the "Rules of Practice" and provide for virtually everything that can happen between the institution of proceedings (starting the case in the court system by getting the registrar to authorize commencement of an action) and obtaining a judgment at the end of the case. One published version of the rules and the summaries of cases that interpret them is over 1,000 pages in length. The rules also provide for appeals, enforcement of court orders and hundreds of other matters—even dictating the colour of paper used in certain situations.

The various levels of court within each province have their own sets of rules as well. A Provincial Court and a Superior Court will each have a different set of rules. (And you thought this was going to be easy!)

By and large, the rules are helpful in keeping everything organized and moving, and provide very much the same procedures for the different courts, with some variations. If used properly they can provide a great deal of control over the progress of a case. Some courts now use a system called "case management," whereby the judge takes a more active role in moving the case forward. The lawyers and clients must perform certain steps within certain pre-set timelines that are laid out by the rules.

The rules prescribe all of the steps that must be taken to move your case from beginning to end, as well as all of the forms that must be used to make the documents acceptable for filing at the court. A system as over-burdened as ours would not last 15 minutes if everyone filed documents in whatever form they wished, so the rules cover everything from the colour and size of the paper to their form and content. The basic steps in any legal proceeding are essentially the same, and include:

1. exchange of letters between lawyers;
2. exchange of legal documents (called pleadings);
3. discovery of each others' cases (questioning under oath);
4. motions (mini-trials on matters from time to time);
5. pre-trial/trial management/case conference (settlement discussion before a trial);
6. the trial;
7. the appeal (if necessary).

The following is a brief summary of what happens at each of these steps.

1. Exchange of Letters

ASSUMING YOU HAVE settled upon a lawyer and completed a retainer authorizing the lawyer to act on your behalf, the matter will usually begin with your lawyer writing to either your spouse or his or her lawyer if one has already been hired. On the other hand, it may be you who receives a letter and consults a lawyer about what you should do in response. These letters often say the following:

"Letter"

Dear Mr./Ms. Spouse:

Re: Family Difficulties

We have been consulted by [Client's name] with respect to your family difficulties. [Client's name] has instructed me to explore the possibility of resolving these difficulties through negotiations that would lead to the signing of a separation agreement containing terms acceptable to both of you.

Please have your lawyer contact me within the next few days so that we can amicably resolve the outstanding problems as quickly as possible.

I look forward to hearing from your lawyer.

Yours very truly,
[Lawyer's name]

Sometimes this type of letter contains a deadline, for example, "If I have not heard from you within 10 days of the date of this letter, I will commence court proceedings." Letters often mention the need to complete financial statements.

These initial letters are important. They set the tone for the negotiations and may list demands and therefore shape the issue. If appropriate, they can open the door to alternatives to the courtroom; such as mediation (see Chapter 11: Alternatives to Court). Given the letter's importance, I suggest that you ask to see the letter your lawyer plans to send. You should also ask about the circumstances under which it will be delivered. For example, it is rarely necessary to have such letters delivered to a person at work, but some lawyers will arrange such a delivery out of thoughtlessness. A person embarrassed at work will not be interested in negotiating anything. Discuss this with your lawyer and make your wishes known. Insist on a personal touch.

I have seen entire Separation Agreements (see Chapter 9: Settling Your Differences) negotiated by letters over a several-month period. In other cases it becomes clear early on that a settlement will not be possible without other methods being used. Do not go from this letter-writing stage to the next stage (legal proceedings) without a written opinion from your lawyer about what happened and what is likely to happen if legal proceedings are started. This opinion should also contain an estimate of fees and out-of-pocket expenses that might be incurred.

2. Exchange of Legal Documents

IF THE LETTERS have not led to a settlement (which would likely be incorporated into a Separation Agreement), your lawyer may recommend starting legal proceedings. All unresolved issues are submitted to the court, saying in essence, "Judge, we cannot decide, so decide for us."

The proceedings can be started a number of ways by using documents described in the Rules of Practice. These are court forms printed by legal stationery companies and are available electronically. Most law firms have special software that will print the client information right into the appropriate form.

Family law proceedings can be started by Divorce Application or Statement of Claim and, in some cases, by Notice of Motion. The names of the forms may vary slightly from province to province, but they all have the same effect and seek to achieve the same goal. That goal is to give the court an orderly and uniform summary of what the dispute is all about. The form will describe the people involved; children, if any; where the clients live; what they want; when they are scheduled to appear to present their case and so on. Sometimes evidence, such as a copy of an income tax return, is included in an affidavit or financial statement.

Once the appropriate forms have been completed, the lawyer's staff will take the material to the court office to be "issued." This means that the clerks at the courthouse examine the documents to see if they have been completed properly, charge a fee, give it a file number and then sign them to make it all official.

Many provinces require the financial statements to be filed before they will issue the proceedings. Given the amount of detail needed, completion of these statements can delay issuance of the claim for several days. The financial statements should give the court (and the other side) a picture of your current financial circumstances and your plans for the future.

Once issued, the documents must be delivered to the spouse (lawyers call this "serving the papers"). If the other side has a lawyer, it may be possible to facilitate service by the lawyer accepting it on the client's behalf. If this cannot be arranged, then a professional document server (bailiff or process server) may need to be hired. Except in the most unusual cases, the service of documents should be done with sensitivity and without embarrassment to the other spouse. (Remember, what goes around, comes around. And it's all at your expense.) Do not serve documents on your spouse. Many courts will not accept this as a valid form of service.

Once the other side has received your pile of material (it can swell to a couple of inches of paper very quickly), they must file material in response. If it is a divorce, they must file an Answer or even a Counter Petition, affidavits and, of course, the financial statements that, more often than not, tell a very different financial story from those issued by your side.

But we are not done yet—you may need to respond to the material you have just received. This can include a Reply, more affidavits and amended financial statements. For historical reasons these all came to be known as "the pleadings," because lawyers used to plead for relief on behalf of their clients. The purpose of responding to the other person's documents has not changed—to narrow the points of controversy until the issues are identified. All of these documents go into what is known as the "continuing record." Each time a new document is added, it goes into the court file so that the proceedings can be tracked accurately.

At the end of this barrage of material, everyone should have a good idea about where the difference of opinion lies. "Everyone" means you as the client. So do not go to the next step (discovery) unless you have received a written opinion from your lawyer telling you what has happened and what is likely to happen. This again should include a bill for the work done and an estimate of the cost of the next step.

In the next five sections, we will examine the most time-consuming and therefore most expensive aspects of family law litigation: discovery (questioning under oath), motions, pre-trials, trials and appeals.

3. Discovery/Questioning Under Oath

DISCOVERY (SOMETIMES CALLED "questioning") includes oral examination of the parties under oath and examination of documentary evidence needed to prove one's case in court. Once the pleadings have been exchanged, each lawyer is permitted to sit down with the other lawyer's client and ask that person questions under oath about the pleadings. The lawyers probe the written version set out in the documents, and discover the evidence in support of it.

Discovery takes place in a small room with a court reporter. Your lawyer is present while the other lawyer asks you questions. Your spouse may even be present while you are questioned. The court reporter takes down all the questions and answers and marks papers as exhibits for ease of reference and to be able to make some sense of the transcript later. (For example, the lawyer may ask you to identify a copy of your mortgage and will ask the reporter to mark it as Exhibit 1 in order to keep track of which documents are being referred to.) If there are many exhibits, the lawyers may bind photocopies of them into a book for ease of reference. This question-and-answer session may take an entire day or only a few hours; it depends on the complexity of the case. This questioning is a good opportunity to evaluate the other side as a witness. Lawyers ask themselves whether a judge would like this person as a witness; would he or she be believed? So, remember that when you are being questioned, you are also being evaluated as to whether you will be a good witness at a trial.

It is unusual for your spouse to be present during your discovery and vice versa. However, sometimes the lawyers may ask for the clients to be present in case it is necessary to consult with them as the questions and answers evolve. Personally, I think the other spouse should not be present, to avoid possible intimidation and to ease the anxiety for everyone.

In advance of this oral discovery, the lawyers should have completed their documentary discovery. This means that if the client intends to rely on a particular document at trial, then a copy of it must be produced in advance of the oral discovery. "Documents" can include tapes, letters, photographs, drawings, financial records, computer files and so on.

Discovery, oral and documentary, is designed to further narrow the issues and prevent surprises at trial. Nobody wants to go all the way to the court to suddenly see a document that proves the other side was right all along. In fact, the court can penalize with legal costs a person who withholds evidence and springs a surprise at trial.

After the discovery, the lawyers will ask the court reporters to prepare a transcript of the questions and answers. Once the transcript arrives, the lawyers review it to evaluate the likelihood of success. They also look to see if there were any questions that the client was unable to answer. In such cases, the lawyer and client sometimes "undertake" or promise to get the information and send it along later. These promises are called "undertakings" and must be kept or you risk being penalized.

Disclosure of documents has become a bit controversial in the family law system, with some people failing to disclose key information, thereby delaying the whole process. In other cases, requests for disclosure have turned into a meaningless fishing expedition where lawyers or people who are representing themselves ask for document after document after document, simply to delay matters or to make it expensive for the parties. Disclosure is supposed to provide information that allows each side to understand the documents that will be used as evidence.

Your lawyer should now prepare a written opinion setting out what has happened and what is likely to happen at the next step. This opinion should include the lawyer's opinion on the likelihood of success. It should speak in terms of "if this matter went to court, I think the court would..."

You are paying the lawyer for his or her opinion on what will happen, so make sure you get it in writing. Do not do anything until you have this opinion in hand. Be prepared to sit down and discuss it with the lawyer, not the student, the paralegal, the secretary or anybody else. You will also want to discuss the expected cost of going to the next step.

4. Motions

A MOTION IS a request to the court for an order on a particular issue. Motions can occur at any time after the proceeding has been issued at the courthouse right up until the time of trial. Lawyers will use motions to sort out interim problems and procedural matters. It amounts to asking the court to settle an issue (like interim custody) until the final trial. A lawyer might bring a motion for a number of things, including forcing disclosure of documents, possession of a home, an advance of interim fees and disbursements, or interim child support.

The motion is held in front of a judge and usually involves the clients. Two documents are needed for a motion: the motion and an affidavit. The motion itself, which is a document that can be two or three pages long, identifies the people involved, describes what they want from the court and sets out a time and date for a presentation to the judge.

Motions are scheduled, since the date and time must be coordinated with the court office and available judge time. They are usually scheduled on certain days of the week. Check with your local court.

The motion is supported by an affidavit sworn by the client. This affidavit is the evidence and takes the place of the client appearing and giving testimony orally. There is nothing to prevent you as the client from attending a motion. I have always found it interesting to watch other lawyers at work when their clients are present. It is a real insight. (Be forewarned, though, there can be a lot of waiting.)

The motion may be adjourned, indefinitely or to a specific day, to allow the lawyers to cross-examine the clients on the contents of any affidavit filed. In such a case, the discovery process is repeated, but only with respect to the affidavit. A transcript of the question-and-answer session may be requested by the lawyer and used as evidence on the motion.

Once the motion is again before the judge, the matter is discussed and the judge makes an order. The motion may be dismissed (rejected), the order sought may be granted, or some other order may be made somewhere in between what the lawyers were asking the court to do. For example, a wife may ask for an order that she have exclusive possession of the home until trial (approximately one year away). The husband may ask the court to order that the house be sold immediately and the proceeds of sale be divided equally, or held in trust until the trial. The judge could order that the wife have exclusive possession until the house is sold and fix the terms of sale to include a stipulation that the deal not close for at least six months. The judge will also order costs to the winner.

If an order is made, the judge will usually just write his or her endorsement on the back of the papers in the file. The lawyer will obtain a photocopy and have it typed into a formal order, which is then approved by both sides as accurate and filed with the court clerks. The order is issued by the court staff and becomes an official order of the court.

Motions may cost thousands of dollars each, not including the cost of disbursements, such as the court reporter's transcript of a cross-examination. Your lawyer should not bring motions without your express consent and then only if there is no other alternative way of solving the problem.

5. Pre-trials/Case Conferences/Settlement Conferences/ Trial Management Conferences

EVERY PROVINCE HAS some method of screening family law cases before they go to trial. In many cases this is known as a pre-trial; in others, a settlement or case conference. A pre-trial takes place once the people involved have indicated that they are unable to resolve the matter and are ready for trial.

A family-court judge or senior lawyer examines the pleadings and meets with the lawyers and their clients. In all but the most unusual cases (for example, where one of the clients lives out of the country), the clients should be available for, and participate in, the pre-trial conference. Once again, the goal of this exercise is to help the people settle part, if not all, of the case. The issues may become narrowed even further or part of the case may be settled simply by having a four-way discussion with a neutral, knowledgeable person.

The pre-trial also allows the lawyers and clients to get a second opinion about their positions. The judge who conducts the pre-trial will not hear the trial, so he or she is free to state frankly how he or she would rule, which can have a powerful effect on a difficult lawyer or client.

In most systems, this type of conference is a pre-condition to being given a trial date. In many jurisdictions there are multiple attempts to assist the parties to resolve the matter. These are called pre-trial case conferences and settlement conferences. There is also a meeting called a "trial management conference" that occurs immediately before trial. This is when the lawyers and clients meet with the judge to actually plan out the trial itself. At this meeting, the clients are expected to know how long the trial will be, how many witnesses they will call, what evidence the witnesses will give, what expert evidence may be required, whether business records will be entered into evidence and so on. Even at that late stage, judges will often work with the clients to try and resolve the matter.

Again, do not go to the next step (trial) unless you have the written opinion from your lawyer about what happened and what is likely to happen next.

6. The Trial

SETTLEMENT DISCUSSIONS MAY have produced nothing, pleadings and discoveries are finished, motions have been exhausted and a pre-trial has not resolved the matter. It may have taken years, but you now stand near the end of the trail—the trial.

Assuming you have actually got a judge, a courtroom, all the witnesses, an opponent and are ready to go, most trials take more than one day. The approximate cost is at least $6,000 per day per client, and therefore it is not unusual to see a three-day trial run $15,000 to $20,000 for each party.

You should understand that everything you have written in affidavits, explained at discovery or achieved on motions must now be recounted for the court orally. From the most obvious questions (What is your name?) through to the most complex (Can you explain the differences between your financial statements for 2013 and 2014?), they will all be traced in public in the courtroom with the goal of persuading the judge that you, after all, are correct and have been since the proceedings were commenced a year and a half ago.

After the evidence has been reviewed by the judge, he or she will render a judgment on the issues placed before the court—custody of your children, access rights, property division and the divorce itself. The judge will also order who must pay the costs of the lawyers and how much, depending on how the case was conducted.

7. The Appeal

ALMOST ANY ORDER or judgment can be appealed to a higher court, although some orders are considered to be of such a minor nature that they cannot be appealed.

Judgments which are appealed must contain some serious error in fact or law to be successful. If an appeal is undertaken, a further six months to one year may be required. A transcript of the entire trial must be ordered, at a cost of thousands of dollars, just to be able to determine whether an appeal is feasible. Never allow a lawyer to undertake an appeal without a written report on what happened, the grounds for the appeal and the likelihood of success, as well as a firm commitment on the cost of the appeal.

CLOSING REMARKS

I HAVE SET out the stages above for one reason: you must appreciate that when a case is not resolved and it goes to court, it must then wind its way through all these procedures. And remember, I have set out a *brief* version of events.

Lawyers who promise quick results in court are either misleading you or haven't been there enough to know better. In either case, think twice about anyone who promises fast results.

You now know as much or more about the legal system and family law than do most law students (and a few lawyers as well). It should be clear why starting proceedings in court is like playing Monopoly: everyone gets a turn, the game often takes a good deal of time and ends only when one person has all the money.

Remember that you will be paying for this with your own (after tax) money at rates in excess of $300 and more an hour. It can be an expensive exercise.

This is not to say that you should never go to court; sometimes it is simply unavoidable. But if you must use the wheels of justice, remember: they turn slowly, grinding up time, energy and money.

MY ADVICE

1. Proof of your case is on a balance of probabilities, not beyond a reasonable doubt.
2. There is a vast network of judges, clerks and other staff working behind the scenes at the courthouse; work co-operatively with them.
3. Rules of Court are critical. They control the process of a case and failing to follow them can cause delay.
4. Keep your communications civil.
5. Complete and accurate disclosure is key.

6. Avoid motions to the court unless absolutely necessary to move the case forward or protect you, your children or your money.
7. Insist on opinion letters at each stage. These opinion letters should set out what has happened, what will happen next, your options and the likelihood of success and the cost of each step.

GETTING A DIVORCE

Dissolving
the Marriage Vows

THOUGHT WE SHOULD start our discussion of the more substantive issues with something easy—the divorce itself. Lawyers and clients sometimes forget during the intensity of a family law dispute that the goal is to actually end the marriage, to dissolve it. This is because the granting of the divorce itself in many cases is the least contentious issue. This wasn't always the case. Before 1985, when significant changes were made to the Divorce Act, couples had to use a list of reasons for divorce that included such things as adultery, homosexual activity, bestiality, prison sentences, rape and so on. Little wonder that people felt they had to defend themselves in a divorce proceeding when such horrible allegations could be made.

The Divorce Act amendments ended many of those disputes by going to an almost completely no-fault system of divorce in Canada. The amendments themselves came into force on June 1, 1986, and apply to all divorces subsequent to that date. We will examine these "grounds for divorce" shortly, but let's consider some background information to put this chapter in perspective.

The Divorce Act is federal legislation and applies only to people who are legally married. It now includes coverage of same-sex couples who have married. If a divorce is sought, the act provides the court with the authority to make custody orders, access orders, spousal support and child support orders, as well as other miscellaneous orders (but not property orders, as they fall under provincial law). In this chapter we will only consider the divorce itself, the order that dissolves the marriage and some related issues.

Tens of thousands of Canadians go through a divorce each year. There have been debates about the level of divorce, but it would seem that about 40 per cent of Canadian marriages end this way. We often hear American statistics stating that one in every two marriages fails, but I do not think that the Canadian level of divorce has yet reached that level. Remember, as well, that many Canadians are now living in common-law relationships, which appear to be much more volatile than legal marriages. (We will consider common-law couples in Chapter 8: Common-Law Spouses Have Rights Too.)

Some days I think that many Canadians might prefer to have the South Korean system of divorce, whereby the couple arrives at the courthouse on a Monday morning, completes some forms—with the help of clerks—and for a few dollars obtains a divorce the moment the papers are signed by a judge. Unfortunately, this easy divorce procedure led to the South Korean divorce rate more than doubling between 1995 and 2005. Canada, sadly, is at the other end of the spectrum, where divorce can be long, drawn-out and expensive.

GROUNDS FOR DIVORCE

THERE IS ONLY one ground for divorce in Canada: "marriage breakdown." The Divorce Act sets out three circumstances in which the marriage will be considered to have broken down:

1. The spouses have lived separate and apart for at least one year immediately preceding the determination of the divorce proceeding.
2. One of the spouses has committed adultery.
3. One of the spouses has subjected the other to intolerable physical or mental cruelty of such a kind as to render intolerable their continued cohabitation.

1. Separation

WHEN WE CONSIDER that the previous Divorce Act required people to be separated for three years, you can appreciate how these amendments have made access to the divorce procedure itself easier. A survey of Canadian lawyers found that the overwhelming majority of Canadians filing for divorce seek the divorce on the basis of the one-year separation.

For a one-year separation to be used as grounds for divorce, the separation must have occurred because there were difficulties in the marriage. A man could not file for divorce because his wife went to study at a university in another city for a year or because one spouse went to work in Saudi Arabia on a short-term contract. At least one of the spouses must intend to live separate and apart because major problems were occurring in the marriage.

If this circumstance of marriage breakdown has occurred, there is no need to describe the problems or lay the blame with anyone for the marriage's difficulties—the fact of one-year separation itself is proof of the marriage breakdown.

Separation need not mean separate houses, although that is certainly the case in most situations. The courts have considered cases in which the husband and wife lived separate and apart, but under the same roof. For example, if a husband and wife had marital problems but could not afford separate accommodations, then they could agree to share their home but live separate from each other in it. This would mean no sexual contact with each other, separate sleeping arrangements, separate meals, separate lives, minimal communication and the leaving of each other to fend for themselves with respect to cleaning and other domestic work.

In most cases, however, the couple separates into their own new lives and it is not difficult to see that they are intentionally living separate and apart from each other. If we were looking for some criteria to guide us in determining whether a couple has actually separated, the court considers the following:

1. Whether there has been an actual physical separation. The separation, as I stated above, can be under the same roof.

2. Whether there has been a withdrawal by one or both of the spouses from their obligations in the marriage. This withdrawal must be intended to end their partnership or repudiate their relationship.
3. Whether there is an absence of sexual relations, but this in itself is not conclusive, due to medical circumstances, for example.
4. Whether the couple continues to discuss and try to work out family problems and communicate. In this respect I sometimes ask couples what their neighbours would think looking from the outside in at their marriage. In other words, do your neighbours think that you're still married? If you've fooled them, then you may not be able to convince a court that you were separated.
5. Whether there is an ongoing performance of household tasks and duties. In other words, is the couple still carrying on as if the marriage was underway?
6. What is the true intent of the individuals involved? In other words, do they consider themselves married or are they simply filing income tax returns as "married" while actually "separated"?

You may have heard the old, melodramatic line in the movies, "She won't give him a divorce!" You will be relieved to know that one spouse cannot deny the other a divorce. Once the separation has occurred, either the husband or the wife can file for divorce. When I say that the separation has occurred, I mean that the day after the separation has occurred, either spouse may file for divorce. The court, however, will not make the divorce order until the full year of separation has expired. If this ground of marriage breakdown is met, the court will grant the divorce no matter what the other spouse says or wishes. Therefore, there can be no withholding of consent to the granting of a divorce. The exception to this general rule is circumstances where custody of the children, possession of the home or child support has not been resolved. In some cases judges will withhold the granting of a final divorce until those issues are resolved.

2. Adultery

ADULTERY HAS ALWAYS been one of the more lurid allegations hurled by one spouse at the other. It is, if proved, considered proof of marriage breakdown and will result in an immediate divorce order. This method of establishing marriage breakdown is being used less and less because of the availability of the one-year separation method.

The spouse who committed adultery cannot start the divorce; only the other spouse may do so. This prevents spouses from going out and committing adultery simply to entitle themselves to an immediate divorce. The only restriction on a divorce based on adultery is that the court is careful to ensure that the spouse who is seeking the divorce did not "forgive" the adultery. Forgiveness will excuse the conduct and prevent the divorce from being granted.

Not surprisingly, there are fewer and fewer cases in the courts dealing with adultery. It is used less and less as grounds for divorce. Interestingly, many years ago in 1921, the court dealt with a situation in which a wife allowed herself to be artificially inseminated without her husband's knowledge. This resulted in the conception and birth of a child. The court considered it to be adultery and granted a divorce on that basis.

Until very recently, homosexual conduct would not entitle a spouse to divorce on the grounds of adultery. Adultery could only be committed with a member of the opposite sex. If a spouse was engaging in homosexual activity that the other spouse found objectionable, it may have constituted mental cruelty but it was not adultery. This changed as a result of recent court decisions where judges have simply said that homosexual activity is adultery. This is a little strange from a lawyer's point of view, because adultery has a specific legal definition that includes intercourse between a man and a woman. This little bit of "judge-made law" became necessary because if same-sex couples were to have access to the same grounds of divorce as heterosexual couples, then the definition of adultery would need to be tweaked. The law evolves with such cases.

3. Cruelty

ONE SPOUSE'S PHYSICAL or mental cruelty toward the other spouse is the third method of proving that the marriage has broken down. The result of the abuse must be that it makes the possibility of living together intolerable. Again, the spouse responsible for the abuse cannot seek the divorce. It must be the abused spouse, and he or she may seek it any time the abuse becomes intolerable.

Law books are filled with cases in which the court has been asked to decide whether or not the physical or mental cruelty is sufficient to render intolerable the continued cohabitation of the partners.

IN A NUTSHELL, you may be entitled to a divorce if you separate for at least a year, if your spouse has committed adultery or if your spouse has been physically or mentally cruel to the extent that you cannot tolerate living together. These rules apply to any marriage, regardless of where it took place in the world. Whether you were married in the United States, Europe, India or elsewhere, as long as you have lived in Canada for at least a year prior to the application for divorce, you may use the Divorce Act.

Is the Marriage Valid?

NOTE THAT SOME of the more unusual forms of marriage may require a second look by a lawyer, if the court is asked to dissolve the marriage. There are a few types of marriage (e.g., polygamous) that we do not recognize for "reasons of public policy." If in doubt, have a lawyer check out the circumstances of your marriage to determine whether it is recognized as a marriage for the purpose of divorce in Canada. A written legal opinion may be required.

"We're Not Legally Separated"

SOMETIMES YOU WILL hear a person say, "I'm not legally separated." It's an odd phrase to use because there is no such thing as being "illegally" separated in Canada. What people usually mean is they are separated from their spouse but they have not concluded their divorce or separation agreement. I mention this only because it causes some confusion in understanding the meaning of separation for the purposes of obtaining the divorce. Once a couple has separated, and again this can include them living separate and apart but under the same roof, the clock starts running for their one year of separation. They do not need to sign an agreement in order to start that clock.

Reconciliation (Hey, Sometimes It Happens)

RECONCILIATION (GETTING BACK together) is always a possibility. I remember a case of a couple reconciling shortly before the court was going to deal with their divorce. They were less than 24 hours from what they thought would be freedom and they decided to give the marriage at least one more try. In one case, a divorce judgment had to be stayed (or "frozen") when the parties reconciled after the divorce judgment was ordered, but before it could take effect.

Some couples try reconciling more than once and this is fine, since no one wishes to discourage people from attempting to work things out. However, we need to keep in mind the effect this will have on the one-year period of separation—either the spouses are separated or they aren't.

The Divorce Act sets a total limit of 90 days of living together. If you go over the 90-day limit, the one-year period of separation is inter-rupted and you must start over again. The 90 days total can be made up of more than one attempt. So, for example, a husband and wife could try for a week in the summer, then a month in the fall and even another month at Christmas and still be entitled to a divorce on the basis that they have been separated for a full year but not reconciled for 90 days.

Regardless of the number of attempts and failures, reconciliation is only possible if both parties agree. It doesn't matter if one spouse really, really, really wants to reconcile; if the other spouse does not, there is no reconciliation.

Incidentally, reconciliation attempts are not considered forgiveness of cruelty or adultery, so couples are given some flexibility in working things out.

A survey of lawyers found that the 90-day re-cohabitation provision was not used much. About one-third of divorcing couples report that they separated but tried reconciling before they gave up and actually went ahead with their divorce.

The Divorce Act has provisions in it that encourage couples to rec-oncile if at all possible. Lawyers even have a legal obligation under the Divorce Act to discuss the possibility of reconciliation with every client who comes to their office seeking a divorce. Lawyers have an obligation to inform the spouses of the availability of marriage counselling or guidance facilities that might be available in the community to help them. We often get some funny looks and outright laughter from clients when we ask the question: "Are you sure there's no chance you two can work it out and get back together?"

THE PROCEDURE FOR A DIVORCE

MOST LAWYERS WILL tell you that there are only two kinds of divorce—contested and uncontested. It can actually be a little more involved than that, but the dynamic of the divorce does depend very much on whether the couple agree to settle matters or not. We will examine in upcoming chapters the consequences of settling or not settling and at this stage will instead focus on what it means procedurally to seek a divorce from the court. Remember, we are thinking now only about the divorce itself, not the custody or access or property division orders.

Since the Divorce Act is federal, only federally appointed judges may make orders for divorce. These judges sit on what are called "Superior Courts" and they have different names depending on the province in question. In Manitoba, Alberta, Saskatchewan and New Brunswick, they are called the "Court of Queen's Bench." In other provinces they are called simply the "Supreme Court." In Ontario it is now known as the "Superior Court of Justice." Regardless of the name of the court in the different provinces, it is these courts that grant divorces.

Whether you use the court in one province or another is dictated by whether one or both of you has been ordinarily resident within the province for at least the previous year. "Ordinarily resident" does not mean the province where your cottage is located or where you took a summer university course. It means the place where you normally have your home. In one case, a young woman moved from Ontario to British Columbia following her husband to attempt a reconciliation. After several months, they realized the marriage would not work and she wished to file for divorce in British Columbia. She was not considered to have been ordinarily resident in B.C. (nor was he) and they could not complete the Application for Divorce. In order to complete that application, at least one of the spouses must have been ordinarily resident for at least a year in the jurisdiction in which the divorce is sought.

As a rule of thumb, the court will consider somebody ordinarily resident in a certain place if that person regularly, normally or customarily lives there in a settled routine. The court is looking for some element of permanence in their lifestyle. This question of ordinary residence is considered to be a question of fact by the court. It is not dependent on citizenship. It is not dependent on immigration status. A person can be ordinarily resident in Canada even if they do not have legal immigrant or other status. With the increased mobility of Canadians, not just from province to province but to and from Canada and other countries, "residency," for the purposes of divorce, will continue to be a difficult point for some couples at the time of separation and divorce.

A Central Divorce Registry in Ottawa collects statistics on divorces filed across Canada and is a critical part of this rule's enforcement. The Registry ensures that where two spouses residing in different parts of the country file for divorce without knowing of the other person's filing, the one who filed first is permitted to continue with the divorce action and the other divorce action is discontinued.

Not only will the residence of the adults affect the location of the divorce; the child's residence is important, too. If a child is affected by the divorce, the court reserves the right to transfer the entire matter to the province that is most convenient for the child. So, for example, where a child is resident in Ontario with his mother and attending school but the father seeks the divorce in Newfoundland, along with a particular custody or access order affecting that child, the Newfoundland Supreme Court could transfer the matter to Ontario. Those best able to comment on the child's life would then be available for the court's consideration.

Uncontested Divorces

IN MANY CASES there are no outstanding issues to be resolved, since any problems concerning custody, access or property division may have been solved by a Separation Agreement. (See Chapter 9: Settling Your Differences.) The parties are then able to ask the court to simply dissolve the marriage and in some cases incorporate the terms of the Separation Agreement into the court's order at the same time. In this procedure, the couple simply fills out the appropriate divorce forms and supporting documents and files them, along with their marriage certificate, with the court.

Years ago, even when the divorce was uncontested, it was necessary to attend court for a hearing. This was considered by many people to be a waste of time and money for the court and people involved. So when the Divorce Act changes came into force on June 1, 1986, the provinces were given the power to create a procedure for granting divorces without the necessity of the people attending a court hearing. Every province has created such a procedure and in some provinces as many as 98 per cent of divorces are granted in this way. Nationally, about 68 per cent of divorcing couples use the no-hearing method.

One positive development with this procedure is the increased speed with which the uncontested divorce can be processed. On average, it now takes about 17 weeks when no hearing is needed. In addition, clients rarely like attending court, so the procedure makes it less of a strain for the people involved. It also tends to generally steer them away from the courtroom in resolving family law disputes and saves on court resources.

Urgently Needed Divorce

IN SOME CASES a divorce is needed on an expedited basis. This usually arises for one of two reasons, and in some cases both. A couple wants to marry but one of them is not yet divorced, or a couple is expecting a child and they wish to marry prior to the birth of that child. Lawyers often hear from clients who have made plans for a wedding, booked a hall, invited guests, but have not obtained a divorce from their previous spouse. It is possible in such circumstances to inform the court that the divorce is required on an urgent basis. I will often include a letter to the court along with the application for divorce and have even gone so far as to include an affidavit with a copy of the actual wedding invitation attached. If a child is expected, I will provide evidence to the court about the expected due date. Judges and court staff are often prepared to expedite the paperwork so that the wedding can go forward, or so that the child can be born to parents who are legally married.

Joint Application for Divorce

AN INTERESTING INNOVATION introduced in the Divorce Act reforms was the Joint Application for Divorce. If the couple can agree on the ground for the divorce and no other matter is in dispute, they are able to jointly issue an Application for Divorce. However, only a small percentage of divorcing couples in Canada have made use of this procedure.

The research available on the use of joint applications suggests that those who use it tend to pay considerably less in legal fees, have their divorce finalized more quickly, are more likely to use joint custody and are slightly more generous with the amount of support paid.

Contested Divorces

A CONTESTED DIVORCE is one in which the parties cannot agree on an issue, forcing them to exchange the "special divorce documents" (revisit Chapter 3: Taking a Look at the Process) for a divorce action. An Application for Divorce must always be issued to start a divorce action. However, what makes the case contested is the need for the respondent to deliver an Answer. In the Answer, the respondent replies to all of the allegations made by the applicant. The respondent also has an opportunity to make a counterclaim in the divorce action.

It is difficult to predict how long it will take to resolve a case once it is contested. Many contested divorces go on for years, particularly, research indicates, if the dispute concerns property. Where custody is an issue and assessments are needed or trials occur, it takes much longer to finalize than an uncontested divorce does.

Regardless of the contested or uncontested nature of the divorce, once the court actually deals with the dissolution of the marriage, it becomes effective 30 days after the judge has made the divorce order. The marriage is over and dissolved on the 31st day. This 30-day period is designed to give either of the people involved an opportunity to appeal. If one of them appeals, the divorce cannot be effective until the appeal is resolved once and for all. Once launched, it can be several months before the appeal is heard.

In some cases, the husband or wife needs the divorce order to be effective before the 31st day; they may, for example, be remarrying. A remarriage cannot take place until the divorce order is final and effective. All jurisdictions therefore allow the couple to have the order made effective sooner if they both undertake in writing not to appeal and if special circumstances require the earlier effective date. Most family law lawyers have witnessed the look of panic on the faces of those who wish to remarry within that 30-day period because the bride-to-be is expecting and the couple wants the child to be born in wedlock. In such a circumstance, the court would abridge the 30-day period and grant the divorce immediately.

What do you get for all this work? A Certificate of Divorce! It is available at the court office and provides an official record of the marriage's dissolution and the effective date of dissolution. The certificate may come in handy if you plan to remarry at a later date. With it, you can prove that your previous marriage is over. You will need it when you apply for any subsequent marriage licence.

Bars to Divorce

EVEN THOUGH THERE are thousands of divorces going through Canadian courts, the court does not always simply rubber-stamp every pile of papers filed with the correct fee. In divorce proceedings, the court has a duty to satisfy itself that there have been no "deals" to facilitate the granting of a divorce that wouldn't otherwise get the approval of the court. So, for example, the court does not want to see that there has been some form of collusion between the applicant and the respondent in order to get the divorce on grounds that don't exist, or sooner than is otherwise legal. More than one individual has arrived at a lawyer's office asking if they can simply agree that they have been separated for a year when they have only really been separated for a month.

The court also tries to satisfy itself that reasonable arrangements have been made for the support of any children of the marriage. The divorce papers require that children be identified, along with their birth dates, schooling arrangements and child support arrangements. If the court doesn't like what it sees, it has the power to stop the divorce from going forward.

The court also has the power to block a divorce where there have been suspicious circumstances. So, for example, a court would probably not grant a divorce if it discovered that one spouse had suggested to the other spouse that they commit adultery to allow a speedy divorce. This would be considered connivance. It is hard to police this kind of deception, but people have been caught and divorce is denied.

Marriages of Convenience

THIS IS AS good a time as any to deal with a growing problem in Canada, that of "marriages of convenience." While no statistics are kept, all lawyers hear frequently about marriages in which a Canadian citizen offers to marry someone in order to facilitate that person's immigration into Canada. Usually the story involves a couple agreeing to marry and then, after an appropriate period, obtaining an uncontested divorce or annulment.

Anyone who is contemplating such an undertaking must be aware of two things: first and foremost, you will be required to go through a form of divorce the same as everyone else, and secondly, sponsorship of the immigrant should not be taken lightly. There are cases in Canada where a husband sponsored a wife's immigration to Canada and agreed to be financially responsible for her for a period of time. The parties eventually separated before the husband could fulfill the entire sponsorship undertaking. At the time of the divorce, the husband was ordered to pay a lump sum to the wife in order to facilitate her retraining and he was also ordered to pay support on a monthly basis.

Entering into marriage, whether for "convenience" or not, entails all of the rights and responsibilities, including a requirement for a divorce, the possibility of spousal support and even the division of matrimonial property acquired between the date of marriage and the date of separation.

There are recent cases where a divorce was denied when it was discovered that the wife had married the husband solely to allow him to immigrate to Canada. The parties had separated virtually on the day of the marriage. In one case, the wife sought the divorce from her husband in order to marry a man who was in Canada illegally because his visa had expired. The wife wished to marry the illegal immigrant to allow him to stay in Canada. The divorce was not granted. In another case, a marriage entered into simply to facilitate immigration status was not dissolved by the court and the couple was forced to stay married.

This problem of marriages of convenience is growing. I have had discussions with judges who are aware of the situation and do not feel comfortable speaking publicly about it. I have met individuals who have paid large sums of money in order to marry Canadian citizens and to gain access to Canada. I have been told of criminals in various communities facilitating these marriages for colossal sums of money. In one case in Toronto, a young girl was kidnapped and killed in an attempt to extort money that would then be used to facilitate an illegal marriage, simply to allow a young man whose visa had expired to remain in Canada.

I have personally seen cases where young women in certain ethnic communities have been cruelly exploited by their families. They are taken from Canada to their country of origin and married to strangers, sometimes in exchange for that individual's family agreeing to marry someone else who will be sponsored to Canada. These women then sponsor the individuals they've married into Canada. Children are born in the marriage and the family is then abandoned. The woman, with the assistance of her family, seeks a divorce, and once it is granted, she is promptly returned to the country of origin to marry again and repeat the process.

This exploitation of women, of immigrants and of our justice system is a disgrace. The federal government has amended immigration law to penalize those who attempt marriages of convenience. Check sponsorship rules based on marriage with Citizenship and Immigration Canada.

Legal Fees for Divorce

WHEN I WROTE previous editions of this book, I was able to say with some confidence that most people are represented in their divorce proceedings by lawyers. At one time, studies suggested that women were four times more likely than men to have legal aid lawyers acting on their behalf.

It is impossible to say with any certainty the actual average cost of a divorce. Most lawyers who see the figures published know that the numbers are not realistic. In some cases, we see posters advertising uncontested divorces for as little as $300. Paralegals are often more than happy to complete those kinds of divorces. The fees alone for filing a divorce can exceed $200. This means that someone is processing simple paperwork for a fee of between $50 and $100. A divorce involving division of property, custody of children or support cannot possibly be done in such circumstances.

I am aware of one particularly sad case in which a woman was desperate for a divorce. She approached a consultant, rather than a paralegal, who completed the paperwork pursuant to her instructions. She sought only a divorce in the hope that she could free herself from a painful situation. The divorce was served on the husband, he gratefully cooperated and a divorce was granted. They had not dealt with their property, however, and since she was no longer married to her husband, their home no longer had the special status of a "matrimonial home" for the Family Law Act of Ontario. This meant that any right to claim possession of that home was lost the minute the divorce was granted. This was a terrible tactical mistake by the woman and it could not be rectified.

Costs are always a concern in divorce and my own view is that the best way to manage cost is to become an informed consumer. There are many free legal resources available online and otherwise, and there is simply no reason in this day and age to make hasty decisions with respect to the important matters of ending your marriage, arriving at a property settlement, dealing with custody of your children or support issues. You may want to review the advice that I give in Chapter 2: Taking a Look at Lawyers. There are many ways to manage the costs, even in difficult cases.

CLOSING REMARKS

WHILE DIVORCE IS in fact the easiest issue for determination by a court, it is linked to many other aspects of the marriage breakdown. I often recommend to clients that they consider getting the divorce last. In other words, deal with all other issues first and then get the divorce. Only if there is some urgent need for the divorce, such as a remarriage or a child on the way, should it be made a priority.

MY ADVICE

1. Legal separation is a meaningless term. The clock for one-year separation starts the minute the parties are separated. They do not need to sign a separation agreement in order to be considered separated.
2. Separation can include living separate and apart under the same roof.
3. To have an effective separation, both spouses must be aware of the separation and that the marriage is ending. Collusion to create grounds for divorce may result in the divorce not being granted.
4. It is possible to reconcile for up to 90 days without interfering with a one-year separation as grounds for divorce.
5. Be cautious in trying to obtain a divorce prior to resolving issues around the home, custody of children and child support.
6. Marriages of convenience are an abuse of women, immigrants and our justice system, and reforms are being implemented to prevent these kinds of marriages from happening.

DIVIDING THE FAMILY'S PROPERTY

Get Your Fair Share from the Marriage Partnership

THE BOTTOM LINE is that marriage now has a bottom line. Certainly entering into marriage means entering into an emotional partnership, but let there be no doubt that marriage creates a financial partnership as well. This partnership begins on your wedding day and ends the day of separation. Any and all assets acquired by the marriage partnership are on the table for division if the partnership fails. Its assets and liabilities must be divided fairly.

Most Canadians own homes and cars, have RRSPs and other forms of savings as well as pensions. In some cases they are lucky enough to have cottages, cabins or recreational property and other interesting assets. A fair division of the assets of the marriage partnership is absolutely critical if both spouses wish to be able to move on to new, independent and financially secure lives. They will be taking away from the marriage this "nest egg," which they must use wisely as they start over.

In this chapter, we will examine what this marriage partnership acquires in the way of property and debt, and how that property is valued and divided along with the family debt. As well, we will consider some of the special circumstances that may arise in some marriage breakdowns.

Property division in a marriage breakdown situation is governed entirely by provincial law and therefore varies from province to province. Because each province has its own property division scheme, this chapter was one of the most challenging to assemble. The number of generalizations that we can make about property division law in Canada is, as a result, limited. So, in this chapter I will attempt to provide a sense of the common goals of property division and examine some of the more practical aspects of this area.

The goal of property division schemes in all of the provinces and territories is to divide fairly, if not equally, the value of all assets acquired by the couple between the date of the marriage and the date of their separation or divorce. The marriage partnership, like any business, sees each partner bring a contribution to it. Assets and liabilities are acquired over the life of the partnership and at its conclusion they are divided fairly between the partners.

This "partnership" arises upon becoming legally married in Canada. (In Chapter 8: Common-Law Spouses Have Rights Too, I examine the very serious limitations on the entitlement of common-law spouses to share property at the end of a relationship.) The rules and guidelines we are discussing in this chapter *only concern legally married spouses,* including same-sex marriages, which now benefit from the marital property division laws in all of the provinces.

While it is difficult to say whether or not married couples are any better off materially now than 20 or 30 years ago, it is safe to say that today's couples are subject to a much more complex scheme of provincial property division. They are also acquiring assets that have a much more complex nature and value.

The complexity of the rules of property division and the types of property that couples own demands the involvement of lawyers and in many cases accountants, appraisers and valuators. Thus, we begin this chapter with a caution that, when it comes to property division, you may need to rely heavily on legal advice. You will be bearing a great deal of the responsibility yourself for locating, describing and valuing your marriage's assets and liabilities.

Property division is one of the issues the court prefers to settle first. Once the family's property has been divided, the court can then turn its attention to questions of custody of the children, access to them, child support and, depending on the amount of property received, spousal support. This is particularly so in determining who will have the matrimonial home.

Time Limitations: Waiting Can Cost You Your Rights

AS WITH ANY claim that can be made in a court, you will face certain time limitations. Each province provides its own cut-off date for claiming things such as property division and spousal support. For example, in Ontario an application to the court to equalize net family properties based on marriage breakdown shall not be brought after the earliest of 1) two years from the divorce or a decree that the marriage was a nullity; 2) six years from separation; or 3) six months after the other spouse has died. If you have separated from your spouse, one of the best reasons to consult with a lawyer as soon as possible is to ensure that you know the time frame within which you must make a claim for property or support.

WHAT IS "PROPERTY"?

THE DEFINITION OF property varies a little from province to province. For the most part, property includes all real and personal property and all interests in property.

The safest approach to division of property and to understanding what can be captured by that word is to simply include everything that was acquired by either of you between the date of your marriage and the date that you separated. This would include the acquisition of property worldwide. Consider the following property as examples of property division in actual Canadian cases:

- household contents
- vehicles
- art collections
- pensions
- cottages and cabins
- time-shares and vacation properties
- severance payments

- a milk quota
- disability pensions
- airline points
- stock options
- shares in companies
- trusts
- sports memorabilia
- recreational vehicles
- sporting equipment
- collections and heirlooms
- books
- pets—and on and on.

An advantage of using the overinclusive approach is that no one will ever accuse a spouse of hiding an asset. Even if it were an honest mistake, the settlement could be set aside if the asset's value was significant and the outcome would have been different had it been disclosed.

WHAT IS DEBT?

JUST AS CANADIAN families acquire property, they also have become adept at acquiring debt, lots of debt. Consider the following examples:
- mortgages
- collateral mortgages
- loans from family members
- judgments by creditors
- credit cards
- lines of credit
- car leases
- unpaid income tax
- income tax penalties and interest
- costs of disposition of assets (e.g., real estate commissions)
- capital gains tax

All debt acquired by the family must be offset against the assets.

Family Loans

ON THE ISSUE of family loans, it is not uncommon to see a financial statement filed showing significant debt to a mother, father or other family member. Sometimes the debt, or the amount of it, comes as a surprise to the other spouse. The spouse is justifiably suspicious that the loan is being shown on the financial statement as a way of decreasing the net worth of that spouse. Courts are equally suspicious of these types of family loans, and require the spouse claiming the loan to produce written evidence of:

- when the loan was entered into;
- what the terms of repayment are;
- whether interest was being charged on the loan;
- whether any repayment has been made and evidence of those repayments; and
- whether other siblings have received similar loans from the parents or family members.

In this last situation, concerning siblings, the court will be interested to know whether the "loan" is simply an advance on an inheritance that is being paid out to children as a part of estate planning. In some cases, the courts have simply disregarded the alleged loan, or significantly discounted its value by, in some cases, as much as 95 per cent.

FINANCIAL STATEMENTS

ALL OF THE above information about assets and liabilities must be captured in a useful way for the lawyers, clients and court. The information is incorporated in the all-important Financial Statement. If spousal support, child support or property division is claimed by either party, sworn Financial Statements must be filed as a part of the proceeding. Only in very limited circumstances of uncontested divorces where all financial matters have been resolved will Financial Statements be dispensed with. Each province has its own particular form of Financial Statement.

It is very likely that the first document your lawyer will present to you, after the Family Law Client History Form, is the Financial Statement.

You will be sent home to complete the form to the best of your ability and return it to the office. So much depends upon the accuracy of this statement. It must be a full statement, complete, up-to-date and meaningful. There is no point in trying to avoid a description of an asset, artificially undervaluing an asset, overvaluing a debt or describing something in such vague terms that it cannot be understood. The content of the Financial Statement will be scrutinized by the lawyer for your spouse and, ultimately, by the court.

It is your job to locate the information and supporting documentation for the Financial Statement. Remember, the form is designed to save time and money by ensuring complete financial disclosure as early as possible in the legal proceedings. It will be updated periodically as the case proceeds.

Your all-important credibility in a legal proceeding is at risk if the Financial Statement is not prepared accurately. The courts look with disfavour upon a party who has neglected to give full and complete disclosure. You should remember that these statements are sworn affidavits. Any attempt to mislead the court can draw a negative inference from the judge.

I have seen a client's case gain strength at trial when they have withstood a probing cross-examination of the Financial Statement and can demonstrate to the judge and the opposing counsel their total honesty and accuracy in completing the statement.

In some cases, clients worry about the disclosure of confidential financial information in a public proceeding. Family law contains provisions in the Rules of Procedure that allow the Financial Statement's contents to be shielded. If this is a concern, you should immediately consult with your lawyer so that you receive that type of protection if appropriate.

On the subject of confidentiality, however, it has come to the attention of family law lawyers that identity theft is occurring because of the detailed financial information put into financial statements in family law matters. Lawyers have told clients for years to be as detailed as possible. Unfortunately, information has been stolen from the financial statements by criminals engaged in identity theft and fraud. For this reason, do not put full credit card numbers, social insurance numbers and other complete bank account information on your Financial Statement. Put enough information to identify the account and the appropriate balances.

In some cases one or both spouses may have interests in privately held corporations. The rules of procedure require the spouse to disclose their interest, but co-owners and/or employers may not consent to the release of confidential corporate information. In such circumstances, spouses may be required to sign confidentiality agreements, undertaking to not release any of the private corporation information, other than for purposes of their separation and divorce.

VALUE OF ASSETS AND LIABILITIES

THE VARIOUS PROVINCIAL schemes for division of property focus not on the physical division of the assets themselves but rather the values of the assets. This means that property that is in the name of either the husband or the wife is valued to determine who has the greater total property value. Once the total values are known, an adjustment is made so that one spouse pays to the other spouse an amount of money (or transfers certain pieces of property) to ensure that each spouse leaves the marriage with approximately the same *value* in assets.

It is the net value of all property owned by either spouse, subject to some very limited exceptions, that is divided between the spouses at marriage breakdown. The values that are divided are net values. This means using the value of an asset *after* deducting any liabilities connected with a particular asset.

So, if a couple owns a cottage that is worth $200,000 but it is subject to a $100,000 mortgage, its net value is $100,000 (assuming there is no capital gain on the sale of the property) and it is that net value that is divided between the couple if and when their marriage breaks down. The same is true for a car that is subject to a bank loan, a home that is subject to a mortgage and even stocks that are purchased on a line of credit provided by a bank. The debts must be repaid first and any remaining value is divided.

How Is Value Determined?

SINCE IT IS not necessarily the asset itself that is being divided but rather its value, one of the arguments that can arise in the area of property division is over the value that should be attached to a particular asset.

The following is a good illustration of how different valuations can be. A man and woman had been married for approximately 30 years and operated a dairy farm. Over the years, the dairy operation was gradually surrounded by housing subdivisions from a nearby city. The dairy operation was successful and the father and mother intended, throughout most of the marriage, to pass on the farm to their children. However, the marriage had difficulties, the couple separated and the value of the dairy farm came into question. The husband pointed out that the dairy operation had a particular "book value" of approximately $700,000 and that he was prepared to divide that value with his wife and later pass on the farm to the children as agreed. The wife, on the other hand, obtained a valuation of the property which concluded that the farm should be valued at $3,500,000.

Why the discrepancy? The wife's valuation was based upon ending the dairy farm operation and selling the land to developers for a new subdivision of homes. Which valuation is correct? Both. Which is the best solution in this particular case? None of the alternatives satisfied all of the people involved, particularly the children who were expecting to inherit the business and property.

The point of the above example is that valuations can be quite different and you will need to explore your alternatives with your lawyer. Some provinces specify that the value to be used is the "fair market value." Other provinces do not specify the basis of valuation and allow each case to be decided on its own facts. This means that in cases involving difficult or unusual assets various approaches will be used, including "current market value," "fair market value," "cost," "book value" and "liquidation value."

Another aspect of valuation is whether or not tax obligations and other costs of disposition should be taken into consideration when arriving at a value for an asset. For example, if a party would incur tax consequences for a particular disposition, those tax consequences would be factored in to reduce the value of the asset as divided.

Similarly, if costs would be incurred to dispose of a piece of property, those costs of disposition should be deducted from the value as divided. So, for example, where a couple own a home and its value is to be divided, but one party does not wish to have the property sold and will, therefore, buy out the other person's interest, a question arises: Should the value be the fair market value of the home after the deduction of an amount for real estate commission? If the property was sold on the open market, a commission would likely be paid, so should the commission be taken into account in reducing the amount that must be shared with the other spouse? For the most part, the answer is yes. When assets are transferred between spouses or when assets must be sold, the courts usually include a reduction to account for the costs of disposition, such as real estate commission. In the case of RRSPs, there is a discount for the future tax consequences of redemption. Discuss with your lawyer the appropriate and fair costs of disposition of particular assets to ensure that the right values are being divided. These are all questions that must be answered in the effort to arrive at an equitable division of the family's property. Remember that valuation methods vary from asset to asset.

Each year, there is some new and interesting challenge for lawyers and courts in trying to establish a value for a particular type of property. For example, valuing airline frequent flyer points can be difficult. Some courts have simply ordered that the points themselves be divided rather than attributing a value to them. Leasing vehicles has become more popular. In some cases, it has been necessary to determine if a vehicle has any equity in it. Stock options have presented some challenges to the courts. In some cases, the stock options are certainly property, but in other cases they are also a form of compensation. Small businesses have also presented challenges. Commercial goodwill, personal goodwill, family farming operations and businesses that have no realistic comparable value have all been considered by the court. Dozens of cases have considered various methods of valuing pensions and even the Supreme Court of Canada has commented that there is no one valuation method that is appropriate and must be used for all cases.

A veritable cottage industry of valuation experts has built up around the family law practice. Experts on pension valuations, stock options, art appraisers, real estate appraisers and so on are all available to assist—for a fee. Valuations can be considerably expensive and it is not uncommon now for one spouse to insist that a forensic accountant/valuator become involved to provide guidance on more complicated asset situations. Determining the value of property can be an expensive proposition.

The cost of valuation can be considerable, whether it is an appraiser valuing real estate, or a valuator attempting to determine the value of a privately held business, or even the extent of a spouse's income from a variety of sources. One spouse may feel at a disadvantage in asking for these expensive expert reports to be prepared. The family laws of each province permit a spouse to ask for money to be advanced to them to meet the cost of such disbursements. The amount will not be ordered automatically, but the court will be interested to know whether it would be impossible for the spouse to adequately understand his or her entitlement without some financial assistance. Rules allow for a spouse to ask for an advance to assist with their legal fees as well. If a spouse can tell from a preliminary calculation that he or she will be receiving a considerable amount of cash as a part of the property settlement, the court may order that some of those funds be advanced to that spouse, so he or she can use those assets to pay for legal fees and disbursements.

WHAT IS NOT DIVIDED? EXEMPT PROPERTY

EACH PROVINCE PROVIDES a list of exceptions—assets that will not be divided upon marriage breakdown. For example, every province allows a couple to exempt property from division by use of a marriage contract. If a couple, at the time they were married, agreed in a marriage contract that a particular piece of property, for example, a family cottage or a family business, would not be shared if the marriage broke down, the property would be exempt. The following types of property are typical of exemption (double-check with your lawyer to see which exemptions are available in your province):

• any property owned in advance of the marriage and brought into the marriage;

- a gift or inheritance received during the course of the marriage;
- a court award or a settlement giving a spouse damages for personal injuries they suffered, for example, in a car accident;
- personal items, such as clothing, basic jewellery and sports equipment;
- family heirlooms and antiques;
- proceeds from a policy of life insurance (e.g., the amount of money received if a husband's mother died and left an insurance policy payable to him);
- gifts from one spouse to the other;
- traceable property (this means property that started out in one exempt category but may have ended up in some other form; for example, if a person took their damage award for injuries suffered in an automobile accident and purchased Guaranteed Investment Certificates, the Certificates are still exempt because they can be traced back to the original exempt category);
- property exempted by virtue of a marriage contract; and
- property that is acquired after the date of separation.

Losing an Exemption

IT IS POSSIBLE for someone to lose the ability to characterize a piece of property as exempt. If, for example, someone received an inheritance that was exempt but they blended that money into the couple's joint accounts, bought furniture for the house and generally mixed it in with the assets of the family, it will be almost impossible to claim an exemption for it. This is bad, since having exempt property can be very valuable at the time of separation and divorce.

Jointly Held Property

THE FORMULAS USED by the various provincial property division schemes rely on each spouse setting out the property and the value of the property that is in his or her name, but sometimes the property is held jointly. This means that the property will appear in both parties' property summaries and it will also mean that the value of the property may fluctuate. So, if a couple owned a property jointly at the time they married and jointly at the time they separated, and the separation took two years for them to sort out, there may in fact be three values for the property. It is not unusual in protracted family law cases for property to be valued over and over again to ensure that the court has the most recent and most accurate valuation.

DATE OF VALUATION

EVERY PROVINCIAL PROPERTY scheme needs to know the value of property that was owned on the date of marriage and the value of the property on the date the relationship ended. Generally, that valuation date is one of three events: 1) the date the parties separated and there was no reasonable prospect that they would resume cohabitation; 2) the date of the divorce or *a nullity* judgment; or 3) the date before the spouse died, where the marriage ends by virtue of one spouse's death.

Figuring out the date of a marriage is easy. Sometimes determining the date of separation is difficult, particularly if the relationship unravelled over an extended period of time. One person may consider the marriage to be absolutely over, while the other is operating under the assumption that they are working at saving the marriage. Reconciliations, trial separations and participation in marriage counselling can blur the line of a date of separation. This means that it can be difficult to pick the date for the valuation of assets. The same is true if the couple lived in the same home but separate and apart. (See Chapter 4: Getting a Divorce for further discussion of the meaning of separation.)

UNEQUAL DIVISION OF PROPERTY VALUES

EVERY PROVINCE PROVIDES an *exception,* a method for the court to divide the net value in a way that is *not equal.* Every provincial legislature recognizes that there may be circumstances in which it would not be fair to divide the family assets equally between the two spouses. They do, however, take a different approach in describing the circumstances in which the court can exercise that discretion.

Some provinces, such as Manitoba, Newfoundland and Labrador, Nova Scotia and Ontario, have provided in their laws that assets should only be divided unequally where to divide them equally would be *grossly unfair or unconscionable*. This is a very high standard. It means that the court would need to find that it was almost shocked by the effect of an equal division for it to depart from that general rule. Other provinces, on the other hand, give the court the discretion to depart from an equal division of the value of the asset where to divide equally would be merely unfair.

I should provide a little reminder at this stage that when the court is considering a division that is not equal, it is not interested in either spouse's complaints about the other spouse's conduct. For example, the fact that a spouse committed adultery is not a reason for the unequal division of property. The fact that a spouse was engaged in conduct that might even be considered mental or physical cruelty is not a reason to divide the property unequally.

What the court is looking for in these cases of unequal division is evidence that if the property was divided equally it would shock the court's sense of fairness. For example, if a wealthy man married a woman and the marriage only lasted six months, the court's sense of justice might be offended if all of that man's property was to be divided equally. In one case, a spouse engaged in reckless conduct (gambling) that basically resulted in him losing all of his property. In addition to losing property, he ran up debts that had to be repaid by both spouses. In a case like that, the court's sense of justice might be offended if what was left over still had to be divided equally. The court will examine the conduct related to the property and how it was acquired, maintained or managed during the relationship.

Because of the existence of this provision in the laws of some provinces, discuss with your lawyer the circumstances under which your provincial legislation will allow the court to depart from an equal division of the property.

THE MATRIMONIAL HOME

THE MATRIMONIAL HOME is a special asset that requires separate consideration. All provinces provide for a restriction on one spouse's ability to dispose of or encumber the matrimonial home without the other spouse's consent. Therefore, one spouse cannot sell the matrimonial home without the other spouse's consent nor place a mortgage on the property without the other spouse's consent. This protects the value of the property for sharing at marriage breakdown.

Most couples starting out acquire their home after marriage. It is usually placed in their names jointly so that one would inherit automatically if the other one died. The house becomes the main asset of the family and is usually divided equally unless there is some very unusual circumstance.

More and more often lawyers are seeing couples in which one has acquired a home in advance of the marriage. If the couple decides to use it as their matrimonial home, then its value may be divided equally. If a spouse brings a home into the marriage, special protection, perhaps through a marriage contract, is something that must be considered.

Another consideration is possession of the matrimonial home at the time the marriage breaks down. Possession does not necessarily relate to ownership of the matrimonial home. For example, Manitoba, New Brunswick, Newfoundland and Labrador, Nova Scotia, Ontario, Prince Edward Island and Saskatchewan all provide an automatic equal right to possession of the matrimonial home at the time of marriage breakdown regardless of ownership of the home. This means that if the couple separates, either or both spouses can apply to the court for an order giving one of them exclusive possession of the matrimonial home. In cases of family violence or where there is a need to keep children in a particular neighbourhood for reasons of continuity, an order for exclusive possession can be a valuable tool. Discuss with your lawyer the availability of orders for exclusive possession in your particular jurisdiction. (For further discussion of exclusive possession and its enforcement, see Chapter 12: Enforcing Family Law Orders.)

Be aware at this stage that you can also obtain an order from the court prohibiting your spouse from dealing with any of his or her property until further order of the court. This allows the court to preserve the assets until the end of trial, if necessary, so that there will be property available to divide and to pay for satisfaction of the judgment.

PENSIONS

ANOTHER SPECIAL ASSET is a pension. It is quite common for one or both spouses to have private pension plans. The pension is a family asset and must be valued and divided like any other asset owned by the spouse. Valuing pensions is a challenge, with values varying from pension to pension and pension holder to pension holder. Since the amount of the pension to be divided will be only the amount of pension accumulated during the marriage, rather than its entire value, it will be necessary to hire someone to provide a specific value for the relevant period.

Different methods used by valuators and accountants include the "termination method" or the "retirement method." In examining the value, the person doing the valuation will also consider mortality tables, the role of interest, early retirement provisions, death benefits that may be available after retirement and the tax consequences of the benefits upon receipt.

Indexed pensions are a separate matter. In some cases, spouses have requested an "if and when" division, whereby a pension is shared if and when it is received by the other spouse. This allows both spouses to share in the actual benefit when the employee receives it under his or her pension plan. This type of division was not really contemplated by provincial laws related to pension division and the courts have struggled to find a way to make such orders. In most cases, they have stressed to the parties that they can consent to such a division, in the process perhaps saving themselves the expense of a valuation.

In the case of *Best v. Best* [1999] 2 SCR 868 the Supreme Court of Canada tried to offer separating couples and lawyers some guidance on pension division. The court suggested that "if and when" division of pensions may be limited to exceptional cases, for example, where most of the equalization entitlement at the end of the marriage is in a pension and where retirement is imminent, forcing someone to make an equalization payment would be a hardship.

The Canadian Institute of Actuaries developed a system called the Deferred Settlement Method. This method is designed to assist spouses in dividing one pension into two pensions after a marriage breakdown.

It requires some cooperation from pension administrators and the consent of the parties, but it may offer an alternative to separating families who are dividing pension assets.

Pension valuations, or valuations of any assets for that matter, are not free. Valuation costs can range from $500 to $2,000. You should receive an estimate from your lawyer in advance before authorizing the valuation of an asset as significant as a pension. Valuations of business interest can cost tens of thousands of dollars.

It is not uncommon to hear a spouse state that if all the property is going to be divided, then they will simply retire and start living off their pension. This does not change the fact that the pension existed as an asset on the date of separation. If a spouse indicates that he or she intends to retire immediately, this has an effect on the value that will be attributed to the pension at the date of separation. The later a person retires, the lower the actual value of a pension at the date of separation. It is not recommended that frustrated spouses cash in their chips and retire or threaten to retire. It is counter-productive for the calculations of a pension value.

In the area of pensions, the Supreme Court of Canada gave an interesting decision in the case of *Boston v. Boston* [2001] 2 SCR 413. This case dealt with the troubling issue of what is known as "double-dipping." Mr. Boston and his wife had divided the value of his teacher's pension at the time they separated. Mr. Boston was ordered to pay spousal support to his wife. They both went their separate ways and several years later Mr. Boston decided to retire. He then began to draw on his teacher's pension and, because he was earning less, asked the court to reduce the amount that he would pay for spousal support. The issue arose as to whether Mr. Boston could look to his teacher's pension again for the purposes of spousal support. It had been divided already at the date of separation. To allow it to be used again for payment of spousal support would in effect be "double-dipping." The Supreme Court of Canada considered the problem and concluded that double-dipping should be avoided and that in the case of Mr. Boston only that portion of his pension that accrued after the date of separation should be used for calculation of any entitlement to spousal support. Accordingly, the amount that he was paying on a monthly basis was reduced.

This case is also important in that it refers to the obligations of the spouses to use the property settlement wisely after the separation and to invest it in a way that contributes to their self-sufficiency. This is an important message to spouses at the time of separation. The Supreme Court of Canada has said essentially that each spouse must take the nest egg and invest it in a way that contributes to their financial independence. The Supreme Court of Canada even went so far as to suggest that the nest egg should be invested in a capital-depleting, income-generating fund, essentially creating a pension for each spouse.

Special Note for Ontario Residents

THE ONTARIO LEGISLATURE passed a law called the *Family Statute Law Amendment Act*, 2009. It concerns the division of pensions in Ontario at the time of separation and divorce. If you are separating and divorcing in Ontario and have a pension, keep in mind the following points and discuss them with your lawyer:

- The new law provides for the immediate settlement of pension benefits on the breakdown of a marriage.
- If the pension plan member is not retired on the date of separation (the valuation date), then payment on account of the value of the pension may be made by way of a lump sum rollout from the pension plan.
- If the pension member was retired before the valuation date, then the retirement income from the pension plan will be divided between the spouses.
- The new law eliminates deferred settlement methods such as the "if and when" arrangements discussed earlier in this chapter.
- The legislation changes the way pensions are valued as property for the purposes of equalization. The pension plan value is calculated by pension plan administrators and is provided to either spouse, if married, on request. Plan administrators charge for this service and fees range from around $200 to $500, depending on the type of plan.
- This approach to division of pensions refers to two values when calculating the pension's value, (1) the preliminary value, which is the value of the plan on the valuation date, and (2) the imputed value, which will prorate the preliminary value for the period of the marriage.

· The value for the plan as determined by the plan administrator will be expressed in pre-tax dollars. That value will not be adjusted by the plan administrator for the income tax impact on the value of the pension. It remains up to the individual to privately obtain the appropriate income tax deduction calculation.

Pension valuation and division is very important for separating and divorcing couples and should be reviewed closely with your lawyer.

Canada Pension Plan (CPP)

ONE PENSION AREA of special interest is the Canada Pension Plan credit-sharing scheme. The CPP was amended in 1978 to provide for the sharing of the pension credits accumulated by one or both spouses during the years of their cohabitation. This sharing of credits takes effect upon the dissolution of the marriage. It was designed to ensure that low- or non-income-earning homemakers whose marriages had ended were provided with some pension coverage.

People who can claim a division of pension credits include married spouses who have been separated for at least one year, as well as common-law spouses whose relationship has ended with the death of one of the parties or a separation lasting at least one year. The general rule is that upon the dissolution of the marriage or the ending of the common-law relationship, all unadjusted pensionable earnings of either spouse during the eligible years of cohabitation are added together, and one-half of the total is credited to each spouse's Canada Pension Plan or provincial pension plan account.

The method by which the credits are divided is related to the contributions made by the respective spouses to the Canada Pension Plan. A wife who never worked and was therefore never eligible to contribute to the Canada Pension Plan but whose husband always made the maximum allowable contribution would benefit to a large degree from the division scheme. If, however, the spouses had incomes throughout the marriage that were relatively equal, their pension credits would remain relatively unchanged. For information about division of Canada Pension credits, see www.canadabenefits.gc.ca or www.womenindivorce.ca.

PAYING AN AMOUNT TO RESOLVE PROPERTY

THE GOAL OF the formula provided by provincial family law is to calculate a sum of money that is owed by one spouse to the other. The
judgment can therefore be paid simply by a cash payment from one
spouse to another or can be paid by the transfer of particular pieces
of property. If, for example, the court finds that the wife is entitled to
$100,000 for her interest in the family property and finds that the mat-
rimonial home has an equity of $100,000, the court could simply order
that the matrimonial home be placed in the wife's name alone in satisfaction of her interest in the family property.

Once the amount owing has been calculated, you and your lawyer
can be creative in satisfying the payment. As mentioned above, it is
possible to transfer a particular piece of property in satisfaction of the
property obligation. However, other alternatives include rolling over
RRSPs, instalment payments, leaving the contents of the home, sale of
a particular asset in an agreement to equally divide anything realized,
and so on.

On the other side of the coin, some families are faced with the prospect of being forced to sell their home to pay debt that accumulated
during the marriage. Many Canadian families, instead of dividing property creatively, struggle with allocating who will take responsibility for
which credit cards, who will pay the line of credit, who will pay income
taxes that have accrued and so on. Although the marriage has come to
an end, in some cases the couple is still connected by their joint obligations on debt.

SOME TAX CONSIDERATIONS

ONE OF THE issues that will arise during your discussions of the way in
which property will be treated in your case is income tax considerations.
I have set out some of those considerations in this section.

Canadian income tax law is affected by changes on an almost annual
basis, so it is important for you and your lawyer to check with your
accountant or financial planner prior to entering into any final agreement. The income tax consequences of property settlements, support

payments, investments, RRSPs and even legal fees can have a significant impact on the net value of the settlement. In the following list, I have set out some of the more common tax considerations. Keep them in mind as you consider your options.

1. Sometimes a settlement of the property and support issues in a separation and divorce will involve the transfer of property from one spouse to the other. The income tax laws generally do not affect such transfers, as they might impede fair settlements of family property claims, but rather work in a way to encourage settlements. However, transfers of capital property between spouses are deemed to take place at the transferor's adjusted cost base (calculated to determine the cost of an investment for tax purposes). For settlement purposes, spouses are sometimes able to "roll over" capital property (transfer without immediate tax consequences). Any tax status of the particular piece of property rolls over from the transferor to the transferee. Whenever property is being transferred from one spouse to the other as a part of a settlement, extra caution must be exercised to ensure that undesirable tax consequences do not flow from the transaction.

2. When dealing with the matrimonial home, it is important to know that each family is entitled to have only one principal residence. A principal residence can be sold and any gain is tax free. If a family has more than one property, then only one property can be designated as the principal residence. Second or third properties will be subject to capital gains. Professional advice is needed where there are two or more possible principal residences. This advice is needed prior to settling the case; after, it will be too late.

3. All or any part of a spouse's RRSP can be transferred to the other spouse's RRSP without any income tax consequences. Again, Canada Revenue Agency has set specific conditions that must be met. Review these conditions with your lawyer and financial planner prior to concluding the settlement.

4. The Income Tax Act also contains a number of rules concerning income attribution. This means that even if one spouse owns a particular property, income from that property (or gain in its value when sold) might be attributed to the other spouse for income tax

purposes. Therefore, an unsuspecting spouse may end up with an unpleasant tax burden. Prior to settling your case, review with your lawyer or financial planner the income attribution rules that govern these transactions.

5. This will come as a shock to many people, but married persons may be held responsible for their spouse's unpaid tax liabilities in certain limited circumstances. For example, if one spouse transfers property to the other spouse by way of a gift or sale, there may be joint and several liability for a spouse's unpaid tax to the extent that the actual fair market value of the property exceeded the amount paid. Again, review these rules prior to settling. Once an agreement has been signed, a spouse who finds himself or herself suddenly saddled with an unwanted tax burden may have little recourse.

6. In some circumstances, legal fees paid may be deductible. Ask your lawyer to identify in his or her bill those fees that are directly attributable to obtaining or enforcing child support or spousal support. This area has recently been open to interpretation and there have been several court cases, so speak with your lawyer to make sure that you receive the maximum benefit.

7. A spouse's release of property and/or support rights in return for a property settlement will not give rise to a taxable disposition of property.

8. As of January 1, 2001, for all purposes of the Income Tax Act, same-sex common-law couples are treated the same as other couples. This means that they are eligible for the same tax benefits. It also means they are subject to the same obligations as married couples and opposite-sex common-law couples.

Every federal budget brings changes to the income tax laws. The above points that I have provided in an overview form are designed to alert you to some of the more common income tax considerations at the time of separation and divorce. These points are up-to-date as of the date of this publication. However, because the income tax laws inevitably will change, I defer to your financial planner and family law lawyer. They will provide you with the most current information and will know how to apply for the maximum benefit in your case. For the most current information about the impact of tax law on separation and divorce visit www.cra-arc.gc.ca/menu-e.html.

CLOSING REMARKS

MARRIAGE IS A financial partnership. The assets and liabilities of the partnership are going to be divided equitably at the time of separation. As we have seen, property has a very broad definition; the valuations of property can vary, and there are special rules governing exemptions for particular pieces of property, and even the possibility of unequal division in limited circumstances. Your lawyer should review with you the various choices and options available to you in seeking to divide your property.

MY ADVICE

1. All forms of property are included in the calculations for division of property at the time of separation and divorce.
2. The goal of provincial property division formulas is to divide the net worth of the couple, as it has accumulated between the date of marriage and the date of separation.
3. Assets and liabilities are divided pursuant to the provincial formulas for property division.
4. These property division rules apply only to legally married spouses for most Canadian provinces. If you are a common-law spouse, see Chapter 8.
5. The right to a division of property can be lost if you delay. Check with your lawyer to find out if there is a deadline for pursuing property claims in your province.
6. All forms of debt are included in calculation of property division, including mortgages, lines of credit, income tax debts, family loans, student loans, credit card debt, judgments and other obligations.
7. Each province provides categories of exempt property, property that does not get shared at the time of separation. Exempt property may include, for example, inheritances, property bought into the marriage and property made exempt by a marriage contract.

8. Mingling exempt property with family property may cause you to sacrifice the exemption.
9. There are a variety of methods for determining the value of a piece of property, including current market value, fair market value, cost, book value and liquidation value. In some cases it is necessary to hire experts to pin down the value of property.
10. The value of jointly held property will float up and down over the course of your discussions. The value as of the date of settlement will be used, rather than the value as of the date of separation.
11. The date of separation is very important, as this is the date upon which most of your assets will be valued. Any change in the value of your asset after the date of separation may not be taken into consideration in settling property unless it is jointly owned.
12. Each province provides the court with the discretion to divide property other than equally if one spouse has engaged in conduct or other circumstances that would suggest to the court that it is unfair to divide the property equally. This power is rarely used.
13. The matrimonial home has special protections in each province.
14. Pensions are considered property and need to be valued and divided. A pension valuator will need to be hired in order to determine the correct value.
15. Canada Pension Plan credits accumulated during the course of the relationship are divided as of the date of separation.
16. The sworn Financial Statement is an important summary of your income, your assets and your liabilities. Make every effort to ensure that it is accurate, as this will speed the settlement and affect your credibility.
17. Check with your accountant prior to concluding any settlement to ensure that the tax consequences of the transfer of property are completely understood.

OBLIGATIONS TO THE
CHILDREN OF A DIVORCE

Every Parent's Top Priority

I T IS SAFE to say that custody of children can be *the* issue in a family dispute. No other issue dredges up such strong emotions or such total commitment by a parent to the achievement of a particular result. It is not uncommon to hear one parent threaten the other with a "scorched earth" policy in the approach to custody of children. Each parent wants a say in the child's upbringing, each parent wants control. It is a recipe for conflict.

In this chapter we will examine the meaning of custody and access, the considerations used by the court in ordering it and some of the more important features of custody and access orders. I have included a section in this chapter called "Hot Spots" to identify some of the real-life problems that parents encounter. We will also examine the methods of dispute resolution and custody, as well as costs and some of the tactical considerations. At the end of this chapter, I have included a section entitled "What Will We Tell the Children?" Read it.

Even though I have been at this work now for over 35 years, I am still shocked at what parents will put their children through at the time of divorce. Perhaps the most incredible aspect of the pain they inflict on their children during divorce is the lengths to which a parent will go in justifying their behaviour. Somehow, everything that parent does is designed to supposedly "advance the best interests of the children." Under that banner, I have seen parents deny their children winter vacations to Florida, block summer vacations at favourite camps, force the sale of homes close to a child's favourite school and best friend, prevent Christmases or major holidays with both sides of the family and worse, all in the name of protecting their child's best interests.

The cause of pain to children at the time of separation and divorce is rooted in one thing and one thing only: conflict between their parents. Certainly, children are heartbroken about their parents separating, but most children can, over time, adjust to separation and divorce. What they cannot adjust to is standing in a no man's land between two fighting parents, both of whom profess to have their best interests at heart.

Canadian family law states that neither parent has a head start in obtaining custody of a child. It is only if the parents cannot agree that the court will step in and decide for them. When the court is asked to step in, it will look to see who can best care for this child. However, the orders that are available to the court are fairly limited. Unfortunately, this has created a foot race between many parents to run each other down in the eyes of the court in order to prove that they alone should have custody of the child and the other parent should only have access. Unfortunately, in many cases, this has become a direct incentive for conflict.

CUSTODY AND ACCESS: UNDERSTANDING TERMINOLOGY

BOTH FEDERAL AND provincial family laws contain provisions with respect to custody of and access to children. The Divorce Act provides the court with the power to make an order for custody of or access to a child at the time it grants the divorce judgment and also on an interim basis until a final order is made. All provincial and territorial family laws contain similar provisions and, as described earlier (in Chapter 4: Getting a Divorce), the application of provincial, territorial or federal law is dictated entirely by whether there is a request for a divorce. Remember, common-law couples are not covered by the Divorce Act. They must use provincial law.

Let's consider some key terms.

Custody

ONE JUDGE DEFINED custody as follows:

> To award one parent the exclusive custody of a child is to clothe that parent, for whatever period he or she is awarded the custody, with full parental control over, and ultimate parental responsibility for, the care, upbringing and education of the child, generally to the exclusion of the right of the other parent to interfere in decisions that are made in exercising that control or in carrying out that responsibility.

The parent who has custody of a child usually enjoys having the majority of the residential time. It is this parent who decides where the child will go to school, what religious faith the child will observe, their medical needs, their dental needs, recreational activities and so on. It is a huge amount of responsibility.

Access

WHEN ONE PARENT is given custody of a child, the other parent typically is given access. This means an opportunity to spend time with the child and the right to have information about what is going on in the child's life. Traditionally, when the courts have made custody and access orders, the court will order that the child be in the custody of the mother and that the father have time with the child alternate weekends from, for example, Friday night to Sunday night and then some midweek visits over night or perhaps only for dinner. The access parent would be entitled to know how the child is doing in school, what their medical/dental needs are and what recreational activities they are participating in.

You will recall my comment at the opening of this chapter about parents wanting a say in a child's upbringing and parents wanting control. You can see from the above allocation of time and responsibility for a child that many parents would not be prepared to accept the traditional custody versus access court order. For many parents, it is simply not good enough to go from living in a home, where there is daily contact with a child and regular involvement in homework and recreational activities, even the day-to-day mundane things like grocery shopping and going to the laundromat, driving them to and from their friends' homes—to visits on weekends every two weeks. As a result the courts and Canadian family law started to develop alternatives.

Joint Custody

IN A JOINT custody situation, the parents share the custodial decision-making responsibility and the child's residential schedule. Some parents have made a distinction between joint physical custody and joint decision-making responsibility over their children. In the case of a joint physical custody arrangement, the child will reside in two homes for fixed periods of time. These fixed periods are not necessarily equal. These residential arrangements can include splitting a week, where the child resides with one parent for half of the week and the other parent for the other half of the week, alternating weeks, alternating months, and, in some cases, alternating longer periods of time.

While the child is in the physical custody of one of the joint custodial parents, that parent has all necessary custodial decision-making power and vice versa when the child changes homes. These types of arrangements work if the parents have a good level of cooperation. For instance, where parents have joint custody and are sharing decision-making, they may allocate different responsibilities to each other, perhaps based on the way in which the home operated when it was intact. So, for example, the father may continue to look after all of the children's recreational activities (getting them to and from sports, music lessons and the like), and the mother may continue to look after the child's medical/dental needs (getting the children to and from their doctor's appointments and dental appointments). Typically in a joint custody arrangement, the parents share the responsibility of getting the children to and from school.

Since joint custody calls for a high degree of cooperation, Canadian courts have become reluctant to impose joint custody on unwilling parents. Unfortunately for some families, this provided an incentive for one parent to be deliberately uncooperative to sabotage any possibility of joint custody. This has led the court into a determination in some cases about whether the only reason joint custody is not possible is because one parent is, in effect, withholding his or her cooperation in the hope of obtaining sole custody.

Shared Parenting

A FURTHER EVOLUTION in the terminology used by families is the use of the expression "shared parenting." This is essentially the same as joint custody but the language of the Divorce Act is abandoned to more accurately describe what is actually going on in this particular family—the parents are sharing the parenting of their children. This can mean a co-operative residential schedule and a similar division of responsibilities for the children's activities and needs. I've also seen some families use the term "co-parenting" or "co-operative parenting."

Parallel Parenting

THE DIVORCE ACT and provincial family laws support the idea of each parent having maximum contact with the child. In some cases, however, one parent will not support a child's relationship with the other parent, and the courts searched for a way to achieve maximum contact with the children but not give either parent sole custody. At the same time, it is clear from the family situation that joint custody will not work. The court's response to this was to establish a form of parallel parenting by which a court order specifies in detail the time the children will spend with each parent and each parent's specific responsibilities while the child is with him or her. The parents are not expected to cooperate. They are simply expected to do their job as a sole custodial parent while the child is with them. These orders for parallel parenting can be very, very specific and contain rules and sub-rules. In some cases the orders are known as "multi-directional orders." Sometimes the court has ordered that one judge monitor the situation as the parents implement the parallel parenting plan.

Nesting Orders

THESE TYPES OF orders are not common but have been used on an interim basis for families that must share one home. The children stay put in the family home—the nest—and the parents alternate their occupation of it. So, for example, during week one the father will stay in the family home and care for the children as if he were a sole custodial parent. At the end of the week he vacates the home and the mother moves into the family home and exercises responsibility as a sole custodial parent. During the week that the parent must be out of the home, he or she finds alternative accommodations—a hotel, staying with a friend or moving in with family. In at least one case that I saw, the parents rented an apartment nearby and alternated use of the apartment during the week that they were not in the family home. In one Saskatchewan case, the parents rotated in and out on a monthly basis until final settlement of the case.

WHO IS A CHILD?

CANADIAN FAMILY LAW defines a child of the marriage as a child who is under the age of majority and is still in the care of one or both parents, or a child who is of the age of majority or over, but is still being cared for by the parents by reason of illness, disability or other dependency. In the case of dependency, it means that the child is unable to withdraw from the care of their parents, unable to obtain the necessities of life on their own. This type of dependency can be caused by a number of things, including a mental or physical disability and so on.

As we will see in an upcoming chapter dealing with child support, Chapter 7: Support, who is a child will be an important determination. Certainly it is easy to understand that a child between birth and age 16 is a child for the purposes of deciding custody and access. However, as a child gets older, this determination can become a little more complicated. For example, here are some real-life challenges experienced by parents:

• A 16-year-old child runs away from home and stays with friends.

- An 18-year-old child goes away to university with mixed success and returns home from time to time after withdrawing from classes.
- A 22-year-old child attends university, but refuses to have contact with one or both parents.
- A 19-year-old child completes high school but develops an eating disorder and is not attending university because medical appointments and hospital stays interfere.

These are the kinds of problems that families must struggle with after separation and through divorce. Intact families would find these problems a challenge, and they are even more onerous for separated families.

Here are some basic guidelines for deciding who is a child and in need of a custody or access order.

- Once a child is over the age of 16, courts are reluctant to make custody orders. Children this age typically vote "with their feet" and will live where they choose to live. A child over the age of 16 can withdraw from parental control (that is a legal way of saying they "ran away from home").
- A child who is over the age of majority and no longer in full-time attendance at school and who does not have any particular medical, mental or other dependency issue will no longer be considered a child of the marriage for legal purposes.
- A child in attendance at school will be considered a child for the purposes of child support up to and including, in some cases, the age of 25. Attendance need not be full time as some children study by way of semesters and co-ops. Many children take time off between schooling commitments to travel or to work to save money to help pay for their education.
- If a child is truly dependent for medical, mental or other reasons, he or she will be considered a child of the marriage for the purposes of support on an indefinite basis. We will see in the upcoming chapter dealing with support how the responsibility for children who are dependent is allocated between parents.

HOW IS CUSTODY DETERMINED?

The Child's Best Interests

PARENTS WILL HEAR the expression "the child's best interests" frequently as they move through a separation and divorce. It is the over-arching criterion for deciding any matter concerning a child. Family laws across Canada have set out considerations that the court should follow when attempting to determine the best interests of a particular child. For example, Ontario's Children's Law Reform Act provides a list of examples of the needs and circumstances of a child that should be considered:

- the love, affection and emotional ties between the child and (i) each person entitled to or claiming custody of or access to the child, (ii) other members of the child's family who reside with the child and (iii) persons involved in the care and upbringing of the child;
- the views and preferences of the child, where such views and preferences can reasonably be ascertained;
- the length of time the child has lived in a stable home environment;
- the ability and willingness of each person applying for custody of the child to provide the child with guidance and education, the necessities of life and any special needs of the child;
- any plans proposed for the care and upbringing of the child;
- the permanence and stability of the family unit with which it is proposed that the child will live; and
- the relationship by blood or through an adoption order between the child and each person who is a party to the application.

Across Canada, the following general considerations have emerged as a guide for the court in making custody and access determinations:

- the physical well-being of the child;
- the emotional well-being of the child and security of the child;
- the plans for the education and maintenance of the child as described by those requesting custody or access;
- the financial position of the parents, so as to be able to apportion responsibility for support;

- the religious or ethical needs of the child;
- the moral and ethical standards of the person seeking custody or access according to local community standards; and
- the sensitivity of the person seeking custody or access as a parent and, in particular, that person's understanding of this particular child's needs.

Status Quo

STATUS QUO IS another expression used frequently in custody and access determinations. It means essentially "what has been going on in this child's life for the last few years." When making custody and access orders, the court is always concerned about making the minimum disruption in a child's life. In determining the status quo, the court will ask:

- "Where has the child been living?"
- "Who has been looking after the child's needs?"
- "Where does the child to go school?"
- "Where does the child pursue their recreational activities?"
- "Where do their best friends live?"
- "How close are they to the school or the park?"
- "Who has been taking them to the doctor/dentist?"
- "Where have they been going to church?" and so on.

This status quo is sometimes described as the "child's universe." While recognizing that this universe will be disturbed by separation and divorce, a court tries to preserve as much of it as possible. The status quo for the child is particularly important in the early stages of separation. If the parents cannot agree on a custody arrangement and a court must intervene, it will be very easy for the court to ask the question, "What is the child's status quo, and why wouldn't we simply preserve that until the court has made a final order?" Establishing this status quo can give an advantage to the parent who is performing all of those functions. By the time the matter is before a court for a final order, a particular status quo may have been in place for an extended period of time.

Primary Parent

ANOTHER QUESTION THAT a court tries to answer in custody/access determinations is, "Who is the primary parent?" or "Who is the psychological parent?" It is not uncommon for a child, particularly a younger child, to have a greater bond with one parent than the other. This may be related in some ways to the child's state of development and the sex of the particular parent.

This determination is sometimes recognized when parents enter into joint custody or shared parenting arrangements. As we will see in an upcoming section dealing with assessments, professionals are sometimes brought in to assist the family in determining who is the primary parent and which parent should take responsibility for certain activities or needs of the child.

The Child's Views and Preferences

THE COURT IS prepared to consider the views and preferences of a child in making custody and access determinations. Typically, when a child is over the age of 10 or 11 years, the court will be prepared to give some weight to the child's opinion. Particularly as children get older, their views and preferences will be determinative in many cases of where they go, what they do, whom they see, and when. It can be difficult for parents to cope with the child's views and preferences as they get older. At exactly a time when a parent thinks that a child will start to express a view that they should be with a particular parent more than the other, both parents learn that the child would rather be with their peers than with either parent.

Since a court is prepared to consider the child's views and preferences once they reach a certain age, it has also become conscious of a parent's attempt to influence the child's views and preferences. The court wants a child's objective views and watches for cases of undue influence with a parent pressuring a child to pick them over the other parent. Parents have tried all forms of influence, including bribery, vague hints at suicide, threats to terminate the relationship and move away, withdrawal of financial resources or, alternatively, "promising a pony/motorcycle."

Related to this issue of the child's views and preferences is the problem with parental alienation. This involves a parent poisoning a child's mind against the other parent to such an extent that the child wishes to limit and/or sever contact with the other parent. It is insidious and the court's attitude toward it has changed somewhat over the last few years. At first, when evidence of poisoning of a child's mind was drawn to the attention of the court, courts were reluctant to get involved and often referred the family to counselling and resisted requests for punitive orders against the parent who was allegedly alienating the child. Quite a different view has emerged and the court has learned that such behaviour must be dealt with quickly and firmly. Parents who seek to alienate a child's affections will be dealt with immediately. There must be consequences to denial of contact; there must be consequences to interference in the child's relationship with the other parent. The ultimate consequence, of course, is the elimination of that parent's influence and a reversal of custody to the alienated parent. These cases are painful for the parents, for the children and for the court. These are among the most time-consuming and expensive disputes seen in our family justice system.

When the court considers it necessary, the child's preferences can be determined in a number of ways:

- calling the child as a witness in court, although most courts discourage children as witnesses in a courtroom;
- arranging a private interview between the child and the judge in chambers (in one case, a judge arranged for another judge in the courthouse to meet privately with the children to obtain their views and preferences and then had that judge report back);
- having an assessment done by a childcare professional who would later report back to the court (more on assessments in a moment); and
- providing the child with his or her own lawyer to assist in determining and describing the child's wishes.

Siblings

ANOTHER CONSIDERATION IN custody and access matters is the presence of brothers and sisters. The general rule, whether under the Divorce Act or provincial law, is that brothers and sisters should not be separated. A strong effort is made to preserve the family despite the absence of one parent. Children often see the presence of brothers and sisters as a very important support during difficult times.

It is difficult to imagine the court concluding, in any but the most unusual circumstances, that the separation of children could be in their best interests. Unusual circumstances where it has occurred include one Alberta case, where a court separated a 15-year-old daughter and a 14-year-old son because they simply wanted to live with different parents. In one Newfoundland case, a judge separated siblings because one parent wanted to move and a child wished to go with that parent. Even when this happens, the courts will try to ensure that some arrangement is made to keep the children in contact with each other and with the other parent.

This raises an interesting point where there is more than one child: if one child expresses a strong preference for a particular parent and the other child expresses a strong relationship with the sibling, then one child's views and preferences may end up governing the outcome of the custody arrangement. For example, a younger brother may be very attached to an older brother and equally attached to both parents. If the older brother insists on residing, for example, with his father, the younger brother may be pulled along as a result.

Tender Years Doctrine

AN INTERESTING CONCEPT that is described in custody and access cases is the "tender years doctrine." This doctrine considered it to be a general rule that the mother was entitled to custody and care of a child during its nurturing years. This came to mean that any child, regardless of who was actually his or her psychological parent, would be given to the mother until at least the age of seven years.

Obviously the tender years doctrine has undergone some revision over the past few decades, with the emphasis now being almost exclusively on what is best for the child, regardless of the child's age. Some courts have commented that the "tender years doctrine" is now irrelevant given the "best interest" test. I still consider this doctrine to be a factor in decisions around very young children.

Behaviour of the Parents

THEORETICALLY THE COURT is not supposed to consider a person's past conduct when making custody or access orders, unless that past conduct is relevant to the ability of the person to act as a parent. Unfortunately, in custody disputes, past conduct is precisely what each parent usually wants to talk about when they seek to sabotage the other parent's claim. The court will be drawn into this concern about conduct if there is some genuine connection between the conduct and the emotional, psychological or spiritual welfare of the child. These concerns can extend to a parent's relationship with a third party (for example, a person convicted of a sexual offence against children), sexual preference, the presence of physical (for example, drugs/alcohol) or mental (for example, cult/depression) addictions, and in one recent Ontario case, whether the parent smoked to such an extent that it aggravated a child's asthma. In that particular case, the judge ordered both parents to not smoke around the child. So while past behaviour is not supposed to be relevant, and someone's awful past is not supposed to be raised in custody disputes, it is in fact very relevant if it affects the child negatively.

HELP FROM PROFESSIONALS WHEN DETERMINING CUSTODY

Assessments

ONE METHOD THAT the court will use to address these questions is called an "assessment." The court can call for it against the wishes of the parties or it can be arranged on a voluntary basis. During the assessment, a skilled professional, often a social worker or psychologist, will meet with the family and the child(ren) to assess the child's needs and the ability of the parents to meet those needs. The assessment can take several visits with those involved and will often produce a recommendation for the court.

Whether through the court process itself or through an assessment, some of the issues that the court and the assessor look for include whether the child's needs are being met in a positive environment, who the child has bonded most closely with, the sexual orientation of the parents, the child's relationship with brothers and sisters and other family members, the child's religious and moral upbringing and his or her biological ties with each parent.

Assessments should be used only in difficult cases and will not be ordered automatically. Assessments are also very expensive and very time-consuming. It is not unusual to see an assessment cost several thousand dollars and become very intrusive to the child's and parent's lives. Assessors will meet with the children's teachers, friends, aunts, uncles, coaches, doctors and anyone else that may have some insight on what would be best for this particular child and this particular family.

Lawyer for the Child

SOME CANADIAN PROVINCES provide legal assistance to the child. In Ontario, for example, there is an Office of the Children's Lawyer. These lawyers are especially trained to deal with the needs and interests of children in separation and divorce, and there is no charge for the service. They are tasked with determining the child's views and preferences and relaying those views and preferences to the court. The lawyer's job on behalf of the child is not to determine what is best for the child, but rather to relay information to the court. In many cases the involvement of a lawyer on behalf of the children has provided a moderating influence on the dispute and the lawyer is able to work with each parent and their lawyers to develop a solution. Unfortunately, these services are sadly under-resourced; only cases referred by a judge will be dealt with and, even then, not every case can be taken.

Parenting Coordinators

THE ROLE OF a parenting coordinator is relatively new to the area of family law. Parenting coordinators work directly with parents to resolve custody and access issues that may arise from time to time. Clients found it expensive to consult lawyers about issues around scheduling, time with the child, Christmas holidays, who would take responsibility for birthday parties or bar mitzvahs, and the like. Similarly, lawyers did not enjoy getting involved in these disputes, and a new professional service arose—the parenting coordinator. In some cases the parenting coordinator may in fact be a lawyer, but in some situations it is a social worker, psychologist or other counsellor.

The parents empower this parenting coordinator to assist them in resolving disputes. So, for example, if two parents agree to alternate or divide equally March Break each year, but for the year in question they have been unable to agree on which parent's proposal for March Break is best for the children, the parents would consult with the parenting coordinator. The mother, for example, would describe her plans to take the children skiing in the United States. The father, on the other hand, would describe his plan to take the children on a trip to Ireland to visit with his elderly and ill parents. The parenting coordinator would assist them in picking an outcome that is appropriate for the children. At the other end of the spectrum, the parenting coordinator may simply be deciding, or helping the parents decide, where the children will spend Thanksgiving. Family life can be complicated when a family separates and divorces and then each parent enters new lives with new families. It is not uncommon now to see children have three separate Thanksgiving celebrations and visits with six different families at Christmas. Parenting coordinators offer a less expensive but effective way of resolving some of the irritants that can arise in custody and access arrangements.

HOT SPOTS

IN THIS SECTION I want to touch on some areas that flare up and cause trouble for families during the separation and divorce and, unfortunately, long after.

Planning Vacations

ALTHOUGH MANY FAMILIES focus their custody fights on the day-to-day residential schedule with the children, vacations can also be a source of trouble. It is easy to forget, in the course of a custody dispute, that Canadian children have between three and four months off during the summer, depending on their schooling, as much as two weeks off at

Christmas, up to two weeks off for March Break, between five and six long weekends, Easter, Thanksgiving, birthdays (child and parents), not to mention Professional Development days from school. Families are dealing with a lot of time, and cooperation certainly makes everyone's life easier, especially the child's.

Vacations can therefore be a hot spot. It is recommended that parents look at the entire year in advance when planning time with the child. Most Separation Agreements and court orders with respect to custody require parents to discuss and pin down their summer vacations by a fixed date early in the year (for example, April 1 or May 1). If children are going to camps during the summer, parents are then working with leftover time to plan their own vacations with the child. Camp registration dates may very well dictate when the child will have time with the parents over the summer. I do not recommend forcing another parent's hand by making plans for vacation without consulting the parent. Some families alternate first picks for vacation times. In other words, in odd years the mother will have first pick on summer vacation time, and in even years the father will have the first pick on vacation time.

Once a trip is planned, in agreement with the other parent, I recommend exchanging detailed itineraries of departure dates, return dates, hotel accommodations, airline flight numbers and times, and contact telephone numbers, e-mails, etc. for emergencies. In the case of younger children, they may wish to stay in contact from time to time with the other parent. Younger children get homesick and this kind of short contact can be facilitated without disrupting vacations.

Travel outside of Canada is a frequent hot spot. Parents should share passports and provide appropriate travel consents so that the child may exit and re-enter Canada easily. The website for Passport Canada provides an example of a form that can be completed by parents when a child is leaving Canada for a vacation. It is a detailed form and, to my knowledge, I have never heard of a border entry official asking for that particular form. It is certainly comprehensive, but other forms of travel consent will be acceptable. For example, parents should set out in written form a travel consent that states the name of the child, the name(s) of the adult(s) with whom the child will be travelling, the child's passport number (if the child has a passport), the method of travel, flight numbers, bus numbers, train numbers, the child's birthdate and so on. The body of the travel consent can say simply, for example, "I am the parent of the child, and hereby give my consent to travel in accordance with the details set out in this letter."

As long as the parents have signed the travel consent and it is witnessed, this is often more than enough for the officials at the border. In some cases parents have their signatures notarized. This is even better than a witnessed letter.

One concern that parents often have is that a parent will not return a child after a vacation. In the chapter dealing with enforcement (see Chapter 12: Enforcing Family Law Orders), I deal with that issue in more detail. At this stage I am simply providing some advice about how to provide travel consents where a child is going out of Canada with the consent of the parent.

Mobility

THIS IS A difficult issue for families. Whether the family is in a custody/ access arrangement or a joint custody arrangement, the need or wish of a parent to move to another city, to another province or to another country can be very problematic. To add to the challenge, Canadian courts have not provided a great deal of guidance to families. This matter has been left entirely to the discretion of a judge, and the test that a judge will use on such a determination is—the best interests of the child. Cases involving a parent's wish to move have gone as far as the Supreme Court of Canada and the court set out four basic rules to assist parents:

1. A court should give great respect to the bona fide wishes of a custodial parent. This does not mean that there is a presumption that a custodial parent can do what he or she wishes at the time of a move.
2. The fact that a move would result in a significant reduction in the other parent's contact with the child (whether through access or a joint custodial residential schedule) is not a reason to deny a move.
3. The parent's conduct is only relevant insofar as it affects the parent's ability to parent the child.
4. The custodial parent need not prove that his or her reasons for wanting to move are "necessary." It is sufficient that the move is proposed

in good faith and that it is not simply designed to interfere with the other parent's time with the child whether through access or a joint custodial residential schedule.

Canadian parents are mobile and courts have been required to deal with hundreds of mobility applications. Some general observations on this particular hot spot are appropriate. Consider the following:

1. There is no guarantee that a court will allow a move no matter how beneficial to the parent or seemingly beneficial to the child. Nothing can be taken for granted when it comes to mobility of children.

2. Whether you were in a common-law relationship or a legal marriage, the same principles apply. The court is concerned about the moving parent's proposal to continue meaningful contact with the other parent if the move is allowed. The court will not accept an attitude of "I'm moving—deal with it."

3. While a joint custody agreement will make a move more difficult for the parent who wishes to move, it is not a guarantee that the court will block a parent's move.

4. Even if parents agreed in a Separation Agreement or a court order to restrictions on the ability to move, the court can still override those restrictions and permit a parent to move.

5. The court will consider a child's views and preferences, but their views are not determinative, as they may not understand the significance of a move.

6. Courts have said that a parent's motive for the move is irrelevant (as long as the motive is not to frustrate the other parent's contact), but certainly courts have enquired into the reasons for a parent's move.

7. The shorter the distance of the move, the more likely it will be supported by a court. However, even short moves have been denied where it would have a serious impact on the child's relationship with the other parent.

8. A parent who insists that they are moving whether the child comes or not may force the court's hand to a reversal of custody to the parent who is not moving. When it comes to mobility situations, the court takes a dim view of parents who set matters in motion in an effort to predetermine the mobility decision. So, for example, where a mother

married a man who lived in another province, sold her home, registered the child for school and then advised the other parent of the impending move, she was shocked to learn that the court would not allow her to relocate.

9. Flight from an abusive situation is more likely to be supported by a court order changing the child's residence.

10. If a parent applies to move from the jurisdiction, they should expect the parent who objects to ask the court to reverse custody.

11. Canadian courts have ordered parents who moved without the benefit of an order to return to the jurisdiction.

12. It is not likely that a court will allow a move to occur pending the final trial, as it may have the effect of predetermining the outcome of the court's decision.

13. If a move is allowed, it may have an impact on the other parent's obligation to pay child support. Courts have been prepared to reduce the amount of child support to allow for the parent's increased costs of exercising their access.

14. Re-read point No. 1—nothing is guaranteed when it comes to mobility of children.

Religion

TYPICALLY THE CUSTODIAL parent is allowed to determine a child's religion and the schools that the child may attend as a result of that decision. So, for example, if a parent decides that his or her child will be raised in the Catholic faith and attend Catholic schools, an access parent cannot object to those decisions. For this reason, parents who feel strongly about religious choices often fight for custody to have a specific say on the religious upbringing of a child. However, it is still open to an access parent to share his or her religious practices with the child during their access time. It is, therefore, not unusual to see a child, for example, raised in the Catholic faith, but on access weekends, attend at the access parent's church. If the issue of religious choice is bringing anxiety and stress to the child, and, therefore, creating conflict between the parents, a custodial parent's decision will be final and an access parent may lose the right to expose a child to an alternative religion.

Of course it is an entirely different matter if the religious practice of either parent is characterized by the other parent as the equivalent of a "cult." Here the court will make a detailed enquiry and make a determination that is in the best interests of the child.

Change of Name

THE RULES WITH respect to changing a child's name vary from province to province. Some provinces give a custodial parent a presumptive right to change a child's name. Other provinces require the other parent's consent or a court order in order to change a name. If a parent has custody, and the other parent has access, the court will enquire into whether it is in the best interests of a child to have his or her name changed. This type of issue generally arises in circumstances of a remarriage where a family wishes to have all children under one official name, for example, for school records. When making these kinds of orders the court has regard to the age of the child, the length of time that the custodial parent has had the sole custody of that child, whether there is a continuing close relationship between the child and the non-custodial parent, and whether there are other siblings who will be affected one way or the other by the change in name.

This issue of use of a name can be a major irritant for a parent, even if there is not an application to change a name. There have certainly been cases where one parent insists on registering the child under, for example, the mother's maiden name, for daycare, for recreational activities and even for school. When the other parent sees reports and records come home without a reference to their name, there can be animosity between the parents. In some cases the courts have ordered parents to use a particular name for all of the child's records for the sake of continuity.

Matrimonial Home

SEPARATIONS ARE NOT often tidy matters. The parents may be living under the same roof and neither willing to move until a custody arrangement has been finalized. Certain lawyers recommend to clients that they not move from the matrimonial home until they have a written agreement with respect to custody of the children, or a court order. This recommendation is provided because, once a parent moves from the home and leaves the other parent in possession of the home with the children, it can be difficult to assert, months later in court, that they should have a joint custody arrangement. You will recall my discussion earlier about "nesting." This concept of parents alternating their time in the home with the children arose because neither parent was prepared to leave the home on an interim basis. In order to avoid conflict, they simply take turns in the home with the children. This can be a hot spot for families because at the time of separation tension naturally arises and the parents can find themselves in conflict in the home. Neither one can move, and the tension continues to rise. Arguments occur, and in some cases, the police are called to the home. If the home is owned jointly, the police will typically advise each parent to go see their respective lawyer, but they will not remove either parent unless there is a criminal charge laid.

Remarriage/New Partner/Blended Families

AS THE PARENTS of a child move on to new relationships, hot spots can arise around the relationship between the child and the new partner. So, for example, when a child returns from one parent's home and advises her mother that "daddy's girlfriend says I should call her mom," sparks will fly. Moving on to new relationships is a reality that both parents must accept. Having said that, parents must exercise some sensitivity and discretion in blending families and blending new partners. It will be difficult for all adults involved and particularly for the children who can find this new development stressful.

Secret Recordings and Surveillance

CANADIAN COURTS HAVE recently expressed the opinion that secret or surreptitious recordings of family members, particularly children, is an odious and repugnant behaviour. Where a court feels strongly that the secret videotaping or recording was unnecessary, they have refused to admit the evidence, and sometimes punished a party by awarding costs against them. Audio recordings to protect oneself from false accusations is one thing, but secret recordings or hacking into email and computer records in order to manipulate or trap the other parent are acts which are seriously frowned upon.

Access

"ACCESS" HAS BEEN defined in court cases as being an entitlement to spend time with a child, and during that time to exercise some of the limited powers of a custodial parent. Other jurisdictions, particularly in the United States, call access "visitation rights." It is improper to characterize the time a parent spends with a child as being merely a visit.

Aside from the right to spend time with the child, the right to access can include, at least under the Divorce Act, the requirement as described earlier that a custodial parent give 30 days' notice of his or her intention to move the child. This new provision is in keeping with the emphasis on giving a non-custodial parent information about the child, whether it be with respect to their health, welfare or education. If a non-custodial parent received such notice of the custodial parent's intention to move, he or she would then have the opportunity to request a variation of the custody order.

Other entitlements to information include the right to be kept abreast of the child's performance in school, the child's medical needs and care, and the child's general welfare. It is not unusual for courts to provide the non-custodial parent with an opportunity to make a contribution to the child's religious upbringing. In fact, there are many cases in which the non-custodial parent was given an opportunity to expose the child to his or her religion.

The wording and details of an access order can be extremely important. For years it was common for the courts and for lawyers, in drafting Separation Agreements and orders, to stipulate simply that one parent would have custody and the other parent would have "reasonable access" or "liberal access" or "generous access" at times to be agreed upon by the parents. Such provisions might be satisfactory where the parents are co-operative and where they can agree on times to be spent with the child. However, the moment such cooperation breaks down, the non-custodial parent is left in a very difficult position, since it is impossible to obtain court enforcement of these vague expressions. In fact, the non-custodial parent is left in a position of returning to court for a variation of the access provision to provide for specific dates and times.

Parents who anticipate difficulties or require some predictability often stipulate the precise days and times for the access to take place. An example could be as follows: every second weekend from Friday at 6:00 p.m. to Sunday at 6:00 p.m.; alternating Wednesdays from 5:00 p.m. to 8:00 p.m.; alternating birthdays, Easter vacations, Christmases, New Year's Eve or other important family events. In the event the access is then denied, the non-custodial parent can point to the specific entitlement when seeking enforcement (for a description of access enforcement difficulties, see Chapter 12: Enforcing Family Law Orders).

Supervised Access

SUPERVISED ACCESS IS sometimes ordered by the court to monitor a parent's time with the child. A neutral third party will oversee the entire visit or in some cases just the exchange of the child. In some provinces facilities will supervise, for a fee, the exchange of the child or the entire visit. It can be ordered or arranged voluntarily and is useful where one of the parents has been accused of sexual or physical abuse. Sometimes the supervision is needed because the custodial parent suffers abuse or the parents cannot be civil with each other at the time of the exchange.

Even where facilities are not available, it may be possible to have an objective, trusted third party supervise the visits. This could be a family member, priest, rabbi, community worker or so on.

Sometimes the restrictions on a parent's access can be limited to the point of transition and the court will order, for example, the use of a neutral location in order to minimize conflict. Parents have used Tim Hortons, McDonald's, police stations, schoolyards and the homes of family and friends to ensure a conflict-free transition.

Generally the court places the onus for proving the need for these restrictions on the parent who wants to restrict the contact. Again, the court has regard to the best interests of the child. If a parent has shown himself or herself to be ungovernable, the court will try to use specific restrictions in order to bring some consistency to access. The specifics around drop-off and pickup times, locations of drop-offs and pickups, limitations on issues that may or may not be discussed and limitations on activities may all be a part of an access order. If a parent refuses to obey those imposed conditions, they will run the risk of losing their access.

Grandparents and Other Family Members

IN AN UPCOMING chapter (Chapter 13: Grandparents and "Other Interested Persons"), we will look at the special role, rights and responsibilities that grandparents and other family members can have at the time of separation and divorce. Grandparents and other family members can be a hot spot because, in many cases, they did not approve of the marriage to begin with and actively support the separation and divorce. This adds to the level of acrimony between the parents. In other cases, they do not understand the reasons for the separation and divorce and for that reason find themselves on the sidelines wondering what impact this separation and divorce will have on their time with the child. Questions around mobility worry not only the parents, but also grandparents and other family members. In many cases in Canada, the grandparents have been providing daycare for the children in question, and they may find that they're not welcome as a daycare provider now that separation and divorce has occurred. One parent or the other may not be prepared to allow that aspect of the status quo to continue, even though it may have a negative effect on the children.

At the time of separation and divorce, it is important to consider the impact on the entire family. These issues are discussed further in the upcoming chapter.

Parenting Plans

THE DEVELOPMENT OF parenting plans is actually more of a solution to hot spots than an actual hot spot in itself. A parenting plan is a very detailed list of rules and guidelines for parents to exercise their parenting. Some plans run to 20 and 30 pages, and prescribe everything from the residential schedule for an entire calendar year to details of vacation time, holiday time, birthday time and even who will take the child out on Halloween. Incorporated into these parenting plans, we sometimes see an agreement to attend family therapy to set out certain principles that will guide communication by telephone, e-mail and even webcam. Often parents need this kind of detailed assistance in order to begin their parenting and, over time, as they build up confidence in themselves, in the other parent and in the child, the rules can be loosened. For parents who find themselves in an acrimonious separation and divorce, a parenting plan can provide a useful work plan for solving many problems. (See Appendix B for a sample Parenting Plan.)

Impact on Child Support

WE WILL BE discussing this issue in greater detail in Chapter 7. In that chapter we will be considering the Child Support Guidelines, which dictate the appropriate level of financial support for a child on a monthly basis. The Child Support Guidelines are driven in part by the amount of time that a child is with each parent. In a traditional custody/access arrangement, where the child is with the custodial parent more than 60 per cent of the time, the Child Support Guidelines apply and a monthly amount is easily calculated. Where the child spends 40 per cent or more of his or her time with the other parent, the Child Support Guidelines do not automatically apply, and an amount other than that provided by the Child Support Guidelines must be calculated.

I mention this as a potential hot spot because both parents are justifiably concerned about the impact of a joint custody residential schedule on the amount of child support. One parent is suspicious that the other parent is only seeking extra time to reduce their child support obligations; the other parent may interpret the reluctance to give more time as simply a way of maintaining a bigger share of child support. This hot spot can often be resolved if parents can agree to their parenting schedule, but continue to follow the Child Support Guidelines whether one parent's time exceeds the 40 per cent limit or not. If they can agree to implement the residential schedule for a one- or two-year period, but maintain full child support, it gives both households an opportunity to settle into a new schedule, make an appropriate budget and then adjust down the road if things are working out. This is often less expensive than a legal dispute over a reduction in child support.

Attending Children's Activities

THE ACTIVITIES OF the children can be a hot spot as it brings the otherwise separated parents into conflict in a public location. School plays, hockey games, graduation ceremonies, swimming lessons, things that could have been attended together suddenly become flashpoints for conflict. This is so especially where a parent is attending these events with a new partner. A father may wish to bring his new wife to the child's highschool graduation ceremony, a mother may ask her new husband to take the children to swimming lessons during her custodial time. Again, sensitivity and common sense and placing the child's interests at the forefront can reduce the likelihood of this type of hot spot leading to conflict.

Variation

THINGS CHANGE. CHILDREN grow older and their universe changes. Canadian family law permits the court to always return to custody and access orders and reconsider what is in the child's best interest. Typically the approach to this is to follow a two-step process. In the first step, the court asks if there has been a significant change in the circumstances of the child and the family. This material change could involve, for example, mobility and the need to move, the health of a parent or a change in a parent's employment or marital status. In some cases the child expresses a different preference. If the court considers that a material change in circumstance has occurred, it then goes on to a second step and attempts to determine whether a change would be in the best interests of the child. At this stage it is starting afresh with a new determination of custody and access and the child's best interests.

A variation is not to be confused with an appeal, and it is absolutely essential that the change in circumstances must be something that was not contemplated or foreseeable at the time the original order was made.

STRATEGIC CONSIDERATIONS

FORTUNATELY, FEWER AND fewer parents are putting their children through the trauma of a full custody trial. The success of mediation in solving custody and access disputes is well known. A detailed description of mediation is in Chapter 11: Alternatives to Court. For a description of the type of process your child will experience, should you decide to go to trial, see Chapter 10: Not Settling Your Differences.

On the issue of a trial, or any disputes with respect to custody, cost is an important consideration. When I mention cost here, I mean the financial not the emotional cost. It is not unusual for lawyers, when taking on a custody dispute, to ask for an advance on fees of between $10,000 and $15,000. Custody trials can consume a great deal of court time with absolutely no promise of a monetary recovery at the end. Consequently, lawyers are anxious to ensure that their fees are secure in advance, as the loser of a custody trial is a notoriously unhappy client.

Another consideration in this chapter is the tactical aspects of custody and access. In order to appreciate the tactical considerations, we need to understand the difference between an interim order and a final order. Interim orders are orders that are made pending the final decision of the court. Naturally, it is necessary to make temporary orders with respect to custody of a child until the court has an opportunity for a full consideration of the dispute. This means that the court must consider on an interim basis where the child should reside and who should have full decision-making power with respect to the child's needs.

The courts have, in the past, been very reluctant to move the child from the home of whichever parent has what is known as "de facto care and control of the child." This means that whoever has the child at the time the interim application is made is very likely to have custody of the child until the trial. The court will only depart from this general rule if it is clearly not in the child's best interests to remain with that parent. At the trial, the judge will often ask, "Where has the child resided pending this hearing?" "How has he or she been cared for?" "Are the child's needs being met?" "Is the child comfortable?" "Does the child go to a neighbourhood school?" "Are friends near by?" "Is daycare near by?"

You can see that the court will be very reluctant to disturb the child's world if it has been meeting his or her needs. As a result, interim custody often means final custody.

In the chapter dealing with property division (Chapter 5: Dividing the Family's Property), I mentioned the strategic importance of the matrimonial home. You will recall that the home can be important in deciding which parent will get custody. The parent who gets custody will in turn get full child support under the Child Support Guidelines. I mention here again the important strategic connection between remaining in the home until a custody arrangement has been concluded. Hasty departures from the home will make it difficult for you and your lawyer to negotiate a fair settlement of the custody-access arrangements and the possession of the matrimonial home. You may wish to take a moment to review that section at the end of Chapter 5.

Sadly, there has been an unseemly development in the area of custody and the matrimonial home concerning trumped-up allegations of domestic violence. Domestic violence is a real and a serious concern in Canadian society and we should enforce the Criminal Code quickly and effectively against anyone who is violent toward their spouse or their children. When charges are laid against a violent spouse, that individual is immediately removed from the matrimonial home, usually placed in jail at least overnight and then released on conditions restricting his or her contact with the spouse and, in some cases, children. In many cases, the release restrictions will prohibit the spouse from going within a fixed distance of the matrimonial home. These rules are designed to protect the victim of the domestic violence and the children. The police are involved, the Crown Attorney's Office is involved and, because criminal charges have been laid, the matter becomes an issue to be sorted out in the criminal justice system.

In some such cases, in the context of the separation and divorce proceedings, lawyers will seek, on behalf of a client, a restraining order. This is an order from the civil courts requiring a spouse to stay away from the other spouse, the children or the home. It is also possible to obtain what is known as an order for exclusive possession of the matrimonial home, which effectively gives one spouse control of the matrimonial home until the matter is concluded. These concepts are explained in more detail in Chapter 12: Enforcing Family Law Orders, which deals with enforcement. The cost of obtaining a restraining order or an order for exclusive possession in the civil justice system can be expensive. Both clients attend, both lawyers attend and a judge must make a decision. It can cost thousands of dollars to obtain those orders. If criminal charges are laid, lawyers are not involved at the outset, because it is essentially a police matter.

It did not take unscrupulous individuals long to figure out that a false or trumped-up domestic violence allegation would result in a free restraining order and order for exclusive possession of the home. Why go to court and argue in front of a judge when you can simply have the spouse picked up and removed by the police?

I would not raise this issue unless the matter was now prevalent. In the last few years of my own practice, I have seen over a dozen incidents in which the police were called to deal with alleged domestic violence under the flimsiest of circumstances. Individuals were arrested, detained in jail, charged and ultimately acquitted after spending great sums of money on criminal defence lawyers when, clearly, the charges should not have been laid in the first place. In at least one incident that I am aware of, when acquitting the alleged perpetrator, the criminal judge commented in his ruling that the charge should never have been laid in the first place.

I am including these comments for a number of reasons. First and foremost, this is a gross abuse of scarce resources that genuine victims of domestic violence need. An individual who calls the police and accuses another parent of domestic violence because that parent knocked on a car window and asked for the baby's car seat (true) or because the other parent was unwittingly at the same movie theatre (true) or, in one particularly horrible case, the parent showed up at a police station with self-inflicted wounds accusing the other parent of having attacked them, only to find out that the alleged perpetrator had an airtight alibi showing he was far away with a group of people at the time of the alleged assault (true). These kinds of allegations are preventing police and Crown attorneys from working on real cases of domestic violence.

The second reason I deal with this in the custody section is that these types of false or trumped-up allegations are usually designed to block a parent's attempt to obtain custody or joint custody of children. This means that the children are being punished by the actions of one parent. In some cases, courts are using the presence of unsubstantiated allegations of violence or abuse as a reason to not give that parent custody. False allegations are an abomination in the family justice system and are no different than looking a judge in the eye and lying outright. It is an attempt to mislead the justice system and thereby undermines the work of many good people in the system.

The third reason I raise this in the context of custody is that I have now met too many individuals who have been arrested, jailed and ultimately acquitted—individuals who should never have been charged in the first place. Many have been devastated by their time in jail. I have sat with men while they cried about their experience in a jail. I have met people who have been absolutely shaken to their core by their arrest and became changed people as a result, and I do not mean changed for the better. These people lose confidence in our justice system. They have a hostility for the police and they have a hostility for the justice system, even if they are ultimately acquitted. This is not right. Lawyers, courts and our policy-makers need to apply their minds to how to deal with situations in which false allegations and misuse of our criminal justice system contaminate the family law system.

In conclusion, whenever I read the news about the system's inability to enforce a restraining order and protect a genuine victim of domestic violence, I think of the resources wasted on trumped-up or false allegations. I wonder whether, if those resources had been targeted more appropriately, that individual or those children would have been safer.

The long and the short of it is that family law lawyers are now advising clients to be extraordinarily cautious at the time of marriage breakdown, for fear that inappropriate use of the criminal-law process will spill into a family law dispute. It is all well and good to eventually be acquitted, but our criminal justice system is slow, and until the charges are eventually dealt with by a court, perhaps many months or even years later, custody determinations and possession of the matrimonial home may be merely academic.

As I said at the outset, custody is *the* issue in marriage breakdown and therefore may be the most emotionally charged. People under the stress of a collapsing relationship may be hard pressed to put their children's best interests first. At a time when they may need to look out for themselves, they must consider someone even more vulnerable. It is a time not for showing how awful someone else may be as a spouse or parent, but rather how good you are as a parent and how you can offer the softest landing to the children displaced by divorce.

Paternity

WHILE NOT AN everyday occurrence, the question of a child's paternity does arise from time to time. In some circumstances it may be a man hoping to establish that he is the father of a child or it could be the mother of a child alleging a man's paternity. In a few cases, it has even been the child attempting to establish paternity.

The reasons for undertaking such a procedure in court vary. One of the very first cases I had when I began to practise involved a young man who had not yet finished high school being confronted by his parents about a neighbour's grandchild. His parents had been enjoying a cup of coffee with the neighbours, admiring their 18-month-old grandchild, who was over playing for the afternoon. When they commented on how cute the baby was, the neighbours dropped the bombshell. "He should be—your son's the father!" When everyone regained consciousness, a paternity suit was launched by the mother of the child alleging that he was indeed the father due to one act of intercourse two years earlier.

In another case, a child needing money for university tracked down her biological father and attempted to prove paternity so she could obtain financial assistance. In another case, a woman who had divorced her first husband and moved away with their two children denied that he was the father of one of them in an attempt to block his access. In return, he sought to prove that he was the father of both of the children.

The law of paternity varies a little from province to province, but the Ontario approach provides a good example of how such issues are tackled by the court. Part III of the Children's Law Reform Act sets out a procedure for "establishment of parentage" by two types of applications:
1. Any person having an interest may apply to the court for a declaration that a male person is recognized in law to be the father of a child.

2. Any person may ask for a declaration that a female person is the mother of a child.

It should be noted that the law has eliminated any distinction—in law at least—between children born inside and outside of marriage.

Once the court makes a "declaration" of parentage, it is good for all purposes and binding on third parties. So, if a man was accused of adultery by his wife and she proved he was the father of someone else's child (while still married to her), that would be conclusive proof of the grounds for her divorce.

The Act establishes several "presumptions" designed to assist the court in reaching a conclusion about paternity. If one of the following circumstances exists, then the court will presume that the man in question is the father of the child. It is up to the man to then disprove the presumption:

- The person is married to the mother of the child at the time of the birth of the child.
- The person was married to the mother of the child by a marriage that was terminated by death or judgment of nullity within 300 days before the birth of the child or by divorce where the *decree nisi* was granted within 300 days before the birth of the child.
- The person marries the mother of the child and acknowledges that he is the natural father.
- The person was cohabiting with the mother in a relationship of some permanence at the time of the birth of the child or the child is born within 300 days after they ceased to cohabit.
- The person has certified the child's birth, as the child's father, under the Vital Statistics Act or a similar Act in another jurisdiction in Canada.
- The person has been found or recognized in his lifetime by a court of competent jurisdiction in Canada to be the father of the child.

The following points should be kept in mind.
- If the presumptions apply to more than one man, then no presumption can be made and the court will need to consider the evidence.
- Both the alleged father and child must be alive at the time of the application.

- The standard of proof is "balance of probabilities" not "beyond a reasonable doubt."
- Any written acknowledgement of parentage by a person may be used as proof of the fact of parentage.
- More often than not, blood tests or DNA testing is used to try to narrow down the evidence.
- If an alleged father tries to abscond (run away), the court can issue a warrant for his arrest.

In the Ontario Act, a procedure is used to gather blood for testing. A person cannot be forced to give blood or to undergo any test. In fact, the order is for "leave" or permission to go and voluntarily obtain blood tests. If leave to obtain the tests is given and the alleged father, referred to as the "putative father," refuses to go, the court can draw an inference. In other words, the court can conclude that, therefore, he must be the father.

The test itself involves the father, mother and child submitting blood samples, which are examined for red and white cell features. The cost can range between $700 and $1,000 for all three. It is not possible to establish with 100 per cent certainty that a man is the father of a child through such testing. Instead, a "plausibility of paternity" is expressed. The result may be that he is 95 per cent likely the father and so on.

If the people are not satisfied with the blood tests, they may decide to try "DNA Finger Printing," which is now available with a simple mouth swab. The turnaround is about four to seven business days. It is more reliable (99.9 per cent proof of paternity, 100 per cent proof of non-paternity) and costs about $700 to $1,000. For more information, check out www.genetrack.com.

The goal of paternity proof is often to establish a claim for financial support and the court will consider making an interim support order pending the gathering of the evidence.

Paternity Agreements

IN SOME CASES where the "paternity writing is on the wall," the couple may wish to avoid the embarrassment of blood or DNA testing and the arguing in court and simply agree to paternity. The provincial family laws provide for what are known as "paternity agreements" by which a man and a woman, who are not spouses, may enter into an agreement for

- the payment of expenses of a child's prenatal care and birth,
- support for the child or
- funeral expenses of the child or mother.

Whether you are the mother or the father of the child, it is important to consult a lawyer before signing such an agreement. Your lawyer can design clauses specific to your own case.

WHAT WILL WE TELL THE CHILDREN?

IN THIS SECTION I would like to deal with what will likely be one of the most difficult moments that you'll have during the separation and divorce: telling the children about your decision. This is a particularly tough challenge for most adults. At a moment when they must summon the most diplomacy and skill, they are also feeling heartbroken, angry, confused, frightened and embarrassed. It is also a time when there is an overwhelming, irrational desire to lash out and hurt the other spouse. Ironically, during this difficult time when some actions are clearly motivated by all the wrong reasons, parents assume that their horrible actions are in the best interests of their children.

I strongly recommend that neither parent discuss a separation and divorce with their children unless they have a clear and honest plan for how this very difficult conversation might unfold. Depending on the ages of the children, there may be some difficult questions to answer. This is not a conversation that can be held two or three times in order to get it right. It has to be done properly the first time. This means thinking about your children, their individual needs and concerns, and your own abilities.

A great starting point in planning this discussion with your children is to try to look at it from their perspective. While divorce is very common in Canadian society, children still feel a sense of shame, embarrassment, confusion and, strangely enough, blame. It is a remarkable feature of divorce that children blame themselves for the divorce itself. Certainly children will have questions and try to assign the responsibility between the parents for the marriage breakdown. They want to know which parent is causing the separation. They want to know who's to blame. They may even ask if one of the parents is having an affair. In many cases, the children have already picked up the vibe and may have preconceived notions about what is going on in their parents' marriage. If there has been fighting, they will have heard it. If there has been a chill in the air, they will have felt it. If there's anger and seething beneath the surface, they will have sensed it. I have been struck in my conversations with children of divorce by how much they knew about the problems in the marriage and how little credit their parents gave them for being aware of the difficulties.

You must be aware as you prepare for this conversation that beneath their probing questions they harbour a distinct impression that they are actually responsible for the marriage breakdown. This seems bizarre to many parents. How could the children possibly think that they're responsible? If we think about it for a few minutes, it actually makes sense. The children have received no explanation for this happening in their home. They know that their parents are angry. They know that they're often the subject of these angry discussions. They know that their parents' anger is often taken out on them. They begin to notice that they rarely see their parents together. Activities seem to be alternated between the parents. No one does anything as a family anymore and, if they do, it can be tense and unpleasant. They are at the centre of the conflict and they somehow must be responsible.

Sadly, these children, who've received no explanation for the problems and who are now blaming themselves, begin to think that if they change their behaviour perhaps the marriage can be saved. I've seen cases in which children begin to act extra good; they do unnatural things to save money for the family; they take on the role of clown, trying to please and cheer up their depressed parents. Of course, none of this can change the problem, and their sense of responsibility deepens.

Eventually these children, especially if they're in the middle of high conflict between the parents, become depressed; their schooling suffers; they begin to act out and misbehave; they may engage in self-destructive behaviour; and they may have generally unhappy lives. Some children find the best answer is to remove themselves from the home, so they end up spending most of their time with friends. This can be particularly difficult if there are younger children at home who depend on older siblings.

Make a Plan

THE WAY TO avoid these problems is to make a plan and provide children with a coherent explanation for what is happening to the family and for what is happening to you as husband and wife. A part of this coherent explanation must be an express statement to the children that *they're not to blame in any way for what is happening*. It does not matter how confident you are that the children will not blame themselves. You must expressly tell them anyway and ask them to specifically acknowledge that they do not blame themselves in any way for what is happening.

When dealing with younger children (say, under the age of seven), it can be very difficult to explain the separation in anything but the most simple terms: "Mommy and Daddy will have separate homes. You'll be spending time with both of us, and we will continue to be your mommy and daddy. We are going to work very hard to make sure that you are happy because you are the most important person in the world to us. Don't worry. We are working on this and everything will be fine." As they grow older, further refinement of the message may be needed from time to time. They will have questions and you should be ready to answer them. I'm not saying that all the gory details must be shared with them, but be prepared to be honest. This is no time for stonewalling and being evasive. Ignoring them and hoping that their questions will blow over will only make matters worse. Give them short, straight answers.

Sometimes families try trial separations. They may honestly tell the children that the separation is temporary. In my experience, few of these separations are really temporary. What the parents are really trying to do is ease themselves and the children into the reality of two households. Unfortunately, the children end up with a false hope that a reconciliation is possible. When the reconciliation does not materialize, the children get a second heartbreak and disappointment. If the separation is genuine and reconciliation unlikely, then be straight with the children so that there are no false hopes.

With older children, parents can be more frank and provide detailed explanations about what is happening to the family. These children are rarely shocked by the announcement. That is not to say that there are not families with children who are absolutely floored by the parents' statement that they will be separating and divorcing. I've seen some modern families where the kids have been kept so busy speeding from one activity to the next that they really have no sense at all of what is going on around them. These children live in a pinball machine rather than a family. They are rarely seeing their parents act as a team in any event, so they do not have many opportunities to witness any actual dysfunction. For them, separation and divorce can be a total shock; however, in most families where the children are over the age of 11 they have a pretty good idea about what is going on. This doesn't mean that they like the idea. They may even say that they knew it was going to happen and wondered why it hadn't happened sooner. They still won't like the idea, but they had a sense it was inevitable.

Older children will have questions about where they will live, how they will stay in contact with both parents, how they will stay in touch with their friends, where their stuff will end up, whether they will continue to go to the same schools and play on the same teams and so on. Their concerns are very practical. What is your separation and divorce going to do to their worlds?

While it is not always practical (in situations where the parents cannot possibly cooperate, for example, where there is violence), it is better if both parents can sit down with the children with a common plan, give a consistent explanation and support each other and the children. I repeat: both parents should be involved. One should not do all the talking. One should not take all the blame. One should not appear to be a victim, nor should one appear to be the villain. A simple, forthright explanation about a need to end the relationship of husband and wife should be given. Similarly, it should be explained in a straightforward way that the roles of mother and father continue forever. Take your time. Watch their expressions. Be attentive to their needs. Be in control of yourself and the meeting. Listen to their questions and be prepared to give them answers.

Now, here's the interesting part—ask them not only for their questions, but also ask them for their suggestions, for their wishes, for their ideas about how this new living arrangement can be made to work in a way that makes everyone happy. Be prepared for them to say that they do not want you to separate and divorce. Stick to your message. Separation is happening. Two households will be created and you need to know what they want and what they need to make that work well.

In the vast majority of cases, the children will tell both parents point-blank they want to see them equally. They will want to spend time at both homes. This will be their number one concern. You must be prepared to address it and assure them that, of course, they will see both parents and spend time at both homes.

It is quite possible that a second and third meeting will be required to deal with their questions. Don't forget to follow up with them. Don't leave them hanging. It's easy to get busy with the details of separation, work and all the other day-to-day chores. Schedule a second meeting.

Perhaps in your family it will be appropriate to meet with the children individually. Some may speak more frankly if they are alone with you. This is when you will need to use your listening skills. They will want to know what their choices are. You can bet that kids in their circle of friends have already experienced separation and divorce. This can be good if those friends will provide a sympathetic shoulder. It can be very bad if those children have been through high-conflict divorces and provide precisely the role model that your children don't need. The more information you give your children, the less likely it is that they will pick up misinformation on the street.

Don't forget that there are many professionals in your community who are skilled in helping children cope with separation and divorce. Some children may need regular counselling. There may be things on their minds that they're not prepared to discuss with their parents. The earlier this type of intervention is used, the easier it will be for the children and the less likely that intervention will be needed on a long-term basis. It's when things are left until they reach the boiling point that the counselling ends up being a long-term, sometimes lifelong, experience for your children.

To this point I've been speaking to the parents who have a reasonable prospect of working co-operatively with each other to ease the pain for the children. Unfortunately, there are parents reading this chapter who cannot work co-operatively. There are parents who are too hurt or too angry or too immature to put a child's interests first. There are parents who will try to manipulate their children. I've seen cases in which a parent tried to make a child feel sorry for him or her; told a child that they will be lonely without the child; promised gifts; told their children that they'll be angry with them if they don't take their side; ran down the other parent; told their children that they (the parent) will be hurt; and told their children that they need the children to take care of him or her.

We hope that our children will intuitively know that they should live with the parent who knows how to look after them and has actually done so; who will make sure that the child stays in touch with friends and family on both sides; who will ensure that the child is able to stay in regular contact with the other parent, whether by telephone, mail, e-mail, FaceTime or in person; who will keep the child's life in place as much as possible by making sure that they attend the same school, if at all possible live in the same house and neighbourhood, and enjoy the same friends, lessons, sports, hobbies and so on; who will have a healthy attitude about his or her own needs and who will be realistic about the changes that are going on in everyone's lives.

In my book *Surviving Your Parents' Divorce: A Guide for Young Canadians* (which is written for children between the ages of 10 and 16), I try to bring children into the picture of divorce by giving them information about their parents' emotional stages and about the system and process of divorce. I hope to ease their anxiety. Consider the following points, which I felt obliged to draw to the attention of the children of divorce:

- Grandparents, aunts, uncles and cousins are all worried about children who must go through the divorce of their parents. They can be a terrific source of support at a very difficult time. In particular, grandparents can be a great help.
- However, it can be difficult for relatives to stay out of the argument between the parents. Family members can also be a source of stress and difficulty as the family goes through the separation. I recommend that children find the aunts and uncles who are helpful and lean on them and avoid the ones who are simply picking sides and causing trouble. I recommend that the children take advantage of the opportunity to get away and stay with relatives if they can.

- Sometimes when one parent gets sole custody of the children, they cut off contact with the other side of the family. This is a very poor choice and is rarely in the interests of the children. I tell children quite frankly to speak up if they want to maintain a relationship with members of the extended family. Just because the roles of husband and wife are ending does not mean that a child should be cut off from half of their heritage.
- They will encounter practical problems when travelling back and forth between houses. Stuff gets lost or it never seems to be in the right place when they need it. I tell children that they have to be more organized. They have to start making sure that they have the right stuff at the right house. This is something they did not have to worry about before.
- Children will have to be careful in scheduling time with their friends or other important events because it may now interfere with an access schedule. The parents may be arguing over who will be seeing the children on a particular weekend only to discover that the children have made their own plans.
- The telephone can be a useful way of staying in contact with a parent. Some kids enjoy talking on the phone; some do not. Long-distance charges can make it even more difficult. Frequent and uninhibited telephone access between children and their parents is an absolute must. Lately this has extended to e-mail and FaceTime contact. It can certainly take a lot of the stress out of the relationship if parents are open and allow free communication.
- It can be very difficult if the child is seeing a parent only on the weekend to catch up about an entire two-week or longer period in such a short period of time. The access parent may have been waiting for two weeks to see the child and may have made big plans and is really anticipating spending time with the child. The child may show up for that weekend dead tired from a tough week at school and just want to crash on the couch and watch television. It can be awkward for both the parent and the child. It can be even worse if the child turns out to be sick and does not feel like going for a visit when it has already been arranged. Access parents have a very difficult life.
- The child may find it difficult to keep up with an entire network of aunts, uncles, cousins and grandparents when they are seeing their

parent only every second weekend. Sometimes the child just wants to spend time with the parent alone.

- Holidays can be a very difficult challenge for families. These include making arrangements around such things as religious holidays, Thanksgiving, March Break, summer vacation, Christmas and other holidays, and even the parents' birthdays. These are supposed to be happy times and all the child hears is argument. Holidays can become a very stressful, unpleasant time for children if the parents cannot work it out. This is never more true than on Christmas Day, which, like the other 364 days of the year, has only 24 hours.

- Children may end up with a feeling of restlessness as they move back and forth between their parents' homes. Some children report that they are never able to really settle in before having to move again.

- Children often end up becoming a very cheap "courier service" between angry parents. I tell them point-blank to avoid this unpaid job. If parents need to exchange messages, they should speak to each other or write and mail confidential notes.

- On the more positive side, some children do tend to notice an improvement in their parents once they are separate and set up into their two new households. Two houses can be special for children. They may have a new room with new stuff in it. They may also have new stepbrothers and stepsisters and, for many families, it means two sets of vacations, one with each parent.

- Children are sometimes a little bit surprised at how much attention they receive after the separation. One child told me that his parents had turned into a couple of "super-parents," each one trying to be the greatest parent ever. It's a shame that it took a separation to cause that to happen.

Here is a list of my suggestions for children:

- Try to remember that divorce is not your fault.
- It is the fault of the adults and it is their job to fix it—not yours. Be patient and let them work it out.
- Don't forget all the emotional stuff your parents are going through. They can get angry and depressed. So will you.
- Be as open and honest as possible with both parents. Once they know what you want, they can plan for what is in your best interest.

- If you are over nine years of age, you have a right to be heard. Your opinion is important and really can influence the way things are handled. Remember, there is more to custody than just where you sleep at night. It also involves making important decisions about your life.
- If you are moving back and forth between two homes, whether for access or because of joint custody, try to make sure everyone is working from the exact same schedule. Make a copy of the calendar each month showing where you should be on each night and weekend. If you see a conflict (your championship baseball game is on the same weekend that your dad is supposed to take you to the cottage), let your parents know as soon as possible.
- Make a list of the stuff you need for the next day or the Monday after a weekend visit. It can help you avoid forgetting stuff that you will need, like homework.
- Try to stay in contact with the other parent, if at all possible. A few short telephone conversations can make the weekend visit a lot more enjoyable. The same thing applies for other family members. Just because your mom and dad split, it doesn't mean you should lose contact with all your cousins, aunts, uncles and grandparents.
- Remember, you cannot please everybody all the time. Don't panic if conflicts come up. Pick the solution that makes the most sense and that suits you best.
- Be good to yourself. Relax. If you need to blow off some steam, do it. Speak honestly to someone you trust.
- Don't get drawn into carrying messages back and forth between your parents.
- Don't get drawn into discussions about money or support. Politely tell your parents that you are not interested. It is the adults' job to solve the money problems.

A WARNING

I WANT TO state frankly to any parent reading this chapter that managing your divorce properly is going to be critical to the future happiness of your children. You face a choice, a very clear choice.

If you fight and put your children through a high-conflict divorce, I guarantee you that as your children grow up they will be depressed; they will do poorly in school; they will be more likely to smoke; they will be more likely to take drugs; they will be more likely to be self-destructive and suicidal; they will be more likely to get into trouble; they will be more likely to have trouble forming intimate relationships both with men and women; and they will be more likely to have eating disorders and other psychological problems. They will also get their revenge and make your life miserable.

On the other hand, you can work co-operatively to have as amicable a separation and divorce as possible. If your children are not exposed to the conflict, then they are more likely to come through your divorce as a survivor.

I'm not saying that they won't be stressed and that they won't be unhappy and depressed at times, but they will have a much better chance of surviving over the long haul than the kids who suffer through bitter divorces. Take my word for it: I have met kids who have been through the good, the bad and the ugly, and it all comes down to choices that were made by their parents. You've been warned. The choice is yours.

CLOSING REMARKS

I HOPE THAT from this chapter you have realized that the custody decisions and choices made will have a profound effect on your children's happiness in the future. In this area, more than any other, you must understand the options that are available to you and your family. Custody choices are related to decisions about the matrimonial home, the division of property and, very importantly, decisions about child support. Prior to going forward with any decisions, make sure that you understand and that your lawyer has explained to you the relative advantages and disadvantages of proceeding. There is room for a great deal of flexibility in resolving custody cases. And because so much depends on making good choices here, you must be an informed consumer.

There is some hope on the horizon that custody and access issues may be determined in an easier, more child-friendly way. British Columbia has recently undertaken an overhaul of its family laws, a part of which includes the use of non-court dispute-resolution techniques and a more prominent role for parenting coordinators. In addition, the terms "custody" and "access" will be replaced with "guardianship" and "parenting time." Instead of "access," the orders of the court will now refer to "contact," and "parental responsibilities" will be delineated in a more customized parenting arrangement. In addition, there will be some improvement in the way in which parenting time is enforced. In an effort to avoid one of the hot spots discussed earlier—mobility—B.C. law will be amended to include a provision for mandatory 60-day notice of a move and specific criteria will be set out to guide the court and the parties regarding moves to different jurisdictions with the child.

There has been talk also of amending the Divorce Act federally to ensure that some of these new concepts find their way into the law of divorce. Whether that happens remains to be seen, but kudos to the Province of British Columbia for attempting to lead the way in improving family law for Canadians.

MY ADVICE

1. Custody, access, joint custody, shared parenting, parallel parenting and bird nesting are all terms used to describe ways of caring for the children after separation.
2. Custody orders are typically made for children between the ages of birth and 16. The court does not like to make custody orders for children who are 16 years of age and older as they tend to vote with their feet.
3. To determine who should have custody, the court looks at the best interests of the child, but is also mindful of the status quo that has been occurring, who is the primary parent, the child's views, the age of the child, what happens with siblings and the behaviour of the parents if it affects their ability to parent the children.
4. If parents cannot agree on custody, professional help is available from professional assessors, lawyers who represent the children and parenting coordinators.
5. Hot spots can occur in the area of custody with regard to:
   • parents engaging in parental alienation

- parents fighting about vacation plans and, in particular, travel consents for the child vacationing out of Canada
- mobility of a parent and moves to another jurisdiction
- religion
- changing the name of a child
- occupancy of the matrimonial home until a final custody arrangement has been achieved
- introducing a child to new partners and blended families
- the role of grandparents and extended families
- the impact of the residential schedule on the amount of child support payable
- attendance at the child's activities, particularly if new partners are also present

6. Detailed parenting plans can address many of the hot spots that may develop around custody and access of children.

7. When it comes to custody of your children, be strategic at the time of separation and, in particular, do not leave the home until you have agreed upon a custody arrangement in writing with the advice of a lawyer.

SUPPORT

Financial Assistance
after Separation

W E HAVE SEEN in the preceding chapters the importance of property division and child custody issues. Just as important, however, is the question of support once the family has separated and gone off to create two new households. It is a difficult fact of life for most families that each spouse and the children suffer a reduction in their standard of living after divorce. Two households cannot be easily supported on the same money that once supported only one household. Discussions about dividing RRSPs, matrimonial homes, cottages and businesses are fine for those who enjoy such assets and wealth, but for many people, the financial burden of separation can only be met through a division of one spouse's income for the benefit of the two new households.

Questions about support, whether child support, spousal support or the relatively new issue of parental support, are important and challenging areas for lawyers and clients. Issues include determining when an entitlement to support arises, how it is paid and when it ends. We will also consider some of the recent changes in the areas of child support and some of the strategic aspects of spousal support and child support claims.

Most seasoned family law lawyers have had the unpleasant experience of explaining to clients that, while fair property division is critical to starting over, child and spousal support obligations, in terms of total costs, can far exceed the value of a modest family home. Consider, for example, a father of three children who earns $100,000 per year. Assume also that the children are all under the age of 10 and that they will all complete university at the age of 22. If we use the Federal Child Support Guidelines in the calculation of child support, this father's minimum obligation for child support alone could exceed $250,000. If the man involved in this scenario also had to pay spousal support, then the cost of his support obligations could easily be double that figure. On the other side of the coin, we have a mother trying to support herself and three children with a monthly amount of child support and a monthly amount of spousal support. That may be the only money that she has to run her household while she retrains to re-enter the workforce. We can see why issues of child and spousal support can become so emotional for families at the time of separation.

As noted in previous chapters, the various laws of the provincial, territorial and federal governments have all provided for the possibility of financial support upon separation. For legally married couples, spousal support is available under the Divorce Act. For common-law couples, provincial family laws provide the right to claim spousal support. In the case of parental support, claims are advanced pursuant to provincial law.

In this chapter, I refer to "marriage breakdown" as a triggering event for the claiming of spousal support. I apply this expression to common-law spouses as well when their relationship breaks down. Consequently, any references to spouses in this chapter apply to both common-law spouses and legally married spouses.

Before entering into a consideration of these various forms of support, recall the all-important financial statements that figured so prominently in the division of family property. Here again, in calculating support, these financial statements play a key role in revealing to the court not only potential sources of support for the two households, but also the budgets within which these households must operate.

As a part of my practice, I regularly meet with clients in advance of separation and divorce. With fairly basic financial information, it is possible to estimate how much child and/or spousal support an individual could be looking at if the separation occurs in the near future. Spending some time with an experienced family law lawyer in advance of your separation is a valuable exercise. As we have seen in the property division chapter, a mathematical calculation can be done there, as well. The court prefers to know how property will be divided before making an order for spousal support. This means that if you gather the correct information and consult with an experienced lawyer, you can obtain a very specific opinion on how much child support, how much spousal support and how much of a nest egg (we hope) each of the spouses will have post-separation.

CHILD SUPPORT

ON MAY 1, 1997, the Federal Child Support Guidelines came into force by virtue of amendments to the Divorce Act. Related amendments were also made at the same time to the Income Tax Act. These Child Support Guidelines were updated as of 2011 to increase the amount of child support payable in the context of separation and divorce.

The Guidelines are a mandatory formula that dictates the amount of child support based on the gross annual income of the non-custodial parent. The rationale for the mandatory formula is threefold: 1) the use of a formula will ensure fairness and consistency in the amount of child support; 2) it will reduce the likelihood of conflict between the parents and their lawyers; and 3) it will provide for a faster, less costly way of resolving the issue of child support at the time of marriage breakdown.

The application of the Child Support Guidelines formula involves the use of tables that establish monthly amounts for child support based on the number of children in question and the paying spouse's gross annual income.

To use the tables, one parent must be the custodial parent or the primary residence parent. This would generally mean that the child spends 60 per cent or more of their time with the parent. We will see in a moment how situations of split custody and joint custody are handled when calculating child support.

Base Monthly Child Support

IN MOST CASES, the children are residing with one parent for at least 60 per cent of the time. The access parent may be seeing the children every second weekend and during overnight visits in the alternate weeks, plus a portion of vacation time. In such circumstances, the gross annual income of the custodial parent is not taken into account to set the monthly child support amount. The Guidelines focus on the gross annual income of the non-custodial parent. As stated before, the gross annual income and the number of children are the sole determining factors for the calculation of the base amount of child support. If the annual income of the parent paying child support is more than $150,000, then a further percentage calculation is added on to the base amount of child support. (See the Federal Department of Justice website, http://www.justice.gc.ca/eng/fl-df/child-enfant/index.html, which provides assistance in calculating the amount of child support.)

The Child Support Guidelines only apply to divorces and agreements that are completed after May 1, 1997. The formula does not automatically apply for orders that predate 1997. It is only if the parents seek a variation of the amount of child support after the May 1997 date that the new Guidelines will be used to calculate child support.

From time to time lawyers still encounter couples who reached their agreements prior to 1997 and are not covered by the Child Support Guidelines. In such cases, the child support is included in the taxable income of the recipient custodial parent and is tax deductible for the non-custodial parent who pays the support. Under the Guidelines, the treatment is quite different. The custodial parent does not include the income in taxable income each year, nor does the non-custodial parent deduct the amount. The figure that changes hands is a net amount. This makes matters much easier for families when completing their income tax returns.

Each province has its own version of the Guidelines for application to the provincial support orders. The Guidelines were designed and tailor-made for each province's respective standard and cost of living. This means that a person paying child support in Ontario will have a slightly different figure on a monthly basis than a person paying child support in Nova Scotia, even though they may have the same gross annual income.

As clients and lawyers work to apply the Guidelines, they are attempting to answer six questions:

1. How many children are involved?
2. What is the custody arrangement?
3. What is the annual income of the paying parent?
4. What does the table set out as the amount?
5. Are there any extraordinary expenses?
6. Will there be undue hardship if the table amount is used?

The use of the Child Support Guidelines has reduced considerably the debate over how much child support should be paid. It is true that parents do get into debates about incurring and dividing other child-related expenses, but for the most part the base amount is no longer controversial and courts will rarely entertain debate about whether the guideline amount should be used.

Special Expenses

I USED THE expression "base amount of support" in the previous paragraphs. This is the amount that is typically paid on a monthly basis to assist the custodial parent with expenses arising from housing, clothing, feeding and meeting the miscellaneous day-to-day expenses of the children.

Over and above this base amount, the custodial and non-custodial parents also contribute to so-called special and extraordinary expenses. These special expenses are usually incurred in consultation and are divided between the parents in proportion to their annual incomes. So, for example, if a child is a talented figure skater and requires special lessons and custom skates and must travel to competitive events, this would likely be considered an expense over and above the base amount incurred each month by the custodial parent. The parents would typically consult with each other, agree on the incurring of the special expense and divide it between the two of them in proportion to their annual incomes.

With respect to special and extraordinary expenses, the Federal Child Support Guidelines offer a few details about what may be considered a special or extraordinary expense. Consider the following:

- childcare expenses incurred as a result of the custodial parent's employment, illness, disability or education or training for employment
- that portion of the medical and dental insurance premiums attributable to the child
- health-related expenses that exceed insurance reimbursement by at least $100 annually, including orthodontic treatment, professional counselling, social workers, psychiatrists, physiotherapy, speech therapy, hearing aids, glasses and contact lenses
- extraordinary expenses for primary or secondary school education or for any other educational programs that meet the child's particular needs
- expenses for post-secondary education
- extraordinary expenses for extracurricular activities

THE COURTS HAVE been asked to interpret the appropriateness of certain special expenses for children, and they have consistently said that the expense must be "reasonable and necessary" in the particular case, having regard to the best interests of the child. The examples set out above were not intended to be exhaustive. The court will look at every situation to determine whether an expense is reasonable and necessary. In one case, the court ordered that vitamins and health supplements could be considered a proper special expense for the child.

Generally, the higher the level of income, the more extensive the availability of extraordinary or special expenses can become. Private school, for some families, may be considered an appropriate special expense. On the other hand, in a Saskatchewan case, the court ruled that piano lessons were too expensive for the particular family in question. In one case (to the horror of the family, I am sure), a judge ruled that a drum set was a reasonable expense in the circumstances. Even though the family finances were tight, the judge thought a small indulgence for the child would help him to cope with the separation and divorce of his parents.

For most families, the typical special expenses that are being dealt with relate to medical costs such as orthodontics, education costs such as tuition or tutoring, and sports activities or camp. Decision-making with respect to special expenses cannot be unilateral. In other words, the custodial parent cannot simply sign up a child and send the other parent the bill. Life is a lot easier if parents work co-operatively around these expenses.

Changes in Income

AS A PARENT'S income changes and as that parent shares annual tax information with the other parent as required by law, adjustments are made to the base monthly child support amount. Each year, they must exchange full income tax returns and copies of the Notice of Assessment. The non-custodial parent father, for example, will reveal his gross earnings for the previous year and the base amount of child support will be calculated. The custodial parent mother, for example, will reveal her gross annual earnings. Those amounts will be relevant to the proportional sharing of special and extraordinary expenses.

The Supreme Court of Canada recently dealt with this issue of updating the amount of child support on a regular basis as a parent's earnings increase or decrease. The motives and circumstances can change from case to case, but it is not uncommon for parents to not stay in touch with each other regarding their annual earnings. A Separation Agreement or a court order may have been obtained after a very acrimonious period of negotiations or litigation, and the parent may not be anxious to rush into an immediate renegotiation simply because somebody's income has gone up or down. They prefer peace.

In some cases, parents continue paying child support that would be a little more than would be called for by the Guidelines. In other cases, they do not report an increase in their income and end up paying less than the Child Support Guidelines stipulate. In the latter instance, we have recently seen parents who did not reveal increases in their incomes being hit with extremely large retroactive obligations to pay child support. In other words, the courts looked at the situation and said, 1) you should have told the other parent about the increase in your income;

2) had you told them about it, the child support would have been at an increased amount; 3) your former spouse and child have been penalized as a result of your failure to disclose increases in income; and 4) not only must you now pay the total amount calculated retroactively but you must also pay interest and legal fees on top of that. In some situations, this has amounted to tens of thousands of dollars in retroactive payments.

The court has sent the clear message to families: update their financial disclosure annually. If you have an increase in your income, disclose it and pay the appropriate level of child support. If you have a decrease in your income, disclose it and recalculate the lower amount of child support immediately.

Variation Applications

IN SOME CASES, it is necessary to return to court to obtain a variation of the child support amount. This is known as a variation proceeding. Either party can return to court to have the amount either increased or decreased, depending on the circumstances of the parents. This type of variation proceeding is required where a parent has not disclosed income changes or is refusing to make a retroactive payment. The parent seeking the payment forces the matter back into court for a determination and a variation of the amount of child support to bring it into line, perhaps retroactively, with the Child Support Guidelines.

WHO IS A PARENT?

THE DIVORCE ACT contains an extended definition of the expression "child of the marriage" and includes any child for whom the person has stood in the place of a parent or any child of whom one is the parent and for whom the other stands in the place of a parent. Essentially this means that biological parents, step-parents and adoptive parents can be obligated to pay child support. In addition, even if a person has not actually adopted a child but has treated the child as his or her own, a support obligation may arise.

WHO IS A CHILD?

AS A GENERAL rule of thumb, child support continues until the child is no longer considered a child of the marriage within the meaning of the Divorce Act. This means that the child has attained the age of majority. So, for example, if a child turns 18 and is no longer in full-time attendance at an educational institution or university, child support will usually end. If the child continues on to university, child support typically continues until the age of 24 or the completion of the child's first university degree.

To continue to receive support, a child need not reside with the custodial parent. In many cases, children have been required to leave home to attend university or college, but still receive financial support via the custodial parent and the non-custodial parent because of their ongoing dependency. There is no firm requirement that a child live with the custodial parent in order to continue to receive support.

It can be tricky for some families if a child is not committed to his or her education. For example, a child might attend university for a year and be entitled to child support, but then decide that the program was inappropriate and take a year off. Child support might be suspended while this child thinks about his or her options and be reactivated if the child returns to school.

Child Withdraws from Parental Control

PROVINCIAL LAW PERMITS the termination of support when a child has withdrawn from parental control. In Ontario, for example, the Family Law Act provides that every parent has an obligation to provide support for his or her unmarried child who is a minor or is enrolled in a full-time program of education to the extent that the parent is capable of doing so. In assessing this obligation to provide support, the court considers the needs of the child. The Act goes on to say, however, that the obligation to provide support does not extend to a child who is 16 years of age or older and has withdrawn from parental control.

Withdrawing from parental control means a voluntary withdrawal, the exercise of a free choice to cut the family bonds and strike out on one's own. The court will not assume that a child has voluntarily with-drawn just because the child no longer lives at home. The court will want to determine whether the child was, perhaps, forced from the home. Were there some unreasonable parental actions that made con-tinued cohabitation with the parents impossible? Was the child driven from parental control by emotional or physical abuse? Perhaps the withdrawal was not voluntary and child support should continue with a direct payment to the child or to another family member who is caring for the child.

A parent cannot expel a child from the home and expect to terminate a support obligation. For this reason, the onus of proving that a child has withdrawn from parental control is on the parents. There are case reports with examples of children whose parents or step-parents have driven them out of their home to live with friends or relatives. The chil-dren have then applied for financial support and received it on the basis that, while they do not live with their parents, they did not voluntarily withdraw from parental control.

In one Nova Scotia case, the applicant was a 14-year-old girl who had experienced difficulties with her mother. The child would not abide by the "house rules" and persisted in staying out very late at night, contrary to her mother's wishes. She then moved out to live with her aunt and uncle for almost a year, but the aunt and uncle soon had the same diffi-culties. After a brief attempt to live again with the mother, the child left on her own initiative to live with her girlfriend's family. When the child applied for support, the court considered her to have voluntarily with-drawn from living with the parents and the parents had a lawful excuse for not providing support.

Illness and Disability of a Child

THE QUESTION OF a child's illness and/or disability can be important. If a child passes the age of majority but for reasons of illness or disabil-ity must continue to be cared for and supported by the custodial parent, there will be a corresponding ongoing financial obligation for the non-custodial parent to pay support.

Step-Parents

IN ATTEMPTING TO determine whether a parent has acted as if he or she was a child's parent even though they are not the biological or adoptive parent, and may have a child support obligation, the courts have asked questions such as the following:

- Did this person provide a large part of the financial support necessary for the child's support?
- Did the person intend to step into the shoes of a parent?
- Was the relationship between the person and the child a continuing one with some permanency?
- Can any inferences be drawn from the treatment the child would receive were he or she living with their biological parent?
- Has the person pertinent to the claim for support ceased to act as a parent of that child?

The court will also consider such things as the affection between the person and the child, the length of time of the association and whether the child has taken the surname of that person and lives in the same dwelling.

HOT SPOTS

THE CHILD SUPPORT Guidelines have brought a great deal of certainty to the area of child support calculations, whether the calculations are being made pursuant to provincial law or the Divorce Act; however, there are points of controversy that the courts have been required to deal with over the last few years. What follows is an overview of some of the common hot spots that have arisen now with respect to child support.

60/40 Custody and Child Support Problem

THE BASIC CHILD Support Guidelines are designed to work with a traditional custody-access arrangement. One parent has custody; the other has access. One parent has the child the majority of the time; the other parent does not. The Guidelines apply. In situations of joint custody, where a parent has the child more than 40 per cent of the time, the Guidelines will not apply and the court has the discretion to vary the amount of child support on the basis that it would be unfair to have a parent pay child support when they have a higher level of expense in caring for the child during their joint custodial time. This is dealt with in section 9 of the Federal Child Support Guidelines. That section stipulates that the amount of child support must be determined by taking into account (a) the amounts set out in the applicable tables for each of the spouses, in other words, the Child Support Guidelines; (b) the increased costs of shared custody arrangements and (c) the conditions, means, needs and other circumstances of each spouse and of any child for whom support is sought.

Questions have arisen around the motives of the parent seeking a reduction in child support, particularly in situations of shared custody. Some observers feel that parents seeking joint custody simply are attempting to reduce their potential child support obligations. In some circumstances, parents with joint custody arrangements have still paid the amount determined by the Child Support Guidelines. For example, a father may have the children 50 per cent of the time but still pay the full amount of child support pursuant to the Guidelines. This may be appropriate in circumstances where the other parent has little or no income at the time of separation. The parents will sometimes agree to use that arrangement until the other parent is able to make a greater contribution to their own self-sufficiency. The bottom line is that the courts have not developed hard and fast rules.

A Supreme Court of Canada case (Contino) dealt with this issue. In the Contino case, the application to vary the child support amount was triggered when the father's joint custodial time exceeded the 40 per cent amount. The reason it exceeded 40 per cent is that the mother asked the father to have the children for an additional night so that she could attend school. The amount of litigation on that issue was, in my view, out of proportion for the money involved. I would certainly recommend that families not treat the 40 per cent level as a threshold that automatically triggers the need for a child support variation. Use common sense and avoid spending money—that might otherwise go for the children—on the lawyers fighting over it. There is little point in arguing about the base amount of child support pursuant to the Guidelines. Unless there are some extraordinary or exceptional circumstances or undue hardship, the Guidelines will be followed by the courts.

In the Contino case, the message to families was basically that determinations of the amount of appropriate child support in shared custody situations would be determined on a case-by-case basis. Many parents simply do a set-off calculation, whereby the mother calculates what she would pay to the father if he had custody, the father calculates what he would pay to the mother if she had custody and one pays the other the difference between the two monthly amounts. For straightforward cases, it works well. If one parent's income and asset picture is considerably stronger than the other, then the court may not think a simple set-off is appropriate. Discussion of joint custody arrangements will obviously have an impact on the amount of child support.

The Supreme Court of Canada suggested that where the parents shared the children about 60 per cent versus 40 per cent and could not agree on the appropriate level of child support, the court would look at the actual spending patterns of the parents, the ability of each parent to bear increased costs of shared custody (this would mean looking at their full asset and liability picture) and also the standard of living for the children in each of the households. The court followed five steps when looking at this shared custody/child support problem:

1. determine the parties' incomes;
2. determine each parent's monthly expenditures attributable to the child;
3. determine the ratio of income between the parents;
4. consider the net worth of the parents and their ability to absorb increased costs; and
5. consider whether there would be a variation in the child's standard of living if there was a change in the level of child support.

Most lawyers have concluded from the Supreme Court of Canada case that there will be less certainty in these shared custody/child support determinations and solutions will be needed on a case-by-case basis.

Split Custody

THE CHILD SUPPORT Guidelines also contemplate the possibility that parents may have split custody, that is, each spouse has custody of one or more of the children. Perhaps the teenage son decides to live with his father and a younger daughter chooses to live with her mother. In such a case, the amount of child support is calculated in a set-off, as described earlier, so the child support order is the difference between the amount that each spouse would otherwise pay if a child support order were sought against each of the spouses.

Undue Hardship

THE CHILD SUPPORT Guidelines also contemplate the possibility that a parent will suffer undue hardship if the Guidelines are used. It is a difficult determination to make, but the court will consider special circumstances that affect a parent's ability to make the ordinary child support payment. So, for example, where a parent has extraordinary costs related to their personal health, or the parent had huge business debts that needed to be paid, then the amount of child support might be altered. Parents should work co-operatively on special and extraordinary expenses. I recommend that no special expenses be incurred unless there is an agreement reached between the parents about the activity being undertaken, the cost of it and the method of payment. It makes no sense for a custodial parent to register children for the most expensive extracurricular activities and simply pass the bill to a non-custodial parent. Cooperation must continue well past the point of separation. If you haven't done so already, you may wish to read the section entitled "What Will We Tell the Children?" in Chapter 6: Obligations to the Children of a Divorce.

Costs of Exercising Access

THE COURT ALSO has the discretion to reduce the amount of support paid if the parent paying child support must incur very high costs in exercising their access. So, if a parent resides in British Columbia but exercises access to a child in Ontario and airplane tickets, hotel costs and so on are a regular factor in exercising access, there may be room for a reduction in child support.

Hiding Income

PROBLEMS WILL ARISE in the calculation of child support from time to time, if parents are secretive about their earnings. Typically problems arise for lawyers when one parent attempts to hide a bonus or special commission. The Child Support Guidelines contain rules for attributing income to parents. When it comes to hiding income in order to keep child support low, many have tried, but experienced family law lawyers will always find a way to obtain the true income figures and will ask a court to attribute those true figures to the parent. During the process, there is a great deal of acrimony and legal expense. It is far better to be open with earnings and negotiate fairly the amount of money that is needed to raise the children.

Cost of the Second Family

THE DEVELOPMENT OF a second family for an individual paying child support is not typically considered to be a reason to lower child support to the first family. The courts will look at this on a case-by-case basis, but they have not been inclined to reduce child support.

Lump Sum Payment for Child Support

IN SOME UNUSUAL circumstances, a lump sum for child support is possible. This is reserved for exceptional situations and has become more and more rare since the implementation of the Child Support Guidelines. In one case, for example, a stepfather was given the option of simply making a lump sum payment rather than continuing to make a monthly payment to a child with whom the relationship had ended.

Determining Income

THE CALCULATION OF the income used for the Child Support Guidelines tables has been the subject of litigation. It is often not easy to calculate what a parent earns; however, the court will take into account income from all sources in assessing the meaning of total income. A starting point is to look at line 150 of the income tax form filed with Revenue Canada. The court will not stop there if it appears that, perhaps, income is being hidden, too many expenses are being deducted or full disclosure has not been made. In addition, where incomes have fluctuated, with a parent earning a great amount one year and then experiencing a decline only to have it return to a different level in a third year, the court may simply turn to an average income for the purposes of child support. And, if the court believes that an individual is underemployed or deliberately keeping their income low to avoid child support, the court has the option of imputing income to that individual and treating him or her as if they earned a level of income appropriate to their standard of living. This litigation can be quite expensive and often involves the need to retain forensic accountants to accurately determine a true level of income.

University Costs

EXPENSES RELATED TO post-secondary education can be a significant expense for families and many questions arise. A non-custodial parent is required to contribute to a child's reasonable post-secondary education expenses. The child attending post-secondary education has an obligation to contribute to their own expenses as best as possible, and the custodial parent also has an obligation to share in this expense. So, for example, in one B.C. case, a court confirmed that money the children had received through a trust fund was taken into consideration in setting the amount that the parents had to contribute for post-secondary education.

These expenses include not just the tuition itself, but also the cost of residence, food plans and even a car or transit pass, if it is necessary for travel to and from school. Computers are taken for granted now as a necessary expense for children attending university. Musical instruments have been considered a special expense, if the child is registered in a music program. In one case, a special expense included a private room for the child, who needed a place to study and practise their music.

The most important question that arises, however, when children attend post-secondary education, is what happens to the monthly child support when the child lives away from the custodial parent's home and, perhaps, lives in residence? Courts do not expect parents to pay "twice"; in other words, to pay a base monthly child support to the custodial parent and pay for residence costs while the child is away from home. The most common way of resolving this is for the custodial parent to not receive child support, or to receive a reduced amount of child support for the months that the child is away from home and full child support for the months that the child is home from university during the summer.

Life Insurance to Secure Child Support

A CHILD SUPPORT obligation continues after the death of the parent who pays it. The surviving child is a dependent of the deceased person. The child support obligation is a first charge on the deceased parent's estate. This can have the effect of disrupting the deceased's intended disposition of his or her property. For this reason, parents obtain or allocate life insurance to secure the child support obligation. If the parent dies, the life insurance is used to continue the child support payments. The life insurance policy may designate the spouse as the beneficiary in trust for the child support. That parent has an obligation to manage those funds responsibly for the benefit of the children. The funds are for the child, not for the parent. If a large amount of life insurance is required initially to secure the child support, because, for example, the children are young and the parent has a high income, then the parent may apply from time to time to have the amount allocated to the child support reduced. So, while a parent may be required to have a $1-million life insurance policy when the children are infants, by the time the children are in university the policy required to secure the remaining child support obligation may be a few hundred thousand dollars, if that.

Rejection of the Parent

SOME DIVORCES ARE so acrimonious that a child will totally reject a parent. This may be caused by parental alienation, or by the bad behaviour of the non-custodial parent. However, child support obligations continue regardless of how poor the relationship between parent and child. In some cases, though, a child's rejection of a parent has been so complete that the parent has asked the court to terminate the child support obligation. "Why should I pay for this child to go to university, when the child will not even speak to me, or respond to letters or e-mails?" Courts have been prepared to tell children in such a circumstance that if they cannot manage even minimal communication with the parent paying child support, they run the risk of the child support obligation being terminated.

High-Income Earners

THE CHILD SUPPORT Guidelines state that where a parent who pays child support earns in excess of $150,000, the court may deviate from a straight application of the Guidelines. If considered appropriate, the court may order that the payor of child support pay the table amount for the first $150,000 of income, and then decide to allocate a portion of the income over the $150,000 for the purposes of child support. For the most part, courts have taken the position that they should only increase or decrease the table amount of support if that amount exceeds the generous limits that constitute a reasonable range, having regard to the circumstances of the family. Is there a point, in other words, at which the court may consider the amount generated by the Child Support Guidelines to be in excess of the children's reasonable needs? There have been some eye-popping amounts awarded for child support for parents who are high-income earners. The law books are filled with cases ordering parents to pay $17,000, $23,000, $35,000 a month, and so on.

How the Support Is Spent

PARENTS PAYING SUPPORT often ask whether they can dictate or influence how the child support payment is spent. The short answer is no, but in exceptional circumstances, a court may be prepared to order that the support-paying parent make payments to third parties on behalf of the child. For example, a parent could pay the tuition for university directly to the institution, rather than to the custodial parent. The court, however, does not wish to oversee how child support is spent on a day-to-day basis by the custodial parent. This can be a matter of great frustration for some parents, who think that their child support payments are actually supporting the adult's lifestyle rather than the children's.

Terminating Child Support

AS WE'VE SEEN from previous discussion, child support can typically end when a child is of the age of majority and no longer in attendance at school. Similarly, if a child goes on to university, completes their first degree and graduates, child support will end. However, the educational path of every child is not always so clear, and it may not be easy to classify whether or not some children are continuing their education. For example, is the child who is 19 years of age and in between high school and university a child no longer in need of support? If that child is taking one or two high-school credits to improve their grades for a university application, are they a child pursuing education? In those examples, I think the court would answer yes. However, what about the child who finishes high school and takes a year off to travel the world without any specific plans about university or college? The court might not consider that child in need of support unless and until the child returns and decides to resume their education. At that point child support would resume. Parents must struggle with the child who "attends university" but is not attending classes, fails consistently and is not on track to complete a degree. Must the child take their education seriously in order to continue receiving child support? Who will assess whether the child is taking their studies seriously? Some children fumble through two or three programs before settling into the appropriate educational path. All of these situations pose challenges for parents who want to see their scarce child support dollars allocated wisely.

While the Child Support Guidelines have brought a great deal of certainty and predictability to the calculation of child support, there are still a wide variety of hot spots that cause problems for Canadian families.

SPOUSAL SUPPORT

THE DIVORCE ACT lists four objectives for orders of spousal support made under the Act (and these objectives apply to the calculation of spousal support for common-law spouses as well). It provides that an order for the support of the spouse should

1. recognize any economic advantages or disadvantages to the spouses arising from the marriage or its breakdown;
2. apportion between the spouses the financial consequences arising from the care of any child of the marriage over and above the obligation apportioned between the spouses with respect to child support;
3. relieve any economic hardship of the spouses arising from the breakdown of the marriage; and
4. insofar as practicable, promote the economic self-sufficiency of each spouse within a reasonable period of time.

In making support orders, the court considers certain factors, including the condition, means, needs and other circumstances of the spouses. These may include the length of time the spouses cohabited, the functions performed by the spouse during cohabitation and any other arrangement relating to support of the spouse. The courts have used a variety of approaches in calculating spousal support at the end of a marriage. Some courts have used what is known as the "income security model," other courts have used what is called the "compensatory model" and other judges and courts have applied the "clean-break model."

In an "income security model," the support obligation is considered to be derived simply from the existence of a spousal relationship. Under a "compensatory model," the spousal support is considered to be a form of compensation for the economic consequences of the marriage, such as loss of career opportunity through the need to care for children in the past. Under the "clean-break model," the objective of the support order is the severing of economic ties between the spouses so that each may go his or her own way. Support is for a fixed period of time that is transitional and then is terminated.

Spousal Support Advisory Guidelines

AS YOU CAN tell from the foregoing paragraphs, there is a great deal of unpredictability around the entitlement to spousal support, its amount and the appropriate date for termination. In response to that unpredictability, a committee of lawyers and judges developed a set of guidelines known as the Spousal Support Advisory Guidelines. Although these are guidelines, the courts in Canada have decided to use them as a reliable predictor of the entitlement, quantum and duration of spousal support. When I say the courts, I mean courts in Ontario, British Columbia and New Brunswick. Courts in Alberta have been less welcoming of the Spousal Support Advisory Guidelines. Instead they have tried to focus on a case-by-case analysis of the needs and ability to pay of the spouses in question. By and large it can be said with some confidence that the Spousal Support Advisory Guidelines will over time become as useful as the Child Support Guidelines. They are, in some cases, persuasive and can be used to guide separating couples to a particular outcome.

The approach in the Advisory Guidelines is to use one of two basic formulas for the determination of spousal support. One formula deals with a situation where there are no children; the other formula deals with a situation where there are children. Both formulas use income sharing as a method for calculating spousal support.

They do not zero in so much on budgets as they do on the ability of the parties to share income. Use of the formulas provides a range for the quantum and duration of support. They do not deal with the entitlement to spousal support.

In essence, the way the courts have used the Guidelines is to see them as a starting point. The necessary information is inserted into the computer programs, that is, the age of the spouses; the length of the relationship; the children, if any, and the children's ages; and spouses' respective annual incomes. That information will generate three pieces of information:

1. a range of amount of spousal support payable on a monthly basis,
2. a period for which the support is presumed to be payable and
3. a description of how the net disposable income of both spouses is being allocated in the range of spousal support given.

Consider the following example of a man, age 64, and a woman, age 67. The man earns $104,000 and the woman earns $35,000. There are no children. There are no special health issues, and the length of the relationship was 30 years. The Spousal Support Advisory Guidelines would suggest a range of spousal support between $2,166 and $2,837 payable monthly, indefinitely. If the couple used the low end of the Guidelines range, then the man would have 55.1 per cent of the family's net disposable income and the woman would have 44.9 per cent. If the high end of the range was used, their division of net disposable income would be 50:50. This is how the Spousal Support Advisory Guidelines work. That type of calculation would be used as a starting point for the court's determination of what is appropriate.

There has been criticism of the Spousal Support Advisory Guidelines, including the fact that they appear too rigid and take a cookie-cutter approach to the calculation of spousal support. It is also felt that the Guidelines are inconsistent with the objectives and the factors in the Divorce Act, particularly with respect to achieving economic self-sufficiency. Experts have suggested that a better approach to the calculation of spousal support would be to consider five matters:

1. Does the person claiming support have the right to make a claim for support? In other words, are they a legally married spouse, or a common-law spouse?
2. Is there any entitlement to support?
3. What form should the support take (periodic or lump sum)?
4. What should be the duration of the support?
5. What is the correct amount of support?

Before considering the question of calculating the amount of support, we should make it clear that the Divorce Act, of course, only applies to legally married spouses, including same-sex couples. A common-law spouse's entitlement to support arises under provincial law only, as is discussed in Chapter 8: Common-Law Spouses Have Rights Too. The principles described in this chapter, however, are applicable to both legally married spouses and common-law spouses. When the court is faced with the need to arrive at an amount for spousal support, it looks at essentially the same criteria regardless of the nature of the relationship.

Spousal support is generally made on a periodic basis, with a monthly payment of a fixed sum directly from one spouse to the other. Family law lawyers would agree that the vast majority of spousal support orders are made from men to women, but we are seeing occasional cases in which a husband has stayed home to care for the children, has lost his job, has suffered health problems or other difficulties and has obtained spousal support from his wife. In the examples in this chapter, I will be referring to the support as payable from the husband to the wife, but all of the principles described should certainly apply without regard to gender.

The making of spousal support orders, whether under provincial family law or the Divorce Act, boils down to the consideration of two key factors: 1) the spouse's need for spousal support, and 2) the other spouse's ability to pay. Thrown into the mix with these two factors is an increasingly controversial consideration—the spouse's ability to provide for his or her own support.

Conduct

BEFORE CONSIDERING THE issues of need and ability to pay, including self-sufficiency, one important aspect of the law should be understood. Family law lawyers often meet with clients who angrily refuse to pay spousal support because their former wife or husband is "undeserving." They also tell hair-raising stories of misconduct that would suggest to most people that spousal support would be completely unfair. However, for the most part, the conduct of the spouses during the marriage and, in particular, at the time of separation is not a factor in calculating the amount of spousal support or the entitlement.

There is a provision in Ontario's Family Law Act that allows a person to argue that no spousal support should be paid because the other spouse's behaviour constituted "a gross repudiation of the relationship." However, this section is rarely used. Until very recently, the courts had confirmed that they were not interested in stories about the misconduct of the other spouse, particularly in the context of setting spousal support. Conduct might be relevant to a person's ability to parent, but it was not supposed to be relevant to one's entitlement to spousal support, the quantum of spousal support or its duration.

Typically, the court wanted to know if there was a need for support and if there was an ability to pay; however, all of this changed dramatically with the Supreme Court of Canada decision in Leskun. This case arose in British Columbia and it involved a husband and wife who split up under very unpleasant circumstances. The wife was older than the husband by some 10 years and part of the reason the relationship broke down was that the husband had started a new relationship with a woman he had met through work. To add injury to insult, the wife lost her job and injured her back. She had made a contribution to the husband's improvement in his education, which, in turn, had led to improvements in his earnings.

Certainly, those facts are unhappy ones, but they are not, by any stretch of the imagination, extraordinary in the context of family law disputes. Experienced family law lawyers have seen situations that involve attempted murder or suicides, serious assaults, frauds and heinous behaviour.

What seemed to make the Leskun situation different from all other unpleasant divorces was Ms. Leskun's response to the separation and divorce. She became obsessed with the litigation against her former husband. That obsession, and what appeared to be her ongoing anger with him, kept her from returning to the workforce. In other words, the husband's behaviour leading up to and at the time of the separation contributed to her inability to become economically self-sufficient.

His behaviour, and its effect on her, therefore, became a consideration in the setting of spousal support. The Supreme Court of Canada specifically noted this in its decision and, as a result, tens of thousands of Canadian divorces were re-evaluated overnight as to whether the awful behaviour of a spouse was a contributing factor to the other spouse's inability to become economically self-sufficient.

The case received a great deal of publicity and clients immediately asked lawyers to comment on whether fault, indeed, had been returned to the Canadian law of divorce. The only answer that lawyers can give is maybe, sometimes, it depends.

There are no happy divorces. Everyone is miserable as a result of the marriage breakdown. No one enjoys the litigation in cases where it cannot be resolved. Everyone is affected in their career by the separation and divorce. No one has a monopoly on horrible treatment of their spouse at separation and divorce.

In determining the spouse's needs, the circumstances of each case must be examined. Much can depend on the nature of the marriage relationship—whether it was a traditional or a more modern marriage. A dependant spouse is entitled to a standard of living that is equal to what she or he could have expected had the marriage continued (where the parties have had a long-term traditional marriage with the result that the dependant spouse is without job skills or income).

Here are some of the key considerations in the area of spousal support, both with respect to assessment of need and calculation of the quantum. It should be noted that these are general rules that apply nationally, but there may be some variation on a province-by-province basis.

- In determining a reasonable standard of living, the court must consider the spouse's ability to pay. In one case, the court decided that it was unconscionable to reduce the husband's standard of living below the poverty level in order to provide the wife with a reasonable standard of living. This was so even though the parties were married for 30 years and the wife was unable to work on a full-time basis.
- A wife asking for support is not expected to take any job in an effort to meet her own needs.
- The objective of a spousal support order is not to equalize the incomes of the two spouses.
- The need for spousal support should be assessed after determination of the division of family assets. If the division of assets leaves the spouse with sufficient means to meet his or her reasonable needs, then the court will not order support, or it will order a lower amount than it might otherwise have done.
- The court will also consider whether the prudent investment of the assets through property division at marriage breakdown and the spouse's qualifications for work will reduce the need for support from the other spouse.
- Spousal support has been denied in cases where there was a lengthy marriage but both spouses were employed throughout and after the marriage breakdown, and the funds from the sale of the matrimonial home generated additional income.

When assessing a spouse's need for spousal support at the end of a relationship, the court is very interested in the outcome of the property division. You will recall from earlier chapters dealing with property division, my characterization of the share of a property settlement as the "nest egg" for future self-sufficiency.

The court has always expected spouses to use their post-separation assets to contribute to their own self-sufficiency. In particular, the case of *Boston v. Boston*, decided by the Supreme Court of Canada, states very clearly that spouses must take their property settlements and invest them in a way that contributes to self-sufficiency. The court went so far as to suggest that spouses, post-separation, have an obligation to take their assets and consider placing them in a capital-depleting, income-generating fund that would create the equivalent of a "pension." The court stated that they were not requiring spouses to have particular investment savvy or to use their property in risky investments, but there is an obligation to use assets to generate self-sufficiency.

In one case, a wife received almost $900,000 in assets at the time of separation. She used some of the assets to purchase a new home; she used some of the balance to do renovations to her new home; and she invested the amount remaining after that in such a way that she could generate nearly $1,500 per month from investment income. The court was interested in her ability to contribute to her own support by making these investments. The question then became how much more spousal support should be contributed by her husband to ensure that her needs were met.

Generally, where a spouse is in her late 50s it can be difficult to expect a significant contribution to her own self-sufficiency if she has been out of the workforce for some time. Perhaps part-time work or modest earnings from some form of employment will help, but there is the possibility that the spousal support will continue indefinitely as the individual need will be continuing indefinitely as well.

For younger spouses in their 20s, 30s and even early 40s, the key question becomes how and when will that spouse become self-sufficient and their need for spousal support thereby terminate. It is these circumstances that lawyers and clients are fighting over daily across Canada. As a general rule, spouses in these age groups are considered obliged to eventually obtain self-sufficiency. This means that they must work and contribute to their own needs as quickly and as effectively as possible.

In some cases, these spouses will need retraining or skills development in order to re-enter the workforce. It is possible that a spousal support order will be made in such a way to allow that retraining to occur. So, for example, if a woman has been out of the workforce for 10 years, but with retraining could return to her work as a nurse, spousal support will be tailored to finance that retraining, as it allows her to return to a position from which she could become self-sufficient.

In some cases, this will call for occupational assessments or other employment reviews. The goal is to find the right occupation for this particular individual and to put him or her on an effective path to achieving self-sufficiency. Many spouses are willing participants in this retraining. They welcome the opportunity to get back to their earlier careers. Child-care needs must be balanced, and in some cases the retraining must even await the children being in full-time attendance at school, but eventually the retraining takes place.

For spouses who are reluctant to retrain, the courts have used a variety of techniques to encourage self-sufficiency. In some cases, the courts have ordered that spousal support will simply be terminated on a certain fixed date. In other cases, the courts have ordered that spousal support is payable for a certain period of time, say three or five years, at the end of which the matter returns to court for review. Some courts have even used the approach of ordering a spouse to pay spousal support at a certain level for a fixed period of time with the amount of monthly support then being gradually stepped down to wean the spouse off spousal support as his or her earnings increase.

It is now rare to see Canadian courts order a fixed termination date for spousal support. Generally, courts are ordering that at the very least the matter return to court for a review. Payors of support are understandably anxious to see their spouses pursue their retraining and return to work. The sooner they attain self-sufficiency, the sooner the spousal support obligation can finish. Recipients of spousal support are understandably nervous about returning to the workforce after extended absences. In my own approach, I try to encourage the payor spouse to invest heavily and at an early stage in the recipient spouse's retraining.

Agreeing to pay spousal support even if earnings from part-time employment are steady and significant can ease that spouse's return to the workforce.

When Does Spousal Support End?

FOR COUPLES WHO have separated, this is one of the most difficult questions to answer. Spousal support should end when there is no longer a need for it. Unfortunately, that point can be difficult to determine. For this reason courts include a provision in support orders giving the couple an opportunity to return to court to have the spousal support entitlement and quantum reviewed. There are no easy answers and each case must be taken on its own facts.

In the past, remarriage has been considered a reason to automatically terminate the payment of spousal support. Lately, however, the courts have not been firm in this regard, and in some cases spousal support has continued even after a spouse has remarried. This comes as a shock to most payors of spousal support.

Spousal Support Release

A VERY CONTROVERSIAL issue that has arisen in the area of spousal support is the ability to release the entitlement to spousal support. A spouse may wish to make a lump-sum one-time payment to another spouse in satisfaction of any and all future claims for spousal support. For some couples, this is a desirable way of making a clean break. A case in Ontario, however, in which a spouse accepted a lump-sum payment in exchange for a full release of spousal support blew up and completely undermined the confidence lawyers and clients have in spousal support releases. In that case, the wife had signed a release but had used up the lump-sum payment. There was a possibility that she might lose her home and she returned to court to have the spousal support release thrown out. On an interim basis (pending the trial), the judge ordered that spousal support be paid even though a release had been signed. It became next to impossible to settle a case using a lump-sum spousal support payment.

New wording for spousal support releases was drafted by the Law Society of Upper Canada and circulated to lawyers to ensure that model wording was used if clients wished to enter into a spousal support release. Now, if there has been full disclosure, independent legal advice and a generally fair result overall, the court will enforce spousal support releases.

This does not mean that lawyers do not remain uncomfortable with spousal support releases, terminations of spousal support and lump sum orders. Lawyers cannot guarantee clients that the release will not be completely disregarded at a later date. The decisions of the courts have injected a great deal of unpredictability into this area.

As a result, more and more emphasis has been placed on the periodic monthly support payment and the methods by which spouses can become self-sufficient. Lawyers and clients are not prepared to take the risk that the release will be completely disregarded at a later date.

One related consequence of this unpredictability is that lawyers find themselves unable to recommend any settlements in the area of spousal support other than indefinite spousal support awards, which at the very most would be reviewed in several years. In the current environment, few lawyers are prepared to recommend that a spouse accept a termination date for spousal support. This, you can imagine, makes it extremely difficult for lawyers to settle cases involving spousal support claims, particularly where those spouses are in their mid to late 40s and their chances for retraining are unknown.

The courts will usually include a cost of living allowance clause, which will increase the amount of spousal support in accordance with the cost of living each year. This reduces the likelihood that the parties will need to return to court for support increases at a later date.

Variation of Spousal Support

JUST AS IN the case of child support orders, it may be necessary for a spouse to return to court for a variation of the amount of spousal support if a material change in circumstance has occurred. For example, where the payor of support has been laid off or has suffered health problems, it may be necessary to return to court to have the spousal support reduced.

Similarly, if the recipient spouse's needs have changed, it may be necessary to return to court to have the amount paid varied upwards.

Earlier I mentioned the case of *Boston v. Boston*. This is precisely the situation that occurred. Long after separation, the payor husband retired and wished to reduce his monthly spousal support obligation. The case went all the way to the Supreme Court of Canada, where it was determined that his spousal support payments should be reduced and that only the portion of his pension that had accrued after the date of separation should be used for the purposes of calculating the monthly spousal support awarded to his ex-wife.

PARENTAL SUPPORT

PROVINCIAL FAMILY LAWS in some jurisdictions now provide that a parent in need of support can obtain it from a child of the marriage.

Ontario's provision states that every child who is not a minor has an obligation to provide support, in accordance with need, for his or her parents who have cared for or provided support for the child, to the extent that the child is capable of doing so.

There have been several cases across Canada that have interpreted the parental entitlement to support. In some cases, the children have been ordered to make a partial contribution to their parents' monthly budget. For example, one daughter was ordered to pay her father's condo fees.

As you can see, such orders could only be made against a child who has reached the age of majority and again the court looks at the parents' needs as well as the child's ability to pay. Support will only be ordered for parents who have cared for or provided support for the child from whom they are now seeking support.

In one case, an adult child had won a million dollars in a lottery and a parent sued the child for support. The court commented that the parent was not entitled to seek an increase in his or her standard of living simply because the child had won a lottery, but it would be reasonable for a child in such circumstances to contribute to any necessary expenses of the parent that the parent was unable to meet on their own.

These cases are complicated, even more so where there is more than one child against whom the support claim can be advanced. Each child may have different financial circumstances, family circumstances and different complaints about the quality of parenting they received from the parent now seeking support.

Again, as we see our population aging, it may not be uncommon in the very near future to see parents seeking support from their children where pension plans and other forms of public assistance do not meet the parents' needs.

CLOSING REMARKS

CHILD AND SPOUSAL support orders are key components of families moving on to new lives after separation and divorce. Thanks to the Child Support Guidelines, the quantum of child support is more adequate and less controversial in cases of separation and divorce. Although the Spousal Support Advisory Guidelines have brought some predictability to the area of spousal support, it will continue to be controversial for some couples, particularly around the issue of duration, and the subject of much debate between husbands and wives—and their lawyers.

MY ADVICE

1. Child support is calculated in accordance with the Federal Child Support Guidelines and includes a base monthly amount and a division of special expenses.
2. This child support can continue until the child is as old as 25 provided he or she is pursuing their education.
3. The Child Support Guidelines are driven by the gross annual income of the parent paying support and the number of children.
4. Special expenses are shared in proportion to the parents' annual incomes.
5. Be cautious with disputes around the Child Support Guidelines and the amount of time that the child is spending with each parent.
6. It is possible to have the amount of child support reduced if the cost of exercising access is very expensive.
7. Life insurance is necessary to secure the child support obligation and to protect the paying parent's estate.

8. A child's attendance at university can be a difficult moment for parents to calculate the appropriate amount of base monthly child support and a division of the child's residency costs while away.

9. Make regular and complete financial disclosure of earnings a requirement for the calculation of proper child support, pursuant to the Guidelines.

10. It is possible to have the amount of child support reduced if there is undue hardship, but the expense of a second family will not typically be considered a reason to lower child support payments to the first family.

11. Spousal support is being calculated with the use of the Spousal Support Advisory Guidelines, which will predict a range of support and a duration. Courts are using the Guidelines as a starting point for determining spousal support.

12. Spouses are expected to use their post-separation and divorce property to contribute to their own self-sufficiency.

13. Be prepared to invest in a spouse's retraining to assist him or her in returning to the workforce to become self-sufficient.

14. Termination dates for spousal support are not typically set by the courts. However, courts are setting review dates, giving the spouses an opportunity to return to court and evaluate any progress that has been made toward self-sufficiency.

15. Remarriage or cohabitation by a spouse receiving spousal support will not trigger an automatic elimination of spousal support.

16. In order for a spousal support release to be binding, and effective, it should only be entered into if the spouse releasing spousal support has received independent legal advice. To do otherwise runs the risk that the court will throw out the spousal support release.

17. The law of Canada now permits parents to sue their adult children for support. The support is calculated in accordance with need and on the basis that the parent claiming the support from their own child cared for and provided support for that child as they grew up.

COMMON-LAW SPOUSES
HAVE RIGHTS TOO

(Just Not the Same as Married Couples)

THE MEANING OF "COMMON LAW"

IN THIS CHAPTER, we will examine the meaning of the term "common law" and the misconceptions that surround it, and identify the rights and obligations of a common-law spouse when the relationship comes to an end. These rights and obligations may include: support, property sharing, pension sharing, custody of and access to children and financial support of children.

What does it mean to live "common law"? Most people would say it means "living together as if you were husband and wife but not actually getting married." The expression appears in few, if any, statutes passed by either the federal or provincial/territorial governments. It seems to have its origins in the English term "common-law marriage," which was a marriage not solemnized in the usual way but created instead by an agreement to marry in the future, which was then in turn followed by cohabitation (living together).

Living in common-law relationships has become very popular in Canada, particularly in Quebec. The results of each census provide more and more evidence that Canadians are prepared to live common law, particularly as a way of checking out whether they want to ultimately marry. Common-law relationships are also very popular among those who are entering second or subsequent relationships.

Common-law relationships are also volatile. Statistics show that first-time common-law couples are twice as likely to break up as first-time married couples. Only about 12 per cent of common-law relationships ever get to celebrate a 10th anniversary. On the other hand, 90 per cent of first marriages last at least 10 years.

Common-law relationships do not always start in the most orderly or legalistic way. For some people, living together arises out of necessity and may grow into a more intimate relationship. For others, it is a conscious choice to avoid the legal obligations imposed by marriage. Still others live together unmarried because they have no choice—one of them is married to someone else and not divorced. They are, therefore, unable to remarry.

Rather than use the expression "common-law spouse" in their laws, several provinces and territories have instead expanded the meaning of the term "spouse" in some limited circumstances to acknowledge that there are consequences for men and women, whether in heterosexual or same-sex relationships, when they choose to live together but do not marry. The definition of spouse for common-law purposes varies from province to province. The federal law, the Divorce Act, has no application to common-law spouses as it applies only to those who took the step of getting married.

Ontario's Family Law Act, which provides for property division and support on marriage breakdown, deals with the common-law spouse issue in an interesting way. Part I of the Act deals with property division and for that part of the Act "spouse" is defined essentially as people who are legally married. However, in Part III of the Family Law Act, which deals with support obligations, the definition of "spouse" includes three categories of couples:

1. people who get legally married;
2. people who live together for three or more years (whether a heterosexual couple or a same-sex couple); or
3. people who live together in a relationship of some permanence and have a child (adopted or natural).

In Ontario this means that when property is being divided after a common-law couple separates, the sections of the Act dealing with property division *do not apply* to them because they are not legally married.

However, it also means that each person *will* be entitled to claim support from the other under Part III if they fit the expanded definition of spouse.

Federal Legislation

WHILE IT IS the provinces that determine division of property for common-law couples, there are many benefits and entitlements or obligations that may arise under federal law. The federal government passed the Modernization of Benefits and Obligations Act in 2000. This Act amended approximately 67 federal statutes so that the benefits, rights and obligations given to married persons would also apply in the same way to common-law couples. The definition of "common-law couple" was set at two persons who are cohabiting in a conjugal relationship, having done so for a period of at least one year. This means that federal legislation treats common-law couples (again, whether opposite sex or same sex) who cohabit for one year in pretty much the same way as it treats married couples.

Let's now consider the rights and obligations of common-law spouses upon the end of the relationship in relation to three important areas: 1) children, 2) spousal support and 3) property division.

CHILDREN IN COMMON-LAW RELATIONSHIPS

ALL THINGS CONSIDERED, this is one of the less complicated aspects of common-law relationships, as all issues concerning the children are decided pursuant to provincial family law. Custody and access issues will be decided in accordance with the child's best interests (see Chapter 6: Obligations to the Children of a Divorce). The Child Support Guidelines apply to child support calculations, regardless of the existence of a legal marriage or a common-law relationship (see Chapter 7: Support).

SPOUSAL SUPPORT

MOST CANADIAN JURISDICTIONS have defined "spouse" in a way that extends an entitlement to or duty to pay support at the end of a common-law relationship.

In Appendix C I have included a chart illustrating the treatment of common-law couples across Canada. This chart shows the provinces in which a common-law spouse has a right to make a support claim as well as the right to make claims against the estate of a deceased common-law partner. If you are cohabiting with someone, I urge you to speak with a lawyer in your province to determine the exact definition of common-law spouse for your purposes. Each province is different, each province has been evolving its own provincial law and each province, therefore, has its own cases interpreting the treatment of common-law spouses.

For example, in Ontario and Manitoba, to qualify as a common-law relationship for the purposes of spousal support requires three years of continuous cohabitation. An exception is a couple who are in a relationship of some permanence and are the natural or adoptive parents of a child. In that case, it does not matter how long the couple has been living together. If they separate, they will be treated as spouses for the purposes of spousal support claims. In Nova Scotia, the required period of cohabitation is two years. British Columbia, as well, requires a two-year period of cohabitation.

Although the period of time of cohabitation is important, the court will also be interested in what the couple was doing while cohabiting—there must be some intimacy and dependency in the relationship. This means that the court will evaluate the nature of the relationship.

When examining a common-law relationship, judges consider a set of criteria based on cases that have gone to court. The court will consider the following:
- Did the partners share accommodations?
- Did one render domestic services to the other?
- Was there a sharing of household expenses? (not necessarily equal sharing)
- Was there sexual intimacy between them?
- What was the nature of their relationship?
- Were they husband and wife for all intents and purposes?

The courts have found that where there has been a relationship of such significance that it has led to the actual dependency of one party on another or the expectation that one will support the other in the event of financial crisis, an entitlement to support arises where there is a case of need.

Assuming the individual qualifies, the amount of the support and its duration is calculated in the same way that it is calculated for legally married spouses who have separated (see Chapter 7: Support). See *The Spousal Support Advisory Guidelines: A New and Improved User's Guide to the Final Version*, Justice Canada, published in March 2010 (see "Spousal Support" at www.justice.gc.ca).

It should be noted that in many jurisdictions, this obligation for support of a common-law spouse may also apply with respect to an estate. That is, if a person dies leaving a common-law spouse as his or her survivor, that person may be able to obtain an order of support from the estate.

To all outside appearances, a common-law relationship and a legally married couple may look exactly the same. However, that little piece of paper—the Marriage Certificate—makes a big difference. Married couples know when they get married because they have an official government document that records the date, establishing the beginning of their marriage. They may argue about when it ended, but they definitely know when it started. The same is not true for common-law couples. Their relationship many need to be put under a microscope to determine when it started, when it finished and if it was, in fact, common-law continuously for the required period. Once all the hurdles are crossed, the spousal support is calculated essentially the same way, but there can be some extra work getting there.

PROPERTY DIVISION FOR COMMON-LAW COUPLES

A COMMON-LAW COUPLE can acquire some significant assets over a few short years—a home, cars, furniture, RRSPs, stocks, a joint savings account—all without so much as a discussion about what would happen if one of them died or if they separated. That is why lawyers consulted by common-law spouses hear the familiar, "Well, I just assumed..." or "I thought we would just share it equally..." or, even worse, "I never intended to share that..." and so on.

With so many Canadians living in common-law relationships and so many of these relationships being volatile, the courts and legislatures have begun to struggle with the question of property division. No laws in Canada—until very recently—extended any property sharing to common-law couples. The presumption was that they would leave the marriage with what they brought in and would leave with anything that was in their name. If they owned a car at the beginning of the relationship and they still owned the car at the end, they would be presumed to take that car with them. If they made a contribution to an RRSP during the course of the common-law relationship, they would be presumed to take that contribution with them. Jointly held property was presumed to be divided jointly unless they could prove that there was a good reason to not divide it jointly.

Again, each province is different and I would refer you to the chart in Appendix C to see which rules apply in your particular province. As with spousal support, it is absolutely essential that you consult directly with a lawyer in your province to determine exactly what your property rights may be as you head into a common-law relationship and, most certainly, as you head out of it.

We cannot review each province individually, but I want to illustrate in the following paragraphs some of the different ways in which common-law spouses are treated in Canada.

When a common-law couple's relationship ends, some of the various provincial laws have nothing to say about the way in which property is divided. They have no statutory property rights. In fact, most lawyers and judges would agree that Ontario takes probably the hardest line in dealing with common-law spouses at the time of separation. If common-law spouses are to gain a share of property that is in the name of the other spouse, they must not only prove that they made a contribution of some kind to that property, but they must also convince a court that it would be unjust to allow that other person to be enriched at their expense. We will talk a little more about this further on, but in Ontario the bottom line for common-law couples when dividing property at separation is that there is no statutory help for dividing their property.

Manitoba tackled the question of common-law couples and property division in a different way. They passed a law called the Common-Law Partners' Property and Related Amendments Act. It came into force on

June 30, 2004. Before that date, a common-law couple splitting up in Manitoba was treated essentially the same way as a couple in Ontario. That is, spousal support rights would apply, but there was no statutory assistance in dividing property. As of June 30, 2004, if a common-law couple splits up, each partner is entitled to half the value of the property acquired by the couple during the time they lived together. This includes division of any pension entitlements. These new laws in Manitoba apply to common-law couples who register their relationship at the Vital Statistics Agency or couples who, if they have not registered, have lived together for a certain period of time (three years, or less if there is a child involved).

This is a huge change in the way in which common-law couples are treated. This means that a common-law couple who lives together three or more years in Ontario and then splits up has no statutory rights, but a common-law couple who lives together exactly the same way for the exact same period of time on the other side of the border in Manitoba will share full division of property.

Nova Scotia adopted a system of registered domestic partnership. In 2000, the Nova Scotia Legislature amended its Vital Statistics Act to permit two individuals who are cohabiting or who intend to cohabit to make a "Domestic-Partnership Declaration." The Declaration must be signed by both people and it must be witnessed. Once the Declaration is made, it is then registered and certain rights flow. The net effect of the changes in Nova Scotia means that there are four categories of cohabiting couples, as follows:

1. There will be married people who have all the rights and obligations given by provincial law to legally married spouses.
2. There are common-law partners who live together for two or more years, whether the couple is opposite sex or same sex.
3. There could be a couple registered as domestic partners regardless of the period of time that they have cohabited. This would apply to opposite-sex or same-sex couples.
4. And finally, there are likely in Nova Scotia some unmarried cohabiting couples who do not meet the statutory test for common-law partners and have not registered as domestic partners. They would not have any property rights.

You can see from the above examples that the treatment of common-law couples in Canada is now becoming more and more confusing. It is also becoming more and more critical for couples to consult with lawyers in their province to determine their exact rights. Do you meet the cohabitation test? Have you been in a conjugal relationship? Could you register your relationship under some provincial legislation and thereby gain rights? Can you sign a Cohabitation Agreement? If you have registered your relationship, can you de-register it? And so on.

These are all extremely important questions and, depending upon the province in which you reside, there will be very different answers. Canadians are also a mobile population. We move from province to province and for common-law couples this means that there could very well be a change in their status. Imagine the surprise of a couple that moves from Manitoba to Ontario in the second year of their relationship. They may have been poised to gain property rights, only to learn upon separating in Ontario a few years later that there is no statutory recognition of property rights for the common-law couple.

The courts have also developed some general guidelines over the years to help common-law couples sort out such property division matters where the law does not do it for them:

- In the absence of an intention to the contrary, each person may leave the relationship with any assets they brought in and any acquired in their name alone during the relationship.
- The court will not allow one person to be "unjustly enriched" at the other person's expense.
- Where one of the persons confers a benefit on the other person and suffers a corresponding deprivation as a result and there is no other legal reason or justification for the enrichment, the court may "correct" the situation through the use of a device called the "constructive trust." A constructive trust is simply a fancy legal way of saying to the spouse who has the property in his or her own name (called having "title"), "You are actually holding that property or part of its value in trust for your partner." The court then orders the part considered to be held in trust to be paid over to the other person.

An example might be helpful. Let's assume a man and a woman decided to live together in Ontario. Over a couple of years, they each saved $10,000 to put down on a home. They bought the house in the man's name with a vague intention to marry someday and live in it. Over the next several years, they moved in, and both paid the mortgage and expenses as best they could, although not equally. A child was born and the woman agreed to stay home to care for the child and the home. She then inherited $50,000 and, rather than start a small business, she agreed to renovate the kitchen and build a playroom. They later separated, with the house still in the man's name. Would the man be unjustly enriched at the woman's expense if he kept the whole house? Did she confer a benefit on him and suffer a corresponding deprivation by renovating instead of starting a business? Would the court correct this by imposing a trust upon him to hold a share of the house's value for her? The answer is yes to all three questions.

The same approach is true of all property acquired by common-law spouses, whether it is the home or the furniture in it. The court will look at their intentions and their contributions and try to achieve a fair split that does not leave one enriched at the other's expense.

The Supreme Court of Canada recently dealt with the issue of common-law couples and how they divide their property upon separation. The Supreme Court suggested that common-law couples approach their assets as if there was a joint family venture. In assessing that family venture, the court will consider four factors: 1) was there a mutual effort, 2) was there economic integration by the couple, 3) was there actual intent to share and 4) what was the priority of the family. If the court found that these factors were present, then an appropriate percentage of the value of the couple's assets could be awarded to the spouse making the claim. The reasoning used by the Supreme Court of Canada allows a common-law spouse to claim a portion of the family's assets that were made possible by their contributions to the relationship, without producing a detailed list of accounting. This case is supposed to bring some certainty to property division for common-law spouses, but it in fact may increase the amount of litigation while lawyers and clients and judges examine these new guideposts for the establishment of a joint family venture and how to compensate a common-law spouse for their contribution.

Other general rules used by the courts when dealing with such cases include the following.

- Each case is different. The size of an interest in a piece of property will depend on the facts of the particular case.
- A contribution does not automatically entitle a person to a half interest. The court will determine what is a fair return on the actual contribution.
- The court prefers a direct connection between the contribution and the property in question. It does not necessarily have to be a contribution directly to the acquisition of the property. It could be some act that preserved the property, maintained it or improved it.
- Merely being a supportive good partner or paying some household expenses will not necessarily entitle one to a share of a property. Remember, there must be the aspect of one being unjustly enriched at the other's expense. The case law is evolving on this point.
- There have been cases that found home, childcare and housekeeping services to have been a "contribution," but in such cases the spouse who cared for the child or did the household duties freed the other spouse to earn and acquire property.
- The court will consider the intention of each person, but does not insist that both have the same intention. It will consider what each person reasonably expected to happen or what interest in the property each reasonably expected.
- If the property is in one spouse's name because it was a gift from the other spouse, then the court will not "correct" the situation. One cannot be "unjustly enriched" by a gift.

Matrimonial Home

IT SHOULD ALSO be noted, in the context of this discussion of common-law property rights, that since there is no "matrimony," there can be no matrimonial home. Again, the provinces vary in their treatment of the home owned by the couple. Some provinces now extend special rights. Other provinces, such as Ontario, do not extend any special protection for the homes of common-law couples. There is no such thing as a common-law couple in Ontario having the right to claim exclusive possession of the home in the same way that a legally married spouse would. This means that it is absolutely essential that a common-law couple preparing to split consults with a lawyer to determine any special rights that may be afforded to their common-law "matrimonial home" or steps that can be taken to protect their home.

Pensions

BEFORE LEAVING THE area of property we should look at one special area that for common-law spouses requires protection—pensions.

Everyone acquires Canada Pension Plan benefits over their working life. The Canada Pension Act provides that persons of the opposite sex who had been living together for at least one year and who have been separated for more than a year may apply to the federal government for a division of pension credits. So, where a working spouse acquires credits, the other spouse may apply to share them. An application must be accompanied by the "necessary details" of course—birth certificate, Social Insurance Number, addresses (current and at cohabitation), relevant dates of cohabitation and separation and, for some reason, the reason for the separation.

Obtain Legal Advice

IT IS PARTICULARLY important to consult a lawyer about division of property when lengthy common-law relationships collapse or where significant assets are involved. Canada Pension credits should also be discussed with your lawyer.

What can be done in cases where the common-law couple wishes to make joint purchases or investments? The best route, of course, is to think in advance about what you feel should happen if one of you died or you separated. It can be a difficult subject to raise because it means confronting two very unpleasant possibilities. Who wants to think about that when things are going so well? You do.

COHABITATION AGREEMENTS

THE BEST WAY, in my opinion, to address the issue of common-law rights and obligations is head-on—"Honey, what would we do if something went wrong?" If the investments are significant or complicated (for example, they involve money from either family), you should seriously consider a Cohabitation Agreement. This type of domestic contract is the equivalent of a Marriage Contract and is designed for people who will not be legally married but will live together.

Cohabitation Agreements are contracts. These contracts are not difficult to prepare (write, sign, witness), but like any contract that affects your property they should be prepared with independent legal advice.

Don't be reluctant to raise the subject. If your relationship is strong, then it will survive this type of planning. Look on the bright side: you can make Powers of Attorney and wills at the same time and save yourself a trip to the lawyer's office.

For more information about Cohabitation Agreements, see my book *Do We Need a Cohabitation Agreement? Understanding How a Legal Contract Can Strengthen Your Life Together.* (For further information about this title, please visit www.michaelcochrane.ca and www.legalintel.ca.)

CLOSING REMARKS

THE PURPOSE OF this chapter is to open the eyes of people in common-law relationships or those thinking about being in one. The rights and obligations are very limited: the right to ask for support and the duty to pay it if the relationship has created a dependency. Sorting out property purchased jointly can be extremely difficult and confusing. If left to the courts, property division can be very rough justice. Custody and access issues are determined in exactly the same way as with the children of legally married spouses. The same is true of the parents' obligation to support their children.

MY ADVICE

1. Common-law spouses do not have the same rights as legally married spouses. Each province has its own approach to dividing the couple's property. In some provinces they are treated as if they were married.

2. But for the purpose of certain government benefits, federal legislation was amended to treat common-law couples the same as legally married couples with respect to all benefits and obligations available through federal legislation.

3. The children of common-law spouses are treated exactly the same as the children of legally married spouses for the purposes of custody, access and child support.

4. Each Canadian province has its own approach to determining an entitlement to spousal support when a common-law relationship ends. The court will be interested in the length of the cohabitation and the nature of the relationship. Was it intimate? Was it dependent?

5. If spousal support is appropriate, the courts will calculate it in the same way as for a legally married couple, by using the Spousal Support Advisory Guidelines.

6. Property division for common-law couples is not provided for by statute in most Canadian provinces. (See the chart in Appendix C for the rights and responsibilities in your province.)

7. If no statutory scheme for property division is provided by the province then, when trying to divide the property of a common-law couple, the court focuses on the facts of the case and in particular, the contribution of each person to the property in question.

8. Common law couples, because they are not married, do not have matrimonial homes. Whether the spouses have access to special rights of possession at separation varies from province to province.

9. Common-law couples do divide Canada Pension Plan benefits, provided the couple has been living together for at least one year.

10. Common-law couples are advised to organize their affairs in a Cohabitation Agreement, which is the same as a Marriage Contract. Independent legal advice is highly recommended prior to concluding any agreement.

SETTLING YOUR DIFFERENCES

Avoiding the Courtroom

ONE OF THE goals of this book is to help you make some intelligent choices about your family's difficulties. Reasonable choices will lead, in the vast majority of cases, to settlement. So, I want to spend a few minutes looking at how and why settlements are reached.

We have already examined the potential emotional obstacles to settlement (see Chapter 1: Taking a Look at Ourselves). Assuming none of those problems are clouding your decision-making, at some point in time you and your lawyer will realize that a settlement is close, that your needs are capable of being met without going to court for an imposed court order.

A settlement should be reached because that is what the people involved want and because it is fair to both of them. Unfortunately, this is not the case for many people in the family law system. Some cases settle for other, less satisfactory reasons. Consider the person who settles because she is worn out emotionally, or frightened of an abusive husband. She settles to avoid further conflict. Or, consider the person who settles because he cannot afford to go to court anymore.

There are too many people who settle because the cost of proceeding outweighs the benefit of an immediate settlement. This can mean either that the person cannot afford to pay his or her lawyer to continue a valid case or that the net amount that can be recovered exceeds that which would remain after a trial. There is no point spending $50,000 on a trial to recover an additional $40,000.

Sometimes a case is settled because it has not been prepared properly. Necessary evidence was not gathered, the case is called for a trial and the lawyer or client is not prepared to go to court. Perhaps they have been tactically outmanoeuvred. These are all unacceptable reasons for a person to settle a dispute.

A case that is settled on such uneasy ground may not be settled for long. I have met too many family law clients who feel they were pressured into a settlement with which they were unhappy. In one case the client was summoned to her lawyer's office to discuss a settlement offer that had just been received by fax on the eve of the court appearance. The offer, as it turned out, was not very different from a previous settlement proposal. The lawyer reviewed the offer with the client after which the following exchange took place.

Lawyer: "I think you should accept this offer to avoid a trial."
Client: "But, it's not what I had in mind. I thought..."
Lawyer: "Well, if you don't accept the offer I will need a $10,000 retainer before we go to court."
Client: "What? $10,000? I can't write a cheque for $10,000. Could you wait until we win the trial? I'll pay you out of what I recover."
Lawyer: "Oh, I can't do that. There's no guarantee we would be successful. In fact, if we lose you may have to pay your husband's legal costs. Your case does have some weaknesses. There are no guarantees, especially in family law cases."
Client: "But I thought we had a good case. You said..."
Lawyer: "Do you want to go to court?"
Client: "What should I do?"
Lawyer: "It's your decision."

Suddenly the case wasn't as good as it seemed six months earlier and the client had the unmistakable feeling of a rug being pulled out from under her. This happens all too frequently, leaving clients unhappy with the process, thinking that the settlement had very little to do with what they wanted or what they were entitled to. Before long, the tainted agreement is being twisted this way and that way by a dissatisfied spouse looking for some advantage to compensate for their unhappiness. Of course, once the agreement is ignored or breached, the whole struggle begins again. Therefore, in this chapter I want to talk about the documents related to the possible settlement of your case:

1. Offers to Settle
2. Minutes of Settlement
3. Orders on Consent
4. Separation Agreements
5. Memorandum of Understanding.

IT MAY NOT always seem obvious, but the lawyers handling the matter actually have a professional obligation to encourage you and your spouse to settle or compromise. Lawyers' rules of professional conduct tell us that we must advise and encourage the client to compromise or settle a dispute whenever it is possible to do so on a reasonable basis. We must discourage the client from commencing useless legal proceedings.

Keep that in mind as your case progresses.

OFFERS TO SETTLE

OFFERS TO SETTLE come in two forms—informal ones, contained in letters exchanged by lawyers, or formal ones, contained in a document prescribed by the Rules of Court. Both are valid and binding, if accepted. As negotiations go on between your respective lawyers, bits and pieces of the case start to get resolved. One letter may confirm an agreement on the sale of the home, another may fix the amount of child support and so on. In some cases, settlement of one issue is conditional upon settlement of another. For example, a father may agree to pay a child's hockey camp expenses provided he has the child for two months each summer. If one part of an offer is accepted, then the other part can be resolved. After the exchange of several letters, a basic agreement may take shape.

Often an experienced lawyer will see fairly quickly an appropriate middle ground upon which the parties can settle. He or she may contact the client to discuss a possible settlement and seek permission to propose it to the other side. A first letter may contain proposals on several matters. With skill and correct timing, it may resolve the dispute; however, in many cases it does not, and more letters are exchanged or proceedings are commenced or moved to the next step. Settling demands a great deal of patience from everyone. Keep in mind the emotional stages discussed in Chapter 1: Taking a Look at Ourselves.

One caution I wish to offer is with regard to the famous "without prejudice" letters. Those words often appear at the top of each letter exchanged between lawyers. Many clients don't understand why those words appear on some letters but not others. The short answer is that we have a system that (we hope) tries to encourage people to settle their differences out of court. To do so, people, including lawyers, need to be able to speak to each other frankly without fear that some remark or admission will be used against them later in court if the matter doesn't settle.

Lawyers have developed a system of shielding discussions designed to settle the case from disclosure in court at a later date. For example, lawyers might say things such as, "My client did not do what your client says he did. However, without prejudice to my client's case at a later date in court, I am willing to recommend that my client pay a fixed amount to your client to settle this matter." By using the words "without prejudice" he prevents the other lawyer from even mentioning the Offer to Settle at a later date.

Consequently, whenever you see a letter marked "without prejudice," it is usually an attempt to resolve the case without admitting the client did anything wrong or to prevent reference to it later.

A more formal type of offer is provided by the Rules of Court. There is even a prescribed form for it. This form is a relatively new innovation and was designed to end arguments that often developed between lawyers over who offered what in the informal letters discussed above. Usually, at the end of a trial, lawyers would stand up with their letters that offered to settle and say that the other person should have to pay all the costs of the trial because they had been offered the same thing (or better) long ago.

For example, a wife may have offered to accept $2,000 a month for support. If her husband rejected that offer, went to court and ended up paying $2,000, then it makes sense that he should pay for the cost of everyone going to court. The trouble was that letters marked "without prejudice" could not be used to tell the court what the offer had been and even if they could, lawyers frequently argued about what the lawyer's letter actually meant. Judges found it confusing and often ordered everyone to just pay their own lawyer and go home.

To solve these problems, the formal Offer to Settle was developed. It operates the same way as the letter but has some important differences. First, because of the Rules, all formal Offers to Settle look the same and follow the same format, meaning there is less to argue about.

Second, the Offer to Settle is made with the specific understanding that it will be drawn to the attention of the judge at the end of the trial. The Offer to Settle means in so many words, "I think the judge will decide the case as follows ... so let's settle the case on that basis. If you don't accept my Offer to Settle and the judge orders the same thing or better for my client, then I intend to show him or her this Offer to Settle."

The Rules of Court provide that if an Offer to Settle is made but not accepted and the judge orders the same terms as the original offer, then the person who rejected the offer must pay all the costs incurred between the date the Offer to Settle was made and the end of the trial. This can be particularly onerous for the person who does not accept it, if an experienced family law lawyer makes a shrewd, but fair, Offer to Settle early in the proceedings. Costs can be a powerful incentive to settlement.

One judge described family law cases as "extremely lengthy and ruinously expensive because of one or the other party's unreasonable and unrealistic demands upon the other." He went on to say that "extended family litigation has become unbearably expensive" and that he would insist on Offers to Settle being made. The Rules now require that Offers to Settle be made in such cases. These offers should also include a deadline for acceptance, or simply be left open for acceptance until the beginning of a trial.

As you can see, the Offer to Settle creates a lot of pressure. It cannot be rejected out of hand and it forces the lawyer and the client to think about their own case and how it might turn out. Whether the Offer to Settle is formal or informal, a lawyer who receives one must tell his or her client about it and provide a recommendation about possible acceptance or rejection. Even if the offer is unreasonable, the client must be told about it. It is not up to the lawyer to judge what the client might or might not accept.

Assuming an Offer to Settle is accepted, the lawyers may recommend incorporating the agreement into Minutes of Settlement, an Order on Consent or a Separation Agreement.

MINUTES OF SETTLEMENT

ANYONE WHO HAS ever been to a business or club meeting knows that someone is usually asked to "take the minutes." This involves making as detailed a record of the discussion as possible. Minutes of Settlement are no more than the details of a settlement discussion that took place, often after legal proceedings have commenced. One of the lawyers might volunteer to draft up a summary of a settlement reached through the exchange of letters, Offers to Settle or even a face-to-face meeting between all the lawyers and the clients. In some cases, the clients may have just finished a court hearing or a "pre-trial" (see Chapter 3: Taking a Look at the Process) and a consensus emerges while everyone is still at the courthouse.

Minutes of Settlement should always be signed by the clients themselves and are usually witnessed by the lawyers. In many cases they are completely handwritten or partially typed and partially handwritten. I have often seen lawyers sitting in hallways, using their briefcases as make-shift desks, furiously scribbling out a settlement just reached in another room. Their haste is often out of fear that one client or the other might change their mind.

Once signed, the Minutes of Settlement are binding and enforceable. To avoid any argument, many lawyers often incorporate the agreement reached into an order of the court made on consent.

ORDERS ON CONSENT

YOU WILL RECALL that the court makes orders in response to requests made by the lawyers and their clients. The request is often in the form of a Notice of Motion and is supported by an affidavit. In many cases, the lawyers have scheduled competing motions to be heard at the same time so that several matters can be resolved at one time.

As the lawyers and clients wait for their turn to be heard, discussion may yield some common ground. By the time the lawyers are ready to stand up and argue in front of the judge, a settlement on one of several issues may have emerged. One lawyer may simply advise the court, "Your Honour, the parties have reached an agreement on this matter and we ask that you make the following Order on Consent." The lawyers are using the time booked at court to record the settlement in an actual court order. This saves time and protects the parties' settlement.

It doesn't always occur while waiting to be heard by a judge. Sometimes the exchange of settlement letters or Offers to Settle produces an agreement that is then incorporated into an "Order on Consent"—an order that everyone agrees should be made.

SEPARATION AGREEMENTS

THE SEPARATION AGREEMENT is by far the most popular method of settling family law disputes. Essentially, the spouses, through their lawyers, sign a contract that sets out the terms of their settlement. We sometimes hear people refer to this as a "legal separation." The alternative, living separate from each other without a written agreement, is not an "illegal separation," as there is no requirement for people to have a written Separation Agreement. There are, as we shall see in a moment, several advantages to a written agreement. It is also worth noting that Separation Agreements are used whether the couple separating was legally married or not. In other words, a common-law couple will also sign a Separation Agreement.

Legal proceedings need not have been commenced in order to use a Separation Agreement. In fact, many people consult lawyers, negotiate and sign Separation Agreements without ever seeing the inside of a courtroom. They are the lucky ones. Others experience the courtroom first, and its related expense, and only turn to the Separation Agreement as a way out of the court system. Mediation (which is discussed in Chapter 11: Alternatives to Court) frequently yields an amicable settlement, which can then be incorporated into a Separation Agreement. So, while the use of Separation Agreements can arise in a number of ways, their purpose remains basically the same—to settle the dispute by contract.

The Basics

THE TECHNICAL REQUIREMENTS for a Separation Agreement are not extensive. The contract must be written, signed by the parties and witnessed. Law firms have computer systems that contain hundreds of model agreements and clauses. As the lawyer identifies the appropriate settlement, he or she simply picks and chooses from a precedent book the necessary clauses and paragraphs. A law clerk or secretary inserts the family details and related information. A hard copy (paper version) is produced and reviewed with the client. We will look at the agreement itself in a moment, but you can see at this point that there is no magic in the "legal separation." It is a contract like any other. If you wish to change or amend it later or even cancel (revoke) it, it must be done by the same method.

The Advantages

LET'S CONSIDER THE reasons for having such a contract. There are several advantages.

- The negotiations themselves have a way of making the couple consider things they might not otherwise have thought relevant. Not only must they resolve the disputes about the past but also think of the future—Where will I live? Can I move with the children to another province? What will happen to my estate if I die? And so on.
- A written agreement that the couple can refer to from time to time offers predictability in the future. There is less room for debate when it is there in black and white. A related advantage is the fact that those among us (you know who you are) who have trouble honouring their verbal promises (you say things like "I never said that!") are less able to walk away from a written promise.
- In every province, Separation Agreements can be enforced like any other contract. They are legally binding. An added advantage in many

provinces is that support provisions in Separation Agreements can be filed with the court or "support enforcement agency" (see Chapter 12: Enforcing Family Law Orders) and enforced as if they were court orders. This can be a great advantage to a person wishing to enforce a promise to pay support.

- Also related to the question of spousal support is the fact that tax advantages will arise if the obligation to pay support is in a Separation Agreement. Revenue Canada permits a person paying spousal support to deduct the amount paid. (No agreement means no tax deduction.)
- A Separation Agreement can considerably speed up any subsequent divorce proceeding. The agreement can be filed and its provisions incorporated into the consent divorce judgment if necessary.

The Details

THERE ARE VERY few limitations on the content of a Separation Agreement. In general terms, the agreement can deal with
- ownership in and division of property;
- support obligations—child and spousal;
- the right to custody of and access to children;
- the right to direct the education and moral training of children; and/or
- any other matter in the settlement of a couple's affairs.

I have reproduced a full Separation Agreement in Appendix A. You may want to take a moment to examine it now. You will note that like any standard contract, it begins by identifying the people who are entering into the agreement. Their names appear in full along with a statement as to their residency. The date of the agreement appears at the top of the first page.

After the introduction, there are several standard clauses. One sets out the particulars of the marriage (Where is that marriage certificate, anyway?) or the period of cohabitation, if it was a common-law relationship. Another paragraph sets out the date and circumstances of the separation. The couple will acknowledge that they intend to continue to live separately and will not interfere with the other person's life.

Each agreement is tailored to the individual needs of the couple. Use the following checklist as an aid.

- custody
- access
- division of household contents
- division of the matrimonial home (sale)
- possession and maintenance of the matrimonial home
- future use of property (for example, cottage sharing)
- child support
- spousal support (amount and duration)
- indexation of support
- restrictions on the mobility of custodial parents (for example, can't move more than 30 kilometres)
- restrictions on changing a child's name without consent
- methods of solving future disputes (mediation or arbitration)
- release of interest in other's estate
- general releases
- releases of interest in specific property
- division of pensions
- interpretation provisions (for example, definitions)
- health and medical expenses
- dental coverage
- automobile division or use
- Canada Pension Plan
- life insurance
- responsibility for debts
- tax consequences
- effect of re-cohabitation
- effect of default
- financial disclosure
- independent legal advice
- responsibility for legal fees

Signing the Separation Agreement

SIGNING (OR "EXECUTING," as lawyers like to say) the Separation Agreement can be quite an experience, although many people have commented that it seems anticlimactic after all the tensions of negotiating it.

The law office staff (law clerks and paralegals) will prepare four identical copies of the agreement, one for each client and each of the lawyers. At the end of the signing "exercise" there will be four duplicate originals. I call it an exercise because it is a bit of a marathon of signatures and initials that goes like this:

- You will sign your name on the last page on the right-hand side above a line and typewritten version of your name as it appears on the first page. In other words, the last page will have a line with, for example, "Michael George Cochrane" typed under it. Place your usual signature on the line. You do not have to write your name out in full—your usual signature is fine. A witness will sign beside your name. This may be a paralegal or other office member, although your lawyer may be the witness to your signature.

- You will then place your initials on each page of the agreement and beside any handwritten changes that have been made at the last minute. (Sometimes a name is misspelled or a birthdate is incorrect.) The same witness will place his or her initials beside yours wherever they appear. The pages are marked with initials for two reasons: to acknowledge that you've read each page, and to prevent anyone from trying to substitute a new—and perhaps different—page later.

- Both people must sign the agreement as I've described above. This is often done on different days at different times. The last page, where the signatures appear, will often show the dates upon which the couple signed the agreement.

- It is the lawyers' task to ensure that the agreement has been signed properly by both sides.

- Once it has been signed by both sides, the agreement is a legally binding contract.

But wait—there's more.

Certificate of Independent Legal Advice

THERE ARE SOME additional documents that are signed at this stage: a Certificate of Independent Legal Advice and an Acknowledgment by Wife/Husband. The Certificate is a sworn statement by your lawyer that he or she is the witness to your signature, that they believe you are the person whose signature they witnessed, and that they believe you understood what you were signing and did it voluntarily. The lawyer will often sign a Certificate of Independent Legal Advice, whereby he or she acknowledges that they explained the nature and consequences of the agreement and that the client signed it voluntarily. The client will then be asked to sign an acknowledgement that they hired the lawyer to advise them about the agreement, that the lawyer did so and that they are fully aware of the consequences of the agreement. It will also state that the person is signing voluntarily. Lots of paper, lots of signing.

You should also note that in some provinces, where Separation Agreements are enforced by the court, you may also need to sign an affidavit at the time of the final signing of the agreement that will facilitate filing with the court or with the police.

The signing exercise takes place only after the agreement has been reviewed, line by line, by you and your lawyer. (Not by you and the secretary, or the paralegal, or the articling student, or the junior lawyer, but the lawyer who negotiated it.) Do not be shy about asking questions. Look at each paragraph carefully. Do you know what it means? What does it accomplish? Don't accept statements like, "That's standard—it's in every agreement." Remember, you are going to be asked to sign the Acknowledgment I mentioned earlier. You are paying a lot of money for this contract, so understand what it does for you. If you don't, you may end up "paying" for years.

Don't be rushed. Sometimes law firms have little interview rooms or a library that can be used. Or ask the lawyer if you can take the draft agreement home to read. Review each draft from beginning to end. Review each new change. Does it do what you thought it would do? Does it accomplish what your lawyer said it would accomplish? If not, he or she should have a good explanation.

Setting Aside a Separation Agreement

THIS BRINGS US to another area—setting aside (or cancelling) an agreement at a later date. Following the technical rules for assembling the agreement will not make it immune to a charge that it was entered into "improperly" or that a special circumstance has changed. An agreement entered into "improperly" could include an agreement signed under duress. In other words, one party forced (through threats) the other person to sign an agreement that they would not otherwise have signed. This is why there is so much emphasis on both people having independent legal advice and acknowledging it in the document itself. It is difficult to challenge an agreement as being involuntary when a lawyer was consulted and gave advice. But it happens.

Another "improper" agreement would be one that was brought about by fraud. For example, if a person has hidden or lied about the presence or value of assets, then any calculations for the division of property would be inaccurate. If it was done to mislead the spouse, the court may set the agreement aside.

The courts will also set aside agreements entered into because of undue influence, material misrepresentation, unconscionable bargain and something lawyers call "non est factum." Briefly, "undue influence" occurs where one person uses his or her power over another in such a way that the more powerful person acquires a benefit. A "material misrepresentation" occurs where one person hides a fact or lies about a state of affairs with the effect of inducing the other person to sign the agreement. In one case, a husband told his wife the agreement was for "tax purposes." In another case, a husband was told it was only "temporary." Both were misrepresentations.

An "unconscionable bargain" may be set aside by a court if it finds that the parties were in unequal bargaining positions and, as a result, the deal was improvident for one of them. This would likely be in situations where no legal advice had been obtained. I know of a case where a husband told his wife that she was entitled to one-seventh of the property because there were two adults and five children. She signed the agreement without legal advice.

Non est factum is a special legal term for what can be quite straightforward—a person signs a document thinking it is one thing but finds out it is something else. It used to be reserved for the blind and illiterate but can now apply to document switches.

Statements of Assets and Liabilities

TO AVOID THESE types of problems, lawyers now insist that the clients exchange sworn statements about their assets and their value. This discourages fraud and allows the lawyers to negotiate a fair agreement. As much as this exchange of information makes sense, there are still clients who will ask lawyers to prepare agreements without having first exchanged full financial information with their spouse. These clients are usually in a hurry, want to save costs or think they already know everything about finances. If this type of client subsequently discovers that the other spouse was not completely honest in his or her disclosure, it is very unlikely that the court will set aside the agreement. The moral of the story is: don't sign a Separation Agreement without seeing a full, sworn financial statement from your spouse. I often attach sworn financial statements to the Separation Agreement as schedules so that everyone knows the basis for the agreement.

Reconciliation

ONE SPECIAL SITUATION deserves mention—what if the people get back together (reconcile) after the Separation Agreement has been signed? The answer is like many in law: it depends. The court will look to the agreement itself and see if that situation was contemplated. It often was and the agreement may provide that its terms expire if reconciliation occurs. It is obvious that there are reconciliations that don't last. The couple may have second thoughts and begin to cohabit again. After a few months the old problems surface and everyone is left wondering what happens now.

The intention to resume cohabitation must be bilateral—that is, both spouses must wish to reconcile. In one case, evidence offered of such an intention was the occurrence of several acts of intercourse, but the court disagreed. One of the spouses testified that they had no intention of getting back together; it was just sex.

Generally, a reconciliation of the spouses will terminate the Separation Agreement with respect to future dealings. If the couple acquires a new matrimonial home or joint savings again and then separate again, they will need to redivide under the family laws. However, all transactions that were intended to be complete are not undone by the cohabitation. Property that was transferred stays transferred. Reconciliation, however, may terminate provisions dealing with spousal and child support.

Separation Agreements are valuable tools for settling family law cases because they record the details of the agreement and provide a method of clear enforcement. Their value is found in recording the agreement the couple wants and needs. This result can only be achieved by understanding the process and giving informed instructions to your lawyer.

MEMORANDUM OF UNDERSTANDING

IN CHAPTER 11: Alternatives to Court we will be considering alternatives to the court and will look at mediation, arbitration and collaborative family law in more detail. At this stage, I only want to mention that another way of recording a settlement is by way of a Memorandum of Understanding.

In a mediation, a neutral third party works with the couple to reach a settlement. If the negotiations and discussions are successful, the mediator will record a summary of the agreement in what is referred to as a "Memorandum of Understanding." That Memorandum will often then be converted into a larger settlement document, the Separation Agreement.

You should also understand that the court does not consider itself bound by any agreement that affects children. The amount or duration of child support, for example, can be changed by the court at any time regardless of what the agreement says. The same is true of custody and access. The court will always try to do what is best for the child.

In the case of spousal support, Separation Agreements often provide that in the event of a "material change of circumstances" (essentially a significant change in some way), the amount and duration of the support can be changed. So, if a wife was receiving $800 per month while working part-time but was laid off, then her support could be increased by the court until she finds a new position.

CLOSING REMARKS

THERE ARE A number òf ways to document the settlement of a family law case—Offers to Settle, Minutes of Settlement, Orders on Consent, Separation Agreements and a Memorandum of Understanding. Each method has its own value depending on the circumstances of your case, but all are based on arriving at a settlement that meets your needs and the needs of your children. Making sure your needs are met is the only valid criterion for settlement. Fatigue or cost or other factors will enter the picture, but they should not obscure your needs. Remember the settlement must last for a long time—maybe forever.

MY ADVICE

1. Family law cases should be settled because the settlement is reasonable. Is it fair? Make sure you are not placed in a position of settling a case because you have been outmanoeuvred or because the necessary evidence has not been gathered to prove your case. At each stage, be prepared to offer to settle the case by providing a clear proposal to resolve an issue and a deadline for acceptance of the offer.
2. Make sure that you understand the consequences of not accepting an offer.
3. In concluding any settlement, be careful to ensure that all the details have been dealt with.
4. Review any proposed agreement carefully with your lawyer present.
5. Make sure that there has been full financial disclosure prior to concluding any settlement, and consider attaching sworn financial statements to any settlement that has been reached.
6. Be aware that reconciliation may have the effect of terminating the effectiveness of a Separation Agreement and could trigger a renegotiation of division of property, custody and support issues.

NOT SETTLING
YOUR DIFFERENCES

Going to Court

I N THE PREVIOUS chapter, we saw how cases can be settled when the people involved find a way to resolve their differences. Not settling means only one thing—going to court for a full trial. This aspect of family law is becoming less common, due in part to the expense of full trials and because clients and lawyers are using more creative methods of solving problems, such as mediation. But there are still many, many courtroom trials every year in every province and territory, at an appalling cost to the people involved.

A trial, at its most basic level, means that the people involved have not been able to agree on a solution to their problem and are left asking the court to solve it for them. All the issues discussed in the previous chapters can be and have been decided by a judge in a courtroom. When people stand back from the process and consider, for example, the meaning of a custody trial, I believe they are in part ashamed of their inability to resolve the problem. They are admitting that they, the child's parents, cannot agree on what is best for this child, so they will ask a complete stranger (the judge), who has minimal familiarity with their lives, to decide on this most important aspect of their lives for them. Yet this is precisely what happens with children, property, spousal support and even the entitlement to a divorce itself.

First, we have to separate reality from the misconceptions created by television. Family law trials in Canada bear very little resemblance to the trials we see on television. I'm always amused by how the TV clients who consult the TV lawyer for the first time at the beginning of the show are having a TV trial by the end of the program about an hour later. We should all be so lucky—most people wouldn't have their financial statements filled out by then, let alone a trial.

TV trials are fast, exciting, filled with tough cross-examinations, lying witnesses, surprise alternative theories ("Isn't it actually true that...") and the obvious "good person" winning over the obvious "bad person." On television, justice is black and white and no one ever seems to pay the lawyers.

Reality? The process is slow, very slow. Some people wait over a year for their trial (that's a whole TV season, never mind one episode), the process is filled with delays, it's often boring in the middle of a trial while technical arguments are made, the process is overblown with much posturing and, unlike television, it is a tense time for you and an even greater burden for your children if they are involved. I think many people justifiably consider a trial to be the most intimidating experience of their lives. You will never meet someone who brags about how great or how interesting or how rewarding their family law trial was. You never hear anyone say, "It was worth every penny..." If anything, most people think it was a complete waste of time and money, on top of which it was a very emotional experience that made them feel vulnerable and out of control.

Having said all that, we cannot simply ignore the trial as a painful lesson in living. Sometimes couples are forced to trial—one person takes an unreasonable position or some aspect of the law is so unclear that a judge's decision is needed. In this chapter, I would like to consider the trial from a few different perspectives so that those who simply *must* go through it can do so with a little more confidence and a little more control.

Before considering any of the technical aspects of a trial, we must consider what unfortunately becomes an overriding consideration—the cost. In advance of the trial, when it appears that a settlement is unlikely, you and your lawyer should discuss the likelihood of a trial. At that time, you should consider the preparation and review of a new retainer that authorizes the lawyer to conduct the trial on your behalf. At the time the retainer is reviewed, the lawyer will undoubtedly inform you that no trial will be possible unless a substantial advance on fees is received before the trial commences. The lawyer will likely explain that the legal fees for a trial are approximately $5,000 per day (minimum), and more if additional lawyers are involved on your behalf. It is not unusual for lawyers to request an advance on fees before the trial in the amount of $10,000 or $15,000. It is highly unlikely that you will find a lawyer who will conduct the entire trial on the understanding that he or she will be paid the legal fees out of the eventual recovery of property at the end of the trial. This is particularly so in cases where the dispute is over custody. The lawyer will insist upon his or her fees in full, in advance.

Assuming that the cost of proceeding to trial doesn't deter you from this option, let us now consider the physical setting of the proceedings.

THE COURTROOM

EXPERIENCED FAMILY LAW lawyers or one of their staff will often take their clients to the court for a tour in advance of the trial to familiarize the client with the layout of the courtroom and to remove any anxiety about the settings in advance of the proceedings.

It is misleading to think of the activity at the courthouse as being confined to the courtroom, although much of the action does take place there. Important things also occur in the court office, the judge's office (called chambers), the lawyers' lounge and even in the hallways.

The courtroom is laid out in a fairly standard fashion, with the judge at the head of the court (usually) on an elevated platform (called the bench). Immediately in front of the judge's bench is the clerk's table, where exhibits are collected and where the court reporter will sit during the trial. The court reporter will likely be a different person than the court reporter who assisted at the examinations for discovery. However, the court reporter's function at a trial is the same—to prepare a transcript of all discussions in the courtroom from beginning to end. A few feet farther away from the judge's bench is a long table called "counsel's table" (sometimes it is two tables, one for each side).

There may be three or four chairs at each counsel table. The lawyers will sit at these tables with their clients and any lawyer assisting on the case or, in some circumstances, a witness with whom the lawyer wishes to confer during the proceedings.

On the judge's left is the "witness box," which can literally be a box with a door at the back through which the witness enters and exits. Inside the witness box are usually a Bible and a Koran for the administering of an oath and a glass of water for the witness.

On the judge's right will sit the clerk of the court. If the lawyers wish to give the judge anything during the course of the trial, they will often hand it to the clerk who in turn will pass it to the judge. The clerk will also mark exhibits during the trial and provide the judge with any necessary assistance upon entering and exiting the court. You may recall the marking of exhibits at the examinations for discovery. Those same exhibits will now be re-marked during the trial, while the new transcript is being prepared.

At the back of the courtroom is a seating area for the public. The proceedings are open unless they have been closed for some special reason, such as protection of a child, but the public is generally free to come and go during the course of any proceeding in a courtroom.

Some courthouses use special smaller courtrooms for family proceedings; however, in many courthouses, the same courtroom is used for family law trials as for murder trials and for other forms of litigation. This means that the courtroom may be equipped with a press box and a jury box, often on different sides of the courtroom. Reporters will take over the press box to cover some of the more spectacular and lurid cases, while the jury box, as mentioned earlier, will always sit empty during a family law trial.

The courtrooms are usually linked by hallways to which only authorized personnel have access. The judges will use these hallways to get to and from their chambers. Court staff and lawyers who have business with the judge will also use these hallways. In some older courthouses, the judge's office may be in another part of the building, so he or she is escorted from the office through the court hallways to the courtroom. In the judge's chambers, the judge works on judgments, reads the court file, makes telephone calls and dresses in his or her robes in advance of trial. It is important to note that this particular judge has likely never heard of you or your spouse and has had nothing to do with the case before the trial. In some circumstances, the judge may have only read the court file a few hours in advance of the trial.

Generally the judge enters the courtroom through a private door behind the bench itself. A clerk will call out "All rise ..." with a reference to the particular court in which the trial is taking place, and when the judge enters everyone in the courtroom will stand. The judge carries a large notebook that will be used for the taking of notes during the trial. Some judges take a great many notes; others appear to only take notes on the most important points. A few judges now use laptop computers.

Lawyers, too, have private dressing rooms in the courthouse. These are called "barristers' lounges" and sometimes look like no more than a locker room. It can be quite an experience in these lounges: settlements are negotiated, victories celebrated, losses mourned, war stories and anecdotes traded; and a lot of socializing goes on. Clients are, of course, not welcome in the lawyers' lounge. It is akin to the local clubhouse in some communities.

When a trial is scheduled to be heard, a lot of time can be spent in the hallways of the courthouse waiting, waiting and waiting. Trials often run overtime; emergency hearings are scheduled, thereby throwing off the judges' plans; judges and court reporters must take breaks and any number of relatively minor but unpredictable events can cause delays. While in the halls, lawyers prepare their witnesses, discuss possible settlements, make telephone calls or just sit and wait. In a busy courthouse, the halls can be a fascinating place to spend a few hours. However, those awaiting trial find it less interesting due to the stress of their own impending trial.

THE PAPER CHASE

YOU WILL RECALL that the courthouse maintains a court file with a copy of everything that has happened during your case. All motions, affidavits, claims, petitions, orders, transcripts and so on are all in the court file to provide a chronological history of the family dispute. In advance of the trial, the lawyers will have prepared a "record," which is a bound collection of all the important court proceedings that will be used like a summary book by the judge during the trial. The lawyers will often have duplicates of this summary in front of them during the course of the trial so that whenever a reference is made to a particular aspect of the proceedings, the judge and lawyers can all refer to the same material at the same time.

The lawyers will also prepare copies of important evidence and exhibit books for use during the trial. The financial statements completed by the couple will likely be out of date by the time the trial arrives and fresh ones will have been completed and filed for use at trial. As you can guess by now, the court file can be quite a monster by the time the trial has arrived. This is particularly so if litigation has taken place over a few years.

The nature of the remaining disagreement between the couple will have an effect on the paperwork in front of the court. If, for example, it is a divorce proceeding that includes a dispute over custody, access, property and the divorce itself, the form of the court proceedings will be dictated by the fact that a divorce is being sought. If some issues have been resolved by the time the trial is to take place—for example, only custody is an issue—the paperwork put before the court may be pared down from the full content of the court file. The bigger the dispute, the bigger the court record and court file used by the judge. The court file is maintained by court staff and delivered to the judge in his chambers by the court staff. All this work goes on behind the scenes in advance of your case actually being considered by the court.

THE TRIAL

THE CIRCUMSTANCES UNDER which your case is "called for trial" can vary from province to province. Some courts use a "fixed date" method, which can add a great deal of convenience to your hearing. At a certain point, the lawyer must certify to the court that the particular case is ready for trial. In other words, the lawyer alerts the court to the fact that this case can be called at any time for trial and he and his witnesses will be ready. When judges are ready to book trials, they look at the list of cases that are ready (called "the ready list") and start to pick and choose trials that will be heard. This often takes place with a few dozen lawyers and a judge comparing their schedules over the next few months.

Depending on witness availability and the expected length of the trial, the cases are slotted into a judge's schedule. In some cases they are given a "fixed date," which means, for example, that Judge Brown will hear *Porter v. Porter* on November 20, 2015. This is very convenient for the parties since they know in advance the date of their trial and can plan accordingly for witnesses to be present and for parties to be available.

Another, but far less convenient, method is to just tell five sets of lawyers to be ready to go to trial "the week of November 20th." The cases are then listed one to five for that particular week. If case number one settles, then case number two must be ready to go. If case number two settles, then case number three should be ready and so on. The judges deliberately overbook and anticipate settlements in such a system. The look of panic on a lawyer's face when he or she finds out on a Friday that they are not number five for the following week but rather number one on Monday morning is unforgettable. There can be quite a weekend scramble in order to be ready for the trial. Unfortunately, this kind of system also forces some less-than-satisfactory settlements on the parties when the lawyers discover that they are not in fact ready for trial.

Regardless of the method of setting the case for trial, let's assume that your case is going to be called on a particular date. You will need to arrange time off work for the entire trial, which may in some cases be several days, and you may also need to arrange for childcare. Your lawyer will be arranging for subpoenas to be served on all the witnesses who will be giving evidence in support of your case. Even friendly witnesses, who have agreed to come to trial, will receive a subpoena and a small sum of money to cover their expenses travelling to and from the trial. While they will only be needed at the time they actually give their evidence, as a witness they are required by the subpoena to be available for the entire trial unless excused by the judge. This can be quite an inconvenience and requires some sensitivity by the lawyer in ensuring that witnesses do not waste their time sitting around in court on days that they are not giving evidence.

It is not unheard of for everyone to be at the court ready to go and suddenly discover that the judge who is supposed to hear their case is now hearing, for example, an emergency injunction application in a labour dispute or some other urgent matter. The trial coordinator tries to patiently explain that the trial cannot go ahead as planned. Sometimes it is put over for a day, sometimes indefinitely. Sometimes the trial begins but is then adjourned. I have even seen cases split in half, with part of the case being heard by a judge in November and the rest of the case being heard by the same judge in the new year. You should not assume that your entire trial will be done in one sitting.

However, let's be optimistic and assume your trial starts when it's supposed to start.

It can be divided into five main parts:
1. introduction and opening statement
2. the petitioner's (or applicant's) case
3. the respondent's (or defendant's) case
4. summation
5. the judgment.

Let's examine each separately.

Introduction and Opening Statement

AT THE OPENING of the trial, after the judge has been ushered in, the lawyer for the petitioner/plaintiff (I am going to refer to the people involved as the petitioner and respondent during this section) will stand up and introduce himself or herself and the other client and other lawyer. This occurs whether the judge knows the lawyers or not and is simply for the record being prepared by the court reporter.

The lawyers will take turns describing the case very briefly to the judge by way of a "thumbnail sketch." They will also tell the judge about anything that has settled in the case or anything that they may have agreed upon to make the trial more expeditious, such as the preparation of a common exhibit book. The lawyers may even give the judge an idea about which witnesses will be called and when they expect to be finished putting evidence before the court. The judge may ask some questions or may simply say to the petitioner's lawyer, "Call your first witness."

The Petitioner's (or Applicant's) Case

THE PETITIONER GOES first and presents his or her story in whatever order he or she feels is most logical. The story is confirmed by witnesses. The rules of evidence are quite complex and dictate the type of evidence that may be given by particular types of witnesses. Expert witnesses are given a little more latitude in the types of things that they may testify about. Virtually all other witnesses may only testify about things of which they have actual knowledge.

Each witness is handled in the same general way. The lawyer or the clerk of the court calls the witness to the witness box. If an "order excluding witnesses" has been made, the witness may be in the hallway. These orders are often made at the opening of a trial to keep the waiting witnesses from hearing each other's evidence and tailoring their answers. While in the hall, the witnesses are not allowed to discuss the case with any witness who has given evidence.

Once in the witness box, the witness is sworn in (or affirmed) and asked preliminary questions, such as their name, address and relation to the parties. The lawyer who has called this witness then asks the witness "open-ended" questions. By open-ended I mean that the questions cannot be leading. For example, the lawyer could not say to this witness, "Is it true that you have worked for the petitioner for 10 years as a chartered accountant and concluded that his 100 business shares are worth only $1 each?" This is a leading question because it suggests the answer to the witness and therefore leads him in a particular direction. The question must be open-ended: "How long did you work for the petitioner?" "Did you calculate the value of his business shares?" "How many shares did he have?" "What method did you use to calculate their value?" "What conclusion did you reach about the value of each share?" The witness is taken step by step through the information he has that is of value to the court and to this particular party's case.

Before the trial, the lawyer should spend some time with the client and the witnesses explaining how to give evidence. The evidence should always be given in a clear voice and directed to the judge if at all possible.

One should only answer the question that is asked and never guess or speculate about a particular answer. It is an absolute must to review the transcripts from the examination for discovery in advance of the trial as a way of preparing and refreshing one's memory about the evidence.

Once the petitioner's lawyer's questions are complete, the lawyer for the other side has an opportunity to test the witness's story through cross-examination. In this situation, if the lawyer is doing the job properly, every question will be a leading question requiring only a "yes" or "no." answer. The conventional wisdom is that a lawyer should never ask a question on cross-examination to which he or she does not already know the answer. Nor should questions ever be open-ended during cross-examination. This can mean hours of preparation for even the briefest of cross-examinations.

One method that a lawyer can use on cross-examination is contradiction of the witness's evidence at trial by demonstrating that the witness made a statement on a previous occasion that is inconsistent with his or her most recent evidence. In other words, the lawyer says to the witness, "What you are telling the court today is not the same as what you told us on a previous occasion under oath." This type of contradiction is called an "impeachment" and is most frequently used against the parties themselves who have had their evidence recorded at the examination for discovery.

Once the cross-examination is complete the petitioner's lawyer, who called the witness in the first place, is given the opportunity to re-examine the witness on any new issue that has arisen during the cross-examination. The lawyer may not ask something that he forgot to ask during the direct examination. It must be something new and it must have arisen during the cross-examination. Re-examination does not take place in every case, but it does allow the lawyer who called the witness to tighten up weak aspects of the evidence that may have been established during cross-examination.

Remember that the judge is making notes through all of this evidence. If he or she does not have any questions, the witness is excused and another witness is called to the witness box. The above process is then repeated, with the direct examination followed by a cross-examination, followed by a re-examination if necessary and questions from the judge. This applies to the witnesses called and to the petitioner. All witnesses are treated in the same way, although the evidence of some is obviously more important than the evidence of others.

The Respondent's (or Defendant's) Case

ONCE THE PETITIONER has called all of his or her witnesses, the respondent takes over. Sometimes the respondent's lawyer will open with a brief statement about the evidence to be called and any other clarifying remarks. The respondent's lawyer then calls all his or her witnesses and the same procedure described above is repeated with respect to each witness.

As witnesses identify documents, each one is marked and entered as an exhibit. The judge examines each document and makes notes about its importance in his or her notebook (whether paper or computer).

That is the procedure in theory, but let's add a small dose of reality.

Consider that the following things may happen while this is underway:

- A witness who was subpoenaed does not show up and the case is adjourned for a day or the order of witnesses is changed.
- A witness shows up but has forgotten to bring important documents with him or her and is excused to locate the documents. Again, either an adjournment is triggered or the order of witnesses is changed.
- People are wandering in and out of the court. They may be lawyers waiting to be heard by this judge in another proceeding, law students monitoring the court lists for their offices, university or high-school students on courthouse tours and even people from other trials. Every time someone walks in, the proceeding is disrupted while everyone turns around to take a look. Why? Because the person might be a witness who should be excluded from the proceeding. The judge or lawyers then ask the person why they are in the courtroom. Once they are satisfied that it is not a witness who has been excluded, the proceeding gradually returns to normal.
- The trial that was originally estimated to take no more than two days is suddenly at the end of its second day and five witnesses have not yet been heard. The trial is then adjourned for six weeks until the next time that the judge is available to continue hearing evidence.

Returning to the trial process itself, once the respondent's case is finished, the petitioner has an opportunity to call evidence in "Reply." This
is like a re-examination of a witness and means that if something new
came up during the applicant/petitioner case that the plaintiff needs to
reply to, he or she can call a witness to provide the court with new information. The petitioner is not permitted to call a witness who should have
been called at the outset as a part of the petitioner's case, but if something new has arisen, the petitioner will have an opportunity to put that
evidence before the court. The process is then repeated for that witness
or witnesses.

Summation

AFTER ALL THE evidence is before the court, the lawyers then stand
up and take turns (petitioner first) summarizing their case for the judge.
The lawyers trace through the evidence, emphasizing strong points and
playing down weak ones. They also weave the relevant law through their
summary. This will involve pointing out cases or sections of legislation
to urge the court in a particular direction favourable to their client. At
the end of each summation, the lawyer suggests to the judge the appropriate outcome in very specific terms.

The lawyer for the respondent repeats this process for his or her client. Once the judge has both versions before him or her, the three of
them may engage in some detailed discussion of the finer points of the
law or the facts of the particular case. The judge will sometimes thank
the lawyers for their work and adjourn the case indefinitely. The judge
will then pack up his or her notes and the evidence and sit down later to
figure out what should happen in this particular situation. Rarely will the
judge give a decision on the spot, and this adjourning indefinitely while
a decision is written is called "reserving judgment." It can put the case
on hold for several months.

The people involved leave the courtroom, the couple goes back to
their lives, the lawyers go on to other cases, and the judge goes on to
new trials, while everyone waits for a decision.

The lawyers may send their clients reporting letters at this stage, providing a detailed synopsis of what happened and what can be expected

in the judge's decision. Sometimes, but not always, the bill is enclosed for the work to date.

The Judgment

JUST WHEN THE client thinks things have returned to normal, the lawyer calls to say that the "Reasons for Judgment" are available. This means that the judge has written out—usually typed—the reasons why the case has been decided in a particular way. The judge will often trace his or her reasoning, making it clear that he or she has accepted either the petitioner or the respondent's theory of the case. Sometimes the judge develops his or her own theory.

The reasons are related to but different from the judgment itself. The lawyers identify what the judge has actually decided by reviewing the reasons. For example, the petitioner gets custody, the respondent gets access on particular terms, the cottage is divided in a particular way, the shares are valued at a certain amount and so on. These essentials are extracted from the reasons and typed into a separate judgment, which is then approved by the lawyers. If the lawyers cannot agree on what the judge has decided in the reasons, they arrange an appointment to see the judge and settle the dispute. Once they have arrived at an agreed form for the judgment, it is recorded at the courthouse and becomes effective.

The lawyers will then usually make an appointment to see the judge to discuss costs (i.e., who will pay the winner's costs and to what extent). This is an important aspect of the case, because the offers to settle that were made earlier (see Chapter 9: Settling Your Differences) are now compared with the actual judgment. If the loser rejected a favourable offer to settle, the costs can be considerable.

Once the court decides who must pay whom, a "bill of costs" is prepared in which the winning lawyer sends his bill to the losing lawyer for approval. If there is a disagreement about the amount, it can be settled by consulting the judge. The court official uses a tariff set by the Rules of Court to decide what is a fair bill from the winner. Losing a trial of four or more days can be an expensive proposition. Not only must the person pay their own lawyer, but they must pay the winner's lawyer as well.

Someone out there is undoubtedly saying "Yes... but if I win, then the loser pays my legal fees and I'm off the hook." Not quite. The "winner" may get about 50 per cent of his or her actual expenses of the trial. So while the loser pays part of the "winner's" bill, the "winner" still has to pay his or her own lawyer the remaining amount.

APPEALS

BEFORE LEAVING THIS area we should deal briefly with appeals. It is not unusual for the lawyers, upon examining the Reasons for Judgment, to discover what they consider to be an error in law by the judge. The judge may have decided the case by using an incorrect principle of law or misinterpreting a section of an Act. It is not unheard of for each lawyer to discover a different mistake and develop two or more reasons as suggested grounds for appeal. These will be pointed out to you in the lawyer's reporting letter. In such cases, the lawyer will often say that he or she has reviewed the judgment and respectfully feels that the judge "erred in finding as a fact that..." or "erred in interpreting the law..." It amounts to a difference of opinion and the lawyer is suggesting that if he or she took it to a higher court, that court would agree with his or her opinion.

Appeals are not free. In fact, they can be very expensive. The cost of a transcript alone, for a trial of several days, can be thousands of dollars. Something very important or valuable must be at stake to even begin to think about an appeal. It should be treated as seriously as your original decision to begin the case, with emphasis on the costs of the appeal and the likelihood of success. As with the original trial, the losing party will pay the winner's costs again if unsuccessful on the appeal.

Appeals do not occur quickly. Depending on the province and level of court to which one is appealing, they can add several months and in some cases more than a year to the litigation. Ask your lawyer how long it will take.

The first appeal is not necessarily the last of the court. If the appeal court changes the trial judge's decision, the other side may be able to appeal that new decision to a higher court. If important new legal concepts are involved, the appeals can go all the way to the Supreme Court of Canada and take years to resolve.

The only advantage to appeals is that they occasionally do correct decisions that were made improperly, and they often enable the law to be "stretched" a little to offer fairness to a new situation perhaps not contemplated by the law. For example, some cases concerning common-law spouses went all the way to the Supreme Court of Canada but made a significant new interpretation of the law available to thousands of people. It may have resulted in numerous settlements of cases that were working their way through the legal system across Canada.

Another small advantage of the appeal process is that there will be minimal involvement by you in the case. The lawyers take over for appeals and clients need not attend the argument of the appeal at the higher court. The lawyers will appear before that court with entirely new, fresh paperwork developed specifically for the appeal. The appeal may be argued before as many as three judges, at which time the lawyers will argue the law as interpreted by the trial judge. Rarely do the appeal judges give their decision on the spot, so yet another "reserved" decision can be expected. The appeal judges will deliver a complete set of reasons for their decision, just as the trial judge did. These decisions are considered most important by the lawyers and are often published in legal reporting services so that other lawyers are aware of them (so much for your privacy).

CLOSING REMARKS

SO, DO YOU still want to go to trial? Are you being forced to go to trial by an unreasonable person on the other side? I don't ask such questions lightly, because the first question you must answer is, "Why must I go to trial?" At the beginning of this chapter I noted that people go to trial when they have not settled their differences. Why haven't you settled yours?

MY ADVICE

Consider the following questions of this Pre-Trial Checklist once you have answered the questions above:

1. Have you received a full written opinion about the case and the issues involved?
2. Does the opinion letter discuss the likely time of trial and expected cost?
3. How long will the trial take?
4. Is it a fixed date?
5. Are you available when the trial is scheduled?
6. What is the theory of the case? How will it be presented to the court? Do you understand the structure of the trial? Have you been briefed in the methods of giving evidence? Have you reviewed the transcripts from the examinations for discovery?
7. Which witnesses will be called?
8. Have you executed a new retainer specifically authorizing the lawyer to conduct the trial?
9. What is the likelihood of success?
10. What Offers to Settle have been made? What effect will they have on costs at the end of a trial?
11. How much of a new retainer will you be required to provide in advance of the trial?
12. If successful, will the retainer cover the costs of collecting the judgment?
13. If custody is an issue, what role will your children play in the proceedings?
14. Do you understand the physical setting of the court? Will your lawyer arrange for a tour of the court in advance?
15. Have all the undertakings (promises to do something like provide copies of documents) been fulfilled and have you done your best to locate any missing pieces of evidence?
16. Have you completed updated financial statements?
17. Do you understand the likelihood of adjournments and delays once the trial is scheduled?

18. What is the difference between your likely net on the last settlement offer and your likely net at the end of a trial?
19. If custody and access are the issues, have you considered the use of mediation to resolve these particular disputes?
20. Once again, why are you going to trial?
21. What happens if you lose?

ALTERNATIVES
TO COURT

Mediation, Arbitration
and Collaborative Family Law

IT IS FAIR to say that until recently we, in Canada, have had a one-dimensional approach to solving family law problems. Our legal system, as you have seen from previous chapters, requires families to solve delicate issues such as custody of children or division of the family home in the same way that responsibility for car accidents, breached contracts or defective products is decided. This adversarial process leads to only one place—the courtroom. It is not a creative process. On the contrary, it encourages lawyers to promote one solution for the entire case and then battle to have their vision prevail.

This approach is particularly unsuited to families in crisis. Like labour disputes, family members must continue to deal with each other after the dispute is finally resolved. It was recognized many years ago that relations between labour and business were important enough that special methods were needed to resolve disputes quickly, inexpensively and without burning every bridge in the process. Mediation and arbitration are techniques well known to those in the labour field and are becoming increasingly popular in family law. In this chapter, we will examine these two methods of dispute resolution with special emphasis on mediation. We will also look at something new called Collaborative Family Law.

MEDIATION

IN MEDIATION, THE couple facing a family problem related to their separation uses a skilled third party to assist them in discussing the issue to reach a mutually satisfactory solution. Instead of having a judge impose a solution, the people design their own. There is no limit on the type of issue suited to mediation: Who should have custody? How should access be structured? Where will we live? How can we divide our furniture, our debts and our property?

Mediation's approach is different from the adversarial courtroom approach because the mediator encourages the parties to look at the problem from different angles and to develop an understanding of each person's needs and interests. The goal is not to develop two competing positions but to determine whether everyone's interests—especially the children's—can be met through some creative solution. Who is better able to develop such a solution than the parties themselves?

Mediation is voluntary and non-adversarial, and works best when a skilled, impartial mediator guides the discussion. Not surprisingly, those who have used mediation note that it provided them with new negotiation skills that then aided them in resolving subsequent dis-agreements. In a nutshell, mediation seems to be faster, less expensive and makes people happier with the agreement to the point of finding increased compliance with it. Mediation is the most important development in family law in decades.

Before looking at mediation in more detail, we should understand what it is not. It is not marriage counselling, which is designed to help a couple sort out difficulties in their relationship with a view to staying together or easing the emotional strain of ending it. Mediation is also not therapy, which is designed to help an individual sort out personal, emotional or psychological problems that affect them and their relationships with others.

Assuming a decision to separate has been made, mediation can offer a family a more humane method of tackling any issue, no matter how big or small. Its goal is joint planning for the future, not argument over the past.

Mediation has become more popular in Canada over the last decade through a combination of word-of-mouth and encouragement of its use by legislation. The federal Divorce Act, for example, was amended in 1986 to place a positive duty upon lawyers to advise clients of the wisdom of negotiating support and custody issues and of the availability of mediation services in their community. This provision has resulted in lawyers encouraging clients to try mediation for these issues.

Provincial laws also encourage the use of mediation. For example, Saskatchewan's Children's Law Act (in force as of October 1990) now mirrors the Divorce Act and requires lawyers involved in custody and access disputes governed by provincial law (you will recall that this happens when the couple is not seeking a divorce but still needs help with custody matters) to inform their clients about mediation facilities that might be able to assist in negotiating a solution. As in the case of the Divorce Act, the lawyer must certify that he or she has complied with this requirement.

Ontario's provincial family laws—the Children's Law Reform Act and the Family Law Act—do not require lawyers to specifically inform clients about mediation, but they do facilitate the use of mediation by allowing the court to order the parties to use it when they both consent.

Most provinces have such a provision in their provincial family laws and every province is governed by the Divorce Act. So, at the very least, husbands and wives who are divorcing and need assistance with custody and access will have mediation drawn to their attention. However, the biggest reason in my view for the growth of mediation is the fact that thousands of lawyers across Canada have taken training to become mediators. Many of these lawyers and others who provide mediation services have also been given extensive training in how to screen potential clients to ensure that there is no history of domestic violence. Violence creates an unequal bargaining power and could preclude the use of mediation.

Let's look more closely at the actual mediation process.

Process

FAMILY MEDIATORS ARE not regulated in any way by either federal or provincial legislation. There are national and provincial associations, however, that organize the membership through voluntary guidelines, accreditation levels, continuing education and so on. There is no requirement that a mediator join these associations prior to offering services to the public, so you must be cautious in selecting a mediator who is experienced and qualified.

An ongoing debate concerns whether mediators need any special educational background in order to assist a family with a problem. Some "mediators" seem to have no other qualification than having gone through a bad divorce themselves.

I was recently involved in a case where a couple went to see an accountant and asked him to act as a mediator/arbitrator in their divorce. This accountant was familiar with the corporate interests of the husband and, in my view, clearly had a conflict of interest in trying to mediate a dispute between his business client and the wife. After multiple sessions, there was a complete breakdown in the process. The accountant made an arbitration order after conducting a hearing in which the wife did not even participate. It was necessary to apply to the court to have the "arbitrator's" ruling thrown out. This was successful, but only at a cost of tens of thousands of dollars.

So while a potential mediator or arbitrator may be empathetic, he or she may not be qualified to conduct a mediation. Many of the best family mediators are lawyers, social workers or psychologists. At the end of this section we will discuss how to find a good mediator, but for now you should understand that the neutral third party who will conduct the mediation should be a qualified professional who brings some special skills to the dispute-resolution process.

The Mediator's Role

THE MEDIATOR'S ROLE includes a variety of functions and obligations. He or she must
  - be impartial (both you and your spouse are clients)

- control the mediation (mediators act more as chairpersons and will never impose a decision)
- keep the discussion on track
- work out a schedule for the meetings
- coordinate the sharing of information between the couple, such as financial information related to support
- keep the process confidential
- be vigilant to ensure that you get help from other professionals as needed (therapists, accountants)
- be careful to act only as a mediator and not, for example, give legal advice (if they are also a lawyer) or psychiatric advice (if a doctor)
- promote cooperation by helping to build goodwill and by reducing tension
- help you to develop your own negotiating skills
- ensure that domestic violence is not present
- compensate for subtle differences in the bargaining positions and abilities of the parties, and
- stay in touch with your respective lawyers to keep them up to date on developments.

Within these general parameters, the mediator leads the couple through the mediation process.

Role of Lawyers

DO MEDIATORS EXCLUDE the need for lawyers? In a word—no. Even if the mediator you have selected is also a lawyer, you and your spouse should each still have your own independent legal advice. The mediator is not there to provide legal advice. He or she facilitates the discussion and helps discover solutions and options. Your lawyer (so carefully selected at the outset, remember?) is there to make sure you understand your rights and obligations under federal and provincial law. He or she will also advise you on the merits of any agreement reached with the help of the mediator. It has been said that people negotiate in the "shadow of the law." This means that people should negotiate a settlement based in part on what would happen if the matter went to court. Lawyers ensure that a fair deal is achieved, one that will hold up over time.

The lawyer's role, therefore, also includes a number of functions and obligations. He or she must:

- meet the obligations imposed by the Divorce Act and, in some cases, provincial law with respect to available mediation services;
- keep up to date on qualified mediators and their professional qualifications and accreditation;
- explain to clients the relative advantages and disadvantages of mediation;
- be cautious to ensure that clients unable to negotiate effectively are not placed at an unfair advantage in negotiation with their spouse;
- stay in close contact with the mediator and client once mediation begins; and
- be careful not to undermine the mediator's work (he or she must scrutinize the agreement to protect the client but also protect the consensus that was achieved).

As you can see, the lawyer and mediator must work together closely to ensure a fair and lasting agreement.

Assuming you have found a mediator, for example, through a recommendation from your family lawyer, and both you and your spouse are willing to give mediation a try, the mediation process will generally move through different stages: identifying the issues, developing options and choices, making choices, developing the agreement and recording it after legal advice on its fairness.

Open or Closed?

AT THE OUTSET, the mediator will ask whether you would like to have the mediation "open" or "closed." If the mediation is "open," then statements made in mediation may be admissible later in court if the mediation fails to achieve an agreement. "Closed" mediation is the opposite—it's confidential. Nothing said in the sessions can be used in court (unless, of course, it is related to evidence of child abuse, which provincial law requires be reported). Some people feel that if the mediation is "open," the people using it will be less willing to speak openly—something that is essential. Mediators, however, report that open mediation does not seem to inhibit the discussions and that people speak freely regardless of it being open or closed. The choice is yours and it is an important one. Consider the choice carefully and discuss it with your lawyer and spouse.

In one case I am aware of, a husband and wife were separating because the husband had developed a relationship with a woman he met through a new church he had joined. There were two children involved, boys age 7 and 10, and they were justifiably anxious about what was happening. The father wanted joint custody (see Chapter 6: Obligations to the Children of a Divorce) of the boys, while the mother, who was quite angry, felt she should have sole custody. To complicate matters, the father wanted the boys to convert to his new faith, while the mother vigorously opposed any further disruption in their lives. Child support was, of course, linked to custody. The mother wished to move to her hometown to be near her family. Unfortunately, that was 2,000 miles away and the father opposed any move away from his good job and new church.

The mediator helped this husband and wife to organize these issues into a logical agenda that could be discussed without losing sight of the children's interests. That is exactly where they began, with a discussion of past childcare routines and parenting for the boys. The father's new faith was explored so the wife understood his new needs. The need for a move was explored, again with the focus on the children and their exist- ing routine.

They agreed to postpone the move and entered into a joint custody arrangement. This freed the mother to retrain to develop job skills, with support from the husband. The boys continued in their regular church but received some exposure to the father's faith, with a view to letting them make their own decisions down the road.

Memorandum of Understanding

THIS COUPLE LEARNED that it is possible to settle problems without one person winning and the other losing. The mediator kept track of the developing agreement and prepared a written memorandum of the final decision. The mediator's memorandum formed the basis of a more detailed Separation Agreement, which was prepared by the lawyers in consultation with the couple and the mediator.

Why, you may ask, did the couple not just sign the agreement prepared by the mediator? It's because there are often technical matters that the lawyers need to build around the clients' basic agreement. The mediator may not have discussed with the couple, for example, the precise wording of releases concerning property claims and so on. The lawyers will ensure that the agreement is legally correct, fair and what you want. It may be useful to review Chapter 9: Settling Your Differences and the section dealing with settling a case by Memorandum of Understanding.

Advantages of Mediation

THE ADVANTAGES OF mediation seem clear:
- You, as opposed to a court, make the decisions.
- The discussions are private and confidential.
- The process is faster than waiting for court dates.
- The solution is tailor-made for your circumstances.
- It can be less expensive than going to court.
- The agreement can be renegotiated if circumstances change.
- The process can teach you new negotiating skills that will help you resolve disputes in the future.
- You still have the benefit of a lawyer scrutinizing your agreement to ensure fairness and legality.
- It is a dispute-resolution method that leaves its users feeling better about themselves and happy about their agreement.

Some Concerns about Mediation

HAVING SAID THAT mediation holds great potential for families that are separating, it is not for everyone. It is a process suited to people who are in a relatively equal negotiating position. If one spouse is at a clear disadvantage, mediation may not produce a fair result.

For example, people who come from homes where there has been violence are unlikely to be able to negotiate with a spouse who has beaten or harassed them. So, violence that puts one spouse in fear of the other and unable to negotiate can prevent mediation. We will briefly examine domestic violence later in this book (see Chapter 16: Domestic Violence).

It is very important that each person come to the mediation prepared to negotiate in good faith. I have seen examples of a mediation process that was abused; one spouse simply agreed to participate in order to obtain disclosure from the other side in advance of attending to legal proceedings.

In yet another case, the spouse simply used mediation to delay matters and increase the expenses to both parties. I have also seen people use a mediation process in order to determine the other side's bottom line. Once that has been put on the table, the mediation is terminated, and the spouse commences legal proceedings.

The only caution, therefore, that I can urge upon you is that, while mediation is valuable, it must be undertaken for the right reasons.

Not every province delivers mediation services in the same way. Some provinces have publicly funded mediation services available for free. Other provinces and territories only have private mediation services on a fee-for-service basis, paid in full by the parties. Still others have a combination of free public services and private mediators.

While mediation is generally available in each province, it may be difficult to find a qualified and experienced mediator close at hand. You have a couple of options when searching for a mediator. First and foremost, if you have selected a good family law lawyer, he or she should have experience with local mediators and should have a list of three or four from whom you can select. In fact, your lawyer will likely provide a recommendation.

When you finally have a list of names to pick from and are meeting with mediators, do not hesitate to ask probing questions about the mediator's background, qualifications, experience and specialties. Some mediators do not deal with financial matters and some will only do custody and access, while still others prefer to do comprehensive mediation—tackling all the issues facing the family. Remember, the mediator is also anxious to see if the "chemistry" is right, so take full advantage of the introductory meeting, which is often free of charge.

You will wish to discuss costs. Most mediators charge an hourly rate ranging between $150 and $500. The cost is often much less than lawyers' fees because the process is faster and less protracted by paperwork and court dates. At the outset, most mediators will have an agreement with the couple about who will pay, how and how much. Usually the cost is split equally and billed directly to the clients. In some cases, the mediator may send the bill on to the lawyers, who in turn pass it on to the clients. I recommend spending as much thought on hiring the mediator as you did hiring your lawyer.

ARBITRATION

A FEW WORDS should be added about arbitration, which has been available for hundreds of years in commercial matters but has only recently found its way into family law. It is another alternative to going to court and is not unlike the use of a private judge. The parties select a private individual, often an experienced lawyer or a retired judge, to hear their dispute in private. After the hearing the arbitrator renders a decision, sometimes within 30 days.

Arbitration is attractive for a variety of reasons. It is completely private. The public and press (if that is a concern) do not have access to your private affairs. It can be significantly faster and more predictable than the public courts, which are busy and subject to delays, such as summer breaks, adjournments and other interferences.

Proponents of arbitration also point to the desirability of being able to select the "private judge" and to be able to have someone preside who is truly interested in a family law matter. This is not the case in the public courts, where judges are assigned to all sorts of cases, family law being about the least popular. Many judges are very devoted to family law cases but some are not, and assignments can be random.

The expense of arbitration is its weakness. The parties are still paying for two lawyers and now "the judge" as well. In the public courts, judges are "free" due to tax dollars paying their salaries. A private judge can cost between $2,000 and $3,000 per day for each day of a hearing. This cost is shared by the parties. However, for those who can afford it, the privacy and speed of the arbitration process can be attractive. Your lawyer will be able to arrange for an experienced arbitrator if you decide to go that route.

MEDIATION/ARBITRATION

WITH ADVICE FROM their lawyers, some people enter into a process that combines mediation and arbitration. In this approach, the individual selected to help the people reach a conclusion acts as both a mediator and an arbitrator. This person will spend the first part of the process meeting with the people and their lawyers, trying to resolve the whole case by agreement. In some cases, they are able to help the parties narrow the issues for the arbitration. However, if they are unable to come to an agreement, the mediation portion ends and the mediator's role changes to that of arbitrator. He or she will now consider the matter that remains in dispute as if he or she were a private judge.

One advantage of this process is that it certainly encourages people to work things out in the mediation phase. One disadvantage is that it can be difficult for an arbitrator to forget some of the things heard in the mediation and become a neutral decision-maker. If mediation/arbitration is being recommended to you, review all of the advantages and disadvantages with your lawyer prior to entering the process.

Another disadvantage to mediation and arbitration is a problem that develops in smaller legal communities, though it can even occur in larger centres. Lawyers prepared to act as mediators and arbitrators can get a reputation for good work and therefore receive numerous referrals. Those same lawyers will very likely continue to represent clients. In other words, one day they may be acting as a mediator/arbitrator, and another day they may be acting as a lawyer.

This has meant that a curiously incestuous situation can arise whereby lawyers who also act as mediators and arbitrators may appear before each other in those different capacities. You can imagine the reaction of a client who learns that on Monday of a given week his lawyer, acting as an arbitrator, appeared before another lawyer, but on Tuesday, roles reversed and that same lawyer, now the arbitrator or mediator, appeared before his lawyer in a case. Clients are justifiably suspicious when they learn that lawyers, arbitrators and mediators are changing hats and appearing before each other in different capacities. I now urge clients to ask a potential mediator or arbitrator whether they have other cases on with the lawyer involved for the other spouse. I believe lawyers are obliged to reveal this potential conflict of interest.

RELIGIOUS ARBITRATION

AN ISSUE AROSE in Ontario about the use of religious arbitrations. For many years it has been well known in the legal community that priests or rabbis will often conduct mediations and, in some cases, arbitrations for members of their faith going through separation and divorce. Some members of the Muslim community have expressed a wish to use Sharia law as a code for determining the outcome of family law disputes within their community. Concerns were expressed that Sharia law might lead to unfair results, and that if Sharia law were applied in private in a family law arbitration, unfair results would never be discovered and rectified. In addition, under the provincial Arbitration Act, individuals could give up the right of an appeal of the arbitrator's decision. This, too, could lead to unfairness.

The solution, in Ontario, has been development of a set of amendments to the Arbitration Act and the provision of special rules for "Family Arbitration." There is a requirement for independent legal advice prior to signing arbitration agreements. There are limitations on the ability to waive a right of appeal, and there is a requirement that family arbitrations take place under the provisions of the laws of Ontario or another Canadian jurisdiction. In other words, parties to an arbitration cannot oust the law of Canada. I expect that other provinces in Canada will enact similar limitations and those individuals going through separation and divorce will feel confident that the same rules apply to everyone, whether they are in a courtroom or a private arbitration.

COLLABORATIVE FAMILY LAW

OVER THE PAST few years, there has been a great deal of discussion about a new approach to practising family law called collaborative family law practice. It bears enough resemblance to mediation that I decided to include a discussion of it in this chapter.

Collaborative family law practice is a blend of soft-advocacy on behalf of a client and well-known mediation techniques. A mediator, as a neutral third party, is not employed by the client; instead, the clients and their lawyers enter into an agreement committing to reach a negotiated settlement themselves.

Importantly, the clients and the lawyers expressly forego any entitlement to litigate the matter in court while the negotiation is underway. This means that the threat of going to court over a particular issue is removed from the negotiations. A lawyer using this approach will undertake not to represent the client if the negotiation is unsuccessful and the matter proceeds to court. The parties are not releasing their entitlement to eventually take the matter into court if it is not settled. Rather, they are making a firm commitment to a negotiated process and are agreeing not to litigate or to threaten to litigate so long as the process is underway and is productive.

The role of the lawyer stays much the same as a usual law practice. The client's rights and obligations are researched and presented in the ordinary course, but the negotiations are characterized by respect among the parties and the lawyers, and good faith and voluntary disclosure of information, documentation and other evidence. The approach includes laying all of one's cards on the table in the hope that a settlement is achieved quickly, inexpensively and in a way that meets the needs of the clients, not to mention their children, if custody issues are involved.

However, I add this caution about collaborative law practice: everyone must be certain that it is not used to simply delay the inevitable. It will be a major disappointment if a great deal of effort and time is placed on a collaborative negotiation to discover that a new lawyer must be hired to start all over again if the matter does not settle. Discuss the appropriateness of collaborative law with your lawyer. In order to use the process, your lawyer will have gone through a special training program as a collaborative family law lawyer.

STRATEGIC CONSIDERATIONS

IT'S NO SECRET that I am of the opinion that the Canadian justice system is letting Canadian families down in the way in which it handles family disputes. While there are certainly exceptions in some courts and in some provinces, for the most part, the family law system is slow, insensitive, ineffective and not cost-effective for anyone.

Evidence of this can be seen in the fact that thousands of people are opting out of the justice system and using mediation, arbitration and collaborative family law. It is common to hear lawyers and clients dis-cussing the advantages and disadvantages of opting out of the system. One of the disadvantages that a lawyer would be required to discuss with the client was the increased cost. Let's face it—your tax dollars have already supposedly paid for the justice system. It is, for all intents and purposes, "free," and it is also your constitutional right. So, when a lawyer discussed with a client the possibility of opting out, he or she would have to explain that there would be an added cost for the media-tor or arbitrator or for the collaborative process, so the cost of opting out was a factor.

I had an interesting meeting with a very good judge, a person who really knows family law and has always shown great sensitivity on the cases before him. Another lawyer and I explained to this judge that our clients, who were involved in a very high-conflict dispute, were opting out to use a private arbitration. This judge raised his eyebrows and said, "That's acceptable if they can afford the expense of an arbitrator."

I explained to him that while they could indeed afford an arbitrator, the problem was that they could not afford to *stay in the justice system*. He looked alarmed as I explained that two lawyers and two clients had basically spent the entire day for the second time waiting to meet with a judge so that they could obtain permission to schedule other days for re-attending at the court. In other words, the clients had spent thousands of dollars paying lawyers to simply sit around waiting for meetings at the court. That money, the lawyers and clients had decided, would have been better spent paying an experienced and sensitive family law arbi-trator to simply deal with the case quickly and effectively. So, ironically, we are now in the position where more and more Canadians are opting out of the justice system because they cannot afford to stay in it.

I fear that we are headed toward a two-tier justice system, where poor, self-represented people stay in the publicly funded justice system (Judge Judy—paid for by taxpayers) and middle-class and well-to-do people simply opt out and "buy private justice" from an arbitrator.

This raises some strategic considerations. Discuss carefully with your lawyer the wisdom of participating in a mediation. The process should be conducted in good faith—it should not be used as a fishing expedi-tion. I have participated in mediations where it became clear after just a few hours that the lawyer and client on the other side were simply using the mediation process to fish out useful information and try to determine our bottom line as an advantage in negotiations. I have also participated in mediations where it was clear the other side was using it as a method of delay and a method to run up costs. I mention these aspects of mediation/arbitration so that you will review these advantages and disadvantages with your lawyer before you go into the process. It must be conducted in good faith or it can be abused.

Another problem that we have seen in the mediation/arbitration area is the very common requirement that the decision be kept confidential. As the process is private, the decision is private. This means that we no longer have a large base of published court decisions to help us resolve cases. Many legal observers are concerned that a vast body of law is disappearing into the private, closed files of lawyers and arbitrators. Sadly, this is a price that the justice system is paying because it is driving people out.

CLOSING REMARKS

MEDIATION/ARBITRATION AND COLLABORATIVE family law have a lot to offer Canadian families. They are more responsive and at times more creative in the way in which problems can be solved. They are certainly more humane processes for families. For a variety of reasons, we will see increased use of these approaches.

MY ADVICE

1. Mediators and arbitrators are not necessarily certified by the government; anyone can offer this service. Make sure you have a qualified mediator or arbitrator.
2. Get recommendations for mediators and arbitrators from your lawyer or provincial associations.
3. You should still use a lawyer for independent legal advice on any agreement reached in mediation.

4. Only use mediation in good faith, and be cautious to ensure that your spouse is acting in good faith. Do not allow mediation to be used for delay, to obtain disclosure or to determine your bottom line.

5. Ask whether your mediator/arbitrator has a conflict of interest or other cases with the lawyers involved.

ENFORCING FAMILY LAW ORDERS

Making an Order Stick

O BTAINING A COURT order for custody, access, support, property division or any other aspect of family law is one thing—enforcing the order can be another matter altogether. One cannot assume that the other person will simply abide by the order of the court; remember, they may feel that they have "lost" in court and that this order is an unwanted imposition. When faced with a spouse who refuses to comply, the spouse with the order may wonder, having gone through the expense and tension of the court proceeding, what to do next.

Enforcement issues can arise in some odd circumstances. Perhaps a custodial parent refuses to allow a child to go for an access visit, or an access parent refuses to return a child on time. Sometimes, child support is not paid, or not paid in full. In other situations, families rely on restraining orders or orders for exclusive possession of the home, and police enforcement may be required. In the most serious situations, children are abducted by a misguided parent and both the criminal and the civil justice systems are asked to respond.

In this chapter we will examine in a general way each of the family orders from the perspective of enforcement.

CUSTODY ENFORCEMENT

Criminal Law Custody Enforcement

IT IS A criminal offence in Canada to abduct a child who is under the age of 14 and who is the subject of a custody order. If the child has been taken from the custodial parent with the intention to deprive that parent of the child, then the abducting person (95 per cent of abductions are by non-custodial parents) may be found guilty and punished with up to 10 years in jail. This is the case whether the "custodial parent" actually has a court order for custody or not. However, if the parent does not have a custody order, before charges can be laid, the parent must obtain permission from the Attorney General of the province in which he or she resides. If an order has been made for custody, the court will look at the terms of the order and whether it provides for sole custody or joint custody, then it will decide whether the "abducting parent" had an intention to deprive the other parent of custody at a time when that parent was entitled to custody.

Problems can also arise even if there is no order for custody of the child, for example, in cases where the parents simply separate or where they separate and agree that the child will live with one of them but they never obtain an order from the court. In other situations, there is a court order for custody that was not made by a Canadian court.

A Wisconsin father who abducted his children and took them to Winnipeg after the Wisconsin court had ordered that the mother should have custody was charged under this part of the Canadian Criminal Code and the children were returned to their mother. These children had been told that their mother was dead.

If the custody order was made by a Canadian court, it can be enforced immediately anywhere in Canada through the abduction provisions of the Criminal Code. However, the abducting parent may have a couple of defences available.

DEFENCE TO ABDUCTION CHARGE: CONSENT OF THE CUSTODIAL PARENT

No conviction will be obtained where the person with custody consented to the child being removed by the other person. It is not uncommon for parents to live in direct contravention of the court's custody order. The order may say that the mother is to have custody, but the child actually lives with the father. This could happen if circumstances changed and, for example, the mother became ill and could not care for the child. There may have been little reason at the time to amend the court order if the intention was that the child would eventually return to the mother's custody. However, if the father decided to move out of the province, the mother would have difficulty alleging that the child was being abducted if she had originally consented to the child being in the father's custody.

DEFENCE TO ABDUCTION CHARGE: IMMINENT HARM

It is also a defence to an abduction charge if the child was taken to protect him or her from "imminent harm." This situation would arise where the non-custodial parent discovers that the custodial parent is mistreating the child. An example would be where the father had custody but could not care for the child and the mother refused to return the child after an access visit for fear that the child might meet with harm. An abduction conviction against the mother would be unlikely in such a situation.

CHILD'S CONSENT IS NOT A DEFENCE

It is no defence to a charge of abduction that the child consented or suggested that the change in custody take place. This prevents the parent from pressuring the child to agree with any suggested changes.

THE BENEFIT OF the Criminal Code provisions is that once a charge is laid, a Canada-wide warrant for the abductor's arrest will be issued to all police forces. The criminal enforcement route is faster, which is critical when the person may be attempting to flee the jurisdiction.

Many provinces have adopted a standard protocol for responding to an abduction of a child. In most, if not all, cases the custodial parent will require a lawyer's assistance. Start with the custody order itself. A legible copy of the order, certified by the court if possible, should be kept in a safe, accessible place at all times.

One of the issues addressed in the standard protocol concerns domestic violence. How can the police and a Crown attorney (who would be called upon to lay the charges) distinguish between an abduction and a parent who is fleeing domestic violence and is simply taking the children with her? Such determinations are made on a case-by-case basis.

Even if the abducting parent is located with the child and criminal charges are laid, it can be difficult to arrange the return of the child. The warrant only brings the abductor back. It is often necessary to involve the local child-protection agencies, which can take custody of the child until the custodial parent or his or her designate can arrive. The best solution, of course, is for the police to coordinate their arrest of the abductor with the presence of the custodial parent.

Parents faced with abductions should also contact Child Find Canada, a non-profit organization with offices across Canada in each province. They will assist in locating missing and abducted children. Call 1-800-387-7962 or visit their national website (which is particularly helpful) at www.childfind.ca, or any of the individual provincial websites, which provide more localized advice. Child Find will assist in reuniting the child and the custodial parent.

Civil Justice Enforcement of Custody Orders

THE CIVIL JUSTICE system can also be used to respond to parental child abduction. The two primary considerations in a civil enforcement case are the child's welfare and a fair and proper administration of justice. Not every case is a clear-cut abduction and in some circumstances the custody order simply needs to be enforced in another jurisdiction.

The provinces and territories have all passed laws to speed enforcement of each other's custody laws. The goal is to enforce, with minimal fuss, the other province's custody orders and return the child to the jurisdiction that made the order. Each province enforces the other province's orders as if they were its own, to discourage the abducting parent from trying to have the order reconsidered in the new province. There are exceptions, of course. If the court thinks the first order was made by a jurisdiction to which the child did not have a strong connection or everyone is now present in a new jurisdiction and a review is appropriate, the court may reconsider the whole matter of custody. Also, if the child might meet with harm if the custody order was enforced, the court may choose to substitute its own order for the other province's order.

THE HAGUE CONVENTION ON CIVIL ASPECTS OF INTERNATIONAL CHILD ABDUCTION

All of the provincial legislatures have adopted The Hague Convention on Civil Aspects of International Child Abduction and enacted legislation to facilitate enforcement of extra-provincial custody rights. This Convention, which has been accepted by many countries, attempts on an international scale to secure the prompt return of children wrongfully removed to, or retained in, a country that has signed the Convention. It also attempts to ensure that rights of custody or access under the law of a country are respected by other countries. It applies to children who are under the age of 16. If a child is wrongfully brought from the country in which he or she habitually resides into Canada, then The Hague Convention can be used across the country. These laws attempt to prevent the re-hearing of custody cases in the new jurisdiction.

The following is a partial list of major countries that will enforce the child abduction provisions of The Hague Convention:

- Argentina
- Australia
- Austria
- Belize
- Bosnia and Herzegovina
- Burkina Faso
- Canada
- Croatia
- France
- Hungary
- Luxembourg
- Netherlands
- Norway
- Portugal
- Spain
- Sweden
- Switzerland
- United Kingdom (England, Northern Ireland, Scotland and Wales)
- United States (extends to American Samoa, Guam, Northern Marianas Islands, Puerto Rico and the U.S. Virgin Islands).

Some countries that do not offer enforcement of The Hague Convention include:

- Egypt
- Japan.

For more information about use of The Hague Convention see the following websites:

- www.hcch.net
- www.freemychild.com

ABDUCTION

IF FACED WITH the abduction of a child, consider the following tips:

- It may be necessary to hire a private investigator to locate the child. Private investigators can be very effective and often have sources of information available to them that others do not. In some provinces, legal aid will pay for the cost of the private investigator if the need for one is reasonable in the circumstances.
- Provincial law provides for an order requiring others to assist in the search for a child. This can enlist the help of other enforcement agencies, such as a local sheriff's office.
- It is a criminal offence to obtain a Canadian passport falsely listing a child as one's own, contrary to a custody order. Sometimes a parent will forge the custodial parent's signature in order to spirit the child out of the country. The penalty for such an offence is two years in jail.
- While the custodial parent may be able to recover costs of locating and recovering the child, he or she cannot sue for damages for emotional distress that may have been suffered as a result of the abduction.
- The federal government enacted the Family Orders and Agreements Enforcement Assistance Act, which will help a custodial parent trace an abducted child through the federal information banks. However, individuals do not have direct access; for reasons of confidentiality, a provincial enforcement agency must request the information.

Thinking about Abduction?

THIS ADVICE IS for parents who have considered abducting their own children. First, as justified as you may think you are, the courts will take an extremely dim view of the abduction. If caught, and there is a great likelihood that you will be caught, the court will be under pressure to make an example out of you to discourage other parents from such actions. Few people will see you as a martyr if you are imprisoned for abducting your own child.

Second, barring some life-threatening situation, it is next to impossible to characterize the abduction as being in your child's best interest. Robbing a child of the other parent can be catastrophic. Lying about the other parent's death or whereabouts will seriously undermine your credibility and the child's confidence in authority figures. Abduction is very rarely a realistic alternative.

CANADA CUSTOMS AND TRAVELLING OUTSIDE CANADA

Travel Documents and Consents

WHEN TRAVELLING OUTSIDE Canada, carry identification for your child regardless of his or her age. This can be a birth certificate, baptismal certificate or passport. Parents who have custody should carry relevant court orders, Separation Agreements or other legal documents. An adult who is not a parent or guardian should have the written permission of the parent as well as the child's identification.

Family law lawyers are often contacted on the eve of a vacation because the parent who will be travelling with children wonders whether there will be a problem at the border. More and more often, there are big problems. It is not unheard of to have families turned around at the border or at airports because they do not have the permission of a non-custodial parent or a custodial parent to be travelling with a particular child after separation and divorce. These permission letters should be obtained in advance of travel. They are not complicated and could read as follows.

To Whom It May Concern:

Re: Travel of (name of child and birthdate as it appears on a passport or birth certificate)

This is to confirm that the above-named child will be travelling with (name of parent as it appears on a passport or birth certificate) in (for example, the United States) between March 15, 201-, and March 24, 201-. I wish to confirm that (name of parent again) is travelling with (name of child again) with my permission. If you have any questions or comments, please do not hesitate to contact me at (telephone number).

Signed this ___ day of _____, 201-.

_____

(Signature of Parent)

_____

Witness

Parents travelling should have an original version of this consent ready with their passport in case a question arises at the time of crossing the border. In some situations, the lawyers will provide a notarized copy of this letter to ensure that the travel takes place without difficulties. Some countries seem to have more respect for the notarized document than a simple original signature.

Canada Customs uses a national database of high-risk travellers, known as the Primary Automated Lookout System (PALS), to verify traveller information. In some cases, they will also use a hand-held computer system that provides images of missing children. As well, their computer has access to the United States Immigration database.

Parent Withholding Consent to Travel?

YOU ARE WELL advised to plan ahead and ensure your travel will take place with the other parent's consent. If that consent is not available, it may be necessary to apply to the court for an order authorizing the child to travel with you. Orders allowing the travel will be made unless there is a very good reason to not permit travel. The courts will not frustrate family vacations simply because someone is being vindictive. If the consent to travel is unreasonably withheld, more often than not, the court will also order legal fees against the parent who is trying to block travel. In other words, if you oppose your child travelling outside the country with the other parent, you should have a very, very good reason, such as fear of abduction.

ACCESS ENFORCEMENT

MANY NON-CUSTODIAL PARENTS have orders that entitle them to "reasonable" or "liberal" or "generous" access. When access is denied, these terms are virtually impossible to enforce. The parent with such an order will be required to return to court to have the access converted into something more specific. If the specific access is then denied, the non-custodial parent is in a position to try to enforce the order.

In most provinces, when access is denied, the non-custodial parent has one remedy: to request a finding of contempt of court against the custodial parent. This means that the non-custodial parent must convince the court that the denial of access was a wilful interference with the non-custodial parent's entitlement to access.

It should be noted that the police will rarely, if ever, assist with the enforcement of an access order, knowing that there are civil remedies available for the enforcement of the access order. They will generally refer you to your family law lawyer.

The standard of proof required on a contempt hearing is higher than for normal civil proceedings (which is on the "balance of probabilities"). The non-custodial parent must prove the wilful denial beyond a reasonable doubt. If successful, the court has two options: jail or a fine for the custodial parent. Neither is appropriate in most cases, since the fine is only depriving the family of much-needed money and the jail sentence is often out of proportion to the access denial itself. The result is that neither penalty is imposed and the access denial goes unpunished.

Courts have been struggling to find ways to improve access enforcement. In some provinces the court has permitted a custodial parent to avoid punishment for contempt by giving them an opportunity to purge their contempt through the provision of "make-up time" with the child. This is simply giving back to the non-custodial parent, on another occasion, the time denied with the child, thereby making up for the time that was lost. If this is done, the contempt is ignored and no penalty is imposed. In other cases, the courts have restructured access to ensure that the contact occurs and that there are regular pickup and drop-off schedules.

The latest and most serious way in which access can be enforced against an interfering custodial parent is to reverse custody. A parent who finds his or her access continually frustrated or denied is sometimes only left with the option of returning to court and asking for custody. As a part of that application, the parent undertakes to the court to ensure that the other parent has regular contact with the child. This is considered an absolute last resort, but it has been done. There is a new attitude toward access enforcement when it appears that the access denial is a form of parental alienation. In the past, courts were prepared to give a custodial parent the benefit of the doubt and suggest that the family go slowly and go for counselling. The new attitude in the court is the opposite—that access denials that appear to be part of a larger parental alienation strategy should be dealt with quickly and firmly. Parents may be found in contempt of court. Parents who deny access may find that the access schedule is much more rigorously set out and enforced, with specific dates and times, as well as drop-off and pickup locations. In addition, courts have been prepared to order supervision of the custodial parent's exchange of the child.

So, with a few exceptions, access enforcement is still undergoing reform in Canada, with contempt power threatened but rarely enforced. The contempt power is slow, expensive (one motion can cost as much as $5,000) and burdensome, and those who use it must seek penalties that the court is reluctant to impose.

Two unfortunate consequences of poor access enforcement concern child support and custody-order compliance. The courts of several Canadian provinces have now made orders suspending child-support orders until access provisions are complied with. In these cases, the court, frustrated by a custodial parent's refusal to permit access, ordered the non-custodial parent not to pay support. This, of course, is a double punishment for the child. Poor access enforcement has long been an excuse used by non-custodial parents for the non-payment of support. This connection may become stronger if non-custodial parents turn to withholding support as a means of access enforcement. Those faced with access denial should not withhold support from the family unless a court has ordered it. Similarly, those with custody should not withhold access because support has not been paid.

The other issue, which is more difficult to assess, is custody-order compliance. Perhaps it is an act of anger designed to punish the custodial parent for their perceived failings in the relationship. There is no doubt that it is harmful to the child, and a non-custodial parent would be hard pressed to justify any abduction. Some people are now asking whether poor access enforcement influences the non-custodial parent's decision to abduct a child. They note that parents who are happy with access are not likely to abduct. Good access-enforcement provisions in provincial laws would certainly help.

To avoid problems, consider the following:

- Avoid access orders that provide only for "reasonable," "liberal" or "generous" access. Have an access entitlement specified, right down to the days, times and specific holidays. The parents can always agree to more access, but at the very least set out a minimum amount of access for reasons of certainty if enforcement is needed.
- Consider calling the arrangement "joint custody" rather than access. The provisions can be the same, but the change in terminology can result in easier enforcement should difficulties arise.

There is no substitute for having an access order set out in very precise terms so that if enforcement is required, there will be no confusion and the court can deal with it swiftly and firmly.

SUPPORT ENFORCEMENT

VIRTUALLY ALL PROVINCIAL and territorial governments, with support from the federal government through complementary legislation, have established "support enforcement programs." These programs have been established at a cost of tens of millions of dollars to provide support creditors with free enforcement of their orders. (By "support creditor" I mean a spouse who is awaiting either spousal support or child support, and by "support debtor" I mean the person who is supposed to be paying either the spousal support or the child support.) Governments have an obvious stake in this service because those who do not receive support tend to rely on public assistance at a cost of further tens of millions of dollars to taxpayers. The justice system is also drawn into disrepute when its orders are considered unenforceable.

Before examining some of the individual features of the provincial and territorial services, we should consider the methods used by the services themselves to enforce support orders. These techniques may vary slightly from province to province, but they are all basically the same.

The most popular method of enforcing a support order is through the attachment or garnishment of wages. The court in this situation allows the deduction of a fixed amount from the pay of the support debtor on a continuing basis. The amount requested is remitted to the Support Enforcement Office, which then sends the cheque on to the support creditor.

Many people are under the mistaken impression that the Support Enforcement Office issues a cheque each month to the support creditor for the full amount of the support order and then begins to enforce the order. This is not the case. The Support Enforcement Office only sends a cheque for the amount actually collected. If nothing is collected (perhaps due to a lack of employment), then nothing is sent. If only half the amount owed is collected, then that amount is remitted to the support creditor. The attachment or garnishment of wages can be an effective method if the support debtor has a regular job. Most jurisdictions place a limit on the amount of wages that can be taken through this method (usually a maximum of 50 per cent). This leaves the support debtor with money to live on while at the same time allowing him to meet his obligations to the family.

Another method of enforcement is the Writ of Execution or Warrant of Distress. These are essentially orders of the court to the local sheriff to seize any land or property owned by the support debtor in order that it be sold to pay the debt owed. This applies to land, furniture, cars, bank accounts and so on. It is effective only against property in the particular province that is enforcing the court order. Few debtors are foolish enough to let property be lost in such a way. When push comes to shove, they make a payment. Even fewer seem to have property available against which the writ can be executed.

The court has the power to imprison a support debtor for non-payment, but this is rarely used unless the debtor can clearly pay but wilfully refuses. Although judges are reluctant to jail people for non-payment, in the few cases where I've seen this used, it was quite effective. After the support debtor spent a few hours in jail, the money was found.

Other methods for collection of support orders include ordering the support debtor to post security that would then be forfeited if he or she did not pay as ordered. Some provinces now permit the support order to be registered on title to property owned by the support debtor. This could, for example, block a refinancing of the property until a support order is paid and ultimately even force the sale of the property to meet the support debt. Driver's licence suspensions are also used in some provinces. Some provinces, through their Support Enforcement Offices, have the power to arrange for the appointment of a receiver for the support debtor's property or business in order to facilitate payment.

But as you can see, the above remedies are only effective when the person actually has property or money. If support enforcement is to be effective, Support Enforcement Offices will need to be able to seize wages quickly and efficiently to impress upon a support debtor the need to pay. Only tough enforcement will form the habits necessary for ongoing compliance.

The Support Enforcement Offices

THROUGH SUPPORT ENFORCEMENT Offices, support enforcement is automatically initiated, monitoring and tracing are available, and government computers and lawyers are there to track down and enforce the support order at no cost to the support creditor.

The type of system may vary from province to province. For example, in Alberta, Manitoba, Ontario and Saskatchewan, all support orders made by the court are automatically entered on the system for enforcement. The support creditor need not do anything other than get the support order in the first place. Furthermore, in Ontario, every order made by the court is required to have a direction in it to the director of the Support Enforcement Office. The couple can opt out under very limited circumstances, such as posting three months' support as security.

By contrast, British Columbia has an "opt-in" system, which requires the support creditor to take the support order to the office and ask that it be enforced. It is the only privately run Support Enforcement Office in Canada.

Regardless of which system is in place, creditors are free to enforce the order themselves with the help of a lawyer in private practice. They do so at their own expense, of course, and would only consider that route if the Support Enforcement Office was failing to respond to their immediate needs.

Once in the system, the support debtor must make all payments to the Support Enforcement Office, which, as already mentioned, remits the amount collected to the support creditor. As you might have guessed, computers play a large role in this type of system. Payments are recorded as they are made; if one is missed, the computer notifies the enforcement personnel, who respond with the most appropriate enforcement procedure—usually a garnishment or wage assignment. In some cases, a "show cause" is needed, whereby the support debtor is summoned before the court to explain, to show the cause of, his failure to pay the order.

An important function of the Support Enforcement Office is tracing. Provincial and federal data information banks can be searched to locate the address, place of work, sources of income and other important information of support debtors. These tracing powers were put in place with great emphasis on the protection of privacy, and the information obtained may only be used for the purposes of enforcing a support order or custody order and nothing else.

At the federal level, there is search access to the Canada Pension Plan data banks and Canada Employment Insurance Commission data banks. Provincially, driver's licence information, health insurance data and other provincial benefits can be searched to assist in the location of a support debtor.

Assuming the search of federal data banks turns up some information, federal monies that may be owing can be garnished to satisfy the support order. Money that can be seized includes:
- income tax refunds;
- EI benefits;
- interest on Canada Savings Bonds;
- CPP benefits;
- Old Age Security benefits; and
- a variety of agricultural benefits payable to farmers.

At the provincial level, similar benefits have been identified for diversion if the support debtor is not meeting the support obligation. In Ontario, a large lump-sum payment to a doctor under the provincial health insurance plan was intercepted for non-payment of support (yes, even doctors don't pay their support).

I strongly recommend that anyone seeking information about support enforcement visit the federal government's website, www.justice. gc.ca. It provides an overview of enforcement and has many useful explanatory notes. As well, you will find a link to each provincial and territorial agency.

One would think that with so much effort, support orders must surely now be paid routinely. No such luck. The reality is that most of these services are overburdened and cannot begin to enforce as vigorously or as effectively as needed.

My personal view is that we need to go back to the drawing board on support enforcement in each of the provinces and across Canada. I was involved in the development and implementation of Ontario's support enforcement system, and the current approach is well beyond anything that was originally imagined when the service was created. In many cases, the enforcement systems simply processed cheques that might otherwise have been paid from one party to another. It's my opinion that the support enforcement system should return to a concentration on difficult enforcement cases and should provide incentives for people who pay directly, in a timely way and in full. I have never understood why our income tax system allows a parent who has been delinquent with child support to continue to deduct spousal support that has been paid.

In my view, there ought to be a method that links the federal tax system with the deductibility of spousal support payments and the failure to pay child support payments so that those who do not pay when they are quite capable of doing so are penalized.

PROPERTY ENFORCEMENT

THE LITIGATION OVER the family property may produce a judgment in favour of one spouse for a significant amount of money if the family assets were of considerable value. As we saw in Chapter 5: Dividing the Family's Property, some potentially large assets are now subject to division on marriage breakdown: pensions, homes, cottages, bank accounts, GICs, cars, boats and so on are all available for division. Judgments can be in the hundreds of thousands of dollars, but, again, the judgment is of little use if it cannot be enforced.

For spouses who are legally married, this can be a relatively easy exercise if the family property is still owned by one of the parties. Most provincial family laws permit the court, at the time of judgment, to order the method by which the judgment is to be paid (or satisfied, as lawyers like to say). So, for example, if at judgment the wife is owed $250,000, then the court can order that certain pieces of property be transferred to her in order to pay that debt. The husband may be ordered, for example, to transfer his interest in the matrimonial home to her in satisfaction of the judgment. This method is very practical and saves the couple further time and trouble with the enforcement of the judgment. Unfortunately, this power is not available for common-law spouses in every province because each system varies.

Assuming property is not transferred at the time of judgment, a spouse who is entitled to money may use a number of different enforcement procedures. These include a Writ of Execution, which is registered on title to land owned by the debtor spouse, garnishment or attachment of wages and, if no assets are readily available, an examination in aid of execution. This is also sometimes known as a "judgment debtor exam."

In this procedure, the lawyer summons the debtor spouse into an inquiry (like the discoveries) in order to examine the debtor spouse, under oath, as to his or her ability to pay a particular judgment. A transcript is prepared and the debtor's assets can be pursued with the information obtained during the examination. Each enforcement step can be expensive and time-consuming. This type of enforcement should not be undertaken unless the creditor spouse has a detailed discussion with his or her lawyer about the cause of this predicament (that is, of having a judgment and no property to seize), what the expected cost of the enforcement will be and what the likelihood of success is considered to be in the circumstances.

The "judgment and no property to execute against" situation raises an important aspect of property enforcement that begins long before the judgment itself is obtained. It is known as the "restraining or preservation order." At any point in the legal proceedings, a person concerned about a particular piece of property in dispute may ask the court for an order restraining the owner of the property from dealing with it in any way. For example, a husband who owned a valuable coin collection could be restrained by court order from selling that coin collection until the trial is finished and a judgment has been rendered. This preserves the property in case it is needed to satisfy the judgment or in case the property itself is ordered transferred to the other spouse. Restraining orders with respect to property should be obtained at the outset of any legal proceeding.

A restraining order may go beyond a prohibition of selling the property to include even using it as security. So, for example, a wife could be prohibited from increasing the amount of a mortgage registered against a cottage that was in her name alone.

Orders for Possession

ANOTHER TYPE OF family law order is the order for exclusive possession of a matrimonial home. This type of order does not affect ownership of the home, but determines who may possess it or live in it during the period leading up to a trial. The criteria may vary a little from province to province, but the goal is the same—to give possession of the home to the spouse who needs shelter and could not find alternative accommodations. It is not uncommon for the parent who is given interim custody of the children to also have possession of the matrimonial home until the case is decided.

The order of possession of the home, as we have seen in Chapter 5: Dividing the Family's Property, prohibits the other spouse from being on the property. In Ontario, for example, the breach of an order for exclusive possession is a provincial offence punishable by a fine and/ or a jail sentence of a considerable length. Subsequent offences are punished even more severely. To enforce such an order, the spouse in possession should always have a certified copy of the order for possession of the home and proof that it has been served on the other spouse. If that spouse then appears at the home in contravention of the order, the police will know in an instant that he or she is aware of the order and can be arrested and removed from the property. In Ontario, the officer may even arrest the offender without a warrant.

The order for exclusive possession is considered to be an important tool for the protection of spouses where there has been violence in the home.

PERSONAL RESTRAINING ORDERS

A DIFFERENT KIND of restraining order is one that restrains a person from doing something. This type of order may, for example, restrain one spouse from "molesting, annoying or harassing" the other spouse and children. It can be a blanket prohibition of contact or a more specific prohibition of contact at all times except those specified in the order. In the latter case, the order may prohibit contact except on, for example, Friday evening at 7 p.m. so that a father may speak with his children or pick them up for access.

In jurisdictions where a specific punishment is not prescribed, the court may enforce orders for restraint of a person through the use of its contempt power. In Ontario, this type of order is enforced the same way as the order for exclusive possession. A breach of the order is treated as a provincial offence punishable by fine or jail and places the offender in a position of being arrested without a warrant.

In some cases, the criminal-law procedure must be used to control a violent or unruly spouse. The Criminal Code allows the court to order that an accused person enter into a peace bond. This means that the spouse agrees to be on good behaviour and to have no contact with the other spouse, directly or indirectly. If the peace bond is breached, the recognizance—usually $500 or $1,000—is forfeited and the spouse can be convicted of breach of the peace bond. A peace bond, therefore, has the same effect as a restraining order.

This procedure has some advantages over the civil restraining order. For example, it is free. The Crown attorney prosecutes the case and the offending party must hire a lawyer to defend the charges. If a restraining order was sought in family court, then the person who wants the order must hire a lawyer, prove the case and then push for enforcement.

However, the criminal peace bond should be used for legitimate situations of criminal behaviour. Inappropriate use can cause matters to escalate out of control—especially if a spouse may face a criminal conviction and a record.

CONTEMPT

TELEVISION HAS FAMILIARIZED everyone with the concept of "contempt of court." Usually, a judge is warning a misbehaving lawyer about some courtroom antic. Again, reality is quite different. The power to find someone in contempt of court is the court's way of controlling its own process, of making sure that people follow the Rules of Court, whether big or small. This type of enforcement is necessary to ensure the smooth and respectful functioning of our courts.

If a person using the court process shows a wilful disregard for the court's rules, the court can punish that contempt in an appropriate way—through a jail sentence, fine or denial of access to the court's remedies. Most provinces have given the court this power through specific legislative provisions or through the Rules of Court themselves. Some courts are considered to have this power inherently and the judge may invoke the power on his or her own, but usually only does so if one of the parties before the court has urged a finding of contempt against the other spouse. Regardless of the source of the power of contempt; it is a potent method of enforcing the court's orders because the judge ultimately has the ability to jail someone he or she considers to be wilfully disregarding the court process.

Because someone's freedom may be at stake, the courts have developed very rigorous standards for making a finding of contempt. If a motion is brought asking the court to find someone in contempt because they have ignored a court order, the person asking for the finding of contempt must follow these standards closely:

- The request for a finding of contempt must be served on the person personally, not through a lawyer.
- The conduct complained of must be clearly wilful. Any confusion will prevent a contempt finding.
- All the facts must be disclosed to the court at the outset.
- Contempt must be proved beyond a reasonable doubt—as if a crime was being alleged.
- There must be no other appropriate way of punishing the conduct.

This power is used rarely and only as a last resort to protect the administration of justice.

Jail sentences and fines are rarely appropriate in family cases and are saved for the most blatant misconduct. Judges, however, have an equally effective method of controlling the process when relatively smaller types of misconduct occur: they can refuse to let the offending person do anything else in the case until the conduct complained of has been remedied. For example, if a husband undertook at the discoveries to produce copies of his income tax returns for the previous three years but has failed to do so, then the court can deny him any court orders until he has produced the income tax returns as promised. If he still refuses to produce them, the court can strike out his case completely (claims and defences) and simply give his wife judgment for her claim. In this way, the court controls the case before it.

CLOSING REMARKS

AS YOU CAN see, obtaining the family law judgment is sometimes less than half the battle. Enforcement can be just as time-consuming and just as expensive. An essential early step in any family law case is the discussion with your lawyer about the likelihood of recovery and the best methods of recovering any final judgment. Don't let someone tell you, "We'll cross that bridge when we come to it." Orders that cannot be enforced are of no value. Concrete plans can be made right at the outset of a case to ensure compliance with any order that is finally made by the court.

MY ADVICE

1. Only the police can use the criminal law to arrest a person for child abduction. Report a suspected abduction immediately.
2. The court will not accept that the child consented to being taken as a defence to abduction.
3. The only defence to a charge of abduction is that the child was in imminent harm or the custodial parent consented to the child being removed.
4. Call Child Find for advice about suspected abduction.
5. If the abduction involves leaving the country then consult a lawyer about The Hague Convention on Civil Aspects of International Child Abduction.
6. Make sure travel consents for international travel by a child are clear and set out a full itinerary.
7. Make sure access orders or agreements are specific. A court cannot enforce "reasonable" or "liberal" access. Put in specific days and times.
8. For support enforcement use the provincial enforcement agencies—they are free.

GRANDPARENTS AND "OTHER INTERESTED PERSONS"

O VER THE LAST 20 years, I have happily accepted an invitation to speak on a Sunday afternoon to a support group for grandparents who wish to maintain contact with grandchildren after their own children have divorced or died, or, in some cases, an intact family is denying them access to their grandchildren.

Most afternoons I estimate the number in attendance to be approximately 30 to 40 people. They come from all across Ontario and some from as far as the United States. Their stories underscore the sometimes forgotten consequence of marriage breakdown, the ending of common-law relationships or, sadly in some cases, the death of their own children. If we remember that there are approximately 100,000 divorces a year affecting nearly 75,000 children, we can safely estimate that there are hundreds of thousands of grandparents who are affected in some way by family breakdown. Many more are drawn into conflict over their grandchildren as a result of death, substance abuse and other personal tragedies.

Grandparents, of course, are not the only ones unexpectedly caught in the legal difficulties of couples separating or other tragedies—aunts, uncles, brothers, sisters and others can all be drawn into the dispute over children.

In this chapter, I would like to examine a special aspect of family law that, although it is really a part of custody and access considerations, merits separate treatment because of its importance to Canadian families.

GRANDPARENTS: A SPECIAL STATUS

THE SPECIAL ROLE of grandparents in a child's upbringing has long been a vital component of Canadian society. Unfortunately, it is taken for granted, and only recently have Canadian courts begun to grasp the importance of a grandparent to grandchildren after separation, divorce or death. The role of grandparents has changed over the years with the increasing mobility of families, the frequency of divorce and the impact of other tragedies, but their special status remains.

It is not uncommon now to see grandparents having a prominent role in their grandchildren's lives. In many families, they are the day-care providers. Grandparents are often an important source of heritage and continuity to a family. Sadly, however, some grandparents have found themselves cut off from their grandchildren by divorce, by tragedy or by some other family dispute. A grandchild can become a chattel that is wielded as a prize to be withheld or granted if the grandparents "behave properly" and comply with their adult children's demands. I have seen cases where families have actually extorted so-called "loans" from their own parents by withholding contact with a grandchild. Many lawyers have seen cases where grandchildren are caught in the crossfire between grandparents and sons and daughters-in-law. What seems like invaluable help one day can suddenly be seen as meddling and interference on another day. Grandparents who are considered a valuable part of a grandchild's life can suddenly have a door slammed in their faces without explanation.

This is not to suggest that all grandparents have some divine right to be with their grandchildren. There have been cases of grandparents who have attempted to use access to a grandchild as a means of disrupting their own children's marriages. Whatever their personal axe-to-grind, these grandparents have placed their children in a position of choosing between an ongoing relationship with their parents and looking after their own children.

In my experience, the problems that grandparents encounter fall into one of four categories:

1. where their children are separating and divorcing, or separating after the end of a common-law relationship
2. where a child has died and the surviving spouse has custody of the grandchildren
3. where there is an intact family and the mother and father of the child decide, for whatever reason, that the grandparents should not have a significant role in the upbringing of the grandchildren
4. where grandparents end up in disputes with third parties, such as the Children's Aid Society (CAS), because their grandchildren have been taken into care, perhaps on an emergency basis, and the grandparents wish to have the grandchildren taken out of foster care and placed with them—and what seems an obvious choice to many may not seem obvious to the CAS

1. Divorcing or Separating

THE FEDERAL DIVORCE Act and various provincial family laws deal with this issue by permitting persons other than the parents themselves to start or participate in legal proceedings affecting a child. Depending on whether the family is undergoing a divorce or is intact, different rules will apply. Let's first consider the situation of a couple divorcing where custody and access to their child is in dispute.

It can be difficult to watch from the sidelines as a son's or daughter's relationship goes sour. This is particularly so if the parents had doubts about the "wisdom" of the union in the first place. Rarely does the problem surface suddenly; more often than not, and well in advance, everyone in the family circle knows the marriage is in difficulty. Opinions and advice may already have been offered, with parents being drawn into the dispute and being asked to take sides.

If the couple's situation is acrimonious and a custody dispute looms, the grandparents may be on pins and needles wondering whether their role with the grandchild can be maintained and whether picking any side, other than their own child's, is advisable. Questions occur to grandparents: What if the son-in-law gets custody and moves back west? What if the daughter-in-law gets custody, remarries and the child has a new stepfather? Will there be step-grandparents? A new world may await the child and adjustments for the family circle will be inevitable.

The Divorce Act, as we have seen, applies only when a legally married couple is divorcing. It does not apply to "intact" families or separating common-law spouses. The Act provides for persons other than the parents to apply for custody or access to a child of the marriage in the divorce action itself. It does not use the word "grandparent" specifically, but the words "other interested person" clearly include grandparents. So, any person, including a grandparent, may apply, but the Act also provides that they must first get the court's permission to intervene. This means that if a couple separated and filed for a divorce, the grandparents could, with the help of their own lawyer, apply for permission to intervene in the divorce action. If permission is granted, the grandparents may ask for custody of or access to the child.

In deciding whether to grant permission, the court will examine the past connection between the child and the grandparents. Is there a real connection between them? Why is the grandparent applying to intervene? What is in the child's best interest? Once permission is granted, the request for custody or access is decided like any other, by asking simply: "What is best for the child in this family?"

A special consideration will be the obvious constraints on the child's time. There is only so much time to be parcelled out to the parents, the grandparents (both sides) and any others who have an interest in this child's life. The issue becomes how much time, realistically, this child has for all of these people. The court will strive to maintain as much continuity as possible in the child's life while the parents try to build new lives for themselves.

2. Death of a Child

WHERE THE CHILD of a grandparent has died and the surviving parent is looking after the grandchildren, no divorce proceeding will be under way, so there will be no action in which a grandparent can intervene. In such a circumstance, the grandparent will have to initiate a court action pursuant to the provincial custody law.

3. Intact Families, Married or Common Law

WHAT IF THE family is not divorcing? Perhaps the marriage or relationship is intact but the grandparents are being denied contact with the child for a particular reason. The problem could be one that surfaced because of the remarriage to a new partner. In this situation, the Divorce Act would not permit the grandparent an opportunity to intervene. However, most provincial family laws offer some recourse to grandparents in this position because they contemplate "other interested persons" applying for an order with respect to children. These laws do not necessarily speak in terms of marriage breakdown or divorce and may thus be used by a grandparent faced with an intact family or a common-law relationship that has ended.

In Manitoba, the provincial law acknowledges that grandparents have a special place in the lives of grandchildren and the law provides an express right for a grandparent to apply for custody or access. Cases that have reviewed the Manitoba law have decided that there is no need for a grandparent to provide some exceptional reason for them to remain involved in a grandchild's life.

Ontario's Children's Law Reform Act provides that a parent of a child or "any other interested person" may apply to a court for an order respecting custody or access to a child. Grandparents seeking access to children in intact families have used this provision. The test applied is, "what is in the best interests of the child," and the court considers all the needs and circumstances of this particular child. The best-interests test includes a consideration of the relationship by blood between the child and each person who is party to the application.

In a British Columbia decision, the judge commented that "any person" might include blood relatives, relatives by marriage, grandparents, aunts, uncles (including in-laws), babysitters, foster parents or daycare workers who have developed some relationship with the child.

Attitudes vary from province to province about the degree of latitude in use of the provisions, and a lawyer should be consulted to determine whether or not a particular province's law has been applied successfully on behalf of grandparents. Dozens of successful cases have occurred right across Canada.

A word of warning, however. Occasionally, grandparents have applied for access to their grandchildren and lost. The court will only do what is best for the child, and there has been one highly publicized case in Ontario where the grandparents came under considerable criticism by the court as being completely unsuitable for contact with the grandchild. Those grandparents were ordered to pay their son's legal costs in defending against their weak claim for access to a grandchild.

In April 2001, the Ontario Court of Appeal gave a decision in the *Chapman v. Chapman* [2001] 15 RFL (5th) 46 case, where a 77-year-old grandmother was attempting to maintain a relationship with two grandchildren, ages 8 and 10. The Chapmans were an intact family who were uncomfortable with the amount of access the grandmother wanted to the grandchildren. They were prepared to allow her to have, at most, six visits per year. The grandmother stated that this was not adequate and the situation deteriorated.

At trial, the judge ordered that the grandparent could have 44 hours of access to be exercised over 6 to 10 visits. The parents were uncomfortable with this and appealed. The Court of Appeal stated that the test was not about what was best for the children in theory, but rather what was in the best interests of the particular children before the court. The court went on to state that a relationship with a grandparent can and ideally should enhance the emotional well-being of a child. When positive relationships are imperiled arbitrarily, as happens when there is a divorce or other re-organization of the family, the court may intervene to protect the continuation of the benefit of the relationship to the children. The court supported the parents' decision to control the amount of access.

Importantly, the court stated that, generally speaking, if parents were behaving in a way that demonstrated capability of looking after the children, then their right to make decisions and judgments about the children's best interests would be respected. This included decisions about who the children would see or not see. Generally, the parents will be allowed to make these decisions; however, the court will intervene if it is only a poor relationship between a grandparent and a parent that is causing the denial of access to the grandchild. Where there is an established record of the grandparents being interested in the child, the court is also more likely to award access. There is almost a presumption that it is best for a child to maintain contact with those who would bring the child's heritage forward. There is a delicate balancing act between the parents' rights and the possible contribution of the grandparents.

Cases before the courts have suggested consideration of a number of questions when looking at these problems:

1. Are the concerns expressed by the custodial parent for denying access reasonable?
2. Is the access that is being denied important to the child's well-being?
3. Is it possible that the denial of access to the third party may have a long-term negative impact on the child?
4. Will the access to a third party have a negative impact on the custodial person's relationship with the child?
5. Will access put undue stress on the parent?
6. Will access be confusing to the child?
7. Is the grandparent showing a controlling, bossy or divisive attitude toward the grandchild and the parent?
8. Will access interfere with the stability of the intact family such that it would eliminate any obvious benefit to the child?

I expect that we will see ongoing judicial and court interpretation of grandparents' rights vis-à-vis their grandchildren. A significant case, known as *Troxel et vir. v. Granville,* 530 US 57, 120 S. Ct. 2054, was decided by the United States Supreme Court. It dealt with the situation of grandparents trying to maintain a relationship with their grandchildren after the children's father committed suicide. The mother did not want them to have access. The United States Supreme Court took the approach that reaffirmed the presumption in U.S. law that fit parents act in the best interests of their children and can therefore control access with grandparents. The court supported the mother.

There may be a tendency to interpret this decision from the U.S. Supreme Court and the decision from the Ontario Court of Appeal as inhibiting the ability of the grandparents to apply to the courts for custody of or access to their grandchildren. I do not agree with that interpretation and would suggest that any grandparent who can demonstrate that an ongoing relationship with the child is in that child's best interest should certainly consider a court application as a possible option. Remember, there have been many cases decided in Canada where grandparents have been given custody of or access to their grandchildren.

Several years ago in Toronto, a panel of senior judges and lawyers considered grandparent access problems. There was near unanimous agreement that where a grandparent has a positive contribution to make to a child's life, access will be ordered. Consult your lawyer about your rights under provincial law.

4. Grandparents Fighting Third Parties

IN OTHER SITUATIONS, the grandparents may find themselves pitted against a Children's Aid Society (CAS). If the parent of the child is suddenly faced with a trauma—jail, a drug overdose, a mental breakdown—or has simply disappeared, the CAS may be called to intervene on an emergency basis. The child could be placed in emergency foster care before the grandparents are even aware of the problem. Once notified, they may find themselves trying to convince the CAS to release the child into their custody. Remarkably, in such cases the CAS officials may ask the parent, if available, what he or she thinks about the grandparents having custody. If the relationship has been strained, they may say no and leave the child with CAS or a foster family. Such struggles can be heartbreaking for grandparents as they realize they must use provincial law to obtain custody of their grandchildren from the provincial authorities.

"OTHER INTERESTED PERSONS"

AS I MENTIONED at the outset, others besides the grandparents may be interested in the children at marriage breakdown. Across Canada, dozens of cases have tested the applicability of the expression "other interested person" in custody and access applications. Consider the following, who have applied—not always successfully—for custody of or access to a child:

- a man who claimed he was the father of a child but whose paternity had not yet been established
- a child's stepfather
- a former common-law partner of the child's mother
- a grandmother and an aunt together
- the child's biological mother after she had given the child up for adoption
- the child's biological father after the biological mother had given the child up for adoption
- a former adoptive father
- a babysitter
- foster parents
- a stepsister and her husband, and
- an adult family friend.

I have seen cases where the paternal and maternal grandparents fought each other for custody of the grandchild and a case where a maternal grandmother fought a great-aunt for custody. The same considerations with respect to the advisability and cost of legal proceedings apply for anyone in these categories.

These cases, whether they involve grandparents or other family members, serve as a serious reminder of the ripple effect of divorce and marriage breakdown. More than the child's parents and the child himself or herself are affected—the child's whole world has an interest.

STRATEGIC CONSIDERATIONS

THIS CHAPTER RAISES some important considerations for grandparents—the advisability of legal proceedings, alternatives to court and the expense of legal proceedings.

The advice in Chapter 3: Taking a Look at the Process, about hiring a lawyer who specializes in family law, applies equally to grandparents who are considering such an application to the court. The commencement of legal proceedings should be seen as an absolute last resort. If the relationship between the grandparent and their own child is beyond the point of no return, the court will do little, if anything, to salvage it. I recommend family counselling in such cases and, if possible, the use of mediation to sort out the underlying problems that have created the barrier to contact between the child and their child's grandparent.

Legal fees can be considerable in these proceedings and should be reviewed, in detail, with the lawyer at the outset. Discuss the likelihood of success based on cases like your own that have been undertaken. If there are none, you may find that you are the test case and much depends on your individual circumstances.

I think a reasonable place to begin is a private conversation between the parents of the child and the grandparents in the absence of the grandchildren themselves. The purpose of the meeting should be to assure the parents about the following:

- that you as grandparents do not sit in judgment on either their decision to separate or their parenting abilities;
- that you as grandparents have had a role in the grandchild's life that has been positive and that you want that role to continue; and
- that the overriding consideration should be what is best for the child and that you want to develop a plan that allows you to contribute to the grandchild's life.

Be patient in approaching these matters. It is certainly advisable to take the long view. It may be that contact with the child will have to be established in small increments. I am familiar with one case where a grandparent painstakingly re-established contact with his granddaughter by submitting to two years of supervised visits. In other words, he had a third person from the local CAS present whenever he had access to his granddaughter. He did not feel that the supervision was necessary and, in fact, felt that it was a little insulting, but he complied. Within that two-year period, the CAS became convinced that he was a very positive influence in the granddaughter's life and recommended an end to the supervision. Later, the granddaughter herself suggested that there was no need for anyone other than her and her grandfather to schedule and arrange meetings and they resumed a normal granddaughter-grandfather relationship. The grandfather was extremely patient and everyone benefited. (After all, aren't grandparents famous for their patience?)

The point of this private conversation should be to let the parents of the child know that you want to understand their decision to exclude you from the child's life and why they think that this decision is best for the grandchild.

Do not threaten to sue, to withdraw financial support, to eliminate inheritances or to penalize the couple in any way. To do so suggests, perhaps proves, that you are not actually acting in the child's best interests after all. If you feel strongly, you are free to make whatever arrangements you wish without them knowing, but I believe it is a mistake to connect those decisions to spending time with the grandchild.

If the meeting is refused or is unproductive, you should seriously consider obtaining legal advice from an experienced family law lawyer about your likelihood of success in a court application under either the Divorce Act or provincial family law. The proceedings may take several months and will be expensive. Certainly, family relations will worsen, but most grandparents in such circumstances realize they have no choice.

CLOSING REMARKS

AN INCREASING NUMBER of these cases will be brought forward. I have noticed that many of the grandparents seeking custody of or access to grandchildren are younger and more and more able to fight to maintain a role in their grandchildren's lives. I have also noticed a genuinely sympathetic attitude among judges when dealing with grandparent cases. One might consider if this is because many of the judges may be grandparents themselves.

MY ADVICE

1. Check your provincial law to ensure that you have the right as an interested person to apply to the court for access to a child.

2. Be strategic in approaching the parent who has custody of the child.
3. Be patient, take the long view and be prepared to maintain or re-establish contact with the child in small increments.
4. Do not threaten to sue or withdraw financial support or eliminate inheritances. If this is a consideration, keep it separate from the access or custody matter and keep it private.
5. Consult with an experienced family law lawyer about legal proceedings, which should be taken only as an absolute last resort.

MARRIAGE CONTRACTS
AND COHABITATION
AGREEMENTS

Managing Your Relationship Contractually

I N THIS CHAPTER, we will briefly examine two other kinds of domestic contracts, the Marriage Contract and the Cohabitation Agreement.
For more thorough information on these topics, please see my other
books *Do We Need a Marriage Contract? Understanding How a Legal Agreement Can Strengthen Your Life Together* and *Do We Need a Cohabitation
Agreement? Understanding How a Legal Contract Can Strengthen Your Life
Together.* (For further information about these titles, please visit www.
michaelcochrane.ca and www.legalintel.ca.)

Marriage Contracts and Cohabitation Agreements have a different purpose than the most common type of domestic contract, the
Separation Agreement (which we studied in Chapter 9: Settling Your
Differences). Separation Agreements are designed to settle disputes that
have arisen over property, custody, access and so on at the time the relationship ends. Marriage Contracts and Cohabitation Agreements are
designed to avoid disputes in advance by setting out the couple's agreed
intentions about important things like property division or support.

Marriage Contracts and Cohabitation Agreements are for people of
different legal status. Marriage Contracts are for those who are married

or intend to marry, while Cohabitation Agreements are for those who are living together or intend to live together.

In looking at these areas, we should never lose sight of the fact that these arrangements are contracts, pure and simple, designed to deal with a specific issue the same way a contract to purchase a car or house is a written record of an agreement that has been reached.

Every province's family law contemplates couples making such agreements, and the technical requirements are not difficult to meet. Just as in the case of a Separation Agreement, these contracts must be written, signed by the parties and witnessed. They can be signed before or after the marriage or cohabitation commences.

With this in mind, let's examine each type of contract in more detail with a view to seeing why they are needed, how they are made and how they are broken.

MARRIAGE CONTRACTS

A MARRIAGE CONTRACT is an agreement entered into by a man and a woman (or same-sex couple) who are married to each other or intend to marry (in which case it is sometimes called a prenuptial), in which they agree on their respective rights and obligations under the marriage or on separation, annulment or dissolution of their marriage or on death.

No one is quite sure how many couples are turning to Marriage Contracts as a planning device for their marriage, but one thing seems clear—more couples are exploring the possibility and in some cases actually signing them. Lawyers report often being consulted about them, although many contracts are left unsigned when the issues touch nerves within the relationship.

The need for a Marriage Contract seems to arise in three circumstances: in anticipation of the marriage, after the marriage has taken place and some new circumstance has arisen or in stitching back together a marriage that is falling apart. Each can produce dramatically different situations for the couple.

I know of an incident where a bride-to-be was presented with a Marriage Contract at her wedding rehearsal. Her fiancé told her, rather sheepishly, to take the contract to a lawyer and have it signed—before the wedding. The message was clear, if not spoken—if it's not signed, there will be no wedding. This is probably the best example of the worst way to handle a Marriage Contract. In fact, weddings have been cancelled or, worse, contracts have been signed under circumstances of virtual blackmail. What a way to start a marriage!

In negotiating a contract before the wedding, people are usually attempting to do one of two things: exempt some specific property (a home, pension, business) from division in the event of separation and divorce or they are completely opting out of the province's scheme for division of property and providing their own scheme. Rarely will you see a couple opt out after the marriage has taken place.

In discussing the proposed exclusion of an asset from division, it is fair to ask why this asset should not be shared. Is there some emotional, financial or other reason to exempt this asset? The most common example would have to be the case of the person entering a second marriage and bringing a home. Perhaps the home was inherited or is the chief asset from the property division after the first marriage. These concerns may be quite legitimate and can probably be met with some creative alternatives.

If the goal of property division at the end of a marriage is to ensure that the fruits of the marriage are shared equally or that one spouse is not left disadvantaged because the other spouse holds all the property, then special assets can be protected through the provision of some alternative security. Perhaps the spouse with the home can take out an irrevocable life insurance policy payable to the other spouse, or some other asset will not be divided equally in order to provide balance. The possibilities are limited only by the assets available and your imagination.

Perhaps one of the most difficult Marriage Contracts to negotiate is where the need for it arises after the marriage has taken place. For example, in Ontario the value of all assets, including business interests, are shareable on divorce. This means that if a person's marriage fails, his or her interest in a company, a partnership or other business is at risk of division in the family property dispute. Business partners or the bank may not wish to expose themselves to the risk of the business being tied up or devalued by the dispute. In such circumstances, business partners have sent each other home to obtain Marriage Contracts from the spouses. In such a contract, the spouse is asked to release any claim he or she may have to an interest in the business. This may be necessary to obtain a line of credit at the bank or other form of financing.

Sometimes the release can be obtained by substituting a full interest in some other equivalent asset. For example, the wife releases the husband's business and he releases any interest in the matrimonial home or her pension. Naturally, values would need to be fairly equivalent. If a separation occurred, he would keep the business and she would keep the house. This example is relatively simple. Situations can be more difficult if the business is the only asset.

Another matter that is often provided for in Marriage Contracts is spousal support. In the contract, the couple agrees in advance how support would be handled if a divorce took place. They may simply agree to not ask for support from each other if the marriage ends, or they may agree to an actual monthly amount and a fixed term, depending on how long the marriage lasted and the need.

On a scale of lesser importance, some spouses have felt the need to provide for the division of household cleaning and childcare responsibilities. Personally, I feel that if you need to put such things in a contract, you have bigger problems than you think. However, there is no legal restriction against including such provisions. I'm not sure how they can be enforced, but if putting it in helps, why not? At least expectations are clear.

A third reason for signing a Marriage Contract is what I refer to as "stitching back together" a marriage that has been in trouble. Sometimes a couple will encounter problems in the relationship and move toward separation. During the course of the discussions between lawyers, it may become evident that the couple could reconcile under certain circumstances. In that situation, lawyers have used a Marriage Contract to deal with the issues that have arisen in the marriage, provide protections for each spouse, and then have the couple continue in the marriage with the new set of rules. If the marriage does not work out, the Marriage Contract comes into force and acts almost as a Separation Agreement for the couple. If the marriage is successful, then the Marriage Contract need never be invoked. This solution is not for everyone, but it has worked for some couples.

On the other side of the coin, there are some things that one cannot put in a Marriage Contract—or if you do put them in, they will not be binding on anyone or the court. For example, a couple may not provide for custody of or access to their children in advance of separation. The child's best interests cannot be ascertained in advance, so such provisions are not binding. Similarly, attempts to set the amount of, or to avoid altogether, child support are not binding.

It is permissible to agree to "child-rearing methods" such as method of education, religious instruction and so on. So, parents could agree in advance of marrying that any children born will be given, for example, a Catholic education or a bar mitzvah.

At the time of separation, legally married spouses are given special rights to ask for possession of a matrimonial home, regardless of ownership of the home. Any attempt to give up the right to ask for possession in a Marriage Contract is not binding. This is designed to protect people from putting themselves in a very vulnerable position without knowing what circumstances they could face when separating. The spouse can give up the right to ownership of the matrimonial home but cannot give up the right to ask for possession of it at the time of separation.

These contracts can have important consequences for one's entitlement to support and property at the end of the marriage, so they should not be entered into lightly or in the absence of independent legal advice. Circumstances will change. Children may be born. Career choices may be made, property may be sold, illnesses may develop and so on. Couples who simply agreed to have separate property at the outset of the marriage have found themselves in an awkward situation 15 years later when one of them has given up a career to raise children. The contract is still binding on them and may only produce a patently unfair result for one of them.

The courts have been more than willing to enforce and uphold these contracts. Where they have been set aside, it has been because the agreements were grossly unfair.

Just a few years ago, the Supreme Court of Canada dealt with a case called *Hartshorne v. Hartshorne*. In that case, the couple signed the Marriage Contract between the wedding ceremony and the reception. Both had had independent legal advice. The wife's lawyer had told her that the agreement was unfair and should not be signed. The wife signed it anyway. Years later, the couple separated and the wife asked to have the Marriage Contract set aside because it was unfair. The court upheld the Marriage Contract, in part because the wife had received independent legal advice and signed the agreement even though she had been advised not to. I think the court took particular interest in the fact that both the husband and the wife were lawyers and perhaps should have known better.

In short, when negotiating a Marriage Contract be cautious, be fair, get legal advice, and think about your future and the need for the contract. An unfair contract will haunt you both.

COHABITATION AGREEMENTS

A COHABITATION AGREEMENT is a contract entered into by a man and a woman (or same-sex couple) who are cohabiting or intend to cohabit and who are not married to each other, in which they agree on their respective rights and obligations during cohabitation or on ceasing to cohabit or on death.

Like Marriage Contracts, we have no accurate estimate of how prevalent these contracts are among cohabiting couples. Based on my discussions with lawyers, they are still relatively rare. Many more people consult lawyers about them than actually sign them.

The purpose of the Cohabitation Agreement with respect to property is to provide a property division scheme where none exists. You will recall from Chapter 8: Common-Law Spouses Have Rights Too that one of the difficulties a common-law couple faces when their relationship ends is the reconstruction of their financial or other contribution to property that they jointly acquired. It is necessary for them to prove who acquired which property for what purposes and with whose money. A Cohabitation Agreement can avoid that type of historical review of the relationship by providing for a particular method of division. Options include:

Separate Property Scheme

EACH SPOUSE KEEPS what he or she acquired in his or her own name. If something is registered in his name, such as the car, it is his. If a piece of property is not registered in any way (furniture), then whoever paid for it keeps it.

Community of Property Scheme

THIS IS ACTUALLY the opposite of the separate property scheme since all property, regardless of registration or source of payment, is divided equally. In effect, the couple agrees to treat their property as if they were married.

Family Asset Scheme

THE COUPLE IDENTIFIES types of property that will be considered "family assets" and would, therefore, be divided equally regardless of registered title or source of payment (home, savings, furniture, vehicles, cottage). Other property (business, pensions, personal investments) would be divided on the basis of a separate property scheme.

Provincial Property Scheme

THE COUPLE OPTS to be treated as if they were legally married and therefore covered by the provincial family law for property division, whatever it may be. Alternatively, they may select a particular jurisdiction's scheme. If they moved to Canada from France, they may want to follow that country's rules.

These are the general options available, but the couple is free to develop whatever scheme they wish. Cohabitation Agreements may also provide for spousal support in the same way as a Marriage Contract. That is, the individuals may waive support or set an amount, depending on their wishes.

The same restrictions discussed with regard to Marriage Contracts and provisions dealing with custody, access and child support apply in Cohabitation Agreements. The court never considers itself bound where children are affected. However, as in a Marriage Contract, the couple can agree to educational and religious training of the child in advance of cohabitation.

Other matters of importance include the following:

- Marriage will turn a couple's Cohabitation Agreement into a Marriage Contract.
- Amendments to either a Marriage Contract or Cohabitation Agreement are made the same way the contract itself is made (written, signed, witnessed).

SETTING ASIDE DOMESTIC CONTRACTS

NO MATTER HOW good one's intentions or how clever one's lawyer, these contracts (and here I include Separation Agreements) can be set aside by the court. Why enter into them at all if the court will just set them aside? While the court has the power to set them (or provisions in them) aside, it will not use that power lightly and will, therefore, do so in very limited circumstances.

The court may set aside a valid domestic contract for the following reasons:

- One person failed to disclose an important asset or liability.
- One party did not understand the nature of the contract.
- Any other reason acceptable in the general law of contract.

Let's consider briefly each one of these reasons.

Failure to Disclose

SINCE THE KEY to the domestic contract is more often than not financial or property arrangements, everything related to the calculations or property division scheme must be revealed. Most lawyers will not allow clients to sign domestic contracts unless each person provides a sworn financial statement setting out all of their assets and liabilities with accurate values.

The court will usually set aside an agreement where the failure to disclose relates to a significant asset or liability that existed when the contract was made. The meaning of "significant" will vary from case to case depending on the full asset and liability picture for the couple. The court looks to see if one spouse is trying to take advantage of the other spouse. Are they being unfair? Is one preying on the other?

The failure to disclose need not be a deliberate attempt to mislead; accidental failures are still valid grounds to set aside the whole agreement or just parts affected by it.

Failure to Understand

IF ONE OF the people signing the domestic contract did not understand the nature or consequences of the agreement, the court may set it aside. This ground is very difficult to establish if both people have received independent legal advice and have signed statements to the effect that they understood what they were doing and were doing so voluntarily. You will recall the affidavits and statements signed at the end of a Separation Agreement that set out the fact of the lawyer's independent legal advice or the availability of it. These same affidavits are attached to Marriage Contracts and Cohabitation Agreements if they have been prepared by a lawyer.

In one case, a man had his wife sign a handwritten summary of how they would like to have a Marriage Contract prepared. In it they summarized their assets and liabilities and exempted some of his property from sharing if they split up. They both signed it and had a friend witness it. When the husband took it to the lawyer, he was told that technically it was already a Marriage Contract. The wife thought that it would be used as a starting point for negotiating between the lawyers. She didn't appreciate that this was a contract (its nature) and that she was giving up property rights (its consequences). The lawyers eventually agreed that the court would probably set it aside, so they started over.

Contractual Failures

YOU WILL RECALL my statement at the outset that domestic contracts are just that, contracts. The general law of contract, therefore, applies to them and any available ground for setting aside a contract will apply to a domestic contract. These grounds include such things as mistake, fraud or public policy reasons. If the couple makes a serious mistake about the law or their assets when negotiating the contract, the court may set it aside. For example, if the couple thought that neither of them was entitled to support after their common-law relationship ended, they would have both made a mistake about the law that likely affected their agreement.

If one deliberately deceived the other to the extent that the contract was actually an attempt to defraud the other, the court will intervene. In one case, a young man moved in with an older woman and, over time, tried to defraud her of her life savings. He had an agreement prepared that he asked "a friend" to witness for them so he could have control over some of her assets. It was a form of a Cohabitation Agreement. No lawyers were involved—until the woman's family found out and stopped the fraud.

There is a general ground available in contract law that allows the court to ignore contracts or parts of them that are "against public policy." This means that if the court considers a particular term offensive, it will ignore it. For example, if a woman promised never to have children for the rest of her life or if someone agreed to be a virtual slave to another person, the court would refuse to enforce it. The meaning or extent of "public policy" can vary as society changes.

Religious Barriers

ONTARIO'S FAMILY LAW Act and the Divorce Act have unique provisions concerning Jewish divorces. These provisions are designed to deal with a curious and unfortunate practice that had arisen within the Jewish community when marriage breakdown occurred.

Briefly, in order for Jews to divorce, the husband must give and the wife must receive what is known as a "get." It amounts to a contractual release from the religious marriage. Without it, Jews cannot remarry within their faith. The husband is under no obligation to provide it and in some cases it is used to unfairly pressure women into inappropriate settlements. Typically, the subject of the "get" would arise during the discussion of the Separation Agreement. The husband would give the "get" only if, for example, the property was divided in his favour or if he was given custody or generous access rights, etc.

The new laws have short-circuited this process by giving the court the power to set aside any agreement in which the giving of the "get" was a factor. The language of the provision in the Family Law Act is general and does not refer specifically to the "get." It speaks in terms of "the removal by one spouse of barriers that would prevent the other spouse's remarriage within that spouse's faith."

The application to non-Jews is considered to be minimal or non-existent, but should be considered by all faiths as possible grounds for setting aside domestic contracts.

CLOSING REMARKS

MORE AND MORE couples are consulting lawyers about Marriage Contracts, particularly where it is a second or third marriage and the couple wishes to protect assets that they have managed to preserve from their first divorce or perhaps after the death of a spouse. No statistics are kept, but my own estimate, based on anecdotal experience and discussions with other lawyers, suggests that less than 10 per cent of Canadians who are marrying or cohabiting enter into Marriage Contracts or Cohabitation Agreements. This is a shame, because not only is a couple passing up an opportunity to design their own method of resolving difficulties that may arise in the marriage or its separation, but they are also passing up an opportunity to do financial planning and potential estate planning. Sometimes it is possible for a couple to not only sign a Marriage Contract or Cohabitation Agreement but to also do their wills and Powers of Attorney at the same time. I hope we continue to see more couples using Marriage Contracts and Cohabitation Agreements.

MY ADVICE

1. Marriage Contracts and Cohabitation Agreements are contracts like any other and are enforceable.
2. It is recommended that independent legal advice be obtained prior to signing a Marriage Contract or a Cohabitation Agreement.
3. Full financial disclosure is required in order to have an enforceable Marriage Contract or Cohabitation Agreement.

4. Marriage Contracts and Cohabitation Agreements will be set aside if one spouse did not understand the nature of the contract, if it is unfair and against the general law of contract or if someone did not make a proper financial disclosure.
5. Be fair with your life partner.

FAMILY LAW AND
YOUR WILL

N THIS CHAPTER, I briefly examine the making of a will in the context of family law. It is not my intention here to provide you with a
blueprint for will making or estate planning. However, there are
some special considerations that should be kept in mind about your will
at the time of separating or divorcing.

MAKING A WILL

THE MOST VALUABLE piece of advice I may be able to offer in this
chapter is simply to make a will. Thousands of people avoid this essential bit of financial planning; however, the fact remains the same—if you
care about your hard-earned money and about protecting your family,
then you should make an appointment with a lawyer who has experience with estate planning and have a will prepared.

Not having a will means that your estate would be considered an
"intestacy," which will mean considerable delay, the hiring of lawyers
and the wasting of your estate's resources by needing to find someone
to distribute the estate for a fee. All law offices have computers that will
produce the necessary clauses for making a will, and the whole exercise

takes very little time. In fact, it is one of the most inexpensive pieces of legal work available from a law firm.

The point of making a will is to plan the distribution of your property after your death. The vast majority of wills provide simply that the property goes entirely to the surviving spouse or to the surviving spouse and the children of the marriage in particular portions.

I strongly urge that when you consult a lawyer about the making of a will, you consider the preparation of two forms of Power of Attorney. A Power of Attorney permits you to appoint a trusted person to make decisions on your behalf with respect to your personal care and/or your property if you're incapable or unable to do so.

Usually lawyers will prepare a separate Power of Attorney for each requirement, so you will have a Power of Attorney for personal care, which allows the person to make decisions about your health, personal needs and, for example, housing, and a second Power of Attorney for property. This second Power of Attorney permits the person you have appointed to manage your bank accounts, real estate investment and the payment of bills.

I strongly recommend that when you consult your lawyer about a separation and divorce, a Marriage Contract or Cohabitation Agreement, or any family problem, you should also have your lawyer prepare the full package containing a will and Powers of Attorney. Once they are prepared, put them in a safe place and let the person you've appointed know where to find that authority if it is needed.

When clients meet lawyers to discuss their wills, two common concerns are expressed from a family law perspective. First, the possible effect of family law property division rules on the planned distribution of the estate and second, the effect of a child's marriage breakdown on an inheritance that the child has received during his or her marriage.

In Ontario, the Family Law Act provides a unique Canadian solution to the potentially inequitable treatment of one spouse after the death of the other spouse as opposed to at separation. As we have seen, family law provides for the equitable division of property upon marriage breakdown and divorce. Is there any reason why a surviving spouse should receive less than a separated spouse? It strikes most people as patently unfair that, for example, a husband could upon his death leave everything to his children, but if he had separated he would have had to share the property with his surviving spouse. In other words, why should separating spouses be treated more fairly than widows and widowers?

Ontario addressed this problem by providing the surviving spouse with a choice (called an election). The survivor could either take the inheritances in the will or take what they would have received in a separation. If they elected to take what was given to them in the will, then the estate would be distributed as planned. However, if they chose to take what they would have received if they had separated, then the estate plan would be thrown into turmoil. For example, if the will left the surviving wife only 10 per cent of the total property value in the estate when she would have received 50 per cent upon separation, then the transfer of the extra 40 per cent will upset the other gifts in the will. Everyone else will have to accept less. In most cases, these beneficiaries would be the testator's children, perhaps children from a previous marriage.

At present, most provinces have provisions in their family laws that state that the death of a spouse has an effect on the division of family property. It is a little different in each province, but the point is a simple one for our purposes: when making a will, it is now necessary to keep in mind the possible effect of provincial family property division rules upon the estate. An estate plan that is turned upside down by an unhappy surviving spouse is worthless.

This has led to lawyers using Marriage Contracts and wills together. The estate plan actually comes in two parts—the will, which sets out the intended inheritances to beneficiaries, and the Marriage Contract, by which the spouses release any interest in particular pieces of property and agree to accept the will without challenge. The releases are often given in exchange for the substitution of some other property or something else of value. In many cases, the spouses make what are known as "mutual wills" and "mutual Marriage Contracts" by which they simultaneously agree to honour each other's wills and develop a joint estate plan through the use of their wills and Marriage Contracts.

A second aspect of wills in the family law context concerns inheritances and children and the effect of a child's divorce on the inheritance. It is not uncommon for a person, when giving a lawyer instructions for a will, to ask whether the inheritances given to his or her children can somehow be protected from that child's spouse in the event of the child's marriage breakdown. For example, a father may wish to leave the family business to his son but wonders whether the business would be jeopardized if his son's marriage broke down. These concerns are not unlike those mentioned by parents who wish to give large wedding gifts to their children but only so long as the marriage works out.

Most provinces have provided in their family property division rules exemptions for gifts and inheritances. Generally, a person who receives a gift or inheritance during the marriage will not have to share that asset with the other spouse at marriage breakdown. In some cases, such as in Ontario, any income earned by the gift or inheritance after it is received can also be shielded from division with a spouse. However, the inheritance must specifically state that the income is not to be shared. This means that in Ontario, if a father wishes to pass on a family business, then it will be critical to also state in the will that income earned by the business is not to be included in the son's family property should the son's marriage break down.

Therefore, when consulting a lawyer about a will, two important considerations are:

1. the ability of the surviving spouse to set aside the estate plan if he or she is dissatisfied with the inheritance in the will and
2. the advisability of protecting a child's inheritance from his or her spouse in the event their marriage should break down after the inheritance is received.

DIVORCE AND YOUR WILL

ASSUMING YOU HAD the foresight to have a will prepared but now find yourself divorcing, an important consideration is the effect of your Separation Agreement on your will. Most Separation Agreements have standard form releases by which the husband and wife release any interest in each other's estate. (See paragraph 28 of the Draft Separation Agreement in Appendix A.) If your will has not been changed, this may mean a direct contradiction between your existing will and the Separation Agreement that you have just signed. Making a new will with a new beneficiary should be undertaken at the same time as the drafting of the Separation Agreement.

Another consideration at the time of separation or divorce is whether any support orders made in the context of the divorce will be binding on the estate of the person paying support. Canadian family law now provides that support will continue to be paid by the support payer's estate. This should be specifically discussed at the time a Separation Agreement or court order for support is drafted.

An important consideration at the time a spousal or child support order arises is the possible impact that order might have on a person's estate plan should they die. Imagine, for example, a man who has consulted a lawyer and carefully prepared an elaborate will and estate plan that parcels out gifts and inheritances to very specific individuals, including family members and children. If that person had a child support or spousal support obligation at the time he died, it would become a charge upon his estate. This means that assets and money from the estate plan would need to be diverted in order to pay the child and spousal support on an ongoing basis. All estate planning may be down the drain. To avoid such circumstances, lawyers and clients have turned to insurance to ensure that a separate fund exists if the support payer dies. That fund will pay the child or spousal support obligation. In some cases, the person paying support simply designates that his or her life insurance policy will be made irrevocably payable to the person in receipt of the support. This means that the person receiving the support will receive a lump sum payment that could, in some circumstances, exceed the actual child or spousal support obligation. If the insurance is inadequate to meet the ongoing support obligations, the support will be a first charge on the deceased person's estate. This is why the payment of life insurance is designed to protect the estate.

An alternative that has developed is a specialized form of insurance that replaces the lump sum with a monthly payment. In other words, if the person paying support dies, this form of insurance kicks in and replaces the monthly payment until the child is no longer in need or until the spousal support obligation ends.

First Meeting with the Divorce Lawyer

AT THE FIRST meeting between a client and a divorce lawyer, some important questions arise with respect to wills that have already been made, death benefits, survivor benefits and beneficiary designations on RRSPs and life insurance policies. It can be a difficult conversation. The individual who has consulted the lawyer has separated or is about to separate. The lawyer must ask this person whether they want their current spouse to inherit or benefit from such things as insurance policies or beneficiary designations.

In some cases, the client is horrified to think that the person they are about to separate from may, for example, inherit under their existing will or be the beneficiary of their RRSPs if they die before the separation and divorce is concluded. Usually the client will say, "You mean if I die on the way home from this meeting, he/she will get everything?" The answer is yes, because if, for example, they own the home in which they live as joint tenants, the surviving spouse will obtain full title to the home. If the spouse is the beneficiary of a life insurance policy, they will receive the proceeds. Similarly, if they are the beneficiary of designations of RRSPs, pensions and other death benefits, they will also receive those funds. In many cases, lawyers must tell clients to go directly to their human resources department or their insurer or their pension administrator and change their beneficiary designations—at least until other arrangements have been made through the separation and divorce. A husband who has taken the wife off his insurance policy as a beneficiary may end up changing it back to her if that life insurance is used to secure the husband's obligation for child and/or spousal support.

I mention these considerations because some couples concentrate so much on issues of custody, access, property division and spousal support that they forget these other details. Make sure you review these issues with your lawyer when you are at that first consultation. Most lawyers have heard stories of husbands and wives separating and one of them dying before an agreement is concluded. The survivor may get it all!

CLOSING REMARKS

WHILE THE ABOVE is not a detailed overview of all the aspects of estate planning for a family, there are a number of considerations both at the time a will is drafted and at the time of separation that are of special interest to Canadian family law issues.

MY ADVICE

1. Make a will.
2. Obtain a Power of Attorney for personal care and a Power of Attorney for property.
3. If you have a will and Powers of Attorney but are divorcing, these documents need to be changed to eliminate references to your spouse. This should be discussed at your first meeting with the lawyer.
4. Discuss death benefits, survivor benefits and beneficiary designations on RRSPs and life insurance policies at your first meeting with the lawyer. These designations should be changed immediately, even if a reversal or other change is required once a Separation Agreement has been signed.
5. In the final Separation Agreement, child support and spousal support obligations may be secured through the provision of life insurance that makes the recipient spouse the irrevocable beneficiary. This insurance protects the deceased person's estate.
6. Once your Separation Agreement has been concluded, or you are divorced, make a new will and Powers of Attorney immediately.
7. A divorce does not automatically revoke a will, but a marriage automatically revokes a will.

DOMESTIC VIOLENCE

A Common Feature of
Marriage Breakdown in Canada

MANY YEARS AGO I was working in my office when a new client, an older woman, arrived for some advice about a separation and a divorce. When I walked into the reception area, I saw her sitting there with three of her daughters. The mother had obviously been beaten up and looked very sad. With the help of her daughters, she got into my office where she explained that her husband of 25 years had beaten her up and thrown her out of the family home. The husband was still back at the house drinking.

I was in shock. As a young lawyer, I had never seen such a case. My initial shock got worse as the woman told her story. I was not the first lawyer that the woman had consulted. The previous week, she had gone to the lawyer who handled the purchase of her home. He was not a family law lawyer and was very busy with real estate work. After talking to her for a while, he suggested that she go home and try to work things out. Court was expensive and slow. Did she really want to separate after all? Her husband had done crazy things before and it had all blown over. Why over-react now? In fact, she was tempted to go back but she didn't. Her daughters persuaded her to see another lawyer. After a lot of work, I was able to obtain for her an order for custody of the children, support and possession of the home. We also obtained a restraining order prohibiting the husband from contacting the family, and she was able to re-establish a normal life when she had extricated herself from the violence in that home.

I continue to be horrified by the violence that goes on undetected in many Canadian homes. Every day the papers are filled with stories of spouses who murder, of children who are caught in the crossfire and of the seeming inability of our justice system to help these families.

In this chapter, I examine the domestic violence that affects thousands of families every day in Canada. Perhaps it has occurred in your neighbour's home or even in your own home.

What do we mean by "domestic violence"? Other terms are used from time to time—"wife beating," "wife battering," "wife assault" and "wife abuse." I have used the term "domestic violence," because it captures two important aspects of this issue—it generally occurs in the home and the term does not leave the impression that it only happens to married women. We are talking about violence by men against women and children and in some cases violence by women again men or violence in same-sex relationships.

One definition that captures the elements of this conduct is as follows: domestic violence involves the intent by a husband or wife to intimidate, either by threat or by use of physical force on the other person or property. The purpose of the assault is to control his or her behaviour by the inducement of fear. Underlying all abuse is a power imbalance between the victim and the offender.

Examples of physical abuse abound, but consider the following: slapping, punching, kicking, shoving, choking and even pinching. Shelter workers report cases of women being burned, beaten with belts, stabbed and even shot—sometimes with fatal consequences. Domestic violence can include sexual assaults, humiliation, forced and unwanted sexual acts or such things as being forced to watch pornography.

It need not be just physical assaults; psychological abuse can often achieve the desired effect. From my own practice I recall a woman who had been hit "only" once, but it was enough to make her feel that one false move would bring a reign of terror against not only her but also her children, her family and her friends. She dared not jeopardize anyone else, because her spouse could make his threats real. She suffered for years thinking that her "walking on eggshells" was actually protecting others. It justified her miserable life. She saw her clothes destroyed and her personal photos burned, suffered humiliations and was forced to beg for money. Threats against the victim, family, children, property or pets can be quite effective.

Her abuser rivalled another husband who responded to his wife's suggestion of marriage counselling with a promise to cut her wedding ring finger off with a pair of tinsnips. She got the message—and so did her daughters. Like others I had met, she described a pattern to the terror in her home—first a period of growing tension, an explosion of violence often triggered by some minor event and then the "honeymoon," when the repenting man becomes the charming person she used to know. Apologies flow, with gifts and lavish attention—until the next period of tension and the cycle repeats itself.

I mentioned the woman whose daughters learned a lesson from seeing their mother assaulted. The lesson was in how to be a victim. Girls who witness violence against their mothers pick up a message about how women are supposed to relate to men. Similarly, young boys who see their mothers being beaten learn that this is how men treat their intimate partners, their future wives and the mothers of their children. The emotional trauma these children experience is well known and has a lasting, damaging effect on them.

In this chapter I offer practical advice on how to identify the pattern of domestic violence, the victims and the perpetrators and, most importantly, how to deal with it, should it happen to you or to someone you know.

VIOLENCE: THE MYTHS

EXPERTS IN THIS area have identified nine common myths about domestic violence. The prevalence of these popular misconceptions has allowed domestic violence to be kept secret for so long, and too long.

1. People who assault their partners are mentally ill.
   Not necessarily. Many function quite well at work and among their friends. This violence is not caused by mental illness.

2. People who assault their partners are drunk.

   Not necessarily. Studies have found that the violence can occur whether or not alcohol is consumed. It does sometimes contribute to the violence, but it is not a cause.

3. Domestic violence occurs only among the poor.

   Dead wrong. Money cannot buy protection from this violence. The spouses of lawyers, doctors and successful businesspeople are all victims.

4. The victim does something to provoke it.

   Yes, something like breathing. The violence has no connection to conduct. Victims who were sound asleep have been beaten.

5. The victim actually enjoys it.

   This is a particularly disturbing myth, because it not only minimizes the violence and blames the victim, but also suggests that the violence is desired. The stream of women and children flocking to shelters should be proof enough that this is simply not true.

6. If the victim didn't like it, he or she would speak up or leave.

   As in the way that hostages on airplanes complain to terrorists that they don't like the way they are being treated? The syndrome that develops from the domestic violence is an invisible cage that keeps the victim from leaving.

7. Abusers who do this are a danger to the rest of the community.

   Maybe in the long term, but day by day they function well and can appear quite charming and friendly to everyone outside the home. They only beat their partners and children because they know that they can get away with it.

8. At least nothing will happen while she is pregnant.

   On the contrary, pregnant women are frequently victims, with blows deliberately aimed at the abdomen.

9. It happens to other people.

   You should be so lucky.

WHY ARE WOMEN ASSAULTED?

IT IS A complex combination of things that has put women in this position. I hope the following is not too much of an oversimplification.

- Our society conditions women to be dependent, to be victims. Many have seen and learned to accept the violence at their parents' knees.
- The privacy of the home allows it to occur out of sight.
- There is pressure to preserve the family. Reporting violence in the home may break it up.
- Those who do report it have found that they are blamed—"What did you do to provoke him?"
- There has been, until recently, little community support when victims of domestic violence finally leave the home.
- Society has not thought it necessary, until recently, to punish the offenders.
- In many cases, the woman and child have been so financially dependent on the male provider that they could not afford to leave.

These factors combine to mould a woman who is afraid and feeling helpless, who blames herself, who feels ambivalent about her life, who has no self-esteem, who prays for a change and who feels inferior to everyone around her. These factors form themselves into a syndrome of domestic violence that keeps her from leaving.

WHY DO MEN DO IT?

AGAIN, A COMPLEX combination of elements of our society has contributed to this problem.
- Society has tolerated it over hundreds of years. Men think it is acceptable to beat those with whom they are angry.
- Given the prevalence of this type of violence in the home, it is likely that thousands of men have learned this behaviour from their own parents.
- Society has also been quick to blame the victim rather than the offender. Why should a man change when "it's not his fault"?
- Men who are violent with their wives and children generally have poor impulse control and an inflexible method of dealing with frustration.

These factors, coupled with poor self-esteem, produce a man who denies he is violent, blames everyone else, is highly emotionally dependent on his partner, is very traditional in his views of male-female relations and handles life in one of two ways—everything is okay or he is furious. This is a man who is emotionally isolated and who lashes out at easy prey—his family.

I was involved in a case recently where the husband/father was particularly abusive. He had been charged and convicted of assault. Part of his probation included taking an anger management course. When I did background research on this fellow, I learned that he had been through a previous marriage and a common-law relationship. We located the court files and read the affidavits and allegations that had been made by his previous partners. They were almost identical to the records in my case.

My client was number three. While the proceedings were underway he met, lived with, abused and left three more women! This fellow was unemployed for most of the three years I dealt with him. He was not particularly good-looking. He had no driver's licence and no property. He could, however, be quite charming and he sought out single women with children.

How can you avoid this kind of person?

If you meet someone who talks about previous relationships that went sour, try to find out what happened. Do a little research. If someone has a conviction for spousal assault, then draw your own conclusions. If you see evidence of the cycle I mentioned, avoid this person. You are placing yourself and your children in danger.

WHAT CAN BE DONE?

AS FRUSTRATING AS this situation appears, there are some things that can be done on a practical level and a legal level.

On the practical side, consider the following suggestions:

- Get out. It won't be easy, but it's possible. Others have done it and so can you. But rather than just walking out, have a plan. You put your life and the lives of your children at risk by staying.
- Protect yourself and your children at all costs. Do not fight back, but do practise self-defence. Be alert to the building tension and stay out of the line of fire if possible.
- Call the police. Press charges. Follow through. One study found that

when the police laid charges, the probability of violence was reduced by half.

- Have a friend available for support.
- Tell your doctor about the violence. Don't make excuses; listen to suggestions and accept support.
- Investigate the availability of shelters in your community. Not every community in Canada has shelters for battered women, but many do. Unfortunately, even when they are available, demand far exceeds available space. In Toronto, for example, shelters are reported to have only one space available for every six requests.
- Keep a record of the abuse and any resulting visits to doctors.
- Develop an escape route for emergencies. Discuss it with the children if necessary. Ask a neighbour to call the police if trouble occurs.
- Set aside some extra money for a cab in an emergency. Try to create an escape fund.
- Leave a supply of extra clothes for yourself and the children at a neighbour's house. Have extra keys made for the house and car.
- When you go, take all your identification: financial records, health insurance numbers, passports, personal ID, credit cards, birth certificates. You will need them if you apply for public assistance.
- Check the availability of social assistance in your community in advance.
- Consult a lawyer about your plans. Check out the availability of legal aid in your community. Some legal aid plans will expedite a request for legal aid where violence is involved.
- Don't wait for him to change. He won't and you know it. In all my experience, I have never seen a person like this change. Courses, books and so on make no difference. Abusers must take responsibility for changing themselves. You cannot do it for them.

As you can see, a great many steps can be taken in advance. Little by little, step by step, you can plan an escape from an abusive home.

On the legal side, consider the following options:

- Press charges. This assault is like any other in that it is a crime and police intervention is necessary. Many forces now have special training for those responding to such calls.

- Every province has a procedure for obtaining a peace bond. This is a relatively straightforward procedure that requires the abusive husband to post a bond subject to certain conditions. If the conditions (for example, keep the peace, stay away from the home) are breached, the bond or money (for example, $500) is forfeited or he may be rearrested.
- All provincial family laws contemplate a court order restraining a spouse from having any contact with his family or, in some provinces, limiting the contact to certain days and certain times. These are called restraining orders.
- Check the availability of legal aid.
- All provincial family laws allow for *ex parte* motions to the court. *Ex parte* means that the court is asked to make the order without notice to the other side of the court appearance. It is used under limited circumstances but is well suited to a situation where a woman fleeing an abusive relationship would be at risk the moment her abusive partner received notice of going to court.
- If your children are at risk, apply for custody of the children as soon as possible. The court will likely grant custody, but may also consider some form of access for the other parent if it will not endanger the children. Ask your lawyer to consider your own risk at the time your husband has access to the children. It is possible to arrange access in such a way that the parents do not have to deal with each other.

If you have been assaulted and injured, consider the availability of compensation from two sources:

1. A civil lawsuit for damages: Essentially, you sue your partner for damages. Damage awards have been made for victims injured by an assault, but relatively few people sue.
2. An application to a provincial Criminal Injuries Compensation Board: All provinces consider the cases of victims of domestic violence applying for compensation.

A number of lawsuits against abusive partners have been successful and I think that people who have been abused or assaulted in their marriage or relationship should sue. I know that someone in this situation has more than enough to think about, but a claim for damages will help the abuser and society get the message—damage has been done.

A Case Study

AN ONTARIO CASE caught my attention in the context of domestic violence and abuse. The case involved a couple, Ms. M. and Mr. D. They began dating in 1998 and were soon engaged to be married. They moved in together, living in and renovating a property that Mr. D. had purchased before they met. They lived together for five years, from 1998 to 2003. In addition to the house that they lived in, Mr. D. bought an empty lot in 2000. The pair worked like pioneers to clear the land and build a cottage on that property. Both properties were registered in the name of Mr. D. alone.

Ms. M. maintained a job, contributing all of her $55,000 annual salary toward paying half the expenses of the household, including mortgage payments. Mr. D. was self-employed and relied on Ms. M. for health benefits. Ms. M. helped with his business and managed the cooking, cleaning and grocery shopping for the household. Unfortunately, she worked a little too hard in this relationship and ultimately developed shooting pains in her shoulder. After multiple visits to the doctor, she was diagnosed with thoracic outlet syndrome, a debilitating shoulder condition. She ultimately went for surgery and began a long path to rehabilitation. The relationship subsequently suffered, as Mr. D. was both unsupportive and unsympathetic to her difficulties. He insisted that, now that she was ill, she was "dragging him down." He refused to help her financially and pressured her to keep up her half of the mortgage and other monthly bills. There were angry outbursts and, eventually, she moved out of the home and back with her family. When she asked for a share of the value of the property she had worked on and contributed to financially, Mr. D. unleashed his fury and accused her of blackmail; claimed that they had never been a couple, but rather that she had been a tenant; reported her to her insurers, accusing her of filing fraudulent benefit claims; dragged out the court appearance; claimed false debts; and ran up debt registered against the properties. He sent menacing letters and threatened to release sexually explicit photos of

Ms. M. to her family. In short, it was a legal and emotional nightmare and a classic case of abuse.

In her claim before the court, Ms. M. asked for a share in the properties upon which she had worked, but she also claimed damages for the abuse suffered at the hands of Mr. D. The court ultimately granted her a restraining order and ordered that the two properties in his name be used as security to make sure that he paid any money owing to Ms. M. Over and above the damages for the abuse, the judge also ordered that Mr. D. pay in excess of $200,000 in legal fees. While I feel sorry for Ms. M. and her experience, I was relieved to see that a court would make an order based on the abuse that she had suffered. I think that in the future we can expect to see more claims for damages joined with the ordinary claims typically seen in separation and divorce—a positive development.

It is not going to be easy, but with organization, planning, support and the right timing, a person and his or her children can escape an abusive relationship. If you are in that position, a lawyer will be absolutely necessary, especially if the full force of the law is to be exercised in your favour. Good luck.

STRATEGIC CONSIDERATIONS

LAWYERS HAVE NOW been trained extensively to try to recognize the symptoms of domestic violence. It's fair to say that we continue to be shocked by what we learn about other people's intimate lives. In this brief section, I want to add some strategic considerations on family violence.

Sometimes it's impossible for a couple to split up and move into separate residences. For financial reasons or for strategic reasons, the couple stays under the same roof. The tension can be unbearable and in some circumstances explosive. All family law lawyers have seen situations where couples call the police to deal with these explosions. The police have been trained to be sensitive to these complaints about domestic violence. Laying the charge can set in motion a series of events over which both spouses lose control.

The police must lay the charge if they are satisfied that there has been evidence of violence. In some cases, the violence has been by both spouses, or at least it has been alleged by both spouses. In such circumstances, the police lay charges against both the husband and the wife. These charges are then passed on to a Crown attorney who must go forward with the charges and will push for a trial. Crown attorneys now have little, if any, discretion to withdraw charges of domestic violence. Policy-makers wanted to ensure that wives who were subjected to violence did not withdraw the charges due to threats from their spouses; therefore, it was thought to be better to take the matter out of the hands of the spouses and leave it with the Crown attorney. As a result, a Crown attorney must go forward with a domestic violence charge.

Once the matter gets to court, each spouse will give evidence in relation to the specific charges and convictions may be obtained, restraining orders may be granted and peace bonds will likely have to be posted. This process takes many, many months. In the meantime, a court may be trying to sort out who should have custody of the children. With criminal charges for alleged domestic violence hanging over one's head, it can be difficult to convince a court that one should be given custody of the children.

I mention this because allegations of domestic violence have now become strategically important in custody disputes. The vast majority of complaints of domestic violence are legitimate. Unfortunately, there have been individuals who have abused the police and the Crown attorney and made allegations of domestic violence in inappropriate circumstances in an attempt to affect the custody determinations. Both men and women have been guilty of this. It is particularly infuriating because it undermines the legitimate complaints that have been made by true victims of domestic violence.

We have something of a crisis developing in the area of family law and domestic violence. I am not the first person to point out that the Canadian justice system does not do nearly enough to adequately protect victims of domestic violence. Over the last few years, there have been numerous incidents of abusers who are subject to restraining orders still managing to viciously attack and, in some cases, kill their spouse. In some particularly horrific situations, attackers have killed their children, as well. This is an ongoing problem in Canadian society. Limited resources are available and not enough is being done about it.

Increasing protection for victims of violence should be a top priority.

Having said that, it is particularly offensive to see these limited resources of our police and our justice system squandered on what can only be characterized as false allegations. The problem is not being tracked or monitored; however, based on anecdotal experience and discussions with other lawyers, it is clear that some spouses have discovered that false or exaggerated allegations of domestic violence can provide a considerable advantage at the time of separation and divorce.

I caution all of my clients who are living separate and apart under the same roof or who are coming into contact on a regular basis with a spouse where there is a great deal of tension: it is in everyone's interest that you avoid violent confrontations. It is, of course, in the interest of your own safety and in the interest of your children, but strategically avoiding violent confrontations is in the interest of everyone trying to advance their case.

Policy-makers are discussing new and more powerful ways to deal with the scourge of domestic violence in Canada. I do not want my comments in this section interpreted in any way as discouraging the reporting of legitimate domestic violence. If you are a victim of violence, then reporting it will contribute to ending the violence and will offer you and your family more protection.

CLOSING REMARKS

DOMESTIC VIOLENCE, UNFORTUNATELY, is still a reality for the area of family law. I wish that I could say I had seen improvements in this area in terms of enforcement. It is certainly an area that requires more resources, and by that I do not just mean more shelters.

For those of you experiencing domestic violence, make a plan to exit safely and to get support, and you will very likely escape your nightmare. For those of you who are faced with false allegations, you may simply be left with no option but to leave your trust in the criminal justice system and pray that you are ultimately acquitted and that, in the interim, your interest in the separation and divorce has not been harmed irreparably.

MY ADVICE

1. Speak with professional counsellors to understand your abusive situation and develop strategies to protect yourself and your children and to exit the relationship.
2. Investigate community resources such as housing support, shelters and legal aid.
3. Develop an emergency exit plan.
4. Consult with a lawyer.
5. Consider laying criminal charges and getting a peace bond or restraining order.
6. Do not try to use a false allegation as a tactic to gain an advantage. You are only stealing resources from those who need them and risking your own credibility not to mention criminal charges against you for mischief.

HOW TO REPRESENT YOURSELF

MY ORIGINAL GOAL in writing *Surviving Your Divorce* was to help clients find a good lawyer and then manage that relationship in an affordable way. Over the years I gradually added more specific pieces of information to support people who are going it alone; that information eventually grew to be this entire chapter because the family law courts are filled with Canadians acting as their own lawyers—"self-reps," as lawyers and judges call them.

Why do people choose to "self-rep"? Reasons are varied—they have no money, no confidence in lawyers or overconfidence in their own abilities, or simply, they are unable to find a lawyer to take their case. Regardless of the reason, these people need help to ensure that they

- advance their own case and protect their property, children and future;
- do not harm their interests and, in particular, the interests of their children; and
- do not cause delay and expense in the administration of justice; after all, there are thousands of other Canadians trying to use this system and delay affects everyone.

It is impossible to cover every aspect of "how to do a case." One version of the *Rules of Court for Family Law in Ontario* is in excess of a thousand pages. Those pages set out for lawyers and judges the laws that concern family law cases (called statutes), regulations (which micromanage the way statutes work), the Rules of Court (which micromanage the day-to-day operation of each case) and short summaries of cases that have interpreted those laws, regulations and rules. There is advice on tactics and strategy as well. It is a lot to handle even for lawyers, and it has been mastered by only a few. So, in this chapter I hope to provide you with at least a framework within which you can do your work and understand how the family law system works.

This chapter is not just for those who are representing themselves though; even if you have a lawyer, this chapter will teach you how to make a contribution to moving your own case forward in a cost-effective, fast and fair way.

In the following sections I set out the way in which lawyers organize their cases. If you are representing yourself, there is no reason why you can't organize your file and your approach to your situation in exactly the same way.

A 10-STEP LEGAL FRAMEWORK FOR YOUR CASE

AS YOU'LL SEE from the following 10 steps, there is no magic in organizing a family law case. It starts with some very basic information, and grows. Most experienced family law lawyers recognize when they sketch out the framework of a case that they will need to come back and fill in new facts, aspects of evidence, issues of law and rejig the approach. I suggest that you do the same thing. Consider the framework that you are building as a draft that will evolve several times as you work on the case.

Step 1: What Are the Facts?

IT IS SURPRISING to see self-represented people in court who do not have a solid grasp of the facts of their own situation, let alone the complicated law and Rules of Court. Every case starts with a mastery of the facts. This means answering the most basic questions: who, what, when, where and why. I organize files by listing chronologically every fact that I know about my client's case. This includes, for example:

- the date the couple began to cohabit
- the date of the marriage
- the date that the couple separated
- their birth dates
- the day upon which they bought their first home
- when children were born
- when jobs were changed
- when counselling sessions were attempted, and so on.

You should expect to amass hundreds and hundreds of facts.

It is best to be overinclusive. Sometimes a chronological listing of the facts provides surprising insight into what happened in a marriage, or what happened, for example, in the acquisition and disposition of property. This collection of facts is not intended to be your memoir, or a speech recounting what went wrong with the marriage or the relationship. There is no need for editorial comment. It is business. It is a simple, straightforward listing of known facts. If a fact is not known, it must be discovered; if there are gaps, you will need to fill in the information. For example, if a spouse claims that the value of an asset that exists on date of separation (for example, an RRSP) should not be shared because the funds used to open the RRSP can be traced to a cash gift from an uncle during the course of the marriage, a paper trail should exist between the date of the gift (for example, a cheque, a cash deposit, etc.) and the opening of the RRSP. Facts should connect those dots. Remember, this summary of the facts will undergo a number of drafts. Come back to it as you accumulate more and more information.

Step 2: Where Is the Evidence?

I'VE NOTICED THAT clients often confuse a fact with evidence. I usually explain it by giving an example. If a client got married on September 21, 2010, that is a fact. If they have a marriage certificate proving that they got married on September 21, 2010, that is evidence. If a couple bought a home in the summer of 2005, that is a fact. If the transfer of that home and their mortgage was registered on July 17, 2005, and I have copies of those transactions, that is evidence. As the summary of facts is built during Step 1, note beside each fact the evidence that establishes it. As you go through this exercise, you will notice that some facts are obvious and would likely be admitted. For example, parents rarely argue about children's birth dates. They will, however, argue about the date of separation, or the value of an asset, or who paid for a particular item or incurred a particular debt. This is where the evidence comes into play.

Evidence can be tricky for a number of reasons. It is one of the more complicated areas of law and frequently trips up even experienced lawyers. There are entire textbooks written about small aspects of the Rules of Evidence. Yet as tricky as the Rules of Evidence can be, family law courts often ignore or bend these Rules of Evidence in an attempt to get to the bottom of each party's story. This is a source of dismay to lawyers who appear before judges with proper legal objections to the admissibility of a particular piece of evidence (for example, *"Your Honour, that letter from the child's schoolteacher is inadmissible because it contains hearsay information"*), only to have the judge state he or she will consider the information and determine if any "weight" should be given to it. In other words, the judge is saying, *"I recognize that the information is inadmissible, but it may help me figure out what's going on, so I will read it and then, if it's of no use, I will reject it or ignore it."*

I recall appearing before an experienced senior judge one morning on a difficult case involving custody of a little girl. The self-represented mother asked the judge to listen to a recording of a telephone message. She had come to court with a tape recorder and what she said was a message left by the father on her telephone. She alleged that when the father was leaving the telephone message, the child could be heard screaming words in the background that would be of great interest to the judge in making a decision. No notice had been given of the intention to admit this evidence, no proof was given of how the telephone recording was made or whether it had been edited, no proof was given of who made the telephone call, and whose voices were being heard, and on top of all those questions, the quality of the recording was very weak. Should a judge base his or her decision on evidence like that? Should custody determinations be made on that basis? These are the kinds of decisions judges face every day in family courts when self-represented people arrive with evidence that may or may not be helpful, but is in complete violation of the Rules of Evidence. This attitude in family courts often turns hearings into evidentiary free-for-alls with numerous pieces of inadmissible evidence landing before the judge. Having said that, this does not mean that self-represented people, or lawyers, can afford to ignore the Rules of Evidence.

As a brief guide to the admissibility of evidence, consider the following:

- Original documents should be used; photocopies may be referred to as long as the original is available for inspection by the court.
- Direct evidence is preferable to second-hand evidence. "Someone told you that something happened" is not acceptable evidence—it is hearsay.
- Evidence should be disclosed by each party; the courts do not like surprises or ambushes.
- Experts are allowed to give opinion evidence to a court, provided they are indeed an expert in that area (which the court will decide) and provided their evidence is in a report that has been shared with the other side well in advance. You will recall the point made above about hearsay evidence; the use of an expert's report is an exception to the rule against hearsay.
- There are special rules for the use and introduction of business records. These rules are designed to make it easier for a court to look at evidence, if the evidence was prepared in the ordinary course of carrying on that business. For example, if a bank routinely enters deposits and debits in a bank book to show the balance in a savings account, then it may not be necessary to call a bank teller to explain how a bank book works. This only applies if the business record is prepared in the ordinary course of business. Unusual letters, documents or statements must be provided by calling as a witness the business person who prepared the record. For example, if a company terminated an employee because of misconduct, the letter of termination might not be considered a record prepared in the ordinary course of business,

and it would therefore be necessary to call as a witness the author of the letter to testify about its contents and the meaning of the contents.

- There is a difference between admitting the authenticity of a document, and admitting that the document is admissible. For example, if a couple signed two Marriage Contracts, one in 1998 and another in 2007, a lawyer may be prepared to admit that both documents are authentic, that is, that they are correct, original documents signed by the parties involved. This does not mean that the lawyer will be prepared to admit that the first Marriage Contract is admissible as evidence. The second Marriage Contract will have replaced the first and that contract's contents may be irrelevant. Just because someone admits that a document is authentic, does not mean that it is admissible.

- The bottom line for all evidence comes down to one word: relevance. The evidence must be relevant to the determination of the issue that is before the court.

- Earlier, I mentioned the judge who said he would admit a document but attribute "weight" to it after he had seen it. If there is any doubt about the admissibility of a particular piece of evidence, it can be a good strategy to suggest to the judge that he or she look at the document and determine later what weight they are prepared to give to it. So, the judge may read the letter from a schoolteacher containing hearsay, consider its contents, but give it little weight in making the final decision. At least the information was available.

- If a piece of evidence is offered to the court but it may be inadmissible, the proper course is for the person who objects to that piece of evidence to stand and say to the judge, *"Your Honour, I object to the admissibility of that evidence."* The judge will then ask the person who has objected to explain their reasons for objecting. That person may answer, for example, *"Your Honour, the letter from the schoolteacher contains hearsay information."* The judge will then ask the other side for their comments about the objection. After hearing those comments, the judge will make a ruling on whether the evidence is admissible or not. Provided your objection is on the record, you have protected yourself in case it is necessary to appeal the decision. Once the judge has made a ruling about the evidence, sit down and do not continue to argue, because the judge will not change his or her mind once the decision is made.

With the above suggestions in mind, go back now and review the facts that you have accumulated in Step 1 and begin to match up pieces of evidence to prove those facts. Examine each piece of evidence and consider whether it is relevant, whether it is admissible, whether it is hearsay, whether it is an original document, whether there is some better evidence that is more direct on the point that you wish to prove. This is how lawyers build cases before going to court.

Step 3: What Are the Issues?

You will want to spend time thinking in advance about the order that you want the court to make. The issue may not be as simple as:
- "Who should get custody of the children?"
- "Who should pay support?"
- "Is that loan really a gift?"

As with the summary of the facts, the way in which the issues are framed may change as you work on the case and think about what you need. So, for example,
- "Who should have custody of the children?" may become "What is in the best interests of the children, who have been in the custody of the mother for the two years immediately preceding this hearing?"
- "Who should pay support?" may become "What is the appropriate level of child support, given the mother's declared annual income of $100,000 and the Child Support Guidelines?"
- "Was the loan really a gift?" may become "Is there evidence that the father's parents loaned him money in 2003 and that they expected repayment?"

As you can see from the above questions, it is possible to frame the issue in a very specific way for the court, to get the judge to focus on the issue that you need resolved.

Step 4: What Does the Law Say?

YOU WILL RECALL from Chapter 3: Taking a Look at the Process that family law is provided by both the federal government, for example, in the form of the Divorce Act, and the provincial/territorial governments, which provide family law property division rules, rules for common-law spouses, regulations and, importantly, the Rules of Court. Here is a brief listing of the names of some key laws:
- the Divorce Act
- the Civil Marriage Act
- the Annulment of Marriages Act
- the Change of Name Act
- the Child and Family Services Act
- the Children's Law Reform Act
- the Family Law Act
- the Family Relations Act
- the Marriage Act
- the Partition Act
- the Pension Benefits Act
- the Succession Law Reform Act
- the Vital Statistics Act
- the Family Responsibility and Support Arrears Enforcement Act
- the Family Maintenance Act
- the Fraudulent Conveyances Act
- the Wages Act
- the Evidence Act
- the Courts of Justice Act.

Each province has its own list of equivalent laws. In the upcoming section dealing with research, I explain how to locate some of these important statutes, regulations and rules.

These laws are important because they set out the legal framework for how the issues that you have identified can be resolved. So, for example, as we saw in Chapter 6: Obligations to the Children of a Divorce, custody determinations are made by looking at what is in the best interests of the children. Statutes such as Ontario's Children's Law Reform Act set out the elements of what is considered to be in the best interests of the child. For child support, the Child Support Guidelines tell us precisely what amount of child support should be paid on a monthly basis given a particular level of income and number of children. For property, provincial statutes set out formulas for the calculation of increases in net worth between date of marriage and date of separation. If a provincial law says that a spouse need not share the value of property that was received as a gift from a third party, then that legal rule must be identified, read and understood before you ask the court to make an order. And if that provincial law applies, then there is little point in asking a court to order that the gift be shared—provided the court has proper evidence that the property was indeed a gift.

The law is generally summarized for the judge in the form of a "factum." The factum contains a summary of your legal framework for the case. It will tell the court basic facts important to the decision being made, list evidence in support of those facts, set out issues that need to be resolved and then tell the court the law that supports the decision you seek. So, as you can see, in these four steps of the legal framework you are essentially building the factum that you can rely upon when speaking to the court.

The law referred to in the factum includes federal and provincial/territorial law, Rules of Court, regulations and cases that have interpreted those laws. We will look at cases in an upcoming section.

Step 5: What Are the Alternative Solutions and the Relative Advantages and Disadvantages to Each?

THERE IS MORE than one way to solve a problem and in Step 5 I invite people to look at various alternatives to solving the problem that the family faces. This is an opportunity to be creative and to think outside the box a little bit after you have summarized the facts, after you have considered the evidence and after you have reviewed the law. Some alternative solutions to the issue may emerge. For example, if it becomes clear that a husband will need to make a $200,000 payment to his wife to satisfy her interest in the family's property, but the husband does not have $200,000 cash, an alternative solution may be needed. If the husband has $300,000 in RRSPs, a solution to the property issue may be to roll over some RRSPs in lieu of a cash payment.

During this phase of considering alternative solutions and relative advantages and disadvantages, settlement options may become evident.

Step 6: What Do You Want?

JUDGES FREQUENTLY ASK a self-represented individual, "What do you want?" On far too many occasions, the person stands before the court and has no answer. In large part, I think this is because they have not done the spade-work that I have set out in Steps 1 through 5.

When asked about the challenges of dealing with self-represented people, judges often state that the self-represented person does not know what to ask for. In court I have seen self-represented people simply start to repeat the facts of the case, describe problems that they have had through the marriage, rail against their spouse and then stand mute when the judge asks, "What do you want?" At that point, you must be prepared to do what every well-prepared lawyer will do—specifically state the court order that you want the judge to make. For example,

> "Your Honour, thank you. I am seeking an order of custody of my daughter Amber, commencing June 1, and an order for child support in the amount of $692 per month based on my husband's declared income of $76,500. I would ask that the court order my husband have access to Amber every second weekend from Friday at 5 p.m. to Monday morning at 9 a.m. when he drops her off at school commencing in September. During the summer, when there is no school, the drop-off can be either at my home or his parents' home, if they are prepared to agree," etc.

As this kind of statement is made, the judge will be writing in his or her notebook exactly what you have asked for. The judge will then ask your spouse or his or her lawyer what they want, and so on.

When the judge is making a decision about the order that will be made, he or she will be reviewing the facts that have been presented, the evidence in support of the facts, the issues that have been framed for his or her decision, the alternative solutions presented and the specific order that the parties have requested.

Step 7: How Should I Organize the Case?

YOU SHOULD ORGANIZE the case as if you were a lawyer. If your case is typical, you should acquire a banker's box, a number of different-coloured file folders and some accordion file folders. My assistant and I divide my files into the following categories, each in its own separate file folder:

- correspondence
- husband's financial statement
- wife's financial statement
- lawyer's notes from interviews
- original documents
- summons to witnesses
- offers to settle
- orders of the court/endorsements
- court briefs
- legal research
- summary of facts
- relevant rules of evidence
- mediation attempts
- confirmation forms for faxes sent to court/opposing counsel
- transcripts
- continuing record
- retainer, and
- file opening information.

These are the standard file folders that are required, but if special issues arise, we open separate file folders to deal with that. For example, if a custody assessment has been done, a separate file folder would be opened to hold information about retaining the assessor, his or her report and notes from meetings with the assessor.

If you spend any time at the court offices you will see lawyers trundling around with their familiar big black briefcases on wheels. You may want to consider acquiring one of these. For most court appearances, everything you need can be placed comfortably in one of these large "offices on wheels." Personally I include in my briefcase a calculator, paper calendars for writing out custody/access schedules, my wallet for identification purposes (there is screening at most courthouses now), extra pens and writing pads, a copy of the Rules of Court, the Child Support Guidelines, a newspaper in case there's some waiting involved, candy and a bottle of water. There can be long waits for things to be heard at court, and you should be prepared for that.

Step 8: How Do I Tell the Court What I Want?

THIS IS A little different than Step 6, which is a determination of what you want to ask the court to do. How you tell the court involves fitting your story into the forms that are dictated by the Rules of Court. There is no other word for this undertaking except "unbelievable." There is a myriad of court forms; each province has its own set, and in some provinces, where there are multiple levels of family court, there are multiple levels of forms. Getting your information into the right form is essential. The courts will not accept your long, single-spaced diatribe against your spouse. These forms were designed to allow the court staff and the judge to quickly assess the basic elements of a case:

- Were they married?
- How long were they married?
- Do they have children?
- How old are the children?
- When did they separate?
- Who has a job?
- How much do they earn? and so on.

The forms allow the court to gather the information at a glance.

Court staff are not permitted to give self-represented people (or lawyers for that matter) legal advice about family law. They are, however, prepared to assist people in understanding the forms that are required to move a matter forward. They cannot assist you in completing the forms, since where a particular piece of information goes on the form can be an important legal decision. Many of the forms required by the court must be sworn. This means that the spouse is stating under oath that everything in that form is the truth. Court staff are prepared to witness those forms. In Ontario this is called "commissioning." If a lawyer has been retained, this is routinely done in the lawyer's office by the lawyer involved or by authorized office staff. If you do not have access to someone who can commission your signature, go to the court office and someone there will ask you under oath whether everything in the document is the truth.

Step 9: How Should I Move My Case Forward?

YOU ARE RESPONSIBLE for your own case. If you want something to happen, you must prod the system into action. The courthouse is filled with tens of thousands of cases, and there is no one in the courthouse lying awake at night worrying about your file. If you do nothing, the file will gather dust. In some cases, doing nothing is a good strategy. If you are content with the status quo, leave it alone. If you want the status quo to change, get busy.

I explain to my clients that a file should be pursued on two tracks at the same time and use the analogy of two trains. One train is on the settlement track: it is moving forward at all times, considering options for settlement, gathering information, being creative and being open-minded and fair. The other train is on the courthouse track: it is gathering facts, gathering evidence, gathering law and framing the issues for the court's decision. The only question is which train gets to the station first. In my view, the harder people work at getting the case ready for court, the sooner the settlement train gets to the station. In other words, preparing for court prepares you for settlement. I have seen clients and lawyers stop working on a case simply because there is talk of a possible settlement; they put down their tools and stop preparing. This can be counterproductive. In my view just because settlement discussions begin does not mean that preparation for court stops. The possibility of court and court orders focuses everyone's mind on the possible settlement. There is a reason so many cases settle at the courthouse. Everyone has prepared (we hope), and everyone knows the options and the likelihood of success. That is when clients are most likely to understand options for compromise and settlement. Reread Chapter 9: Settling Your Differences. The documents discussed in that chapter are signed because people understand their case and are ready to settle.

Step 10: What Do I Do in Court?

I WANT TO provide some general comments about the perils of self-representation, but also some specific tips for handling yourself as the matter goes forward.

- Be reasonable. Self-representation can be frustrating. You will be tempted to lash out. You're going to be asking people to help you. Do not turn around and be difficult the minute you think you can take advantage of them. Just like in real life, what goes around comes around in the justice system.

- Do not expect everyone in the "system" to ignore deadlines, paperwork requirements, rules and legal procedures simply because you are unrepresented. To be frank, the system does not like self-represented people. You slow things down, you make it harder for everyone, you ask too many questions, you expect favours. Self-represented people are a nuisance as far as the system is concerned. Don't expect anyone to do favours for you and you won't be disappointed.

- Don't be surprised if the lawyer on the other side is reluctant to talk to you. When lawyers and law office staff from opposing firms talk to each other, there is an understanding about certain things being "off the record" and "without prejudice." This understanding allows us to work more freely, but it cannot be extended to self-represented people. We as lawyers have to assume that anything we say or do to a self-represented person will end up in front of a judge somehow. Lawyers live in constant fear that they will be in front of a judge and a self-represented person will stand up and tell the judge something totally in breach of the Rules of Evidence and Rules of Procedure. The statement usually begins *"Yes, Your Honour, but Mr. Cochrane said that I should..."* I may or may not have said it, it may or may not be accurately repeated by the person, it may or may not have been understood by them in the first place, it may or may not be in compliance with the Rules and, most importantly, it may or may not jeopardize what I want the court to do that particular day. So for a lawyer in my position, it is simply better to deal as little as possible with self-represented people. Certainly lawyers will avoid discussing the case on the telephone with self-represented people. I personally ask for all communication to be in writing or by e-mail so there is at least a record that can be shown to the judge. You make the lawyer's work harder and more expensive.

- Do not tape telephone calls with lawyers and your spouse. No one will ever listen to them and it just makes everyone very reluctant to talk to you. Judges are rarely impressed when they hear about telephone tapings or videos being made. Be polite and respectful with everyone. Outrageous letters, faxes and e-mails will all come back to haunt you. Foul language and tough talk will get you nowhere. If something important needs to be said, put it in a short, to-the-point letter, fax or e-mail.

- Be patient. The system involves waiting. Very few things happen when they are actually scheduled. If the court is scheduled to start at 10 a.m., be there at 9:30 a.m. and be prepared to wait until 11 a.m. before you are dealt with in the most preliminary of ways.

- When in court, remember the judge knows very little about you. He or she may or may not have read the file. Their gut reaction is one of caution in dealing with you. You are a problem, remember? Every minute that a judge must spend explaining procedures to you is a minute not spent on cases that require his or her decision as opposed to his or her advice.

- Call all judges "Your Honour" and refer to the lawyers in the case as Mr. or Ms. and use their name. The courtroom may be filled with people and the judge needs to know to whom you are referring.

- Remember, when you are given an opportunity to speak at some point in court, it is not a chance to tell your life story or to try to convince the judge how awful your spouse has been. Make your points and offer to answer any questions the judge may have. Tell the judge what you would like to have happen. Try to have a plan and ask the judge to assist you in implementing it. I have seen some self-represented people do an absolutely fantastic job in court. I saw a man make a clear, articulate, fair and well-reasoned presentation. I was shocked to discover that he was representing himself and was, in fact, a recently laid-off business executive. On that day in court he got the job done very effectively.

- Don't get fancy and think that you are "as good as any lawyer" simply because you have accomplished one or two steps in a proceeding. I saw a self-represented person get very full of himself in court. He was referring to rules and evidence and was really going out of his way to try to make life difficult for the lawyer and for his spouse. He was being unreasonable and the judge saw right through it. Within a few minutes, he had been cut down to size and had really hurt his position. Reread my first point.

- Be prepared to be physically and emotionally drained. Even lawyers who go to court often feel drained after a day there. There is a lot of waiting; it is stressful and courthouses are not known for their stimulating environments. I have seen more than one person get sick from the stress and the wear and tear on their nerves. Over the course of a divorce case, there may be multiple court appearances and proceedings, and things can get quite drawn out. It can be a difficult burden to carry when your own life, your property and the happiness of your children is on your shoulders. Remember the old saying that lawyers are taught in first-year law school: "A lawyer who represents himself has a fool for a client."

- Try not to think of things in terms of "winning" and "losing." It doesn't really work like that. Rarely is someone a clear winner in the family law system. Focus instead on goals, have a plan, be flexible and don't get lost in the details that may not really matter in the long run. Keep your eye on the ball.

- Consider consulting with a lawyer from time to time to see if you are on the right track. It may cost a little, but it could save you in the end.

- Be prepared to compromise. Offer to settle and put it in writing. If the offer is only available for a limited period, then say so. For example, an offer to settle might be available for acceptance until Thursday at 5 p.m., after which time it is withdrawn.

- Reread this book from time to time. I have heard many readers say that they had to read a chapter in the context of what was actually happening to them in order to fully appreciate some of the information.

50 TIPS FOR YOUR DAY IN COURT

1. Get a good night's rest.
2. Before going to court, try practising your presentation on a friend. Accept suggestions that might improve it.

3. Eat normally. It can be a long day and you're going to need to keep your strength up.

4. No drinking or drugs. (That seems obvious, but we regularly encounter people at the court reeking of booze, thinking they have disguised it with mouthwash.)

5. If you smoke, have one before you head into court.

6. Be prepared for an emotional day. It is very stressful.

7. Bring a friend for moral support.

8. Make sure your witnesses have details about which court and the time to appear. Show them all of the points on this list.

9. Bring your entire file with you.

10. If you have documents for the court, bring two copies of each—one for the other side and one for the judge.

11. Bring change for photocopy machines. Depending on the court office, they may have a photocopier in the library or in the space outside the courts.

12. Make sure that you have a notepad, pens and other supplies.

13. Be aware that you cannot record the court proceedings or take photographs in the courtroom.

14. Bring your legal framework with you (do not give a copy to the other side).

15. Bring some food.

16. Don't bring your children.

17. Make sure you know where you're going, including the address of the courthouse, the floor that you're on, the courtroom you're in.

18. Is the courthouse served by public transit?

19. Is there parking? A meter will not do.

20. Leave time for traffic. Arrive early.

21. Have the contact number for the court office in case you are delayed.

22. Be prepared for delays at the security check/metal detector screening.

23. Present as a calm person, not an angry person.

24. Turn your phone and pager off in the courtroom (although a court will be prepared to allow you to turn it on to access an electronic calendar).

25. When you arrive, check in with the court clerk. There is a sign-in sheet.

26. If you need an adjournment, tell the other side in advance and be prepared to explain to the court why the adjournment is required (for example, I do not have the relevant documents and my case would be prejudiced without them).

27. Ask the clerk how the list is proceeding and what number you are on the list. Be prepared to give the clerk an estimate of how long your case could be.

28. Ask the court clerks or staff for information while you are there, but not advice.

29. Seek out a duty counsel, if any is available, and obtain free advice. You may have to put your name on a list, but it's worth the wait.

30. If you get to see duty counsel, ask for information or insights about the judge in front of whom you will appear.

31. Be prepared for delays. One day I was ready to enter the court on a complicated matter, and someone pulled a fire alarm that emptied the entire courthouse for over an hour. Things happen.

32. If you arrive early, try to sit in the courtroom and watch how other cases are dealt with.

33. If there is a lawyer on the other side, seek him or her out and politely introduce yourself.

34. Bring a book or a newspaper to pass the time. I've noticed lately that a lot of sudokus get done at the courthouse.

35. See if there is a law library that you can use to do research while you wait. If you've signed in, you will be paged when your case is reached.

36. Dress neatly in clean clothes. You do not need to buy a new suit or clothes. Be conservative and respectful in your dress and behaviour (for example, avoid T-shirts with offensive messages; wear proper shoes).

37. In court, do not chew gum, eat, read a newspaper, sleep, wear a hat, listen to music or chat with other people.

38. Once the court proceeding begins, address all comments directly to the judge. Do not address your spouse or the other lawyer directly. All communication flows through the judge.

39. Address the judge as Your Honour.

40. Remember to speak loudly and clearly, and to only one person at a time.

41. When the hearing is complete, get a copy of the judge's endorsement.

42. After the judge has made his or her decision, tell the judge about any offer to settle that you made.

43. Ask for costs if you are successful. Even though you have not incurred legal fees, you may have taken time off work. Ask the judge for $1,000 to compensate for your time. If you don't ask, you won't receive any costs.

44. If you don't understand something that has happened, ask the court to explain. (For example, *"Excuse me, Your Honour, I didn't understand the last comment that you made about going forward. Could you explain what you meant? Thank you."*)

45. Sit down and make a note to yourself about what happened: what went well and what went poorly.

46. Ask the judge for clarification on what will happen next.

47. At the end of the hearing, thank the judge.

48. Is there a date to return to court?

49. Is it necessary for you to approve the form of any order made by the court? Sometimes the judge will make an endorsement on the record in handwriting, but the order will then be typed up by a lawyer to make it an official document. In most cases you will need to see that typewritten version and confirm that it captures what the judge has written in the record. It will be necessary to compare the endorsement with the typewritten version.

50. Take a few minutes to relax and decompress.

DEALING WITH LAWYERS

AS I MENTIONED in the previous section, you should not be surprised if lawyers are reluctant to talk to you and insist on everything being in writing. My advice to you is to be unfailingly civil with lawyers, as much as you may resent steps that they take on behalf of their client. Matters will only become worse if communications become acrimonious. I recommend that all communications be written as if the judge will read them. Marking a letter "without prejudice" in an attempt to shield some ugly comment may not protect the communication. Remember, letters that are marked "without prejudice" are designed to allow the parties and lawyers to communicate for the purposes of settlement.

I have noticed that swearing and foul language is often an issue in communications on family law cases. Lawyers are often as guilty of it as clients. Many of my clients will attest to the fact that I actively discourage the use of foul language because it adds an ugliness to the matter. There is enough tension without further poisoning the air. I recall a trial that I did in which the wife testified about the foul language the husband used in his communications with her. Her lawyer asked her to tell the judge word for word the kind of abusive language her husband used. It had a withering effect on the husband's case.

Keep all communications in writing. Keep those communications professional, and keep copies of all communication.

There will be times when you will need to communicate face to face with the lawyer at the court office. Again, these communications should be civil no matter how emotional the issues. Angry yelling is never a solution. If anything, it could trigger the intervention of security personnel. One day I watched as a wife engaged in a screaming match with a lawyer in the hallway. The lawyer was concerned for her own safety and summoned the security personnel. When the case was ultimately heard, the woman in question sat in court with a police officer on either side of her. You can imagine the impression this made on the judge.

DEALING WITH COURT STAFF

AS I'VE MENTIONED earlier, court staff cannot provide advice, but they can provide information. The same general rules that apply to communication with lawyers apply to the staff. They must be treated with courtesy and patience. They have a difficult job to do, looking after thousands of cases and scheduling matters for multiple courtrooms. Treated properly, they can be of great assistance.

DEALING WITH THE JUDGE

IN THE LIST of tips for your day in court, I have mentioned that the judge should always be referred to as "Your Honour." Remember that, as you sit in court, the judge is sizing you up. I have noticed in cases where the opposing client has been representing himself or herself, that even while I am making a presentation to the judge, he or she is often glancing over at the self-represented person to measure their reaction to my comments. During presentation of the case, I recommend that you avoid any histrionics such as rolling of eyes, shaking of your head or other gestures. These will only have a negative influence on the judge. I have even seen judges tell self-represented people to stop making gestures. Similarly, it is inappropriate to interrupt the other side while they are speaking. If they've said something to which you object, make a note, and then when they have finished their presentation, stand and tell the judge that you need to comment on some points that were raised. The last thing a judge wants to see or hear is a self-represented person shouting out, "That's a lie!" or "I never said that!" These kinds of outbursts undermine your credibility.

By watching the judge during the court case, you can often tell what is catching his or her interest. Address the things in which the judge shows interest. If the judge asks questions about child support, deal with those questions. Do not try to change the subject to custody because that is more important to you. It seems trite to say this, but self-represented people need to listen to the judge. In trying to understand each side's position, the judge asks a question because he or she is trying to get a handle on a certain aspect of the case.

GETTING HELP FROM LAWYERS: THE LIMITED RETAINER

PART OF THE justice system's and legal profession's response to the rise of self-represented parties has been the provision of selected pieces of legal advice under a "limited retainer." The client does not hire the lawyer to do the case from start to finish, but rather hires the lawyer to provide, for example, a memorandum of law on a particular issue. A client may hire a lawyer to prepare court materials. In some cases I've seen lawyers hired simply to make the court presentation, based on documents that were prepared by the client. If there is an important stage in your case that would benefit from a lawyer's opinion, consider the use of a limited retainer. Judges appreciate lawyers chipping in, even part-time, on cases.

LEGAL RESEARCH

IT MAY BE hard to believe, but for all the details we have covered in the preceding chapters, we have only scratched the surface. You may want to do further reading on the various subjects I have covered, and I encourage you to do so. In this section, I have collected a list of materials and resources you may find useful.

Some of the books will be available at the local public library, some are available in university or law school libraries and some are available free from the provincial, territorial or federal governments. A great deal of material is available on the Internet.

Before going any further, I want to add a short note for those who might be adventurous enough to try a law school library. Every province has a law school (Ontario has six) and you should feel free to use their library—your tax dollars have paid for every one of them. Having said that, take note that law students can be a tense bunch, with a lot on their minds—especially around exam time. I know, because I have taught at Osgoode Hall Law School, the University of Ottawa Law School, Carleton University's Department of Law, as well as Ryerson University. I have always found the staff at the various libraries to be very co-operative. They will be more than happy to help you use the indexing system, now computerized at all schools, and locate the appropriate resource. Once you have it, find a nice quiet spot away from the fuss of studying students and settle in for a read. You cannot remove books from these libraries.

Law books often contain case citations—codes to help locate actual reported decisions in cases that have been to court. These cases are likely located right there in the library and can be found with a little help and some digging. Not all cases are reported, but the most significant ones are routinely published. (Remember those "Reasons for Judgment.")

The following are the more popular sources of actual family law cases as reported:

- *Ontario Reports* (O.R.) and other provincial series, such as the *Manitoba Reports* (MAN.R.) or the *Western Weekly Reports* (W.W.R.)
- *Reports on Family Law* (R.F.L.)
- *Dominion Law Reports* (D.L.R.)

A typical case citation would be as follows:

Pettkus v. Becker (1980), 117 D.L.R. (3d) 257 or (1980), 19 R.F.L. (2d) 165
Gordon v. Goertz (1996), 19 R.F.L. (4th) 177 S.C.C.
Contino v. Leonelli-Contino, 2005 SCC 63

The names are the names of the people involved, and the year refers to the year in which the case was reported (not necessarily the same as the year in which it was decided). The next number is a reference to the volume of the particular service (for example, Vol. 117 of the *Dominion Law Reports* or Vol. 19 of the *Reports on Family Law)*. These volume numbers are printed on the spine of the book near the name of the reporting service. The next bit of information describes which edition of the service carries the case. All editions are filed chronologically. Be careful you don't pick up the right volume number but the wrong edition. The last number is the page reference.

Usually, but not always, the case names are the same, for example, *Brown v. Brown, Porter v. Porter* and so on.

If you want some experience locating family law decisions in a law library, try locating the following volumes:

- *Andris v. Andris* (1984), 40 R.F.L. (2d) 315 (Sask.)
- *Brockie v. Brockie* (1987), 5 R.F.L. (3d) 440 (Manitoba)
- *Moss v. Moss* (1916), 5 R.F.L. (3d) 62 (Nfld.)
- *Chapman v. Chapman* (2001), 15 R.F.L. (5th) 46 (Ont. C.A.)
- *Walsh v. Bona*, [2002] 4 S.C.R. 325

Note: When asking for a case, describe it as "Andris and Andris" not "Andris versus Andris."

May I also suggest that you take a moment to read the case *Bruni v. Bruni*. This case is reported in the *Ontario Reports* for (2011), 104 O.R. (3d) 254, which can be found at www.canlii.org. It is a decision of the Superior Court of Justice, Justice Quinn. It was decided in November 2010 but is reported in 2011. It involves two individuals, each appearing in person and representing themselves. Justice Quinn's decision begins with the words, "Paging Dr. Freud. Paging Dr. Freud. This is yet another case that reveals the ineffectiveness of family court in a bitter custody/access dispute where the parties require therapeutic intervention rather than legal attention. Here, a husband and wife have been marinating in a mutual hatred so intense as to surely amount to a personality disorder requiring treatment." Justice Quinn's colourful Reasons illustrate a textbook case of how not to represent yourself in family court.

There are other terrific resources available in the law library. For example, track down a book called *Ontario Family Law Practice* by Justice Craig Perkins, Justice David Steinberg and Esther Lenkinski (published by LexisNexis Canada). It is an exhaustive collection of laws and cases related to family law in Ontario. A similar publication exists in each province, whereby the province's laws are collected along with cases that interpret them. I have a book for lawyers and law clerks called *Family Law in Ontario* (published by Canada Law Book), which is available in many law libraries and law firms. I am not recommending that you purchase these books—they are very expensive—but you should use them for research purposes.

It can be a lot of fun doing research in a law library. If you get bored with family law cases, try *Canadian Criminal Cases*—you won't want to go home until you have registered for law school!

INTERNET RESOURCES

THE INTERNET AND other technology have dramatically changed the availability of legal information to the average person. Virtually everything is now accessible online. Some of it is free and some of it requires subscriptions. For your purposes, more than enough is available absolutely free—but you need to be careful. A lot of it can be unreliable.

Many law firms have websites. These "electronic brochures" at least allow you to get a sense of the firm without actually going to the office. Larger law firms maintain very elaborate websites. They often publish papers on those websites to demonstrate their expertise in particular areas. These papers are written by experts and are often very readable, as the lawyers have sometimes prepared the papers for their clients. This information is excellent and it is reliable, so by all means, go to law firm websites. You will more often than not find a menu item called "Members of Our Team." Here you may find one or more family law lawyers. Under their names you may find articles they have written, which can be of use to you and your case. Remember, these articles should not be filed with the court as proof of the law, as judges generally only want to hear about other court decisions or the actual provisions of the law. The articles, however, can assist you in understanding how certain areas of the law are intended to work, and it's all absolutely free.

In the area of self-help information, I need to add a little caution. There are services in the marketplace that sell books and tapes, and offer access to lawyers and tips on family law. Some of the sources have very weak materials and have caused some general harm to consumers; some tend to have an "angry" aspect to their marketing, and their pitch is often gender-focused. I recommend that you steer clear of such services. I have had to fix more than one mess created by some very bad advice. In two cases, it cost more to fix the mess than the actual service that was required in the first place. In conclusion, by all means use both self-help and free resources, but be very careful when somebody asks for your cash or credit card. Avoid anyone who seems to be hawking angry or spiteful advice. You need help, not fuel for the fire!

I recommend the following Internet resources for general legal research:

- The Canadian Legal Information Institute: www.canlii.org
- Department of Justice Canada Family Law: www.justice.gc.ca/eng/fl-df/
- Department of Justice Canada Homepage: www.canada.justice.gc.ca/eng/index.html
- *Divorce Magazine*: www.divorcemag.com
- Duhaime Law Dictionary: www.duhaime.org
- Family Lawyers Association: www.flao.org
- *Family Matters* online television program: www.familymatterstv.com
- Federal Court of Appeal: www.fca-caf.gc.ca
- Law Now: www.lawnow.org
- UpToParents, www.uptoparents.org, an interactive website of articles, videos and exercises that is child focused and provides links to related sites such as www.whileweheal.org and www.proudtoparent.org for common-law parents.
- www.ourfamilywizard.com and www.google.com/calendar are websites that can assist parents to communicate and plan their children's schedules.

The Ontario Ministry of the Attorney General has established an interactive website to assist Ontarians to fill out 11 of the most commonly used family and civil court forms, www.ontariocourtforms.on.ca/english. British Columbia has an excellent website maintained by the Legal Services Society, see www.familylaw.lss.bc.ca, or see Alberta's www.albertacourts.ab.ca/familylaw. New Brunswick also has a site for its citizens: www.familylawnb.ca. Check to see if your province has an equivalent online assistant for completing forms. Other resources include:

- Alberta: www.albertacourts.ab.ca
- British Columbia: www.courts.gov.bc.ca
- Manitoba: www.manitobacourts.mb.ca
- New Brunswick: www.gnb.ca/cour
- Newfoundland and Labrador: www.court.nl.ca
- Northwest Territories: www.justice.gov.nt.ca/en
- Nova Scotia: www.courts.ns.ca
- Nunavut: www.nucj.ca
- Ontario: www.ontariocourts.on.ca/coa/en
- Prince Edward Island: www.gov.pe.ca/courts
- Quebec: www.jugements.qc.ca
- Saskatchewan: www.sasklawcourts.ca
- Yukon: www.yukoncourts.ca
- Association of Family and Conciliation Courts Ontario, www.afc-contario.ca, is a multidisciplinary organization for lawyers, judges, psychologists, psychiatrists, counsellors and mediators.
- Centre for Public Legal Education Alberta: www.cplea.ca
- Families Change, www.familieschange.ca, is a website developed by the Justice Education Society of British Columbia.
- Legal Aid Ontario: www.legalaid.on.ca
- Legal Aid Ontario Family Law Information Program: www.legalaid.on.ca/en/getting/flip.asp
- Nova Scotia Barristers' Society: www.nsbs.org
- Great, accessible information about the impact of tax law on family law: www.duffandphelps.com

If all else fails, try Wikipedia, which may take you to some general information that, in turn, could lead you to some specific sites. However, do recall my cautions about ensuring that the information you receive applies to the jurisdiction in which you reside and about being circumspect regarding any information you receive from questionable sites. Under no circumstances quote any of these Internet resources as an authority for doing something in court. These are simply online vehicles for you to find legal information. Judges in court are interested in statutes, rules, regulations and cases interpreting those categories. They are not interested in an article written by a lawyer for his or her website, blogs or other commentary.

HOW TO COMPLAIN

MY GUESS IS that despite all of the advice, forewarning and caution set out in this book, you will still probably be disappointed in some way by a part of the system, the people in it or the outcome of your case.

Experience tells us that one or more of the following may give you cause to complain. If so, there is usually something you can do.

- If you are unhappy about your lawyer's conduct or competence, then contact your provincial law society.
- If the judge mistreated you, make a complaint in writing. For federally appointed judges, contact the Canadian Judicial Council in Ottawa; for provincially appointed judges, contact the appropriate provincial judicial discipline body for judges in your province.
- If the court system let you down, then contact your provincial Ministry of the Attorney General.
- If the mediator didn't do a good job, then forward your complaint to the appropriate provincial association and also send a copy to Family Mediation Canada.
- If the children's lawyer didn't help, then contact your province's Attorney General's Department.
- If the law needs to change, then contact your provincial Attorney General or the federal Minister of Justice.
- If your spouse let you down again, how should you complain? You already know how to do that.

One of the most difficult aspects about complaining is that it is time-consuming and forces you to continue to think about a part of your life that you would just as soon put behind you. In many situations, your complaint may not change the outcome of your own case. So, why do it? Because even though complaining is hard work, it's often worth it.

CLOSING REMARKS

IF YOU ARE undertaking self-representation you will have your hands full. That does not mean it is impossible. I have seen many self-represented people do a terrific job in court. They have handled themselves in an organized, clear and rational manner. If you follow the 10 steps, use the legal research tools available to you and take the approach of doing what is best for your children and your own future, you will certainly minimize your emotional stress and costs.

I wish you good luck.

MY ADVICE

1. Develop a clear and organized framework for your case based on accurate facts, evidence, your issues and what you want a judge to do for you.
2. Organize your materials and documents as if you were a lawyer with labelled file folders, tabs to identify documents and even a special briefcase to carry it all around.
3. Conduct thorough legal research and, even if you're representing yourself, consider hiring a lawyer for a bit of advice on what you're doing.
4. Review the 50 tips over and over—before you get to court.
5. Remember to tell the judge what you want.
6. Only represent yourself as a last resort. It can be very draining emotionally and physically. There is a lot at stake.

APPENDIX A

Some Important Paperwork

MOUNTAINS OF PAPER will be exchanged in family law cases, everything from letters between lawyers, faxes, copies of e-mails, pleadings, evidence, Offers to Settle and affidavits, to Separation Agreements and divorce judgments. I wish I could provide you with an example of each one, but space considerations simply won't permit it. Instead, I have selected three key documents for your consideration: a retainer form, a Separation Agreement and a Client History Form. Before each one, I have provided a brief annotation about its purpose and where in the text you can find more information about its role.

Please note: In the following sample documents, [ ] means you should insert name, address, geographical, age or title information, if not otherwise specified.

A RETAINER FORM

THIS IS YOUR contract with your lawyer. In it, he or she should describe the work that will be done on your behalf and the estimated (or maximum) cost of the work. Retainers vary from lawyer to lawyer, but they should have, as a minimum, the amount of detail contained in the following example. You should always have a written retainer with your lawyer. For more information on retainers, read Chapter 2: Taking A Look At Lawyers and see the definitions in the glossary.

Sample Retainer Form

I, [CLIENT'S NAME], of the City of [city name] in the Regional Municipality of [municipality name] hereby retain and employ Messrs. Cochrane & Cochrane, [City/Province] as my solicitors and hereby authorize them to [purpose] and to take such actions and conduct such proceedings as they may consider necessary or proper for the conduct of such action on my behalf.

DATED this [ ] day of [ ], [ ].

Witness: _____

_____
[Signature of client]

Sample Fees and Disbursements Policy

FOR THE INFORMATION of clients, the firm's policy in regard to fees and disbursements is as follows:

1. All services performed by lawyers and students on behalf of a client are ordinarily recorded on a time-occupied basis and charged against the client on that basis at rates ranging from $500 per hour down to $75 per hour. The hourly rates are reviewed on an annual basis. Time in court may be charged in certain cases at rates in excess of $5,000 per day depending upon the nature of the case, its complexity, and the lawyer or lawyers involved.

2. Most matters require the disbursement of money by the firm on the client's behalf. These disbursements will be billed regularly to the client as they are incurred on an interim statement of account entitled "Disbursements Only."

3. HST will be billed as a separate item and fee quotations do not include HST.

4. In most litigious and other matters, clients will be requested to provide an advance on accounts of fees and disbursements, which sum will be held in the firm's trust account to the client's credit to be applied towards such disbursements and fees incurred in connection with the matter.

5. It is recognized by this firm that many clients are unfamiliar with the manner in which lawyers bill and, further, are unfamiliar with the amount of fees that may be owing from time to time during the course of a particular proceeding. In the circumstances, clients are encouraged to discuss fees at any time with any representative of the firm and, in particular, to discuss the method of billing when the firm is originally retained.

Sample Note to Litigant

IN VIEW OF the fact that [lawyer's name]'s practice involves a great deal of court work, he/she may be out of his/her office, or on occasion, out of the City and thus sometimes unavailable on an immediate basis for appointments or reception of telephone calls. On those occasions, his/her secretary and other members of the firm who are familiar with your case will be of as much assistance to you as possible.

[Lawyer's name] will, of course, attend to your problem at his/her earliest opportunity.

Note: Fees (exclusive of HST and disbursements) will not exceed $ without prior written authorization.

Barristers & Solicitors

City

Telephone Number

Note: Whether the lawyer's preprinted form includes it or not, I recommend placing a limit on the maximum fee that could be incurred without prior authorization. Write it in by hand if necessary.

A SEPARATION AGREEMENT

THE SEPARATION AGREEMENT is the most common of the three types of domestic contracts (the other two are Cohabitation Agreements and Marriage Contracts). All three contracts must be written, signed and witnessed. A Separation Agreement acknowledges that the parties are living separate and apart and intend to do so from now on. It sets out important details about their background, their marriage, children and so on. It then describes, in as much detail as is required, the terms upon which the parties will end their marriage. It can deal with all or only some of the outstanding concerns. It may describe who will have custody and access, who will have which pieces of property, possession of the home on an interim or permanent basis, responsibility for family debts, life insurance, and so on. The agreement can be final or interim (temporary).

The following example of a Separation Agreement is not a complete document, but shows a selection of typical provisions and some alternatives. Law offices have draft clauses and agreements in their computers. Legal secretaries prepare a first draft by filling in the blanks. While the following is not necessarily a model agreement for your situation, it will help you to understand how comprehensive an agreement can be.

Sample Separation Agreement

THIS IS A SEPARATION AGREEMENT MADE ON [day/month/year].

BETWEEN:
[husband's name]
–and–
[wife's name]

1. INTERPRETATION
1. In this Agreement,
    (a) "husband" means [name], who is one of the parties to this Agreement, whether or not the husband and the wife are subsequently divorced;

(b) "wife" means [name], who is one of the parties to this Agreement, whether or not the husband and the wife are subsequently divorced;

(c) "child" means [child's name], born on [date], or, [child's name], born on [date], both of whom are the children [ ] or who is the child [ ] of the husband and the wife [ ];

(d) "cohabit" means to live together in a conjugal relationship, whether within or outside marriage;

(e) "matrimonial home" means the buildings and lot located at [address];

(f) "cottage" means the buildings and lot called [address];

(g) "Family Law Act" means the Family Law Act (or relevant provincial law);

(h) "property" has the meaning given by the Family Law Act.

2. An Act of the Legislature or Parliament referred to by name will mean that Act in force at the material time and includes any amendment or any successor Act that replaces it.

3. The proper law of this contract shall be the law of [appropriate province], and this contract shall also be deemed to be valid and enforceable in accordance with the law of any other jurisdiction. The parties intend all of their affairs and property to be governed by this contract and the law of [appropriate province].

4. The parties agree that the contract is valid and enforceable in [appropriate province] and that they intend it to be a domestic contract in accordance with the Family Law Act, and that it is legally binding.

2. BACKGROUND

This Agreement is entered into on a basis of the following, among other facts:

1. The parties were married at [location], on [date].

2. The parties have [ ] child [ ], born on], and [ ], born on [ ].

3. The parties have no children.

4. The parties are living separate and apart from each other since [date], and there is no reasonable prospect of their resuming cohabitation.

5. The parties desire to settle by agreement all their rights and obligations that they have or may have with respect to:

- the custody of, and access to, their child [ ],
- the support of their child [ ],
- possession, ownership and division of their property and
- support of each other.

3. AGREEMENT
Each party agrees with the other to be bound by the provisions of this Agreement.

4. DOMESTIC CONTRACT
Each party acknowledges that this Agreement is entered into under s. 54 of the Family Law Act [or appropriate provincial law] and is a domestic contract, which prevails over the same matters provided for in the Act or its successor.

5. EFFECTIVE DATE
This Agreement will take effect on the date it is signed by the last of the husband or the wife.

6. LIVING SEPARATE AND APART
The parties will live separate and apart from each other for the rest of their lives.

7. FREEDOM FROM THE OTHER
Neither party will molest, annoy, harass or in any way interfere with the other, or attempt to compel the other to cohabit or live with him or her.

8. CUSTODY AND ACCESS (SOLE CUSTODY/ACCESS)
1. The wife will have custody of the child, subject to reasonable access by the husband on reasonable notice to the wife of his intention to exercise such access.
2. The husband will have access to the child [ ] as follows:
   (a) (Be very specific: days, times, holidays, special events, total number of days per year, make-up times.)
   (b) The husband and the wife each acknowledge that it is in the best interests of the child [ ] for [ ] to have frequent contact with [ ]

father and to spend time with him. Accordingly, the husband and the wife will each use their best efforts for the child to have frequent and regular periods of access with the husband, consisting of a combination of both daytime and overnight visits appropriate to the needs and stage of development of the child.

(c) In making plans for access, the husband and the wife will give the needs and convenience of the child primary importance and will give their own needs and convenience only secondary importance.

(d) The parties will keep each other fully informed of all matters touching the interest of the child and they will confer as often as necessary to solve any difficulty raised by or on behalf of the child.

8. CUSTODY (JOINT)

(a) The child [name] shall be in the joint custody of the husband and the wife. The child shall have [his or her] primary residence in the home of the [ ].

(b) The husband and wife each acknowledge that the other is a devoted and loving parent. The [ ] acknowledges that it is essential to the welfare of the child [ ] that [ ] have as close communication and contact with the [ ] as is reasonably possible, commensurate with the best interests of the child [ ].

(c) The husband and wife agree and undertake that in all matters relating to the custody, maintenance, education and general well-being of the child, the child's best interests and wishes shall at all times be paramount.

(d) The husband and wife shall conscientiously respect the rights of one another regarding the child. The husband and wife shall continue to instill in the child respect for both of the parents and grandparents, and neither the husband nor wife shall by any act, omission or innuendo, in any way tend or attempt to alienate the child from either of them. The child shall be taught to continue to love and respect both parents.

(e) The husband and wife shall have the right to communicate with the child by telephone and letter at all reasonable times, provided that such telephone communication shall not interfere with the private life of either the husband or the wife.

(f) The husband and wife agree that there shall be full disclosure between them in all matters touching the welfare of the child, and they agree that they shall confer as often as necessary to consider any problem or difficulty or matter requiring consideration touching the welfare of the child.

(g) The [ ] shall have generous and regular access to the child. It is acknowledged that the kind, frequency and duration of such access should be established in advance, and made as certain as existing circumstances permit, in order to enable the child, the husband and the wife to make plans for their day-to-day living.

(h) If special occasions, holidays, excursions or other presently unforeseeable opportunities become available to the child, neither the husband nor the wife will unreasonably insist that visiting arrangements be adhered to without exception. On the contrary, the husband and the wife shall at all times maintain a reasonable and flexible position respecting the visiting arrangements with the child, and at all times, the best interests of the child shall prevail.

(i) In any matter of contention between the husband and the wife that the husband and wife cannot resolve between themselves by mutual agreement, the parties agree to mediate any such disagreements or differences of opinion through a mediator that the parties may hereafter agree upon. If the parties are not able to agree on a mediator or if the mediation is unsuccessful, the parties acknowledge that either one of them may bring an application to a court of competent jurisdiction to resolve the outstanding matters between them.

(j) The husband and wife acknowledge that the wife may wish to change her residence from the Province of [Ontario] as a result of remarriage or career opportunities. The husband acknowledges that provided that the wife is leaving the Province of [Ontario] for such reasons, he will not take any action that would prevent the wife from leaving the Province of [Ontario] or unduly insist on exercising the access as set out in this Agreement in order that the wife be prevented from changing her residence from the Province of [Ontario]. The wife agrees to give the husband at least sixty (60) days notice of any intention to change her residence from the Province of [Ontario] for the reasons set out in this paragraph so that the parties may make alternate arrangements with respect to access to the children, or

(k) Neither party shall move more than thirty (30) km from the city of [ ] without the consent of the other.

(l) Neither shall change the child's name without the consent of the other.

9. FINANCIAL PROVISION (SPOUSAL AND RELEASE)

1. Both parties accept the terms of this agreement in full satisfaction of all claims and causes of action which he or she now has or may in the future acquire against the other for support whether under the Divorce Act, the Family Law Act, the Succession Law Reform Act, or otherwise, under presently existing legislation or future legislation whether in this jurisdiction or any other jurisdiction and releases the other from any such claim. They each intend this agreement to be forever final and non-variable.

2. Each of the parties, and "w" in particular, releases all rights to claim from the other or obtain from the other, and releases the other of any obligations to provide support, interim support, maintenance, interim maintenance or alimony for himself or herself pursuant to any statute or law or the common law.

3. This agreement has been negotiated in an unimpeachable fashion and fully represents the intentions and expectations of the parties. Both parties have had independent legal advice and all the disclosure they have asked for and need in order to understand the nature and consequences of this agreement and to come to the conclusion, as they do, that the terms of this agreement, including the release of all spousal support rights, constitutes an equitable sharing of both the economic consequences of their relationship and its breakdown.

4. The parties agree that the terms of this agreement substantially comply with the overall objectives of the Divorce Act now and in the future and the parties' need to exercise their autonomous rights to

achieve certainty and finality. In particular, the parties acknowledge that they have taken into consideration the factors and objectives set out in section 15.2 of the Divorce Act and applied those considerations to their current situation.

5. The terms of this agreement and, in particular, this release of spousal support reflect their own unique particular objectives and concerns. Among other considerations, they are also depending upon this spousal release remaining in full force and effect upon which to base their future lives. As a result, each party recognizes that the other party is relying upon the provisions for spousal support not being changed from as set out in this agreement and will be arranging his and her affairs accordingly.

6. The parties acknowledge that they have been advised of the significance of the decision rendered by the Supreme Court of Canada in the case of *Miglin v. Miglin*. They have applied their minds to the negotiation of this agreement as they understand a married couple should do when separating. In that regard, they each specifically acknowledge and confirm that this agreement was prepared with the advice of experienced family law lawyers acting for both parties and in circumstances without any kind of pressure or undue influence from the other. There was an ample period of time for each party to receive full and complete legal advice and each party has sought and obtained that advice.

7. "h" and "w" do not want the courts to undermine their autonomy as reflected in the terms of this agreement, which they intend to be a final and certain settling of all issues between them. They wish to be allowed to get on with their separate and independent lives, no matter what changes may occur. "h" and "w" specifically anticipate that one or both of them may lose their jobs, become ill and be unable to work, have additional childcare responsibilities that will interfere with their ability to work, find their financial resources diminished or exhausted whether through their own fault or not, or be affected by general economic and family conditions changing over time. They each also recognize that the financial circumstances of the other may improve modestly or dramatically. Changes in their circumstances may be catastrophic, unanticipated, or beyond imagining.

Nevertheless, no change, no matter how extreme, will alter this agreement and their view that the terms of this agreement reflect their intention to always be separate financially. "h" and "w" fully accept that no change whatsoever in their circumstances, or the circumstances of the other, will entitle either of them to spousal support from the other.

8. This agreement and this section in particular may be pleaded as a complete defence to any claim brought by either spouse to assert a claim for support.

9. FINANCIAL PROVISION (CHILD SUPPORT)

1. Commencing on the [ ] day of [ ], [year], and on the [ ] day of each and every month thereafter, the husband shall pay to the wife for the support of the child [ ], the sum of [ ] per month (per child), being a total of [ ] for the support of [ ] in accordance with the child support guidelines based on a gross annual income of $[ ], until one or more of the following occurs:

   (a) the child becomes eighteen (18) years old and ceases to be in full-time attendance at an educational institution,

   (b) the child ceases to reside with the wife,

   (c) the child becomes twenty-two (22) years old,

   (d) the child marries or

   (e) the child dies.

2. In clause (b), "reside" means to live in the home of the wife and the child does not cease to reside in the home of the wife when the child is temporarily away from home to attend an educational institution, to work at summer employment, or to enjoy a reasonable holiday.

3. The parents agree to share the child's special expenses in accordance with the child support guidelines and will divide them annually in proportion to their respective gross annual incomes.

9. FINANCIAL PROVISION (ALTERNATIVE SPOUSAL)

1. Commencing on the [ ] day of [ ], [year], and on the [ ] day of each and every month thereafter, the husband shall pay to the wife for her own support, the sum of [ ] per month, until one or more of the following occurs:

(a) the wife remarries or cohabits,

(b) the wife dies or

(c) the husband dies.

2. The husband and wife agree that the spousal support will be paid each and every month until the [ ] day of [ ], [year], at which time it will be reviewed on application to the court [or alternatively that it will be terminated at that date].

10. INDEXING SUPPORT

1. The amount of support payable under this Agreement for the support of:

   (a) the wife will be increased annually on the anniversary date of the effective date of this agreement by the indexing factor, as defined in subsection 2, for November of the previous year.

2. The indexing factor for a given month is the percentage change in the Consumer Price Index for Canada for all prices of all items since the same month of the previous year, as published by Statistics Canada.

10. INDEXING SUPPORT (ALTERNATIVE)

1. The support payments outlined in paragraph [ ] shall be increased annually in each year commencing in [ ], [year], for so long as spousal [ ] support is payable under this Agreement, by an amount equal to the lesser of the [ ] annual percentage increase in the cost of living of the preceding year and the annual percentage increase in the husband's salary [ ]. The increase shall be calculated according to the Consumer Price Index for Canada for prices of all items since the same month of the previous year, as published by Statistics Canada.

2. The wife shall deliver to the husband a notice in or about the month of [ ], [year] with respect to the increase in spousal [ ] support based on the cost of living increase. If the husband alleges that his increase in salary is less than the said increase in the cost of living he shall provide such evidence of the salary increase to the wife within thirty (30) days of the delivery by the wife of the notice to him. If the husband fails to deliver such evidence to the wife, the increase shall be in accordance with the cost of living as set out in paragraph [ ] herein.

11. WAIVER OF RIGHT TO INDEX SUPPORT PAYMENTS

Each party hereby:
- (a) waives any right and
- (b) releases the other from all claims

that he or she has or may have to require that the amounts or any amount payable for support under this Agreement be increased annually, or at any time, by an indexing factor as provided in the Family Law Act, or by any factor or percentage.

12. MATERIAL CHANGE IN CIRCUMSTANCES

1. The husband and wife intend paragraphs [ ] to be final, except for variation in the event of a material change in circumstances. If such change occurs, the husband or wife seeking the variation will give to the other a written notice of the variation he or she is seeking, and the husband and wife will then confer either personally or through their respective solicitors to settle what, if any, variation should be made.

2. If no agreement has been reached thirty (30) clear days after notice has been given under paragraph (1), variation relating to custody, access and support of the child and wife may be determined at the instance of either the husband or the wife by an application pursuant to the Family Law Act, or the Divorce Act. Any such application by a party shall be deemed to be an application for maintenance or support pursuant to the Family Law Act or the Divorce Act.

13. HEALTH AND MEDICAL EXPENSES

1. The husband warrants that he is maintaining in force for the benefit of the wife and child a plan of insurance established under a health insurance plan to protect them against the costs of health services.

2. The husband agrees to continue this insurance or equivalent insurance,
    - (a) in the case of the wife until one or more the following occurs:
        1. the marriage is terminated or
        2. the wife cohabits with another man.
    - (b) in the case of each child so long as he is obligated by this Agreement to support the child.

3. If the husband fails to maintain this insurance or equivalent insurance, he will pay the costs of all health services that would have been paid by the insurance.

14. DENTAL AND ADDITIONAL MEDICAL COVERAGE

The husband agrees to continue a dental and medical plan for the benefit of the wife and child through his place of employment as long as he is able to obtain coverage for such plans through such employment, for the wife until the husband and wife are divorced and for the child so long as he is required to provide for [spousal or child] support under this Agreement.

15. MATRIMONIAL HOME AND CONTENTS

1. The parties acknowledge that they hold the matrimonial home as joint tenants.
2. The parties agree that the wife may remain in exclusive possession of the matrimonial home until one or more of the following occurs:
   (a) five years elapse from the date of this Agreement,
   (b) the wife remarries,
   (c) the wife cohabits with another man,
   (d) the wife ceases to reside on a full-time basis in the premises or
   (e) the husband and the wife agree in writing to the contrary.
3. During the period of her exclusive possession of the matrimonial home, the wife will be responsible for paying all mortgage payments, taxes, insurance premiums, heating, water and other charges related to the matrimonial home, and will save the husband harmless from all liability for those payments.
4. The wife will keep the matrimonial home fully insured at her expense to its full replacement value against loss or damage by fire or other perils covered by a standard fire insurance extended coverage or additional perils supplemental contract and will apply any insurance proceeds to reasonable repairs. The insurance will cover both the husband's and the wife's interest in the matrimonial home. If the husband demands it, the wife will produce proof of premium payments and of the policy being in force. The husband and the wife will direct the insurer to send notices of premiums to both of them.

5. The parties will bear equally the costs of major repairs to the matrimonial home, but only if the repairs are undertaken with the consent of both parties. No consent will be unreasonably withheld.

6. During the period of her exclusive possession of the matrimonial home, the wife shall not change the use of the home, shall maintain its "principal residence" status within the meaning of the Income Tax Act, and shall so designate the home (and no other property) pursuant thereto. If the wife, contrary to this Agreement, sublets the matrimonial home, changes her use of it, does not maintain its "principal residence" status for tax purposes, or does not designate it (or other property) as her principal residence, with the result that the husband becomes liable to pay any tax or penalty under the Income Tax Act, then the wife agrees to indemnify the husband with respect to the liability or penalty.

7. When the wife is no longer entitled to exclusive possession of the matrimonial home, it will immediately be sold. Upon the sale of the matrimonial home, the proceeds will be divided equally between the parties. The wife may continue to remain in exclusive possession of the matrimonial home until the closing date of its sale. Any difference between the husband and wife on the method in terms of sale shall be resolved under the section of this Agreement providing for the solution of differences.

8. The husband and wife agree to divide the contents equally between them as they may agree.
(Or)

9. The husband and wife acknowledge that the contents have been divided between them to their mutual satisfaction and that each is entitled to the contents in his or her possession.

16. COTTAGE

1. Each party acknowledges that the cottage was held by the parties as joint tenants until the transfer referred to in subsection (2) was made.

2. Contemporaneously with the execution of this Agreement, the parties have transferred the cottage from themselves as joint tenants to the husband as sole owner.

3. The wife waives any right she has or may have to, or any interest she

has or may have in the cottage, and releases the husband from any claim she has or may have to any such right or interest.

17. PRINCIPAL RESIDENCE DESIGNATION

1. For the purpose of the "principal residence" designation provided for in the Income Tax Act, the wife will designate the family residence as her principal residence for the years from the date of acquisition up to and including [year], and the husband will designate the cottage as his principal residence for the years from the date of acquisition up to and including [year].
2. Both the husband and wife will designate the family residence as their principal residence for each of the years after [year] to and including the year in which this Agreement is executed.
3. Neither the husband nor the wife will designate any other residence or property as his or her principal residence in any of the years after [year] to and including the year in which this Agreement is executed.

18. AUTOMOBILES

(a) (as may be agreed) (identify vehicle specifically)

19. CANADA PENSION PLAN

The wife may apply under the Canada Pension Plan for a division of pension credits.

20. PRIVATE PENSION PLANS

(a) (as may be agreed)

21. INVESTMENTS AND OTHER SAVINGS

(a) (as may be agreed)

22. LIFE INSURANCE

1. Contemporaneously with the execution of this Agreement, the husband has delivered to the wife (a certified copy of) the following policy [ ]
   (a) Policy No. [ ] of [ ] Insurance Company, having a face value of $[ ] and

(b) Policy No. [ ] of [ ] Insurance Company, having a face value of $ [ ].

2. The husband warrants that he has irrevocably designated the wife as the sole beneficiary under the above policy and that he has filed the designation with the principal office of the respective insurer in accordance with the provisions of the Insurance Act. (Ontario)

3. The husband will pay all premiums when they become due and will keep the policy in force for the benefit of the wife as long as he is required to pay support or maintenance for either the wife or child.

4. Upon the happening of any one of the events described in subsection (3), the husband may deal with the policy as he deems fit free from any claim by the wife or her estate.

5. The husband will deliver to the wife, within fourteen (14) days from the date when it is demanded, proof that the policy is in good standing. This proof may be demanded at any reasonable time and from time to time.

6. If the husband defaults in payment of any premium, the wife may pay the premium and recover from the husband the amount of the payment together with all costs and expenses that may be incurred in restoring the policy to good standing.

23. HOUSEHOLD GOODS AND PERSONAL EFFECTS

Each of the parties acknowledges that:

(a) the contents of the matrimonial home, including furniture, furnishings, household goods, silverware, china, glassware, rugs, books, pictures, bric-a-brac and all other household effects have been divided between the parties or have been purchased or the value set off against the value of other property by one of the parties to the satisfaction of each of them,

(b) each has possession of his or her jewellery, clothing and personal effects and

(c) each may dispose of the items possessed by him or her as he or she deems fit.

24. DEBTS AND OBLIGATIONS

1. Neither party will contract or incur debts or obligations in the name of the other.

2. If, contrary to subsection (1), either party contracts or incurs debts or obligations in the name of the other, he or she will indemnify the other from all loss or expense that results from or is incidental to the transaction.

25. NO PROPERTY TO BE DIVISIBLE ASSET

No property owned by either party or by them jointly on the effective date of this contract or at any later time is or will be:
  (a) family property or
  (b) property subject to division otherwise than according to owner-ship, under the Family Law Act and the laws of any jurisdiction.

26. PART II OF THE FAMILY LAW ACT

Each of the parties releases and discharges all rights and claims he or she has under Part II of the Family Law Act.

27. RELEASE AGAINST PROPERTY

Except as provided in this Agreement, the husband and the wife each acknowledge and agree that:
  (a) all their property has been divided between them to their mutual satisfaction,
  (b) each is entitled to property now in his or her possession, free of any claim from the other,
  (c) each may dispose of the property they now possess as if they were unmarried,
  (d) each releases and discharges all rights and claims relating to property in which the other has or may have an interest, includ-ing all rights and claims involving:
      1. possession of property,
      2. ownership of property,
      3. division of property and
      4. compensation for contributions of any kind, or an interest in property for contributions of any kind.
  (e) This section is a complete defence to any action brought by either the husband or the wife to assert a claim to any property; wherever situated, in which the other has or had an interest.

28. RELEASE AGAINST THE ESTATE OF THE OTHER

Without restricting the other waivers and releases in this contract, and subject to transfers or bequests that may be made, each party

(a) waives all rights and

(b) releases and discharges the other from all claims that he or she has or may in the future acquire under the laws of any jurisdiction, and particularly under the Family Law Act and the Succession Law Reform Act and their successors, entitling him or her upon the death of the other

1. to a division of property owned by the other or to one-half the difference between their net family properties or to any other share of this difference, or to any share of the property of the other,

2. if the other party dies leaving a will, to elect against taking under the will in favour of receiving an entitlement equalizing their net family properties, or in favour of any other benefit,

3. if the other party dies intestate, to elect to receive an entitlement in intestacy or to receive an entitlement equalizing their net family property,

4. if the other party dies testate as to some property and intestate as to other property, to elect to take under the will and to receive an entitlement in intestacy, or to receive an entitlement equalizing their net family properties,

5. to share in the estate of the other under a distribution in intestacy in any manner whatsoever and

6. to act as executor or administrator of the estate of the other.

29. GENERAL RELEASE

1. The husband and wife each accept the provisions of this Agreement in satisfaction of all claims and causes of action each now has including, but not limited to, claims and causes of action for custody, child maintenance or child support, maintenance, support, interim maintenance and interim support, possession of or title to property, or any other claim arising out of the marriage of the husband and wife, EXCEPT for claims and causes of action:

(a) arising under this Agreement and

(b) for a decree of divorce.

2. Nothing in the Agreement will bar any action or proceeding by either the husband or the wife to enforce any of the terms of this Agreement.

30. ATTRIBUTION

(a) The parties hereby elect under clause 74(7)(b) of the Income Tax Act that subsection 74(2) (gain or loss deemed that of the transferor) of the Income Tax Act will not apply to a disposition of any property that has been transferred between the parties pursuant to this Agreement, or to any property substituted therefore.

(b) Contemporaneously with the execution of this Agreement, the parties have executed in duplicate a separate form of joint election according to Schedule "A" [not actually attached / attached] to this Agreement.

(c) Each party authorizes the other to file an executed copy of the form of election completed according to the form in Schedule "A" with his or her return of income for the taxation year in which this Agreement is executed.

(d) The parties will indemnify each other for any tax liability imposed upon one of them by any taxing authority or government, resulting from the transfer of or disposition of property transferred pursuant to the terms of this Agreement.

(e) Specifically the parties agree to indemnify each other with respect to any liability or charge resulting from:
   1. any tax arrears of one enforced as against the property or income of the other and
   2. any attribution of income or capital gains from one to the other after separation.

(f) The parties will not designate any other property except the matrimonial home as their principal residence, for the period up to and including the year of this Agreement.

31. RESUMPTION OF COHABITATION

If at any time the parties cohabit as husband and wife for a single period or periods totalling not more than ninety (90) days with reconciliation as the primary purpose of the cohabitation, the provisions contained in this Agreement will not be affected except as provided in this section. If the parties cohabit as husband and wife for a single period or periods totalling more than ninety (90) days with reconciliation as the primary purpose of the cohabitation, the provisions contained in this Agreement will become void, except that nothing in the section will affect or invalidate any payment, conveyance or act made or done pursuant to the provisions of this Agreement.

32. AGREEMENT TO SURVIVE DIVORCE
If at any future time the parties are divorced, the terms of this Agreement will survive and continue in force.

33. EXECUTION OF OTHER DOCUMENTS
Each of the parties will execute any document and do all further things, at the cost of the other, that are reasonably required from time to time to give effect to the terms and intent of this Agreement.

34. CONTRACT TO PREVAIL
This contract prevails over:
  (a) any matter that is provided for in the Family Law Act [or relevant provincial law], where the contract made provisions for such matters and
  (b) any matter provided for in a subsequent domestic contract between one of the parties and another person other than the other party, where the present contract makes provisions for such matters.

35. GOVERNING LAW
This Agreement will be governed by and construed according to the laws of Ontario (or relevant province).

36. GENERAL
  1. The husband and wife will each execute any document or documents reasonably required from time to time to give effect to the terms and intent of this Agreement.
  2. The husband and wife each warrant that there are no representations, collateral agreements or conditions affecting this Agreement other than as expressed in this Agreement.

3. This Agreement may be amended only by a further instrument in writing signed by the husband and by the wife.
4. The provisions of this Agreement are binding on the respective heirs, executors, administrators or assigns of the husband and the wife.

37. SEVERABILITY

The invalidity or unenforceability of any provision of this Agreement will not affect the validity or enforceability of any other provisions and any invalid provision will be severable.

38. DEFAULT

If either of the parties is in default with respect to the payment of support pursuant to this Agreement, including any provision with respect to indexing of support payments, the other party may register the Separation Agreement in the [name of relevant family court] and the parties hereby consent to this Agreement being registered.

39. FINANCIAL DISCLOSURE

Each party:
   (a) has fully and completely disclosed to the other the nature, extent and probable value of all his or her significant assets and all his or her significant debts or other liabilities existing at the date of this contract, and in addition to this disclosure,
   (b) has given all information and particulars about his or her assets and liabilities that have been requested by the other,
   (c) is satisfied with the information and particulars received from the other and
   (d) acknowledges that there are no requests for further information or particulars that have not been met to his or her complete satisfaction.

40. INDEPENDENT LEGAL ADVICE

Each of the husband and the wife acknowledges that he or she:
   (a) has had independent legal advice,
   (b) understands his or her respective rights and obligations under this Agreement,
   (c) is signing this Agreement voluntarily and

(d) believes this Agreement is fair and reasonable and that its provisions are entirely adequate to discharge the present and future responsibilities of the parties and will not result in circumstances unconscionable to either party.

41. LEGAL FEES

The husband will pay the wife's solicitor's fees for the preparation and execution of this Agreement.

(Or)

The husband and wife will each bear their own legal fees incurred in the negotiation and execution of the Agreement.

TO EVIDENCE THEIR AGREEMENT, each of the husband and the wife has signed this Agreement under seal before a witness.

SIGNED, SEALED AND DELIVERED
in the presence of:

_____   _____
Witness as to the signature of   [name]
[wife] [Date]   [wife's signature]

_____   _____
Witness as to the signature of   [name]
[husband] [Date]   [husband's signature]

Caution: Please do not attempt to adapt these contracts to your situation without the advice of a lawyer. Many of the clauses are alternatives to each other and would not necessarily be applicable to every case. This Agreement also has an Ontario emphasis. It is reproduced only as an example or guide. Using it as a drafting guide would be a good way to gather information about your situation.

THE FAMILY LAW CLIENT HISTORY FORM

MANY LAW FIRMS will ask a client to complete a family history form. This form facilitates the collection of family details and prevents people from overlooking important details. The following is a modified form that you may wish to use as you sort out your own predicament. A completed form will give any lawyer a big head start on behalf of the client.

Sample Client History Form

Date: _____

Your Full Name: _____

Your Address: Home: _____

Office: _____

Telephone: Home: _____   Office: _____

Fax: _____   E-mail: _____

Date of Birth: _____   Place of Birth: _____

Date of Marriage: _____   Place of Marriage: _____

Date of Separation: _____

Your Status Before Marriage: Wife: _____

Husband: _____

Divorced: _____   Decree Available: _____

Surname of Wife at Birth: _____   At Separation: _____

If 2nd Marriage for Either of You, Give Details of Earlier Marriages

_____

_____

_____

When Did You Come to Canada? _____

Length of Residence in Province: _____

Prior Residences in Last Year: _____

Names of Children, Dates of Birth, Grade and School
1. _____
2. _____
3. _____

Special Needs: _____

Surname of Your Spouse at Birth: _____

Surname of Your Spouse at Separation: _____

Spouse's Date of Birth: _____

Spouse's Place of Birth: _____

Name, Address, Fax and Phone Number of Spouse's Lawyer:

_____

_____

_____

SOCIAL HISTORY OF MARRIAGE:
(Includes courtship, cohabitation date, lifestyle, conduct, present status and counselling details. Complete in detail. Use additional pages as necessary.)

_____

_____

ECONOMIC HISTORY OF MARRIAGE:
(Includes education, financial position before marriage, history of matrimonial homes, net worth of both of you, employment records, fitness for employment, and contributions by spouses to the marriage. Complete in detail. Use additional pages as necessary.)

_____

_____

_____

CUSTODY AND ACCESS:
(The positions of you and your spouse, the allegations and expected cross allegations. Complete in detail. Use additional pages as necessary.)

_____

_____

_____

YOUR IMPRESSION OF THE SITUATION:
(Complete in detail. Use additional pages as necessary.)

_____

_____

_____

WHAT DO YOU WANT?
(Complete in detail. Use additional pages as necessary.)

_____

_____

_____

APPENDIX B

(To Be Attached to a Full Separation Agreement)

The ___ Family
Parenting Plan

A. DEFINITIONS

FOR CLARITY, WHEN the children are with their mother, she will be referred to as the "resident" parent, and when they are with their father, he shall be referred to as the "resident" parent.

B. PARENTING GUIDELINES AND PRINCIPLES

1. In relation to any dispute, conflict or concern pertaining to the children, the needs of the children shall be paramount.
2. The parents shall recognize the children's need for good and ongoing relationships with their parents. The parents shall make every effort to actively foster and facilitate children's positive relationships with the other parent, with step-parents, with siblings and with members of the other parent's extended family. The parents shall ensure that the children spend the scheduled time with the other parent.
3. The parents shall exert their best efforts to work co-operatively and to make parenting arrangements with the children's best interests at heart.

4. The parents shall openly and/or subtly support the Parenting Plan as outlined below and ensure that the children spend the required time with the other parent.
5. The parents shall refrain from any subtle or open denigration of the other parent and/or members of the extended family in any communication with the children and/or in the presence of the children. In addition, the parents shall not speak to or in front of the children in a critical or disparaging way about the other parent. Further, the parents shall make every effort to protect the children from the parent's anger and/or frustration regarding the other parent. Children find conflict stressful. Parental conflict compromises their adjustment and their self-esteem. The parents shall advise others to maintain the same standard and to refrain from criticizing the other parent in front of the children. The parents shall also advise others not to question the children about their relationship with the other parent, step-parent or siblings.
6. The parents shall not speak with the children directly about specific parental differences and disagreements, including those related to financial issues, specific concerns about the other parent and parenting arrangements. The parents shall not show children documents related to their conflict.
7. When the children ask questions, the parents shall reassure them that the parents are working on the problems, taking into account the children's feelings and thoughts.
8. The parents shall refrain from any manner of conflict, subtle or open, in the presence of the children and, accordingly, shall relate to one another in a reasonable and cordial manner in all instances in which the children are present or nearby, even when the parents think the children are probably asleep.
9. The parent shall not ask the children to relay information from parent to parent and the children shall not be letter carriers for the parents.
10. The parents shall respect each other's privacy, and as such, refrain from engaging the children in any discussion or questioning about the other parent's personal life or activities.

11. The parents shall refrain from any form of interference, direct or indirect, open or subtle, into the life, activities or routines of the other parent. In this regard, neither parent shall schedule activities for the child requiring their active involvement or involvement by the other parent during periods in which the children are in the care of the other parent, without the consultation and consent from the parent.

12. The parents shall make all practical efforts to ensure the children's attendance at any or all structured activities or special occasions involving peers and/or extended family/step-family. While it is understood that this may not be feasible, when possible the parent will schedule these events when they know the children will be with them. In facilitating this and to ensure continuity of the children's schedule of residence and routines, "make-up time" is encouraged, especially when the usual or holiday parenting time has been impeded by the other parent.

13. In the event that the children complain to the resident parent about the other parent, the children will be encouraged to talk directly to the other parent about the concerns. If the children express difficulty with this, we shall raise the issue with the other parent and/or assist the children to express their concerns to the other parent. The parents recognize that children frequently express to parents what they believe they wish to hear about the other parent. The parents will take this into full consideration before coming to any conclusion regarding the other parent.

C. PARENTAL COMMUNICATION

1. All communication shall be in writing (e-mail, fax, text). In the event of a true emergency or time-sensitive issue, the parents may contact each other by phone or, preferably, text.

2. The parents shall use reasonable discretion in minimizing the extent of such communication. To this end, the principle of forwarding only that information which is necessary to ensure that the children's needs are being met shall be adhered to. E-mails and faxes shall be accumulated and sent no more than twice a week on Thursdays and Sundays. E-mails shall be checked and responded to within 24 hours. If a reply to a request cannot follow by then, an e-mail shall be sent

advising that the requested information cannot reasonably be ascertained by then, and as to when a response can be expected.

3. Given the children's ages/needs and their adjustment, and in an effort to foster consistency and stability for them, the parents shall make every effort to communicate about the children's routines, activities and experiences. This shall be done through the use of specific headings (i.e., Schedule, Medical, Homework, Major Accomplishments and Significant Challenges) and any other headings the parents deem applicable.

4. It is understood that each parent has different routines and activities. Each parent shall make good efforts to respect the basic routines (and individual schedules of the children) of the other home, even if they do not rely on the exact same approach. If the children comment that the other parent does it differently, the parent shall respond by saying that "sometimes parents do things differently."

5. The parents agree not to communicate about issues or other non-emergency arrangements at transition times, activities or special events. The parents shall greet each other and remain cordial, courteous and respectful in front of the children and shall only discuss pleasantries in front of the children. If one parent considers that the discussion is not courteous, both will discontinue the conversation and will take the issue up later (when the children are not present, nearby and/or awake) by voice mail, e-mail, in a "business meeting" or with the assistance of a third party.

D. RESIDENTIAL SCHEDULE

1. The children's time with each parent shall be as per the following two-week cycle:

	MON	TUES	WED	THU	FRI	SAT	SUN
Week 1							
Week 2							

E. RECOMMENDED HOLIDAY SCHEDULE

THE HOLIDAY SCHEDULE shall be as follows:

BIRTHDAYS

1. The parent with whom the child is not resident that morning shall spend time with the honoured child and their siblings on the child's birthday from after school until 7 p.m. If the child's birthday falls on a Saturday or Sunday during the summer, the parent with whom the child is not resident that morning shall spend time with the children on their birthday from 2 p.m. until 8 p.m.
2. Each parent will plan the children's family parties during their own time and at their own expense.

MOTHER'S DAY/FATHER'S DAY

The children shall spend time with the honoured parent from the Sunday morning at 10 a.m. for the remainder of the weekend until the regular schedule resumes.

THANKSGIVING LONG WEEKEND

In even years, the children shall be resident with the father from Friday after school until the children are dropped off at school on Tuesday morning. In odd years the children shall be resident with the mother from Friday after school until they are dropped off at school on Tuesday morning, unless otherwise agreed.

EASTER LONG WEEKEND

1. The Christian weekend begins Thursday from after school and ends Tuesday morning.
2. The Easter weekend will fall as per the usual schedule.

CHRISTMAS EVE, DAY AND CHRISTMAS SCHOOL BREAK

1. The father shall have the children for the first half of the Break in even years and the mother shall have the children for the first half of the Break in odd years. The Break will be defined in accordance with the children's District School Board's schedule.

2. Christmas Break shall be shared equally. Christmas holidays shall be considered a two-week holiday (14 days) and the parent's week shall be attached to his/her regularly scheduled weekend, in order that the parent's regular rotation of weekends remains undisturbed. *(To further explain: should it be the mother's year to have the first week of Christmas Break, and the mother, on the regular weekend has the first weekend, her week would begin on the Friday at school dismissal and would continue until the next Friday at 4 p.m. At that time the father would have the children from that Friday at 4 p.m. until the next Friday at 4 p.m. The mother would then resume her regular parenting time for that last weekend. In the above scenario, should it be the mother's year to have the first week of Christmas Break and the first weekend is the father's regularly scheduled weekend, the father would have the children in his care for his regular weekend, and the mother's week would begin on the Monday morning at 9 a.m. until delivery to school on the following Monday. In this way, the rotation of the weekends is not interrupted).*

FAMILY DAY

As per the usual schedule with the weekend extended to include Family Day with drop-off at school on Tuesday morning when the schedule will resume.

MARCH SCHOOL BREAK

1. The March Break will be defined as the board's scheduled holiday plus that parent's regular weekend. The March Break will be shared equally or alternated as may be agreed.
2. If either parent chooses to travel with the children during the March Break, notice shall be given to the other parent no less than 60 days in advance.

VICTORIA DAY LONG WEEKEND

As per the usual schedule with the weekend extended until Tuesday morning.

SUMMER SCHOOL BREAK AND VACATION

1. The parents will follow the regular schedule for the summer subject to each parent taking an equal number of holiday weeks with the children.
2. Each parent will have a minimum of two and a maximum of four weeks of summer holidays with the children.
3. The parents will agree on their respective holiday time no later than May 1st each year and will work around the children's scheduled activities such as camp.

CANADA DAY

Canada Day shall be as per the usual schedule.

AUGUST CIVIC HOLIDAY AND LABOUR DAY

These weekends shall be as per the usual schedule, adding on the statutory holiday until the regular schedule resumes.

F. CHANGES TO SCHEDULE

THIS CHANGE APPLIES to when the non-resident parent would like to have the children for a special occasion and when the scheduling of these occasions is out of the control of the non-resident parent. Examples are: family weddings, work Christmas party, family birthdays, special anniversaries, etc. The parents shall communicate by e-mail about a request for a change or modification to the usual and/or holiday schedule, when the need for a change arises and with as much notice as possible. A response shall be provided within 48 hours of receiving the e-mail. If an answer cannot be given within this time, the parent shall advise when he or she expects to be able to advise about whether or not the change is agreeable. Agreement to changes shall be finalized in writing.

G. DECISION-MAKING

THE PARENTS WILL share in the responsibility for care, rearing and decision-making according to the following:

DAILY/ROUTINE MEDICAL

1. The parents shall continue to use the services of the same family physician and dentist.
2. The parents shall provide each other with the names, addresses and phone numbers of all physicians and health care professionals (e.g., psychologists, social workers, counsellors, occupational therapists, orthodontists, etc.) providing care to the children.
3. Changes to the children's health care professionals shall be mutually agreed to by the parents.

MEDICAL/DENTAL (long-term medication/treatments, surgery, orthodontia work, therapy/counselling by a mental health professional, etc.)

1. The parents shall notify each other as soon as feasible of an emergency child visit to a physician, specialist and/or hospital. Both parents may attend. Both parents shall make emergency decisions unless, after a concerted effort, one parent cannot be reached, in which case the present parent may make emergency decisions in consultation with the medical professionals.
2. The parents shall supply each other with copies of all medical and/or professional reports they have pertaining to the children. The parents may also request any relevant records/information from the children's physicians directly.
3. Major and non-emergency medical decisions are usually infrequent. Since they are serious, it is in the children's best interests for both parents to be involved in major medical decisions, with the assistance of expert third parties, who are typically relied upon (e.g., medical specialist, dentist). The parents shall notify each other of any potential major medical decisions as well as provide the other with the name and phone number of the attending physician(s). The parents shall consult with the relevant physicians together, gaining second opinions as necessary. The parents shall arrive at major medical decisions mutually in accordance with consensus professional opinion. In the event that there is no consensus professional opinion, the parents shall abide by the terms of the Future Dispute Resolution clause (Dispute Resolution Section L).

EDUCATION (school selection, psycho-educational testing, remedial assistance, report cards, parent/teacher meetings, etc.)

1. The children shall attend their current public schools unless the parents agreed otherwise.
2. Any changes in schools shall be mutually agreed to by the parents.
3. The parents shall attend the routine parent-teacher meetings together, if at all possible based on their schedules, or separately if this is not possible. Additional individual meetings with the school and/or teacher may be arranged.
4. The parents shall advise each other if the school calls regarding a significant child-related matter.
5. The school shall have both parents' names to call in case of an emergency.
6. A school calendar is available from the school. It is each parent's responsibility to stay up to date on any relevant educational matters (e.g., professional activity days, special events, field trips, concerts, parent-teacher meetings, etc.). Each parent shall request from the school that he/she be provided with all the notices, report cards, etc.
7. Notwithstanding, upon receipt of information or notices, the resident parent shall advise the other parent by e-mail of any special events or meetings at the school, with special attention paid to those notices that are time-sensitive (i.e., for events that same week or the beginning of the following week.)
8. For additional cross-checking, notices brought from school by the children shall be initialled by the resident parent and returned to the children's knapsack. Once a parent sees that the other parent has initialled the notice, it may be discarded.
9. The parents shall notify each other of any potential major educational decisions and provide each other with the name(s) and phone number(s) of the attending educational professionals. The parents are entitled to contact these professionals. In consultation with the professionals, the parents together will reach a consensus of major educational decisions. If the parents are unable to reach a mutually agreeable decision they shall use the Dispute Resolution process (Section L below).

H. EXTRACURRICULAR ACTIVITIES AND LESSONS

1. The parents and their extended families may attend special extracurricular activities and events, such as hockey, gymnastics, concerts and the like. The parents shall remain cordial, courteous and respectful to each other and to extended family during these events.
2. The children's preferences regarding their activities and lessons shall be taken into account and given substantial weight when selections are made.

I. TELEPHONE AND E-MAIL COMMUNICATION

1. The children may telephone or e-mail the non-resident parent whenever they wish.
2. The parents shall encourage the children to feel comfortable calling the other parent and shall afford the children the privacy to do so.

J. TRAVEL

1. When a parent travels out of town with the children, the parent will provide a contact phone number to the resident parent in case of a child-related emergency and/or if the children want to contact the travelling parent.
2. The location(s) and phone number(s) of the children's whereabouts when travelling with the resident parent out of town shall be provided prior to departure to the non-resident parent in case of an emergency.
3. The children may travel with either parent outside of [province] as per the usual and holiday schedules, with written notice to the other parent as soon as knowledge of travel is available but with no less than three weeks' notice. A full itinerary (i.e., destination; airline name, flight number and phone number; times of travel; hotel name and phone number; etc.) shall be supplied at the time written notice is provided.
4. The written notarized consent required by customs/immigration and the necessary documentation required for travel (i.e., birth

certificate, passport) shall be provided to the travelling parent no less than 48 hours prior to departure. The non-travelling parent will be responsible for the securing and costs of notarized consent.

K. RESIDENTIAL AND JURISDICTIONAL MOVES

MAINTAINING TWO RESIDENCES within a reasonably close proximity is preferable as it enables a smoother implementation of the Parenting Plan and allows frequent access to both parents. The distance between residential homes shall not exceed 20 kilometres. Moves beyond that noted shall be as per the parents' mutual agreement, or otherwise resolved through the alternative Dispute Resolution Process (see Dispute Resolution Section L).

L. FUTURE DISPUTE RESOLUTION

ANY ASPECT OF the parenting plan may be changed upon mutual agreement of the parents.

In the event of an impasse, such as a change in custody, residential schedule or mobility, the parents shall first attempt to resolve the matter with each other. If a mutually acceptable resolution does not occur, the parents will enter into a mediation/arbitration process conducted by a lawyer or mediator/arbitrator.

We agree to follow this Parenting Plan and adapt it as necessary as our children's lives and our lives evolve.

Dated this day of, 20___

_____   _____
[Mother]   [Father]

_____   _____
Witness   Witness

APPENDIX C

Table of Common-Law Rights
and Responsibilities

PROVINCE	COMMON-LAW STATUS?	SPOUSAL SUPPORT?	PROPERTY?	ESTATE RIGHTS?
B.C.	After 2 years or upon birth of child while cohabiting	Yes/1 year to apply	Yes—statutory rights after two years of cohabitation	May apply to court
Alberta	Yes, but not called common law	Yes—Adult Interdependent Act	No statutory rights	No
Saskatchewan*	Treated same as married people	Yes	Yes—statutory rights	Yes
Manitoba*	After 3 years or upon birth of child while cohabiting	Yes	Yes—statutory rights and may register a common-law relationship	Yes
Ontario	After 3 years or upon birth of child while cohabiting	Yes	No statutory rights	No
Nova Scotia*	After 2 years	Yes	No, but may register a domestic partnership	No

PROVINCE	COMMON-LAW STATUS?	SPOUSAL SUPPORT?	PROPERTY?	ESTATE RIGHTS?
New Brunswick	After 3 years of substantial dependence	Yes	No property rights	No
Newfoundland and Labrador	After 2 years or upon birth of child while cohabiting	Yes—called a "partner"	No property rights	No
P.E.I.	After 3 years or upon birth of child while cohabiting	Yes	No statutory rights	Yes
N.W.T.*	After 2 years or upon birth of child while cohabiting	Yes	Yes—property rights	Yes
Yukon	Relationship of some permanence	3 months to claim	No statutory rights	Yes
Quebec	No common-law rights	None	None	None
Nunavut	After 2 years or upon birth of child while cohabiting	Yes	No statutory rights	Yes

*These provinces and territory have special rules for common-law spouses. For example, in Manitoba and Nova Scotia, there are laws which permit common-law couples to register their relationship and to thereby qualify for extra rights and protections. Check with a family law lawyer in those provinces to discuss the value of registering your relationship in addition to, or instead of, a cohabitation agreement.

In Manitoba see www.gov.mb.ca/justice/family/law or call 1-800-282-8069 ext. 3701.

In Nova Scotia see www.gov.ns.ca/just/flic.

A GLOSSARY OF
FAMILY LAW TERMS

Access The opportunity to visit with a child. Under the terms of the Divorce Act, a spouse exercising access rights is also entitled to information about the child's health, welfare and education, unless a court orders otherwise. *

Adultery Sexual intercourse by a husband or wife with someone of the opposite sex who is not his or her spouse. Adultery is one of the ways marital breakdown can be established. *

(Note: Until recently, a gay or a lesbian relationship would not constitute adultery, but as a result of some recent court decisions, the definition of adultery has been "modified" to account for these types of extramarital affairs.)

Adversarial System Canada's court system is designed to resolve disputes between two opposing parties. The parties present their respective sides of an issue through evidence. The judge acts as an impartial arbiter, weighing the evidence and deciding how the law applies in each specific case. *

Affidavit A sworn statement, typed and signed by a person involved in a family law matter. It is witnessed by someone, usually a lawyer, and filed in support of a motion.

Alimony An old expression used to describe spousal support. Now that you know what it is, don't use it. Call it spousal support.

Appeal When a person affected by a judge's decision believes that the judge has made a mistake, that person can ask a higher level of court to review the decision. The court reviewing the decision can uphold it, change it or send the matter back to the original court for reconsideration. There are strict time limits on this type of review. *

Application A court proceeding starts with the filing of certain documents with court officers and the serving of copies of these documents on other persons affected. Details of the material to be included in the application, the document format and the filing fees are determined by provincial and territorial rules of court procedure.

Arbitration A third party is asked to decide a case for two people who cannot agree. This person acts as a "private judge," with rules and procedures made to the likings of the parties involved. It is not mediation. A decision is imposed because the people agree to be bound by whatever the arbitrator decides.

Best Interests Test This is the overriding consideration in custody and access matters. The court searches for that which will best serve the child's interests.

Child The Divorce Act defines a "child of the marriage" as a child of both spouses, a child of one of the spouses toward whom the other spouse acts as a parent or a child towards whom both spouses act as a parent. Biological children, adopted children and children looked after by the spouses may all be considered children of the marriage. The custody and support provisions of the divorce law apply to a child of the marriage who is under 16 years of age or who is over 16 and remains dependent on his or her parents because of illness, disability or other reasons. *

Cohabitation Agreement A domestic contract signed by a man and a woman who are living together or intend to live together but not marry.

In it, they may provide for ownership and division of property, support and any other matter affecting their relationship except custody of and access to children.

Collusion An agreement or conspiracy to fabricate or suppress evidence, or to deceive the court. If evidence to support a divorce application is the result of collusion, the application can be rejected. *

Common-Law Spouse Almost all the provinces recognize that some men and women live together without getting married. While the precise definition varies from province to province, it means achieving the status of a spouse for some legal purposes, such as support, in the province.

Condonation The forgiveness of a matrimonial offence with full knowledge of the circumstances, followed by an acceptance of the offending spouse back into the family. A forgiven offence cannot be revived at a later date as a basis for a divorce. A legal opinion may be necessary to decide if a matrimonial offence has been condoned by the subsequent actions of the other spouse. *

Confidentiality People in certain relationships are protected by law from having to give any evidence in court regarding communications between them. Communications between lawyers and clients have this special protection. A court-appointed reconciliator also has this protection with regard to communications made in the course of attempting to reconcile spouses.

Most professional associations have ethical guidelines regarding the confidentiality of communications between members and their clients. These guidelines form a very important part of the professional relationship; however, they do not necessarily provide protection from disclosure in court.

The laws regarding the relationship between other professionals and their clients, such as clergy and their parishioners and doctors and their patients, vary across the country. These professionals may be called upon to testify in court. *

Connivance The marital misconduct of one spouse caused by, or knowingly, wilfully or recklessly permitted by, the other spouse. Connivance in creating a basis for a divorce application can result in the application being rejected. *

Consummation of a Marriage The "completion" of a marriage by an act of sexual intercourse by a husband and wife after the marriage ceremony.

Contempt of Court A method the court uses to control its own process. It is wilful disobedience of a court order, punishable by fine or imprisonment or both.

Contested Divorce If either the husband or wife disputes the grounds for divorce, or if the spouses are unable to agree on child or support arrangements, a court will have to resolve these matters. A hearing will be held and both sides of the dispute will be entitled to present evidence supporting their view. The judge will consider the evidence presented and impose a solution. *

Corollary Relief Under the terms of the Divorce Act, people involved in a divorce proceeding can ask the court to make supplementary orders pertaining to financial support for a spouse or child, or for the custody of, or access to, a child of the marriage. *

Costs Sums payable for legal services. When matters are contested in court, a judge has the discretion to order that the losing party pay a portion of the successful party's legal costs. *

Custody Control over a child given to an adult by the court. This control generally includes physical care of the child and the responsibility to make decisions regarding education, religion and health care, and to provide food, clothing and shelter. *

Decree Absolute Under the Divorce Act of 1968, a divorce only becomes final when a court grants a decree absolute. A decree absolute can be granted by the court three months after the day on which the court allows the divorce action. If the parties agree not to appeal the divorce decision, and if special circumstances existed, the court could shorten the three-month period. *

Decree Nisi Under the Divorce Act of 1968, the court that allows a divorce grants a temporary order called a *decree nisi.* The divorce is not final until at least three months later when the court grants a decree absolute. *

Dependant A person who relies on someone else for financial support. In the context of divorce law, it may include a spouse or child. *

Desertion The failure of a husband or wife to live with his or her spouse. It must be a unilateral act carried out against the wishes of the other spouse. Desertion was a ground for divorce under the old divorce legislation. Under the current divorce law, it would be evidence of the separation period. *

Disbursements Out-of-pocket expenses incurred in a family law matter, such as the cost of paying for the petition to be issued at the court office or the cost of paying someone to deliver it to your spouse. It could also be the cost of a family law assessment.

Discoveries A step in legal proceedings where lawyers get to ask the opposing client, under oath, questions about things said in the legal proceedings, especially in affidavits and pleadings. It is done in the presence of a court reporter and a transcript of all questions and answers can be prepared.

Divorce The termination of the legal relationship of marriage between a husband and wife. *

Divorce Certificate The actual piece of paper that officially describes the termination of the marriage. It is needed as proof of the divorce in order to get a marriage licence.

Domestic Violence The intent by either spouse to intimidate, either by threat or by use of physical force on the person or property. The purpose of the assault is to control the person's behaviour by the inducement of fear.

Fees and Disbursements The bill of account. This is a statement you will receive monthly, periodically or in one lump sum at the end of the proceeding. The fee is for the lawyer's time, which is calculated by multiplying the hourly rate by the number of hours worked on the case. Disbursements are out-of-pocket expenses. HST is extra.

Final Order An order that is not interim. Interim orders are effective until the end of the trial. The final order is intended to last indefinitely or until changed by the court.

Garnishee A legal procedure that allows for the seizure of money owing to a person who has not paid a court-ordered debt. A court may order the debtor's bank, employer or anyone else who may owe money to the debtor to pay the money into court to help pay the debt. *

Get A religious divorce necessary for observant Jews. It is needed in addition to a civil divorce in order to dissolve the marriage.

Indexing To increase the amount of a support order or provision in a Separation Agreement by a fixed amount each year. The increase is usually tied to changes in the cost-of-living index. It is also known as a "cost of living allowance" or COLA.

Interim Orders There may be a considerable period of time between the initial filing of a divorce application and the date on which a court is able to grant a divorce and related support, custody or access orders. On request, a court can make a temporary order for the interim period to stabilize custody or access arrangements or to provide financial support for a spouse or child. *

Joint Custody A mother and father can continue to share responsibility for making major decisions that affect their children, regardless of which parent the children actually live with on a day-to-day basis. Such arrangements require a commitment on the part of both former spouses to cooperate for the benefit of the children. Joint custody does not eliminate the obligations of both parents to provide financial support for the children. *

Joint Petition A special form of divorce petition that can be used by two spouses who wish to have an uncontested divorce. It is one request for divorce filed by two people.

Judgment The final decision by the court on any issues put to it during the trial. The formal piece of paper that describes who has been successful or not and on which issues.

Limitations Time limits imposed by the laws and rules of court. If certain things are not done (claim support, division of property), then the right to claim is lost unless the court grants special permission.

Litigation Resolving a dispute by using the courts and the adversarial process.

Marriage The voluntary union for life of two people to the exclusion of all others. In Canada, marriage involves a religious or civil ceremony that complies with the procedural requirements of provincial or territorial laws where the marriage takes place. Marriage creates the legal status of husband and wife and the legal obligations arising from that status. *

Marriage Breakdown The sole ground for legally ending a marriage under the terms of the Divorce Act. Marriage breakdown can be established in three ways: Through evidence that one spouse committed adultery; physical or mental cruelty; or that the spouses intentionally lived separate and apart for at least one year. *

Marriage Contract An agreement between a husband and wife outlining the spouses' respective responsibilities and obligations. Some contracts also include agreements as to how property and ongoing obligations will be shared if the marriage breaks down. *

Matrimonial Home Where the married couple has resided and comes with special rights to possession at the time of separation. It is possible to have more than one such home at a time. (Whether a common-law couple has the same rights with respect to their home at separation varies from province to province. Check with a lawyer in your province.)

Mediation A process by which people in situations of potential conflict attempt to resolve their differences and reach a mutually acceptable agreement.

Neutral third parties, or mediators, can often help the parties retain a focus on the problems to be solved and possible solutions, rather than on areas of personal disagreement. *

Minutes of Settlement A method of settling a case by writing out and having the parties sign an acknowledgement of how they want their problem resolved.

Motion A request to the court for a particular order pending trial, such as interim custody or support. Filed with an affidavit.

Order The court's decision on a matter that it was asked to resolve. *See* Motion; Affidavit.

Parental Support A request by the parent of a child for financial support from that adult child if the parent is in need and has provided for the child's upbringing.

Parties The husband and wife, or anybody else who is named in the case before the court and asking for an order of any kind.

Pension A fixed sum paid regularly to a person or surviving dependant following his or her retirement. There are both public (Canada Pension Plan) and private (from one's own employer) pensions. Some provinces consider a pension that is not yet being paid at the time of marriage breakdown to be property that must be divided.

Petition for Divorce The formal document by which one person asks the court to dissolve his or her marriage to another and for corollary relief.

Pleadings The typewritten description of each person's claims in a family law matter, which must be prepared in accordance with the province's Rules of Court.

Possessory Rights Some provincial family laws give each legally married spouse an equal entitlement to possession of a matrimonial home upon separation. This right exists regardless of actual ownership of the home by one or the other. The court will fix, or the couple will come to an agreement over, the appropriate period of possession. It usually continues for the period leading up to the trial.

Procedure The technical rules that lawyers must follow to get a case through the civil justice system. They are contained in the province's Rules of Court.

Questioning *See* Discoveries.

Restraining Order An order that prohibits contact between two spouses and in some cases their children. It can be a blanket prohibition or it can provide for specific contact at specific times and under specific circumstances.

Retainer The contract by which you hire a lawyer to take your case. It can also mean the sum of money you give the lawyer to be applied to fees and disbursements.

Rules of Court *See* Procedure.

Separate To cease living together as man and wife, possibly under the same roof but usually not. Done with the intention not to live together again.

Separation Agreement A contract signed by the parties to settle their differences. It can deal with property, custody, access, support and any other matter. A form of domestic contract.

Shared Parenting Another term used instead of custody and access. It describes a sharing of the decision-making that usually is given solely to the custodial parent.

Solicitor-Client Privilege The lawyer's obligation to keep secret everything you tell him or her.

Spousal Support An order that one spouse pay the other a sum of money either in a lump sum or periodically for a set period of time or indefinitely.

Spouse A married individual.

Statute A law passed by the legislature of a province or the federal parliament (e.g., the Divorce Act).

Uncontested Divorce If neither the husband nor wife disputes the grounds for divorce, and if they are able to reach an agreement regarding child care and financial arrangements, it may be possible to ask a judge to grant a divorce without a lengthy court hearing. In some provinces and territories, it may be possible to get a divorce without having to actually appear in court at all. *

Variation If the circumstances that justified making a particular support, custody or access order change, a person affected by the order can ask a judge to alter the order to make it fit the new circumstances. *

Note: The definitions in the glossary that are followed by an asterisk (*) are from a Government of Canada, Department of Justice publication entitled *Divorce Law for Counsellors*.

INDEX

abduction, 246–51, 253, 255
acceptance, emotional stage, 21–22
access. *See* custody and access
accountants, 84, 92, 97, 101, 166, 232–33
adjournments, 222, 238, 327
adultery, 24, 33, 34, 67, 68, 70–71, 72, 73, 79, 95, 137
affidavits, 59, 61–62, 88
age of majority, 159, 160, 169, 180
airline points, 86, 91
Alberta
    common-law relationships, 375
    online resources, 335
    siblings, 116
    spousal support, 171
    Superior Courts, 74
    support enforcement, 257
alcohol, 6, 10, 34, 118, 300, 326
anger, 3, 8, 10, 15, 18, 301, 305
annulment, 79, 279
Annulment of Marriages Act, 317
"Answer," contested divorce, 77
appeals, 64–65, 77, 225–26, 335

Application for Divorce, 48, 74, 77
appraisers, 84, 92
arbitration, 238 *(See also* mediation/ arbitration; religious arbitration)
Arbitration Act, 240
assets/liabilities
    division of, 83
    value of, 89
    (See also property division)
audio/visual taping, 126, 324
authenticity vs admissibility, 315

bailiffs, 58
balance of probability, 14, 50, 253
bank accounts, 260
bankruptcy, 15–16, 33–34
bargaining, emotional stage, 19–20
bars to divorce, 78–79
best interests of child(ren), 107, 113–14, 117, 129, 131, 132, 139, 251, 276, 316, 317–18
Best v. Best, 97
"beyond doubt," 49
birthdays, 119, 121, 128, 130, 146

blaming the victim, 301
blended families, 126
blood tests, paternity, 138
boats, 260
book value, 90
Boston v. Boston, 176, 180
British Columbia
    common-law relationships, 186,
        375
    grandparents' rights, 270
    mobility, 148–49
    online resources, 335
    spousal support, 171, 174
    support enforcement, 258
Bruni v. Bruni, 332–33
burden of proof, 49
business interests, 91–92, 280, 283–84,
    292–93
business records, 314

cabins, 85
Canada Customs, 252
Canada Employment Insurance Com-
    mission, 258
Canada Pension Act, 193
Canada Pension Plan (CPP), 100–2,
    193, 258
Canada Revenue Agency, 102, 166
Canada Savings Bonds, 259
Canadian Bar Association, 32
Canadian Institute of Actuaries, 97–98
Canadian Judicial Council, 336
capital gains tax, 86, 102
career retraining, 176–77, 179
cars, 83, 85, 89, 91, 260, 284
case citations, 331, 332
case conferences, 63
case management system, 55
Central Divorce Registry, 75
Certificate of Divorce, 78

Certificate of Independent Legal
    Advice, 206–7
Certificate of Legal Aid, 37
change of name, 125
Change of Name Act, 317
Chapman v. Chapman, 271–72
child
    adoptive, 113
    de facto care and control of, 132
    defined, 159
    disclosure of divorce to, 139–47
    domestic violence, 299, 304
    illness/disability, 160
    impact of divorce on, 106–7, 116,
        140–41, 147–48
    in common-law relationships,
        185
    lawyers for, 116, 119, 336
    make-up time with, 253–54
    more than one, 103-4
    name change, 125
    religious orientation, 127
    residency status, 75
    views/preferences, 113, 115–16
    withdrawing from parental control,
        159–60
    (See also best interests of child(ren);
        custody and access)
Child and Family Services Act, 317
Child Find Canada, 248
child of the marriage, defined, 111–12
child support
    base monthly, 154–55
    changes in income, 157–58
    concerning fairness, 151–53
    duration, 159–60, 169, 210
    enforcement, 255–57
    estate planning, 293–94
    hiding income, 165
    high-income earners, 168

how spent, 168–69
life insurance to secure, 167
lump-sum payment, 165
rejection of parent, 168
relocating, 124
self-representation 316
60/40 split, 161–63
special expenses, 155–57
tax considerations, 103
undue hardship, 154
university costs, 166–67
updating amount, 157–58
variation applications, 158
Child Support Guidelines, 33, 130–31,
    133, 152, 153–55, 317–18, 348
Child's Law Reform Act, 136–37
child's universe concept, 114
child–protection agencies, 248
Children's Aid Society (CAS), 268, 273,
    275
Children's Law Reform Act, 47–48,
    113, 317, 318
children's lawyers, 116, 119, 336
Christmas, 128, 146
citizenship, 75
Citizenship and Immigration Canada,
    80
civil justice system, 49
Civil Marriage Act, 317
clean-break model, spousal support,
    170
clerk of the court, 53, 215
Code of Professional Conduct (CBA),
    32
Cohabitation Agreements, 193–94,
    278, 279
    amendments to, 285
    community of property scheme, 284
    described, 283
    family asset scheme, 284

impact of marriage on, 285
    provincial property scheme, 284–85
    separate property scheme, 283–84
collaborative family law, 240–41
collections, 85, 261
collusion, 78, 79
commissions, 91
common-law relationships
    children in, 185
    Cohabitation Agreements, 193–94
    CPP, 100
    defined, 193–94
    Divorce Act, 107
    federal legislation, 185
    grandparents' rights, 269
    legal advice, 193
    property division, 84, 187–92
    rights/responsibilities, 375–76
    seeking legal advice, 193
    spousal support, 152, 172, 186–87
    tax considerations, 103
community of property scheme, 284
compensatory model, spousal support,
    170, 171
complaints process, 336–37
computerized record books, 53
confidentiality, 31–32, 88, 243, 250
conflict of interest, 239
constructive trust, 190–91
contempt (of court), 253, 263–64
contested divorce, 74, 77–78
continuing record, 59
contracts. See Cohabitation Agree-
    ments; Marriage Contracts;
    Separation Agreements
contractual failure, 286–87
control, 11, 15, 106, 213, 298, 337
co-operative parenting, 110
co-parenting, 110
cost of living allowance, 179

costs
    appeals, 65, 225
    arbitration, 238
    arbitration/mediation, 241, 242
    assessments, 118–19
    contempt (of court), 254
    disposition of assets, 86, 91
    exercising access, 164–65
    Offers to Settle, 199–200
    proving paternity, 138
    restraining orders/order for exclu-
        sive possession, 132–33
    self-representation, 328
    trials, 64, 132, 213–12, 224–25
    uncontested divorce, 80–81
    valuation, 92, 98, 99
    (See also legal fees)
cottages, 85, 89, 92, 260, 261, 284
Counter Petition, 59
countries, Hague Convention, 249
court file, 216–17
Court of Queen's Bench, 74
court order enforcement. *See*
    enforcement
court personnel, 50–54, 321, 329
court record, 217
court reporters, 53–54, 214
courtroom, 214–16
Courts of Justice Act, 317
court
    alternatives to, 57, 230–43
    discovery/questioning under oath,
      59–61
    exchange of legal documents,
      57–59
    exchange of letters, 56–57
    pre-trials/conferences, 63
    (See also appeals; Rules of Court;
      trials)
credibility, 88, 251, 307, 330

credit cards, 86, 101, 303
Criminal Code, 46, 133, 246, 247,
    262–63
Criminal Injuries Compensation Board,
    304
criminal justice system, 46, 48, 49,
    134–35
cross-examination, 221
Crown attorney, 49
Crown Attorney's Office, 133
cruelty, 33, 71–72
current market value, 90
custody and access
    access defined, 108–9, 127–28
    access denial, 254–55
    assessments, 118–19
    attending child's activities, 131
    change of name, 125
    contested divorce, 77
    costs of exercising access, 164–65
    custody defined, 108
    domestic violence, 304, 307
    enforcement, 253–55
    grandparents' rights, 129
    matrimonial home, 125–26
    mobility, 122–24
    planning vacations, 120–22
    religion, 124–25
    remarriage/new partner/blended
      family, 126
    self-representation, 315
    Separation Agreements, 210
    strategic considerations, 241–43
    variation, 131
custody—determining child's best
    interests, 107, 113–14
    child's views/preferences, 115–16
    general considerations, 113–14
    help from professionals, 115, 116,
      118–20

parental behaviour, 118
primary parent, 115
siblings, 116–17
status quo, 114
tender years doctrine, 117
custody–order compliance, 255

debt, 83, 86–87
declaration of parentage, 137
defaulters. *See* support enforcement
agencies
Deferred Settlement Method, pension
division, 97–98
delays, 53, 213, 216, 219, 222, 223, 224,
310, 322, 324, 326
denial, emotional stage, 17–18
dependant, defined, 111, 112
depression, 16, 20–21, 118
disbursements, 36, 39, 92 *(See also* fees
and disbursements, sample)
Disbursements Only account, 39
disclosure of documents, 61
discovery, 59–61
dispute-resolution skills, 15, 24
dissolution, date of, 78
divorce
causes of, 23–24
grounds for, 67, 68–70
rates, 68
Divorce Act, 46–47, 48, 67–72, 73–76,
107, 110, 127, 152, 153, 158, 269,
287, 317
Divorce Application, 58
divorce order, effective date, 77–78
DNA Finger Printing, 138
document servers, 58–59
documentary discovery, 60
domestic contracts
and failure to disclose, 285–86
and failure to understand, 286

contractual failures, 286–87
religious barriers, 287–88
setting aside, 285
(See also Cohabitation Agreements;
Marriage Contracts; Separation
Agreements)
domestic violence, 16, 247–48, 297
defined, 298–99
escaping, 303
false allegations of, 133, 134-35,
307, 308
lawsuits/compensation, 304
myths, 299–300
Ontario case, 305–6
reasons for, 300-2
self-defence, 302
shelters, 303
strategic considerations, 306–8
Domestic-Partnership Declaration, 189
double depression, 20–21
double-dipping, 98
driver's licences, 257, 258
drugs, 10, 34, 118, 148, 273, 326
due diligence, potential partner, 15–16
duty counsel, 327

education, 108, 112, 113, 127, 156, 157,
159, 166, 282, 284
"election," surviving spouse, 291–92
e-mail, 38, 121, 130, 144, 144–45, 168,
323-24
emotions, at time of divorce/separa-
tion, 9–10
(See also marriage breakdown, emotional stages of)
empathy, 14–15, 24–25
enforcement
custody/access, 246–48, 253-55
property, 260–62
support, 255–57

estate planning, 290–96
evidence, 218, 220, 312–16
Evidence Act, 317
ex parte motions, 304
exchange of legal documents, 57–59
exchange of letters, 56–57
exempt property, 92–94
exhibits, 60, 214, 215, 217, 222
extended family, 145, 145–46 *(See also* "other people")

factum, defined, 318
failure to disclose, 285–86
failure to understand, 286
fair market value, 90
fairness, 94, 95, 152, 224, 226
false allegations, 133, 134–35
family arbitration, 240
family asset scheme, 284
family business, 1, 92, 293
Family Law Act of Ontario, 47, 48, 81, 173, 184, 287–88, 291, 317
family law cases, sources, 331–32
Family Law Client History Form, 32–33
Family Law Insurance Centre, 294
family law system described, 46–48
  guides, 11
  in crisis, 10
  process, 10–11
  users, 9–10
family loans, 5, 87
Family Maintenance Act, 317
Family Mediation Canada, 336
Family Orders and Agreements Enforcement Assistance Act, 250
Family Relations Act, 317
Family Responsibility Act, 48
Family Responsibility and Support Arrears Enforcement Act, 317

Family Statute Law Amendment Act, 99–100
family therapy, 130
farms/farmers, 90, 91, 259
Federal Court of Appeals, 334
federal divorce law/provincial family law, interconnection, 46–48
Federal Orders and Agreements Enforcement Assistance Act, 48
fees and disbursements policy, sample, 339–40
file folders, self-representation, 320–21
final order, 132
financial disclosure, 157–58, 166
financial statements, 58, 87–89, 209, 217, 285
fixed date method, trials, 52, 217, 218
forgiveness of adultery, 71, 73
forgiveness of cruelty, 73
forms, 58, 321, 338–63
  online resources, 334
foster care, 273
fraud, 16, 88, 208, 209, 286–87 *(See also* false allegations)
Fraudulent Conveyances Act, 317
full disclosure, 285 *(See also* financial disclosure)

gambling, 34, 95
garnishment, wages, 256, 258, 260
"generous" access, 253, 255
"get," *See* Jewish divorce
GICs, 93, 260
gifts, 93, 103, 144, 192, 293, 299, 312, 316, 318
grandparents, 30, 144, 145–46, 147, 266–67
  adversarial, 267

and access, 129
and divorcing or separating,
    268-69
death of a child, 269-70
fighting third parties, 273
intact families, 270-73
role of, 267
special status of, 267-68
strategic considerations, 274-76

Hague Convention Civil Aspects of
    International Child Abduction,
    249-50
hallways, courthouse, 214, 215-16, 220
Hartshorne v. Hartshorne, 282
heirlooms, 86, 93
hiding income, 164, 165
high-risk travellers, 252
holidays, 146, 255 *(See also* vacations)
homes, 83, 260 *(See also* matrimonial
    home; property division)
homosexual conduct, and adultery, 71
household contents, 85

identity theft, 5, 88
"if and when" division, 97, 99
illegal immigrants, 79-80
illegal marriage. *See* marriages of
    convenience
immigrant sponsorship, 79, 80
immigration, 75, 79-80
imminent harm abduction, 247
impeachment of witness, 54, 221
"improper" agreements, 208
impulse control, 301
income
    and Child Support Guidelines,
        153-58
    determining, 166
    hiding, 164, 165

high, 168
(See also financial disclosure; gar-
    nishment, wages; taxes)
income attribution, 102-3
income security model, spousal sup-
    port, 170
Income Tax Act, 102, 103, 153
independent legal advice, 31, 206-7,
    240, 282-83, 286
indexed pensions, 97
informed consumers, 6-9
inheritances, 87, 93, 291, 292-93
insurance, and estate planning, 294,
    296 *(See also* life insurance, obliga-
    tion child/spousal support)
interim order, 132, 138-39
Internet resources, 1, 333-36
interprovincial travel. *See* mobility
intestacy, 290-91
investments, 24, 42, 99, 102, 193 *(See
    also* self-sufficiency)
isolation, emotional stage, 17-18
issuance of claim, 57, 58
itemized statement of account, 40

Jewish divorce, 287
joint accounts, 93
Joint Application for Divorce, 77
joint custody, 33, 77, 123, 255
joint tenants, and estate planning,
    295-96
jointly held property, 93-94
judge's chambers, 214, 216
judge-made law, 71
judges
    addressing, 51-52, 324
    and self-representation, 329-30
    complaints against, 336
    final decision, 48, 224-25
    (See also private judge)

judgment debtor exam, 260–61
juries, 54

law firms, websites, 333–34
law libraries, 331–33
Law Partners' Property and Related
    Amendments Act, 188
law schools, 331
Law Society of Upper Canada, 278
Lawyer Referral Services, 28
lawyer/client relationship, 11, 13–14,
    15–17, 27, 31–32
lawyer's bill, in dispute, 40–41
lawyers
    as mediators/arbitrators, 231
    billing method, 39–40
    choosing, 11, 28–31
    court personnel, 55
    dissatisfaction with, 37–41
    fathers' rights, 30
    firing, 41–44
    for child, 116, 119, 336
    initial interview, 30, 32–34, 45
    junior, 30
    legal aid, 80
    negative image of, 27
    professional misconduct, 32
    relationship with colleagues, 54
    retainers, 34–37
    with admitted bias, 30
lawyers' lounges, 216
leading questions, trials, 220, 223
legal aid, 37, 250, 303
legal fees, 80–81, 92, 103, 214, 224–25,
    275
legal proceedings, initiation of, 57–58
legal research, 44, 80, 331–33
legal separation, 72
Leskun case (BC), 174
liabilities. See assets/liabilities; debt

"liberal access," 253, 255
life insurance, obligation child/spousal
    support, 93, 167, 280, 294, 295
limited retainers, 330
lines of credit, 86, 89, 101, 281
liquidation value, 90
loans, 5, 86–87, 89

Manitoba
    common-law relationships, 188–
        189, 190, 375, 376
    grandparents' rights, 270
    matrimonial home, 96
    property division, 94
    Superior Courts, 74
    support enforcement, 48, 257
marriage
    date of, 94
    of convenience, 79–80
    polygamous, 72
    preparation courses, 15–16
    validity of, 72
Marriage Act, 317
marriage breakdown, emotional stages
    of, 14–15, 17–22
Marriage Contracts, 92, 278
    property division, 93, 283
    spousal support, 281, 283
    wills, 292
marriage counselling, 73–74, 94
material change in circumstance, 131,
    179–80, 210
material misrepresentation, 208
matrimonial home, 81, 84–85, 95–96,
    101, 102, 125–26, 133, 134, 192–93,
    281, 282
mediation, 8, 57, 132, 210, 243
mediation/arbitration, 239
Memorandum of Understanding, 210
mental cruelty, 71, 95

mental health, 10, 16, 34, 299
mini-trials. *See* motions
Minutes of Settlement, 201
mobility, 75, 122–24, 129, 131, 149, 190
Modernization of Benefits and Obligations Act, 185
mortgages, 86, 89, 261
motions, 61–62
multi-directional orders, 110
murder, 50, 298, 307
mutual wills, 292

name change, child, 125
nesting orders, 111, 126
New Brunswick
    common-law relationships, 376
    matrimonial home, 96
    online resources, 335
    spousal support, 171
    Superior Courts, 74
Newfoundland and Labrador
    common-law relationships, 376
    matrimonial home, 96
    online resources, 335
    property division, 94
    siblings, 117
    Supreme Court, 75
90-day re-cohabitation provision, 73
no-fault divorce, 67
no-hearing method, 76
Northwest Territories, common-law relationships, 376
note to litigant, sample, 340
Notice of Assessment, 157
Notice of Motion, 58, 201–2
Nova Scotia
    child support, 154–55
    common-law relationships, 186, 189, 375, 376

matrimonial home, 96
online resources, 335
property division, 94
nullity judgment, 94
Nunavut
    common-law relationships, 376
    online resources, 335

Offers to Settle, 198–201
Office of the Children's Lawyer, 119
Old Age Security, 259
On Death and Dying (Kübler-Ross), 16
one-year separation rule, 33, 69–70, 72, 73, 100
online assistance, by province, 334–35
    (See also Internet resources)
Ontario
    child custody, 113
    child support, 154–55
    common-law relationships, 184–87, 188, 189, 190, 375
    domestic abuse case, 305-6
    estate planning, 291–92, 293
    grandparents' rights, 270, 271, 272–73
    law schools, 331
    lawyer for child, 119
    Marriage Contracts, 280
    matrimonial home, 96
    online resources, 335
    Orders for Possession, 262
    parental behaviour, 118
    pension valuation/division, 99–100
    personal restraining orders, 262
    property division, 85, 94–95, 192–93
    religious arbitration, 240
    spousal support, 171, 178
    Superior Courts, 74
    support enforcement, 257–58, 259

Ontario Act, 138
Ontario Court Forms Assistant, 335
Ontario Court of Appeal, 271, 272–73
open-ended questions, trial, 220
opinion letters, 57, 59, 63, 72, 174
oral discovery, 60
order excluding witnesses, 220, 223
Orders for Possession, 132, 134,
    261–62
Orders on Consent, 201–2
ordinarily resident designation, 74–75
"other interested persons," 269, 273–74
out-of-court settlement, 52
out-of-pocket expenses, 36, 57

paralegals, 53, 61, 81, 206, 207
parent, definition, 158
parental alienation, 116, 143
parental behaviour, 106–7, 118
parental control, withdrawal from,
    159–60
parental support, 151, 152, 180–81
parenting coordinators, 119–20
Parenting Plan, 5, 129–30
    sample, 364-74
Partition Act, 317
Passport Canada, 121
passports, 250, 251–252, 303
paternity, 136–38
peace bond, 262–63, 304, 307
Pension Benefits Act, 317
pensions, 5, 83, 85, 86, 91, 97–100,
    189, 193, 281, 284, 295
permission letters (for travel), sample,
    251–52
pets, 86
physical abuse, 95, 128, 160 (See also
    domestic violence; sexual abuse)
physical cruelty, 71–72
physical separation, 72

plan administrators, 99
"plausibility of paternity," 138
pleadings, 43, 59
Powers of Attorney, 194, 291
premature litigation, 36
prenuptial agreements, 279–80 (See
    also Marriage Contracts)
presumptions, paternity, 137–38
pre–trials, 63, 201
Primary Automated Lookout System
    (PALS), 252
primary parent, 115
Prince Edward Island
    common-law relationships, 376
    matrimonial home, 96
principal residence, 102 (See also matri-
    monial home)
private investigators, 250
private judge, 238, 239
property, defined, 85–86
property division
    Cohabitation Agreements, 283
    common-law relationships, 84, 184,
        187–92
    complexity of rules, 84
    contested divorce, 77
    CPP, 100
    debt, 86–87
    enforcement, 260–62
    estate planning, 291
    exempt property, 92–94
    financial statements, 87–89
    goals of, 84
    jointly held property, 93–94
    Marriage Contracts, 93, 280, 282,
        283
    matrimonial home, 95–96
    paying amount to resolve, 101
    pensions, 97–100
    provincial law, 194, 284, 293

same-sex relationships, 84
tax considerations, 101–104
time limitations, 85
unequal division of property values,
    94–95
valuation, date of, 94
value of assets/liabilities, 89
property value, determining, 90–92
provincial law societies, 28, 336
provincial laws
    access enforcement, 254
    child abduction, 247
    child custody/access, 107, 109
    child support, 47, 152
    custody law enforcement, 248
    matrimonial home, 95, 96
    paternity, 139
    property division, 84, 89, 92, 93,
        94, 95, 99–100, 185, 284,
        292–93
    property enforcement, 260
    spousal support, 47, 153
    support enforcement, 255
    websites, 334–35
provincial/federal provisions, 46–47
psychological abuse, 298
psychological parent, 115, 117
psychologists, 118
public policy, and contracts, 287

Quebec
    common-law relationships, 183,
        376
    online resources, 335
questioning under oath. See discovery

reactive depression, 20
ready list, 218
real-time transcription, 53–54
"reasonable" access, 253, 255

"reasonable and necessary" expenses,
    155–57
Reasons for Judgment, 224, 225–226
reconciliation, 73–74, 94, 209–10,
    281
recording, 126–27, 313
recreational vehicles, 86
re-examination, trial, 221
registrars, 52–53
regulations, 311, 317, 318 (See also
    Rules of Court)
religion, 5, 124–25, 127, 282, 284
religious arbitration, 240
relocation. See mobility
remarriage, 78, 125, 126, 178, 288
"reserving judgment," 52, 223, 226
restraining orders, 133, 134, 135, 261,
    262, 297–98, 304, 307
retainers, 35–37, 214
    form, 338–39
retirement method, valuing pensions,
    97, 98
Revenue Canada. See Canada Revenue
    Agency
reversal of custody, 123–24, 254
robes (judicial), 54, 216
RRSPs, 83, 91, 101, 102, 295, 312, 319
Rules of Court, 54–56; 263, 311, 317,
    318
Rules of Court for Family Law, 311
Rules of Evidence, 313
Rules of Practice, 55, 58

same-sex relationships, 67-68, 184,
    185
    Cohabitation Agreement, 283
    domestic violence, 298
    grounds for divorce, 71
    property division, 84
    tax considerations, 103

Saskatchewan
    common-law relationships, 375, 376
    matrimonial home, 96
    online resources, 335
    Superior Courts, 74
    support enforcement, 257
savings, 83, 284
self-blame, 301
self-esteem, low, 301
self-help information, 334–35
self-representation, 11, 81, 310–11
    costs, 328
    dealing with court staff, 329
    dealing with judge, 329–30
    dealing with lawyers, 328–29
    legal framework outline, 311–37
    limited retainers, 330
self-sufficiency, 152, 172, 174, 176–77
Separation Agreements
    advantages of, 203–4
    described, 204–5
    financial statements, 209
    function of, 204
    negotiated by letters, 57
    reconciliation, 209–10
    sample, 341–60
    setting aside, 207–8
    signing, 205–6
    technical requirements of, 198–201
    wills, 293–94
separation counselling, 23
separation date, 94
service of documents, 58–59
settlement conferences, 63
settlements, 196–97
    Memorandum of Understanding,
        210
    Minutes of Settlement, 201
    Offers to Settle, 198–201
    Separation Agreements, 202–10

severance payments, 85
sexual abuse, 128, 298
sexual relations, absence of, 70
shared custody/child support, 161–63
shared parenting, 33
Sharia law, 240
shelters, battered women, 303
shorthand, 53
"show cause," support debtor, 258
siblings, 87, 116–17, 140
silent typewriter, 53
60/40 custody and child support,
    161–63
social assistance, 303
social workers, 118
sole custody, 33
South Korea, divorce system, 68
special divorce documents, 77
split custody, 164
spousal conduct, 174
spousal support
    clean-break model, 170
    Cohabitation Agreement, 284
    common-law relationships, 186–87
    compensatory model, 170
    concerning fairness, 161–62
    conduct, 173–78
    end of, 178
    enforcement, 255–57
    estate planning, 293–94
    guidelines, 171–73
    income security model, 170
    income tax, 259–60
    lump sum, 179
    Marriage Contracts, 281, 283
    objectives, 170
    Separation Agreement, 210
    tax considerations, 103
    time limitations, 85
    variation of, 179–80

Spousal Support Advisory Guidelines, 171–73
spousal support release, 179
spouse, defined, 184
standard of living, 151, 163, 175
Statement of Claim, 58
status quo, determining, 114
statutes, 311, 317, 318
steno mask, 53
step-parents, 158, 161
stocks, 86, 89, 91
subpoenas, 218, 222
Succession Law Reform Act, 317
suicide, 115, 174, 272
Superior Courts, 55, 74
supervised access, 128–29
support. See child support; parental support; spousal support
support creditor, 256
support debtor, 256
support enforcement agencies, 48
support enforcement offices, 257–60
Supreme Court of Canada, 8, 91, 97–99, 122, 157, 162–63, 191, 174, 176, 180, 225–26, 282–83
surviving spouse, election, 291–92

taxes, 70, 86, 101-4, 157-58, 260
telephone
    communication, children/parents, 145, 147
    returning calls, 38
tender years doctrine, 117
termination method, valuing pensions, 97
terminology, family law, 377–86
Thanksgiving, 121, 146
time dockets, 39
time-shares, 85

traceable property, 93
travel, documents/consents, 121–22, 251–52
trial coordinators, 52, 219
trial management conferences, 63
trial separation, 94, 141
trial(s), 64–65, 213–14
    components, 219–25
    costs, 64, 132, 213–14, 224–25
    paperwork, 217
    setting the case for, 217–18
    (See also appeals)
Troxel et vir. v. Granville, 272
trusts, 43, 86
two-tier justice system, 242

"unconscionable bargain," 208
uncontested divorce, 74, 75–76, 79, 81
"undertakings," 60–61
undue hardship, 164
undue influence, 208
United States, divorce rate, 68
United States Supreme Court, 272–73
universities, 166–67

vacations, 1, 120–22, 128, 154, 251, 253
    (See also holidays)
valuation costs, 98
valuation date, 94, 99
valuators, 84, 92
variation, 1, 131, 158
victims of violence, protection, 307–8
Vital Statistics Act, 137, 317

Wages Act, 317
Warrant of Distress, 256–57
webcams, 130
websites, self-help assistance, 334–35
wedding vows, 17, 23
weddings, 15, 76, 78

weight, evidence, 313, 315
wills, 283, 290–95
withholding consent to divorce, 70
"without prejudice" letter, 199–200
witnesses, 54, 219–23
women
    exploitation of, 80 *(See also* mar-
        riage of convenience)
    lawyers, 29
Writ of Execution, 256–57, 260
written opinions. *See* opinion letters

Yukon
    common-law relationships, 376
    online resources, 335

Notes

Notes

Notes

Notes